DAILY LIFE

DAILY LIFE

DAILY LIFE

JOHN KENNEDY

Jointly Published by

GOSPEL LITERATURE SERVICE

Bombay, India.

and

WEC Publications

Gerrards Cross, England.

DAILY LIFE

John Kennedy

© Gospel Literature Service, Bombay — 1982
Revised Edition   — 1992

Published in India:
Gospel Literature Service
Udyog Bhavan, 250-D, Worli
Bombay - 400 025, India.

Published in UK:
WEC Publications
Bulstrode
Gerrards Cross
Bucks, SL 9 852 England.

ISBN 0 900828 65 X.

Printed at GLS Press, Bombay - 400 075, India.

CONTENTS

CONTENTS

PREFACE

There are many excellent books of daily readings, so producing another one calls for some word of explanation.

Most books of daily readings are devotional in character. DAILY LIFE aims to be more expository, and its main purpose is to teach basic Christian doctrine and practice in a way that is easily understood. It is designed either for individual use, or for the use of the older, more mature Christian family.

In all, fifty-two subjects are dealt with, one for each week of the year. Roughly half of these are doctrinal in character, and the remainder practical. Doctrinal and practical subjects are alternated throughout the year to prevent the subject matter from appearing too heavy or difficult to assimilate. Each subject is divided into six parts, each part dealing with a different and important aspect. The seventh day of each section is given to a Bible character whose experience illustrates the particular truths that have been explained.

Each day's reading commences with a short portion of Scripture which should be read preferably in a modern translation. Then follows the comment on the passage. At the end are listed five verses from different parts of the Bible relevant to the subject under consideration. These are meant to be used as memory verses. If, for example, a family of five is using DAILY LIFE during their period of daily family prayer, it is suggested that each member of the family learn a different verse. If the book is used for five years all the verses will be committed to memory by each person. Anyone who has learned the 2054 verses listed will find that he has not simply memorized so many isolated texts, but he has learned some sizeable portions of the Scripture.

The readings in DAILY LIFE are taken from every book of the Bible, and thus demonstrate the relevance of all Scripture to our daily living. The readings have also been selected to provide expository comments on large sections of the Bible, and in some cases on whole books. In the course of the year some of the New Testament Epistles are completely covered, as well as very large sections of other books.

The index of Scripture portions at the end of DAILY LIFE enables it to serve as a basic commentary on the portions used, and the general index provides a guide to Scriptural teaching on important aspects of practical daily living.

It should be unnecessary to say that DAILY LIFE is not intended as a substitute for Bible reading. On the contrary, it is hoped that it will stimulate those who use it to search the Scriptures more keenly to find in them the abundant life our Lord promises to those who follow Him.

All Scripture quotations are taken from the Revised Standard Versions of the Bible unless where otherwise indicated.

J.K.

Index of Main Subjects

x

God

THE PERSONAL GOD

Reading: Ephesians 1. 1-10

The God of the Bible is a person. He is not an impersonal force, nor is He the sum total of everything. He exists separate from His creation, and though He is infinitely greater than man whom He has made, He is able to enter into relationship with man as one person with another. When He speaks to us, as He does throughout the Bible, He says, "I", and we can respond to Him by saying, "You".

Mind, emotion and will are three distinguishing marks of personality. All of these exist in God. God thinks. God feels. He shows love, joy, sorrow and other emotions. God wills, that is He turns His thoughts into purposeful actions.

In his letter to the Ephesians the apostle Paul explains some of the profoundest truth found anywhere in the Bible. He begins by emphasising the fact that God is a person. If God were not a person, the blessings Paul describes would be impossible, the purposes he says God has for His children would be meaningless. All these things are possible only because God is who He is, a personal God. A personal God is the foundation of all the great truth of the Ephesian letter.

Notice the marks of God's personalness in our reading. He blesses us (v. 8), that is He acts in kindness towards His people. V.4 tells us that He chose us to be holy and blameless. God's purpose or plan is mentioned again in verses 5, 9, and 10. Here we see His concern for righteousness, an indication of His own moral character. Not only is God Himself good, He is deeply grieved over every act of evil. Yet He loves (v. 5), and forgives (v. 7). We know God is like this because He has made Himself known to us (v. 9). God is not a distant, disinterested spectator, looking with unconcern upon the joys and sorrows, the triumphs and defeats of our lives. He is deeply, vitally concerned. He has a plan for each one which He wants to make known and to work out. Let us thank Him for it and pray that we may understand more fully what it means to be related to a personal God.

Lev. 19. 2; Ps. 103.7; Isa. 64. 4; John 3. 16; Eph. 1. 3

God

THE TRINITY

Reading: 1 Peter 1. 1-12

The fact that God has revealed Himself to man shows that He wants us to have as clear an understanding of Him as possible. Yet we always need to remember that we are creatures standing before our Creator. Our finite minds can never fully grasp His infiniteness, and human language can, at best, but incompletely describe His greatness. Nowhere is this more evident than in the doctrine of the trinity.

The Bible never attempts to explain the trinity, but the fact of the trinity is clearly stated. In the Old Testament there is the suggestion of a plurality of persons within the Godhead in the word 'Elohim', one of the words used for God. Elohim is a plural word, yet it is used with a singular verb. In the New Testament, the first actual statement of the trinity is in the Lord's great commission (Matt. 28.19). Apart from this the three persons are mentioned together many times as they are in Peter's introduction to his first letter.

In v.2 not only are the three persons clearly mentioned, Father, Son and Holy Spirit, but Peter also sets down the distinctive function of each one. We are 'chosen and destined by God the Father'. As the one who predetermines our ways, the action of the Father is the basis of all else. The Son unites us with the Father through the work of the cross (vs. 2,11). The Holy Spirit enlightens (v. 12), and sanctifies (v. 2).

These three functions must not be taken to mean that there are three Gods. Both Old and New Testament are equally emphatic that God is one. Yet within the unity of the Godhead are three persons of full deity, all equal, and each with His complementary function. The Son and the Spirit, nevertheless, are subordinate to the Father. The limitations of our language is obvious in the use of the word 'Son'. It does not mean that our Lord had a beginning but that He enjoys a personal relationship of sonship with the Father.

The trinity may remain a mystery to us, but we can thank God for who He is, for the work of Father, Son and Holy Spirit, and pray that we may go on to experience His working in an ever fuller measure.

1 Peter 1. 2; John 14. 16; 1 Tim. 2. 5; Isa. 48. 16

God

THE GOD WHO REVEALS HIMSELF

January 3   Reading: John 1. 1-14

We can know the truth about God because God has revealed Himself to man. Most philosophies and religions begin with man who speculates about God and the nature of life, but man's ideas are seriously restricted by his own human limitations. The Bible, however, begins with God as John 1. 1 tells us. God has spoken.

John introduces us to one of the great names of our Lord, the Word. Through the Word all things were made (v. 3). 'And the Word became flesh and dwelt among us' (v. 14). Words are the most adequate means we possess of expressing ourselves. A child who has not learned to speak may try to express himself by an action, perhaps by pointing at something, but he cannot accurately communicate to others what is going on in his mind. Our Lord is called the Word because, through His life and speech, He has shown to us accurately what God is like, His desires and His purposes.

From the very beginning of history there has been some expression of the Word, though most of these expressions have been inadequate, like a child's cry or sign-language. God has revealed Himself in nature. The existence of the world in which we live is an indication of God's existence. God has revealed Himself in history, particularly the history of the nation Israel. This is the subject of the Old Testament. He has shown us His standards in the law given to Moses, in the sacrifices and offerings He instituted, in the details of the tabernacle. Yet all of these were but shadows of the reality.

Finally, God came Himself in the person of His Son. His coming was like a light (v. 5), dispelling the darkness of our limited understanding. God has shown us what He is like not merely by giving an explanation of Himself in a book, or by sending someone to tell us, but by coming Himself and actually living in this world as we do ourselves. The Bible, particularly the New Testament, is an account of the life and teaching of the Word made flesh. It is an expression of the living Word. By reading it we know what God has said, what He desires, and how He acts. God has revealed Himself to us in the plainest possible way. Let us thank Him for doing so.

John 1. 14; John 14. 8-9; Heb. 1. 1-2; Ps. 19. 1; Amos 3.7

3

God

THE CHARACTER OF GOD—HOLINESS

In trying to understand God we can divide His characteristics into two types, those characteristics which He communicates to men, and the characteristics which are strictly His own and man cannot possess.

In our reading, the Psalmist speaks of the Lord's law and testimony (v. 7), precepts and commandments (v. 8), fear and ordinances (v. 9), all of which he describes in words which indicate perfection and holiness. In v. 10 he speaks of how desirable they are. Then in vs. 11-14 he applies them to his own living and prays for victory over attitudes which would hinder them from being revealed within himself. This is one of many Scriptures which show us not only the holy character of God, but show us also that He purposes to impart that same holy character to His people.

The holiness of God is stated again and again in the Old Testament. In fact all God's dealings with the people of Israel served to emphasise it. God's holiness is shown through the law, through the perfection required in the sacrifices, through the words of the prophets condemning sin and upholding righteousness. In the New Testament God's holiness is demonstrated in the life of our Lord Jesus Christ, and through our Lord's redemptive work holiness is effectively imparted to His people.

In the work of the cross we see two aspects of God's holiness, His love and His justice. In God these virtues, alongside His others, are perfectly balanced. In His people they perhaps never are. David expressed this in his prayer, "Keep back thy servant also from presumptuous sins" (v. 13). He was well aware how difficult it was to judge aright, or how easy it was to allow his love to triumph over his sense of justice. His relationship with his son Absalom is but one example of this problem.

So while God does impart His holiness to His people, we show forth but a faint expression of the matchless holiness of God Himself. Nevertheless, that expression should be growing day by day. In vs. 11-14 the Psalmist shows his longing for more of God's holiness. Let us pray that God will give us the same longing.

Ps. 19. 13; Eph. 2. 10; Heb. 12. 14; Mal. 3. 3; Ex. 15. 11

God

THE CHARACTER OF GOD—TRANSCENDENCE

January 5

Reading: Nahum 1. 6-13

Transcendence is rather a technical word, but it means simply that the eternal God exists outside His creation and is much greater than everything He has made. There is a philosophy which teaches that the universe is God, but this finds no support in the Bible whatsoever.

Nahum was chosen to predict God's final judgement upon Nineveh, an empire which had deliberately rejected God's mercy. In our reading Nahum clearly portrays God's transcendence, the fact that He is supreme over His creation. He also suggests other related aspects of God's character. God is all-powerful and all-knowing.

God's almighty power is implied in the question of v. 6, "Who can stand before His indignation?" and in the statements of vs. 7 and 12. No one is able to stand against Him or thwart His purposes. Vs. 9-11 point to the all-knowing nature of God. Nahum derides those who would presume to plot against the Lord. "What do you plot against the Lord?" (v. 9). He shows the utter foolishness of those who imagine that by scheming or in any other way they can deceive God and hide their condition from Him. God knows all, future as well as present.

Throughout the passage there is also a sense of God's presence in every situation, whether it is His presence in judgement, or His presence to uphold those who really trust Him (v. 7). While it is true that God is other than His creation, it is also true that God is ever present. We must be careful to keep these two truths in balance. A stress on God's transcendence alone has led some people to think that God is far off, and what happens in day to day life is unimportant. This is wrong. On the other hand, some so stress God's presence in our lives that they think everything they do or say is of God, so ascribe to God their own weaknesses and sins. This is equally wrong.

God is other than His people and His church. Individual and church alike must bow before Him in worship. At the same time, God is ever present as Nahum shows us. Let us thank God for His greatness, and pray that we may recognize the solemnity of His presence in our lives.

Nahum 1. 7; Acts 17. 24; Isa. 40. 25; Ps. 139. 3; Eph. 4. 6

God

GOD'S CREATION AND PROVIDENCE

January 6   Reading: Isa. 40. 21-29

Isaiah here presents us with two great truths, first that God is the Creator (vs. 22,26,28), and secondly that He is the preserver of what He has created (vs. 23-24,29). This is what we mean by God's 'providence'. God has not only made the world. He is also in absolute control of it and everything in it.

God's creation extends not only to the earth (v. 28), but to the whole universe (vs. 22,26). This is stated in the first chapter of Genesis. The Bible is not meant to be a scientific text-book, and creation is described in language understandable in every period of history. There are, however, certain facts which the Bible makes clear. 1. Creation was accomplished by a series of definite supernatural acts of God. This is indicated in the Hebrew word for 'create'. 2. The material world is not eternal. It had a definite beginning. 3. It was created by God out of nothing. The very material of which it is made up was itself created by God (Heb. 11.3).

God's providence includes the whole of nature (vs. 22,24), history (v.23), and individual people (v.29). The world and the universe do not keep going automatically. They are dependent upon the will and power of God who controls everything according to certain unchangeable laws. We call these the 'laws of nature', and they show God's concern for His creation down to the most minute detail. But God also controls the affairs of men, both historical events and the destiny of the individual.

Many people find it difficult to reconcile the providence of God with the free-will of man, but a little thought will show how dependent we are upon God's providence. Man's free-will is really a very small part of his situation. What we are or observe today depends upon a past chain of events, a slight change in any one of which might have brought us to a vastly different situation. God's providence teaches us that He has been in control of each one of these circumstances. Nothing happens by chance. Let us thank God for His creation and for His sure hand upon all our ways.

Isa. 40. 28; Isa. 40. 29; Rev. 4. 11; Heb. 11. 3; Rom. 8. 28

God

ABRAHAM

January 7   Reading: Genesis 12:1-8

In this account of Abraham's call we see a number of the characteristics of God we have already been considering. More than that, we see the very practical effects of God's call in the life of this man who was to become the father of the nation Israel.

The word 'Lord' is a translation of the greatest of God's titles in the Bible. It signifies the sovereign God who ever was, is and shall be, the God before whom all must bow unconditionally. Abraham's reaction to the Lord's call was trust, obedience (v. 4), and worship (vs. 7-8). These attitudes were to characterize the rest of Abraham's long life.

God's personalness is seen not only in His speaking to Abraham (v. 1), but in His loving concern for him (v. 2). God had a purpose for Abraham, and indicated that He would take decisive measures to see it fulfilled (v. 1). As a condition of blessing God called Abraham to separate himself from the familiar environment of the previous seventyfive years. God wanted to make a fresh start in refashioning Abraham's character more in the likeness of His own. We see the depths of Abraham's faith in his willingness, as an already ageing man, to leave his established routine and to follow God, 'not knowing where he was to go' (Heb. 11:8).

The providence of God too is clearly seen in these initial dealings with His servant, and it can be traced throughout Abraham's subsequent experience. In how many different ways Abraham might have been led astray apart from God's sovereign hand upon him. Within his own family circle was one person, his nephew Lot (vs. 4-5), who was the cause of constant friction. Whether God wanted Lot to be in the party which left Haran, or whether Abraham allowed him to accompany them in a fit of misguided emotional affection, we do not know. The resulting difficulties certainly could have had serious effects upon the whole of Abraham's future life apart from God's steadying, controlling hand, and Abraham's continuing response of faith.

We thank Thee Lord that thou art still the same. Guide us, and give us the obedience and faith of Abraham.

Ps. 32. 8; Jer. 29. 11; Heb. 11. 8; Rom. 4. 20; Phil. 3. 20

Worship and Thanksgiving

THE BLESSING OF A THANKFUL HEART

January 8   Reading: 1 Thessalonians 5. 12-23

Paul's three exhortations, "Rejoice always, pray constantly, give thanks in all circumstances" (vs. 16-18) follow advice on our attitude to others, and come before advice on our relationship with God. Prayer and thanksgiving should always go together. To be asking constantly without a sense of appreciation for what God has done is a symptom of spiritual selfishness.

The Thessalonian church was suffering from problems which could have been a threat to the unity of the assembly. Thanksgiving draws God's people together, and it should encompass all the relationships Paul mentions. Elders are to be respected and esteemed highly (vs. 12-13). They should have a constant part in the prayers of the church, and their ministrations should be accepted with thanksgiving. Part of their duty is to give needed admonition (v. 12). Have we learned to give thanks to God for this? Thanksgiving when our failures are pointed out to us is the first step to victory over them.

Always there will be idlers to be admonished, fainthearted to be encouraged, weak to be helped (v. 14). Do we tend to despise such people, or do we thank God for the opportunity of ministering to them, and thank Him too for the spiritual potential that is in them? Only then can our ministry to them be effective. Do we return evil for evil, or do we really seek the benefit of those who do us wrong and thank God for the opportunity of displaying His grace?

Thanksgiving is dependent upon our obedience to God. This is the force of Paul's exhortation in vs. 19-22. There is no ground for thanksgiving unless the Spirit is free to do His work within us (v. 19), or if we are unresponsive to the Word of God (v. 20), or are unconcerned about righteous living and our testimony before others (vs. 21-22). We have no right to go our own way and thank God for our defeats, imagining them to be victories. Thanksgiving is always ready for correction. If it is true spiritual thanksgiving, and not merely a spirit of self-congratulation, it will open our eyes to our own needs and contribute to God's work of sanctification in us.

Lord, give us obedient hearts, and a spirit of thanksgiving for what You want to do in us, and in others through us.

1 Thess 5. 5; 1 Tess. 5. 19-22; Col. 3. 15; Phil. 4. 4; Ps. 100. 4

8

Worship and Thanksgiving

THE DEPENDENCE OF WORSHIP

January 9   Reading: 1 Chronicles 16. 23-35

Worship is dependence. Worship is giving God the place of supremacy which is His right. The whole of our reading is a commentary on the words, "The Lord reigns" (v. 31). We depend on Him for salvation (v. 23). We depend on Him within the circle of the family and in all our relationships (v. 28). We depend on Him to control the ways of the nations (v. 24). We depend on Him to sustain the course of nature (v. 30-31). We depend on Him to restrain and finally to judge wickedness (v. 33). We depend on Him to maintain a testimony of holiness upon the earth through His people (v. 35).

Where the Lord reigns there is order. Where He does not reign there is chaos. In worship we recognize that the Lord has the right of supremacy in every sphere of living. The modern world is a terrible object lesson of what happens when God is debarred from His place of rulership and man presumes to occupy it. Among the nations there is enmity which frequently errupts into warfare, bringing suffering to countless thousands of people. Families are divided and homes are broken through selfishness. Nature seems to work against man in frightening natural catastrophies. Wickedness of every kind often appears to have free rein. Even amongst the people of God there is sometimes little holiness and little testimony. All because men have not learned the spirit of worship and have taken over God's place to rule.

There can be no true worship without humility, because in recognizing that God must reign in all our affairs we admit our own inability to order our lives aright. Man is naturally proud and full of self-sufficiency. It is humbling to realize that even within the circle of his own family he is incapable of alone establishing peace and order. The same applies in the life of the church. How many believers proudly think that they have something important to contribute to the life of the church, and blame others when their ministry is not accepted or effective. A spirit of worshipful dependence upon God is the basis of living a life to His glory. Let us thank God for His sovereignty, and pray for greater dependence upon Him in everything.

1 Chron. 16. 23; Chron. 16. 25; Prov. 16. 18; James. 4. 10; 1 Tim. 1. 17

Worship and Thanksgiving

REJOICING IN TRIBULATION

January 10   Reading: 1 Peter 4. 12-19

Peter's first letter is, in the New Testament, what the book of Job is in the Old. It was written to explain why God allows His children to suffer. Suffering is part of life, and God has nowhere promised to exempt His people from it. In fact our Lord repeatedly emphasised to His disciples that to follow Him would mean suffering beyond what they might otherwise expect.

There is a suffering which legitimately befalls those who commit crimes against society. Punishment of evildoers is one of the responsibilites of human government as God ordained it. If a believer disobeys the law of the land, he has no right to expect God to save him from the just punishment of his misdeed, nor is the punishment a privilege for which he can thank God (v. 15). No believing Christian should ever have cause to suffer in this way.

Peter is here speaking of the suffering which God's people endure when they accept identification with their rejected Lord. It may be the suffering of scorn, or the suffering of being denied one's rights, or actual physical suffering as was the case with many of the people to whom Peter was writing. We need not be surprised when called to suffer in this way (v. 12), for the Lord suffered in the same way. We can give thanks for the privilege of sharing in some small way our Lord's travail (v. 13).

But there is another aspect of tribulation in which we can rejoice. Even when our trials seem to be thrust upon us by the hands of godless men, we have the confidence that God is working out His purposes through them. "The time has come for judgement to begin with the household of God" (v. 17). Through suffering God cleanses His people and raises a testimony to His holiness in their midst, a testimony which brings transformation to the lives of others.

The early churches won their way in the world through their testimony of holiness. Though severely persecuted they rejoiced, and demonstrated a quality of life higher by far than that of those who opposed them. Let us thank God for our trials, and pray that in them we might be a testimony to others.

1 Peter 4. 12; 1 Peter 4. 14; 1 Peter 4. 17; Matt. 5. 11; John 15.11

Worship and Thanksgiving

WORSHIPPING TOGETHER

January 11   Reading: Hebrews 10. 19-25

The writer to the Hebrews emphasises the importance of those who believe in the Lord Jesus Christ meeting together for worship (v. 25). Worship, as we have seen, is based on our humble dependence upon the Lord as individuals, but one of the most important ways this can be shown is in the gathering together of believing Christians to worship publicly.

Public worship is important for three reasons. It is important for our own personal, spiritual welfare (v. 23). We will never grow strong in the confidence of God's great purpose for us, and progress in that hope, if we neglect our relationship with other believers. Secondly, meeting with the Lord's people gives us the opportunity of demonstrating before all where our loyalty lies. It is an open confession that we belong to Christ. Thirdly, we will never be able to encourage others, or grow ourselves in the things of God (vs. 24-25) if we are ashamed to confess our faith openly.

Public worship, however, does not consist merely in the act of gathering together. It is the gathering together of people for whom the Lord Jesus Christ has done something decisive, and who accept their responsibility to obey Him. The writer tells us two great facts about our Lord. First, it is through the rent body and shed blood of our Lord Jesus Christ that we can enter the presence of God (vs. 19-20). By His work on the cross He opened up the way for all who put their trust in Him. Secondly, Jesus is our Great High Priest (v. 21). As the function of the Old Testament priesthood was to be a bridge between God and man, so Jesus shows us the way to God and introduces us to His presence. Knowing this we can have confidence (v. 19), and full assurance of faith (v. 22).

These are our privileges, but, as with all privileges, they entail certain responsibilities. We are responsible to maintain our relationship with our Lord, for only He can give us a conscience which is clean and void of offence (v. 22). We are also responsible to order our lives aright by the 'water' of the Word which cleanses us as we obey it (v. 22). Then our public worship will be a testimony to God, a strength to ourselves, and a blessing to others. Let us pray that God will make it so, and let us thank Him for the privilege of entering His presence.

Heb. 10. 22; Heb. 10. 25; Eph. 5. 26; John 1. 7; Ps. 40. 10

Worship and Thanksgiving

MUSIC IN WORSHIP

January 12   Reading: Nehemiah 12. 27-30

The book of Nehemiah is the story of the rebuilding of the wall of Jerusalem after the return of some of the Jews from captivity. Under the leadership of Nehemiah the work was carried on and completed. Our reading tells of the dedication of the wall and of the singers and instrumentalists who took part in the service of praise.

Not only here, but in other books of the Bible, particularly the book of Psalms, music both vocal and instrumental is mentioned as part of the worship of God. There are some Christians who decry the use of instruments in church gatherings. It is true that in the New Testament there is no specific reference to musical instruments being used on such occasions, but their use is in harmony with the tenor of Scripture teaching.

V. 30 states a very important fact. "The priests and the Levites purified themselves, and they purified the people and the gates and the wall." It shows that there was nothing superficial about the worship they offered. Whatever instruments were used, the praise was a heartfelt expression of thanks to God which sprang from a desire for His glory on the part of all who gathered.

There are important lessons for us in this simple passage. Music and singing can be to the glory of God, but it can also easily degenerate into an expression of human emotion and fleshly enjoyment. This can be so whether singing is accompanied by musical instruments or not. There are many modern hymns and choruses in which the words are little more than an accompaniment to a jaunty tune. Music can sometimes be so loud and prominent that the words are lost altogether. The dangers of this kind of music are seen when time is occupied with singing under the guise of worship to the neglect of prayer and the ministry of the Word.

The practice of allowing unconverted instrumentalists to lead the praises of God's people is something else which is bound to bring spiritual loss. In the dedication of the wall of Jerusalem all who took part had a heart for God. Let us thank God for the gift of music, but let us pray that we may use it as an expression of genuine love for the Lord, not as an expression of mere fleshly enjoyment.

Isa. 52. 11; Col. 3. 16; Ps. 149. 1; John 4. 24; Phil. 3. 3

12

Worship and Thanksgiving

THE ATTITUDE OF WORSHIP

January 13   Reading: Micah 6. 6-8

This is one of the greatest declarations of a spiritual faith in the Old Testament. The prophet Micah had a clear insight into the nature of worship. He saw that it was not merely a form, but an attitude of heart which should characterize the every-day living of a child of God.

Micah speaks first of the offerings instituted by God through His servant Moses (vs. 6-7). He shows that God is not satisfied with the mere observance of these offerings. They had been given to the children of Israel as illustrations of spiritual truth, and unless the people saw beyond them to the grace of God, they were of no value.

Christian people today do not observe the sacrifices and rites of Old Testament times, but there are other things which can become just as much a stumbling-block as the offerings were to many of the Children of Israel. How easy it is for our Bible reading, our prayers, our Christian gatherings to become mere forms. Unless through these things we meet with God, they are of little value and may even blind our eyes to our dire spiritual need. Every right act originates in an inner thought or attitude. Unless our hearts are right, what we do cannot be truly good. This is what Micah understood so clearly.

"He has showed you, O man, what is good" (v. 8). Our worship of God and our relationship with Him is not simply a matter of the outward act, though our actions are important. (We must never make the mistake of claiming that what is in a man's heart is all that matters, and what he does of little consequence.) To do what is just springs from a love of kindness (v.8). When our hearts are right with God, our actions will be glorifying to Him. Micah combines both in the final phrase of the verse, 'to walk humbly with your God'. A walk with God controls the whole of life, its inner expression known only to God and ourselves, and its outer expression seen by the world around.

This walk with God is the basic aspect of worship. Worship is not just the act of kneeling or standing, of saying or singing words to God. If we do not have the attitude of worship we cannot perform a true act of worship. Let us thank God for His faithfulness, and pray that He might help us to walk with Him in an attitude of constant worship.

Micah 6. 8; 1 Sam. 16. 7; Prov. 3. 5; Luke 12. 1; Matt. 23. 23.

13

Worship and Thanksgiving

HANNAH

January 14   Reading: 1 Samuel 2. 1-11

In Hannah's prayer we find many of the characteristics of true worship. She knew the blessing of a thankful heart (v. 1). She had sought the Lord for a child, and the Lord had given her Samuel.

Hannah's dependence upon the Lord did not end, as is the case with so many, once her request was answered. She did not try to back down on her promise to give her son back to the Lord. As a mother, relinquishing Samuel to the care of Eli must have caused her deep, natural sorrow, but her obedience to God brought rejoicing. "The Lord makes poor and makes rich: He brings low, He also exalts." There was no denying Hannah's understandable sadness as she returned to an empty home, but she was enriched in the knowledge of doing the will of God.

Eli was a priest, but Hannah had little reason to have confidence in him to bring up her own son. He was a weak man, unable to control his own family. His sons were a disgrace to the holy office they occupied, and not only was Eli unable to restrain them, but he was unwilling to discipline them by ejecting them from the priesthood. All this was well known, and Hannah and Elkanah her husband certainly did not thrust their little boy lightly into such a situation.

But Hannah knew her responsibility. She had made a promise to the Lord (1 Sam. 1. 28), and that promise could not be broken. Her leaving Samuel in the custody of Eli was the measure of her confidence and faith in God. She knew that the Lord would take care of her son (vs. 9).

Hannah walked with the Lord. She had not abandoned her son and ceased to feel concern for him. Each year when she went with her husband to offer the yearly sacrifice, she took for Samuel a little practical token of her love and care. She had given him as an act of worship, and her constant attitude of worship enabled her to face her sacrifice day by day with thanksgiving.

May the Lord enable us to worship Him in a similar readiness to give Him the best we have.

1 Sam. 2. 8; 1 Sam. 2.9; Ps. 37. 5; Matt. 6. 33; Eccl. 5. 4

The Person and Work of Christ

THE DEITY OF CHRIST

January 15   Reading: John 20. 19-30

Doubting Thomas gave voice to one of the greatest ascriptions of deity found anywhere in the Bible. His demand for proof that Jesus had risen from the dead was forgotten. His heart triumphed over his head. He could do no other than cry out, "My Lord and my God" (v. 28).

The Christian faith stands or falls on the deity of our Lord Jesus Christ. The New Testament plainly states that our Lord existed prior to His incarnation at Bethlehem. John tells us that He was in the beginning with God, and that He was God (John 1.1). In His last great prayer our Lord speaks to the Father of 'the glory which I had with thee before the world was made' (John 17.5). Not only was He there in the beginning, John speaks of Him as the Creator (John 1.3). Paul makes a similar claim. "In Him all things were created" (Col. 1.16). Jesus Himself speaks of being one with the Father (John 10. 30).

In His public ministry our Lord claimed divine authority, and He exercised powers which belong to God alone. He forgave sins, which brought upon Him a charge of blasphemy from some of the Scribes (Matt. 9. 2-3). He accepted worship from His disciples (Matt. 14. 22-23). He claimed to be the giver of life (John 10. 10), and to be the judge of all the earth (John 5. 26-27). His claim to authority was substantiated by the people who heard His ministry (Luke 1. 22), and countless thousands have experienced His saving and transforming power down to the present day.

To the early Christians Jesus was a living Lord. He had risen from the dead, as was witnessed by all the disciples as well as by many others. These same disciples saw Him ascend bodily into heaven (Acts 1.9), and from that experience a band of twelve insignificant men went out to see the Gospel proclaimed throughout the known world within the space of one generation. The deity of Christ, who was alive for evermore, was the source of their life and power.

As afresh we acknowledge Jesus as our Lord and our God, may we go forth, as did His disciples, to live and speak for Him.

John 16. 28; John 1. 1; Col. 2. 9; John 11. 25; Titus 2. 13

15

The Person and Work of Christ

THE HUMANITY OF CHRIST

January 16   Reading: Hebrews 4. 14-5. 10

In this passage the writer begins by stressing the deity of our Lord Jesus Christ (4.14). Then he goes on to show our Lord's humanity. The work of a high priest was to bring man into the presence of God, and to do so he had to be fully in touch with both. Jesus perfectly fulfilled this condition. He was God, yet He was like us in all things, sin apart.

The very fact of our Lord's sinlessness made Him feel more acutely than we ever can the temptations which beset us. He felt the whole weight of the tempter's power, a weight God never allows to fall upon us, because it would crush us completely. But our Lord withstood all the strain and anguish and can sympathize with us in temptations as a man who has gone through the experience Himself. He was truly and completely human, as He was truly and completely divine.

In the Old Testament the High Priest had to offer up sacrifices for his own sins before he made offerings for the sins of others (5.3). Jesus had no need to offer a sacrifice for Himself, but in giving Himself for the sins of others His prayer in the garden of Gethsemane clearly shows His humanity (5.7). As a man, He did not want the suffering of the cross. As a man, He experienced the agony of the anticipation of calvary.

A further mark of His humanity is that He learned from the experiences through which He passed (5. 8-9). Jesus accepted human limitations, but He was a perfect man. When the writer says that He was 'made perfect' (5.9), he is not speaking of being made morally complete. Our Lord was already perfect in that sense. The word used here means 'perfectly fitted for a task'. Through His experiences of life as a man Jesus was perfectly fitted for the work of bringing eternal salvation (v. 9)

The divinity and humanity of our Lord in one personality is a mystery, but the Scriptures plainly teach that our Lord Jesus Christ was both God and man. At no time did our Lord lay aside His deity, yet in His life on earth He was at no time less than a perfect man.

Let us thank God for the humanity of our Lord Jesus Christ through which He perfectly understands, sympathizes with us and helps us.

Heb. 4. 15; Heb. 5. 8-9; Heb. 2. 14; Gal. 4. 4; Phil. 2. 7

The Person and Work of Christ

PROPHET PRIEST AND KING

January 17   Reading: Hebrews 1. 1-9

The letter to the Hebrews is concerned with the work of our Lord Jesus Christ as Mediator between God and man. In the opening verses the writer mentions three important aspects of our Lord's mediatorial work. He is Prophet, Priest and King.

A prophet is one who speaks the word of God to men. "In these last days he has spoken to us by a Son" (v. 2). We tend to lay great stress on the death of our Lord Jesus Christ as the means of our salvation, but we must never forget the work that He accomplished in His life. Both are of vital importance. In His life He taught the truth about God, and He promised that, after His death, He would continue to teach this truth to men through the Holy spirit. The woman of Samaria recognized this aspect of our Lord's ministry when she said "Sir, I perceive that you are a prophet" (John 4. 19).

Man, however, needs more than to know the truth about God. He needs forgiveness of sins and cleansing. This is the work of our Lord as Priest. "When he had made purification for sins, he sat down at the right hand of the Majesty on high" (v.3). Christ offered the sacrifice of Himself on the cross for our sins, so His work as Priest relates particularly to His death. It continues, however, from 'the right hand of the Majesty on high' where He acts as our advocate, interceding for us on the ground of His perfect and complete sacrifice on the cross.

Christ is also King. His kingship was recognized even at His birth when the wise men came to look for the 'king of the Jews' (Matt. 2. 1-2). He is, however, king in other respects. He is king of the lives of His people. He is king over the affairs of this world which He rules in the interests of His glory. A day is coming when He will be undisputed King, and every knee will bow to Him.

The work of our Lord as Prophet, Priest and King has a very practical meaning for our every-day lives. May He help us to learn more of Him, realize our constant need of His priestly work, and let Him reign as King in our lives.

1 John 5. 20; Heb. 9. 14; 1 John 2. 1; Heb. 7. 25; Eph. 1; 22-23.

The Person and Work of Christ

HIS LIFE AND RESURRECTION

January 18   Reading: 1 Corinthians 15. 1-14

It is of tremendous importance to recognize that the Christian faith is based upon unassailable historical facts. This is what Paul is here emphasizing. He states that these facts 'are of first importance' (v. 3). Why is this so? It is so because our Lord's life, death and resurrection set before us God's standards in a way that would otherwise be impossible. If our Lord had not come and lived on earth, we would be left to our own imagination as to what God is like and what He requires of us. If our Lord had not died, we would be without hope of forgiveness and salvation. If our Lord had not risen, we would be without assurance of God's power to save us and enable us to live to His glory.

The life of our Lord provides us with norms. How do we know what is right and what is wrong? People who do not know the Lord Jesus Christ have no really satisfactory answer to this question. To the believing Christian, something is wrong, to tell lies for example, because God disapproves of it. How do we know God disapproves of it? We know because of what Jesus did and taught. His life and words are our norm, our standard. If He had not lived we would be without norms. We would have no clear sense of direction how to live.

The death of our Lord Jesus Christ shows us the seriousness of sin and the greatness of God's love. God did not merely say that He hated sin. He judged it. God has not merely said that He loves us. He died for us. Calvary has shown that God's love and justice are not just theories. They are facts of history which serve as a warning and an example for our own day to day living.

Paul lays great stress on the resurrection. He recounts the appearances of our Lord to the eleven, to over five hundred brethren, to James and the apostles, and finally to himself on the Damascus road (vs. 4-8). If Christ has not been raised, he says, our preaching and our faith are vain (v. 14). The resurrection was a demonstration of God's power to give newness of life. That power was available not only in the resurrection of our Lord Jesus Christ, but through Him it is available to us all. Without it, the possibility of living to the glory of God would be a vain hope, and the assurance of salvation only a dream. But Christ has risen indeed. May the Lord help us to live in the power of His resurrection.

1 Cor. 15. 3; 1 Cor. 15. 22; Rom. 5. 10; 1 Peter 1. 3; Rom. 1. 17-18

The Person and Work of Christ

HIS WALK AND MINISTRY

The walk and ministry of our Lord were completely consistent. He lived what He preached. Our reading is the first part of what we call 'the sermon on the mount'. Some Christians feel that the standard of our Lord's teaching here is so high that it can only be fulfilled in a coming millenium. This, however, is not so. Our Lord was laying down principles which he Himself demonstrated, and are guidelines for His people today.

One of the most obvious things about this passage is how completely different our Lord's thinking is from the normal thinking of the world. "Blessed are the poor in spirit.... those who mourn.... the meek.... those who hunger and thirst after righteousness". The world thinks in almost exactly opposite terms. It sees the road to success in self assurance, in not allowing ourselves to be too moved by the suffering around us, in not being too concerned about truth and righteousness. The child of God has to realize that he belongs to a world of different standards, standards which appear foolish to others, and standards which require a price to be paid to maintain them.

Our Lord paid this price, not only in His death, but in His life. He was despised and rejected of men, criticized and spurned because He refused the standards of the world. His crucifixion, from the human angle, was but the culmination of a rejection He daily had to suffer because of His righteousness which showed up the sin of the world around.

The kingdom of heaven (vs. 3, 10) is first and foremost a matter of peace of heart. Many people from king Solomon to the present age have found that riches and material plenty often go along with empty and frustrated living. Abundant life is never the product of our own selfish way, but of our Lord's way.

"You are the salt of the earth" (v. 13). "You are the light of the world" (v. 14). This is so as we live in the way of the Lord. This alone makes the world worth living in. If everything which originated in the walk and ministry of our Lord Jesus Christ were removed from this earth, it would be little less than hell. Whatever spiritual light there is in this world comes from Christ through His people. May the Lord help us to fulfil our privileged position, to be the salt of the earth and the light of the world.

Matt. 5. 5; Matt. 5. 6; Matt. 5. 8; Matt. 5. 13; Matt. 5. 16

The Person and Work of Christ

HIS INCARNATION

January 20

Reading: Matthew 1. 18-25

The coming of our Lord into the world was not the same as that of an ordinary man. It was both the birth of a man and the incarnation of the Son of God. It is not, therefore, surprising that the mode of His birth was unusual. Matthew tells us that our Lords's conception was miraculous, that the agent was the Holy Spirit, and that Mary was a virgin (v. 23). The transmission of sin, which has been the heritage of natural man since the fall, was interrupted in the case of our Lord. This does not mean that the virgin birth alone was sufficient to enable Him to be born without sin, but we can appreciate His sinlessness more readily when we consider the unique circumstances which surrounded His birth.

Most of the passages of Scripture which refer to the incarnation do so in connection with redemption (v. 21). Our Lord was born to die the death of the cross. Without the cross redemption would have been impossible, but we must not view the cross in isolation from the rest of our Lord's life. The one who died on the cross was one who displayed perfection in the previous three decades of His life amongst men. He was born to be the perfect man, and that entailed living a life in the circumstances all people have to face.

In his first letter to the Corinthians Paul speaks of our Lord as the 'last Adam' (1 Cor. 15. 45). Just as the first Adam was the head of a race of sinful men, so the last Adam has become the Head of a new spiritual race of redeemed people. For this reason He took a body similar to our own, and lived a life of complete obedience to the divine standard in the midst of the trials and temptations of the world. He is fully able to guide those He has redeemed, and worthy to be their Head.

A further important reason for the incarnation was the manifestation of the character, wisdom and love of God in a way that we can all readily understand. We see this clearly in the Gospel records, but it was also evident in the thirty hidden years between our Lord's birth and His baptism, as the voice of God on that occasion suggests (Matt. 3. 17). Let us thank God for the miracle of the incarnation, and pray that we in our lives may show forth something of the character, wisdom and love of God.

Matt. 1. 21; 1 Cor. 15. 49; Isa. 7. 14; 2 Cor. 5. 21; 2 John 7

The Person and Work of Christ

THE CENTURION AND JOSEPH OF ARIMATHEA

January 21   Reading: Luke 23. 44-56

Here we see the effect upon two different men of the crucifixion of our Lord. One was an officer of the Roman army, described simply as 'the centurion' (v. 47). The other was Joseph of Arimathea, 'a good and righteous man' and a member of the Sanhedrin (v.50).

The centurion, the officer in charge of the crucifixion, was a Gentile, and a man no doubt well used to the horrors of war and of execution. Whether he had any previous contact with our Lord Jesus Christ we do not know, but his observation of our Lord from the time of His condemnation to the time of His death made a most dramatic impact upon him. Luke tells us that he 'praised God' and said, "Certainly this man was innocent" (v. 47). Matthew in his account tells us that the centurion and the other soldiers with him said, "Truly this was the Son of God" (Matt. 27. 54). Luke's remark of the Centurion's praising God suggests that he could have been one of the 'God-fearers' of whom we read in the Acts of the Apostles, Gentiles who, disgusted with the evils of heathenism, sought truth in the Jewish synagogue. He was certainly convinced not only of our Lord's innocence, but of His godly character. The false accusations and fanaticism of a section of the crowd could not dim the witness of the life of our Lord to a man whose heart was open to the truth.

Joseph of Arimathea had longer contact with Jesus. John tells us that he was a secret disciple (John 19. 38), but he was not without courage. He had refused to vote in the Sanhedrin for the death of Jesus, a fact which appears to have been known publicly, and Luke speaks highly of him as a man who 'was looking for the kingdom of God'. It must have taken considerable courage for Joseph to ask Pilate for Jesus's body, but our Lord's death, and no doubt the memory of His life as well, had done something for Joseph. He could be a secret disciple no longer. Tradition tells us of Joseph living the rest of his life in the service of Christ. Whether this was actually the case we do not know for sure, but it may well be so. The life of our Lord Jesus Christ demands a response from us all. The response of the Centurion and of Joseph of Arimathea was a positive one. Let us pray that the Lord will embolden us to follow Him more faithfully.

John 21. 21-22; Luke 9. 23; Matt. 10. 32; Mark 1. 17; John 8. 12

Fellowship

THE IMPORTANCE OF FELLOWSHIP

January 22   Reading: Philippians 1. 1-11

Paul was writing to the Philippians from prison in Rome. News of the Philippian church had reached him through the visit of Epaphroditus (2:25), and it seems that the Philippians were facing problems which were threatening their fellowship together. Paul knew the vital importance of Christian fellowship, so he is anxious to write to the Philippians in order to help them in their difficulties.

The difficulties Paul himself was facing were much greater than those of the Philippians, but he is far more concerned about them than he is about himself. Not only is he concerned to be of help to them, he is also very much aware of the help he receives from them through their prayers and love, even though they are far apart. Again and again in Paul's letters we see how he treasured his oneness with all the people of God. Their unity was no mere theory. It was a means of tremendous spiritual strength both to them and to himself. He still looks upon the Philippians as partners in the gospel (v. 5).

All of us have such a long way to go spiritually. Paul realized this of himself as well as of others. When we look back in our spiritual experience, we may seem to have come far, but when we look ahead to the perfection of our Lord we have to admit that we have only begun on the way. This is what Paul says in v.6. God will complete the work He has begun. Nevertheless, we are still only beginners. When we understand this we will have much more patience with our fellow believers, and we will begin to realize how much patience they need to have with us.

Fellowship is important because through it we grow together in the Lord. Difficulties there will always be, but we learn by facing them, not by sweeping them aside or trying to escape from them. Notice Paul's prayer in vs. 9-11. Fellowship can only be fostered in love, in a real heart-concern for one another. When we love we will try to understand (v. 9). When we try to understand, we will become more perceptive of right and wrong (v. 9), and less hasty to jump to conclusions (v. 10). Our own characters will be purified, and we will be a blessing, not a stumbling block to others (v. 10). Fellowship enables us to exercise the life of Christ within us, and makes us more like Him.

Phil. 1. 6; Phil. 1. 9; 1 Cor. 1. 9; 1 John 4. 11; John 17. 20-21.

Fellowship

THE BASIS OF FELLOWSHIP

January 23   Reading: 2 Timothy 2. 14-22

When Paul wrote his second letter to Timothy, there was widespread declension within the church. It was often difficult to know who was a child of God and who was not. Paul sets down basic principles to help us in such circumstances.

Fellowship is not just the idea that all who belong to the Lord Jesus Christ are one, though this is true. Fellowship is something very practical, and is to be seen principally in the life of the local church. We need, therefore, to be able to recognize those with whom fellowship is possible, otherwise our attempts at fellowship will end up in confusion.

What is the basis of fellowship? In v. 19 Paul says, "The Lord knows those who are his." In other words, the final judgement as to who belongs to the Lord and who does not, is not in our hands. It is in the hands of God. We have no right to arrogate to ourselves the claim that our own little company are true believers and others are not. God will eventually make that judgement, and He will make no mistakes. We do, however, have the responsibility of discerning those who make up the fellowship of the local church. Our discernment is aided by the Spirit of God, yet it still contains that human element which makes us liable to err, so though we cannot be dogmatic in our judgement, we still have solid ground on which to base our fellowship.

What are the factors we are responsible to discern? First, a concern for practical righteousness (v. 19). If a person does not have an obvious desire for righteous living, we have no grounds to accept him as part of a Christian fellowship, whatever professions he may make. He should be a person who calls 'upon the Lord from a pure heart' (v. 22). In other words, he should be someone we are confident has a real heart for the Lord. Together we aim to grow in 'righteousness, faith, love and peace' (v. 22). The believing Christian should be a person of spiritual, not selfish aims. The ministry of the Word is of prime importance (v. 15). So is freedom from pettiness which Paul calls 'disputing about words' (v. 14), 'godless chatter' (v. 16), and 'youthful passions' (v. 22). Let us thank God that He has given us clear guidelines for our fellowship, and let us pray that we ourselves may be more worthy of the fellowship of the church.

2 Tim. 2. 19; 2 Tim. 2. 22; 1 John 2. 4; James 3. 17; 1 John 3. 24.

Fellowship

THE RESPONSIBILITIES OF FELLOWSHIP

January 24 Reading: Romans 12. 9-21

Paul here explains some of our responsibilities as members of the fellowship of the body of Christ. In his exhortations there is a balance between attitudes and actions. We may pride ourselves on doing what is right and treating others fairly, but if our attitude is wrong our actions will not foster fellowship. Many of the problems we have in fellowship are due to wrong attitudes, not wrong actions. We cannot judge the attitudes of others, for we have no means of knowing them unless they show themselves in acts, but we are responsible to face up to our own attitudes before God and to judge them.

There is a spurious love that is motivated by gain, or seeks to get more than it gives. Christian love is completely sincere (v. 9). Paul uses strong words when he says, "Hate what is evil, hold fast to what is good" (v. 9). What many people hate is the consequences of evil rather than evil itself. They avoid evil lest they be inconvenienced by its results, and they do good only to the extent that it enhances their own prestige. This is not a Christian attitude. The Christian must decisively repudiate evil and have a passionate concern for what is good. Some of the attitudes we are responsible to foster are, a right attitude towards God's people as members of the same family (v. 10), a right attitude towards God which loves to serve Him (v. 11) and counts every trial a privilege (v. 12). Serving God means, among other things, serving His people (v. 13) and praying for them (v. 12).

In vs. 14-21 Paul points out the need to be able to identify ourselves with others (v. 15), and to preserve a right spirit when we are treated unjustly (v. 17). The attitude of humility so prominent in the previous verses is the key. To 'weep with those who weep' may be easy. Rejoicing with those who rejoice is often hindered by jealousy and envy, those subtle symptoms of a proud heart. We may imagine that there is little injustice in a company of the Lord's people, but it is a sad fact that believing Christians can, and often do speak and act towards their fellow believers in a way which must bring great grief to the heart of God. Our responsibility is to bless (v. 14), to take thought for what is noble in the sight of all (v. 17), and evil will be overcome with good (v. 21).

Rom. 12. 9; Rom. 12. 15; Rom. 12. 11; Rom.•12. 17; Rom. 12. 21

Fellowship

THE PROBLEMS OF FELLOWSHIP

January 25   Reading: 3 John 9-15

3 John was written to a brother named Gaius, apparently an elder in a local church, and a man respected for his testimony and hospitality. John mentions three characters in this little letter, Gaius himself, Demetrius (v. 12) another brother known for his godly life, and 'Diotrophes who likes to put himself first'. There are very few assemblies without a Diotrophes, and, fact, there is something of the spirit of Diotrophes in all of us, the spirit of self-love and self-importance.

The problem in the church was not theological, otherwise John would almost certainly have exposed it. It was a problem of personality and personal ambition such as all too often disfigures the local testimony. The evils of Diotrophes' attitude are clear. He had a spirit of resentment against John whom he considered a rival. He was unwilling to learn or receive correction from John (v. 10) or from anyone else. He resorted to slanderous gossip in an attempt to discredit John (v. 10). He refused to receive brethren of good testimony who were welcomed by the rest of the church (v. 10). Not only did he refuse to accept them himself, but he sought to drive a wedge between them and their fellow-believers (v. 10). He even went as far as presuming to separate from the church those who would not bow to his wishes (v. 10).

What is to be done in such dire circumstances? John makes quite clear his intention to speak out against the evil (v. 10), but beyond that he does not counsel stern action. The church is not to give in to Diotrophes, but it is not to retaliate in the same contentious, proud spirit that he displays. "Beloved, do not imitate evil but imitate good" (v. 11), and he mentions Demetrius as an example of spiritual behaviour (v. 12). Demetrius was exalting the Lord. So was Gaius. They should continue to minister fellowship and hospitality, not give in to evil, but hold fast to truth and God-honouring conduct.

The problems of Christian fellowship are real. The answer to them is in steadfastly following a straight path and exalting the Lord. Lord, help us to uplift Thee in our words and actions, and prevent us from being drawn into fleshly disputings.

3 John 11; Rom. 12. 9; Mark 10. 43; Mark 10. 45; 1 Peter 5. 2-3.

Fellowship

THE SELF-GIVING OF FELLOWSHIP

January 26   Reading: Philippians 2. 14-29

One of the principles of Christian fellowship which Paul explains in his letter to the Philippians is the principle of self-giving. In the great passage at the beginning of ch. 2 he shows how our Lord gave Himself to the extent of dying the death of the cross. In the second part of ch. 2 we see the spirit of self-giving in Paul himself.

Paul does not set out deliberately to show the Philippians his own self-giving spirit. In fact he was probably quite unconscious that what he said demonstrated this aspect of his character. After all, if we are always congratulating ourselves on what we do for others, it means we are more concerned with ourselves than with those we profess to serve. Virtue is spontaneous, not self-confident. Otherwise it ceases to be virtue.

Paul was in prison awaiting his trial before Caesar, but his concern is for the Philippians, not for himself. He is concerned for their public testimony (vs. 15-16), and if the end of his ministry is that he be called to pay the price of his life, he considers it abundantly worth while if, through his fellowship, the Philippians have learned to know the Lord more deeply (v. 17).

There is sorrow in Paul's heart as he thinks of people who profess to belong to the Lord, yet who 'look after their own interests, not those of Jesus Christ' (v. 21). This was completely the reverse of the life Paul had experienced in Christ. It was a denial of the gospel. On the other hand, there is joy as he mentions Timothy. Paul is full of appreciation for Timothy's loyalty to him (v. 21), but it was not a self-seeking loyalty which excluded others. Timothy had a heart of concern for all the Lord's people, including the Philippians (v. 20).

Finally there is Epaphroditus. Epaphroditus had come from Philippi with news and gifts from the church. He too was a man who gave himself for others, and had probably volunteered to be with Paul to serve him as he awaited his trial (v. 25). Paul could have kept Epaphroditus to minister to his needs, but after Epaphroditus had recovered from a severe illness, Paul thinks first of him and the Philippians who were worried over his illness. He sends Epaphroditus back to Philippi.

Let us thank the Lord for such faithful believers, and let us pray that we may have more of the spirit of self-giving.

Phil. 2 13-14; Rom. 12. 10; Gal. 6. 2; 1 Cor. 10. 24; 1 Peter 4. 8.

Fellowship

THE EXTENT OF FELLOWSHIP

Reading: 1 John 5. 1-5

Fellowship is expressed most fully within the local curch, but we also need to remember that the family of God is much wider than the local expression. Paul and the other writers of the New Testament epistles had a very deep sense of the breadth of Christian fellowship. We today are often faced with opportunities to cooperate with others in the extension of the kingdom of God. Should we retreat into our own shell and refuse to have anything to do with other Christians? Or should we try to cooperate on every opportunity that presents itself?

God has given to each local church its responsibilities which it should faithfully fulfil, and the church's main energies should be expended in this work. Beyond this, however, opportunities of witness along with others should not be neglected. They can be a means of spiritual enrichment as well as of testimony to others. There must, however, be a proper foundation for cooperation.

John's first letter sets down for us the marks of a true child of God. John emphasises three factors which he repeats a number of times in the course of his epistles. In ch. 5. 1-5 these three factors are drawn together. They are right belief, right living, and a right attitude to the brethren. To put them another way, right doctrine, righteousness, fellowship.

Our fellowship cannot extend to any who do not accept that Jesus is the Christ, the Son of God (vs. 1, 5). We cannot overlook any denial of the basic fundamental truths of the faith. But that is not enough. What is professed must be practised. A child of God should show in his daily life evidence of obedience to the Lord and victory over the world (vs. 2-4). Furthermore, there should be evidence of a genuine love for all the people of God (vs. 1-2). One of these characteristics alone is not sufficient, but where all three coincide in the life of an individual or an assembly, we should recognize them and respect them as children of God, and there is a sure foundation for practical fellowship in Christian witness.

The Lord has united us together in a wonderful family. Let us thank Him for it and pray that we may show forth oneness wherever we meet those who believe in Him, live for Him, and love His people.

1 John 5. 1; 1 John 5. 2; 1 John 5. 4; 1 John 3. 10; 1 John 3. 7.

Fellowship

EUODIA AND SYNTYCHE

January 28   Reading: Philippians 4. 1-7

There must have been some good reason for Paul to mention Euodia and Syntyche by name in this letter. They were two mature and highly respected sisters who had made a significant contribution to the work of the gospel (v. 3). Were Euodia and Syntyche perhaps the centre of the fellowship problem in the Philippian church? We cannot know for sure, but it is very probable. Obviously their own fellowship was not as it should have been, or Paul would not have written to them to 'agree in the Lord' (v. 2). This is a warning to us all how easily we can be the cause of marring the fellowship of the Lord's people, even though we may feel we have reached some measure of spiritual maturity.

From Paul's commendation of Euodia and Syntyche it is inconceivable that their difference was of a trivial nature. A careful reading of the epistle suggests that the problem may have been of a doctrinal nature and one in which loyalty to Paul himself was involved. These two factors, doctrine and personal loyalty, frequently enter into church problems, and very often they are found together. In our disagreements with one another it is easy for each one to claim that he is standing for the truth and thus to condemn the other. Seldom, however, are our difficulties matters of straightforward right and wrong. If they were, a solution would be much easier than it is. Usually there is some emotional involvement as well, perhaps a matter of loyalty, or a spirit of resentment over the way something was said or done. When this is so the doctrinal question may be settled, but the problem still remains, and very easily it can affect the whole life of the church.

Paul entreats Euodia and Syntyche to agree 'in the Lord' (v.2). This is a significant phrase. It points to their unalterable relationship in Christ. When problems arise, this is something on which we need to lay hold. We may disagree, but God has put us together, a fact far greater than all our difficulties. When we realize this we will find something in the other for rejoicing (v. 4), and will begin to learn forbearance (v.5).

Let us thank the Lord for putting us together, and let us pray that, whatever our difficulties, we may never lose sight of this great fact.

Phil. 4. 5; Phil. 4. 6; Eph. 4. 2; Col. 1. 9; Rom. 14. 19.

The Holy Spirit

HIS PERSONALITY AND DEITY

January 29   Reading: John 14. 1-17

John chs. 14-16 are part of our Lord's final discourse with His disciples. They are, therefore, chapters of great importance. Jesus was preparing His disciples for His departure (vs. 1-3), but the ministry of the gospel He had come to initiate was not going to cease. It was to be carried on by the Holy Spirit (vs. 16-17). John chs. 14-16 are basic chapters for an understanding of the Holy Spirit's person and work.

In the first part of John 14 Jesus assures His disciples that His departure is not in any sense going to be a loss to them (v. 12). Whatever they had found in the fellowship of our Lord during the three and a half years they had been with Him, they would continue to find in the new era they were soon to enter. After giving these assurances, the Lord mentions the Holy Spirit, (vs. 15-16). In introducing His disciples to the Holy spirit, Jesus uses the word Counselor which literally means a person called alongside to strengthen and help. In this we have an indication of the Holy Spirit's personality. We must never think of the Holy Spirit as merely an influence or the breath of life. The description of His work and His relationship to us both here and elsewhere in the New Testament indicates characteristics which belong only to a person, intelligence, will and emotion. He is no less a person than God the Father and God the Son.

The Holy Spirit is also God. Jesus tells His disciples that the world cannot receive the Spirit (v. 17). The world is that section of people who live as if God did not exist. They rejected God the Father; they rejected God the Son; and they would reject the Holy Spirit too since God was of no concern to them. V. 16 ascribes omnipresence to the Holy Spirit, a quality of deity, and our Lord identifies Himself with the Spirit in saying, "He dwells with you" (v. 17). At the same time, in saying that He 'will be in you', Jesus shows the Spirit's separate personality.

The Godhead is a mystery beyond the capacity of our finite minds to understand, but the deity and personality of the Holy Spirit who is one with the Father and the Son are clearly shown in the Scriptures. Let us thank God for His Holy Spirit.

John 14. 15; Matt. 12. 32; John 15. 26; Eph. 4. 30; Job 33. 4.

The Holy Spirit

THE SCOPE OF HIS WORK

January 30

Reading: John 16. 1-14

Many believers make the mistake of holding a far too limited idea of the work of the Holy Spirit. This is usually so because they leave out of their consideration much of what the Bible says about the Holy Spirit, particlarly the teaching of John chs. 14-16. There Jesus tries to impress upon His disciples the advantages of the Holy Spirit's coming (v. 7). When He was with them, Jesus was voluntarily bound by human limitations. The Spirit would know no such restrictions. Wherever a child of God might be, the Spirit would be there with him, and believers would begin to learn to live not by seeing the Lord bodily, but by faith.

Vs. 8-11 is a wonderful summary of certain aspects of the Spirit's work. It shows us first that the work of the Holy Spirit begins in the world (v. 8), long before anyone comes to know the Lord in a personal way. The Spirit is at work, bringing him to see his need, convicting of sin. Through the Spirit we come to realize the righteousness and worth of the Lord (v. 10), that He is who He claims to be. Through the Holy Spirit the fact of judgement is brought home to us. We see God's attitude to sin and learn that the judgement was borne on calvary. All this is the work of the Holy Spirit in the world (v. 8). As we look back in our experiences we can often discern the working of the Spirit as He led us to a place of faith in Christ, though at the time we were probably unconscious of His work or even of His existence.

But the work of the Holy Spirit continues. One of the main emphases of our Lord's talk here with His disciples is the permanent place that the Holy Spirit occupies in the life of the believer. "He will guide you into all the truth" (v. 13). Our knowledge of truth should always be growing if we really know the Lord, and it is through the Holy Spirit's teaching that this knowledge increases. Not only does He teach, He glorifies Christ (v. 14). He takes the truth and applies it to our daily lives that we might live for Him.

Let us pray that God will help us to understand the breadth and greatness of the Holy Spirit's work in the lives of His people.

John 16. 7; John 16. 8; John 16. 13; John 16. 14; Rom. 8. 11.

The Holy Spirit

THE BAPTISM OF THE HOLY SPIRIT

January 31

Reading: Acts 2. 1-12

Before our Lord ascended He said to His disciples, "Before many days you shall be baptized with the Holy Spirit." Acts 2 recounts the fulfilling of this promise. V.4 tells us, "They were all filled with the Holy Spirit." The word 'baptized' is not used here, but we cannot doubt that this is the experience to which our Lord referred.

The first thing we need to notice is that this was a corporate, not an individual experience. At the time, the disciples were 'all together in one place' (v. 1), and the symbolism of the tongues of fire indicates that the fire came from one source and demonstrated the unity of the disciples as belonging to that one source. The power of the witness of the early church lay in the unity of the Lord's people.

Pentecost was a unique experience. It was the birth of the church in which all human barriers were broken down. God showed this by three other extensions of the experience of Pentecost, in Acts 8. 14-17 where the Holy Spirit is revealed to the Samaritans, in Acts 10. 44-48 where He is revealed to the Gentiles, and in Acts 19. 1-7 where He is revealed to some disciples who had not progressed beyond the teaching of John the Baptist. In the first and last instances the work of the Holy Spirit is accompanied by speaking in tongues. In Acts we have no other accounts of the baptism of the Holy Spirit. Paul, however, in writing to the Corinthians says, "For by one Spirit we were all baptized into one body—Jews or Greeks, slaves or free—and all were made to drink of one Spirit" (1 Cor. 12.13). He shows that the baptizm of the Spirit is the Holy Spirit's uniting of each believer to the rest of the body of Christ.

The teaching of the New Testament points to Pentecost as the foundation of the church, an experience, therefore, which cannot be repeated. Now as the Holy Spirit brings a person to birth in Christ, He baptizes that person into the unity of the church. This is not water baptism. Baptism signifies identification, and the baptism of the Spirit is the act of the Spirit who adds to the church such as should be saved. Let us thank the Lord for having baptized us with the Holy Spirit into the fellowship of the church.

Acts 2. 1-2; Acts 1.8; 1 Cor. 12. 13; Eph. 2. 14; Gal. 3. 28

31

The Holy Spirit

HIS WORK THROUGH THE WORD

February 1   Reading: John 14.18-26

How does the Holy Spirit do His work? The Holy Spirit may work in many ways. He may speak through the counsel of another believer. He may speak through circumstances. He may speak through something we are reading. But basic to every means the Holy Spirit uses is the Word. He never says or does anything that is inconsistent with the Word of God.

As the Lord prepares His disciples for His leaving them, He has quite a lot to say about His Word, or His words. He speaks of the love of His disciples (vs. 21, 23) and the proof of their love which is obedience to His words. Whenever a person truly loves the Lord Jesus Christ he should have a deep concern for His Word and a desire to obey it. So when the Holy Spirit comes He will bring to remembrance 'all that I have said to you' (v. 26). To put it another way, the Spirit will work through the Word. Our Lord was, of course, here referring to what He was actually saying to His disciples. We do not have the Lord physically with us today, but we do still have His words written in the pages of the Bible, and it is through the Bible that the Holy Spirit does His work.

There are many pairs of things in the Bible which always go together, faith and works is one example. When God puts two things together we must be careful never to separate them. The Holy Spirit and the Word of God go together. Whenever we emphasise one of these to the detriment of the other we get into difficulty. Some people talk of the Holy spirit as if they had His ear in a special way which makes the Bible unnecessary. What they claim to be the voice of the Holy Spirit is usually the voice of their own desires, perhaps even selfish and unspiritual desires. On the other hand, when a person tries to use the Bible without dependence upon the Spirit, he becomes a legalist and he finds in the Word bondage instead of liberty.

Since the Holy Spirit works through the Word, we cannot expect Him to do His work in us unless we ourselves are people of the Word. Let us thank God for His Word and for His Holy Spirit who speaks through it, and let us pray that He will make us people who love and live in the Bible.

John 14. 23; John 14. 26; John 8. 31-32; John 15. 26; Prov. 14. 12.

The Holy Spirit

HIS PURPOSE IN THE BELIEVER

February 2   Reading: John 15. 1-8

John 15 is often spoken of without reference to the Holy Spirit. It is true that the Holy Spirit is not mentioned till v. 26, but the chapter is part of our Lord's last discourse in which He is preparing His disciples for His departure and the Holy Spirit's coming. What He says here is illustrative of the Spirit's work.

The illustration of the vine was familiar to the disciples, for it is used of Israel in the Old Testament. There, however, it is always used of Israel's unfaithfulness Isaiah and Jeremiah both see the vine of Israel as having gone wild (Isa. 5. 1-7; Jer. 2. 21). In contrast to this, the Lord says that He is the 'true vine' (v. 1), and His people are the branches (v. 5). What was impossible through a system based on law, is possible through the relationship of Christ with His people. This vine will bear good fruit.

Fruit-bearing is the end to which the Holy Spirit is working in the life of the believer, and the fruit is the character of the Lord Himself. Paul gives a list of the fruits of the Spirit in his letter to the Galatians (Gal. 5. 22-23). A well tended vine grows prolifically, but it requires a great deal of attention if it is to bear a maximum yield. All of us should realize the tremendous amount of work the Holy Spirit has to do in each one of us in order to fulfil God's purpose. The vine illustrates some of the means which the Holy Spirit uses. Like a vine, our lives require pruning. Pruning entails the cutting way of what is unnecessary. What is removed may not always be bad in itself, but it may retard what God wants to do. Often the good is the enemy of the best. The Pruning of discipline is not pleasant, but through it we learn and grow as we never could without it.

The Spirit's work through the Word is also implied in v. 3. Constantly we need to subject our thoughts, our words, our actions to the scrutiny of God's Word, and to accept its judgement as the Spirit applies it to us. In the acceptance of its judgement there is cleansing. Acceptance is really what our Lord means when He says, "Abide in me." To abide in Him is to accept the work He wants to do, and to accept whatever means He uses. Let us thank God for the purpose He is accomplishing in us through the Holy Spirit, and let us pray that He will help us to abide in Him.

John 15. 2; John 15. 4; John 15. 8; John 15. 6; Isa. 60. 1

The Holy Spirit

HIS WORK IN REGENERATION

February 3   Reading: Titus 3. 1-7

Paul casts his mind back to his pre-conversion days and reminds Titus that they were both very much part of a fallen world (v. 3). "But," he says, "when the goodness and loving kindness of God our Saviour appeared, he saved us." Then follows an expression of the transforming work of the gospel in which the Holy Spirit plays a prominent part. In vs. 4-6 all three persons of the trinity are mentioned. All are active in the dramatic work of regeneration, but the most direct activity is attributed to the Holy Spirit. He carries out a two-fold work, regeneration and renewal (v. 5).

We have already seen that the Holy Spirit begins His work in the world, that is before a person is brought into a vital relationship with Jesus Christ. Through the Holy Spirit, the person is led up to the point of that relationship. Now we find the Holy Spirit active in the forging of that relationship, the work of regeneration. Regeneration is a decisive act of God in which He implants within men the principle of new life, a life whose bent is towards holiness. Scripture looks upon the Holy Spirit in particular as the bestower of life, and as the one who produces the fruit of holiness, so it is no surprise to find Him here in the work of regeneration.

Regeneration and renewal (v. 5) are an expansion of the phrase 'he saved us' earlier in the same verse. The Greek word for 'saved' is one of the great words of the New Testament. It denotes a work which affects the entire man, spirit, soul and body. The regenerating work of the Holy Spirit is basic to all that He subsequently has to do. From it follows the process of renewal, an activity in which the Holy Spirit is engaged throughout a believer's life-time. So within the compass of two words we see something of the all-embracing nature of the Spirit's work in the life of every child of God. He is there at the beginning, initiating new life, and from that point on He is at work developing and sustaining it.

Let us thank the Lord for the regenerating work of the Holy Spirit, and let us pray that we may be constantly open to His continuing work of renewal.

Titus 3. 5; Rom. 8. 9; John 3. 5; John 3. 6; 1 John 3. 24

The Holy Spirit

STEPHEN

Reading: Acts 7. 44-60

Stephen was a man 'full of the Holy Spirit' (v. 55). We first read of him in Acts 6 where he was one of the seven chosen to oversee the distribution of benefits to the widows of the church. There we are told that he was 'a man full of faith and of the Holy Spirit' (v. 5). Scripture uses the term 'filled with the Spirit' occasionally to describe a person's general spiritual condition. Our Lord was 'full of the Holy Spirit' from His baptism (Luke 4.1), and John the Baptist was 'filled with the Holy Spirit even from his mother's womb' (Luke 1.15).

More often, however, the expression is used of a specific experience granted to a person at a time of particular need, an experience which may be repeated many times over. It is never used of a climatic spiritual experience which guarantees an automatic continuing spiritual power. It is also significant that Stephen did not himself claim to be filled with the Spirit. The testimony is based on the observation of others and of Luke who wrote the book of Acts. Stephen's enduement of the Spirit in Acts 6 obviously granted him a very practical concern for the needs of others, and an enabling to deal with others with wisdom and grace. It is in his defence before the Jewish council that the characteristics of this Spirit-filled man stand out most clearly.

In his defence, Stephen recounts the history of the nation from the time of Abraham, and draws certain lessons from it. A person filled with the Spirit will be able to learn from the experiences of others. Stephen also recognized the spiritual implications of what he learned, another mark of the Spirit's powerful presence. He saw God's deeper purpose where David and Solomon had failed to do so (vs. 45-48). They had built a temple which, twice reconstructed, still obsessed the Jews of Stephen's day, but what God wanted was a spiritual house.

Stephen's message was one which could not be ignored. It had either to be accepted or rejected, and he was completly committed to the Lord whatever the cost of his faithfulness might mean. In death he prayed for his persecutors and forgave them. Let us thank God for the example of Stephen, a man filled with the Spirit, and let us pray that the marks of the Spirit may be evident in our lives also.

Eph. 5. 18; Eph. 3. 16; Luke 1. 15; 2 Cor. 4. 7; 2 Cor. 3. 18

The Fruit of the Spirit

THE FRUIT OF THE SPIRIT

February 5   Reading: Galatians 5. 16-26

Paul contrasts the 'fruit of the Spirit' (v. 22) with the 'works of the flesh' (v. 19). In this way he emphasises the transforming power of the Spirit's work and shows that the fruit of the Spirit is the only and inevitable proof of the work of the Spirit.

The works of the flesh fall into three general divisions. 1. Sensual sins (v. 19). 2. Sins in the religious realm, 'idolatry, sorcery' (v. 20). 3. Sins of relationship (vs. 20-21). 4. Personal excesses, 'drunkenness, carousing, and the like' (v. 21). In this list which, of course, is not exhaustive, the sins of relationship form the biggest category. They are the inner attitudes from which the other more blatant sins flow. Let us look into our own hearts and ask ourselves how far we have victory over the sins of personal relationship. This is an indication of the extent to which we walk in the Spirit.

Paul's use of the words 'works' and 'fruit' is significant. The flesh is a weed which produces nothing of value, but the Spirit produces fruit, something of value and of intrinsic good. Nine fruits of the Spirit are enumerated. They can be divided into three sets of three, and depict a believer's relationship to God, to others, and to himself. In the fall, man was separated from God and His fellow men, and his own inner harmony was lost. In the fruit of the Spirit we see these relationships restored.

Love, joy and peace (v. 22) find their basic and deepest expression in our relationship to God. Our love of God and our peace and joy in Him are the foundation of our relationship to others and of our own inner harmony. Patience, kindness, goodness (v. 22) indicate our relationship to others which should be characterized both by right attitudes and right actions. The last three virtues, faithfulness, gentleness, self-control (vs. 22-23) describe the spiritual man himself, faithful and humble, both descriptive of self-control.

The fruit of the Spirit still has to grow much more in us all, but it should appear in some rudimentary form as the outflow of the Spirit's working in the life of every child of God. Let us pray that the fruit of the Spirit may mature more and more in each one of us.

Gal. 6. 16; Gal. 5. 22-23; Gal. 5. 24; Gal. 5. 25-26; Eph. 5. 9

The Fruit of the Spirit

LOVE

February 6   Reading: 1 Corinthians 13. 1-7

There are two words in the New Testament translated 'love'. It would not be too much to say that the word used here and in Gal. 5.22 is the distinctive word of the Christian faith. It is used to express the essential nature of God (1 John 4.8), His attitude to His Son (John 17.26), to the whole of mankind (John 3. 16), and particularly to His children (John 14.21). It also expresses the attitude God wants His children to show to one another (John 13.34), and to all men (1 Thess. 3.12). This love is not merely an emotional impulse, above all it is not self-seeking, but is concerned with the welfare of others.

Paul shows us the absolute necessity of love (vs. 1-3) and then goes on to enumerate its characteristics (vs. 4-7). The Corinthian church was gifted in many ways (1 Cor. 1: 5-7), but it was deficient in the one essential Christian characteristic, and the result was confusion. Without the attitude of love, all else is worthless, be it dramatic spiritual gifts (v. 2), or extreme sacrifice (v. 3). These things which are so often considered the marks of true spirituality are of no value whatever if they are not based on love towards God and others.

Vs. 4-7 stress the self-effacing character of love. To read honestly through these verses is to realize how very far short we are in our experience of the love of God. "Love is patient and kind" (v. 4). It accepts injury without thought of revenge. It returns good for evil. "Love is not jealous or boastful; it is not arrogant or rude" (vs. 4-5). Love is happy when God blesses and uses others. It does not make itself out to be superior to others or try to dominate over them. "Love does not insist on its own way; it is not irritable or resen ful" (v. 5). Love is not self-seeking. It can accept disagreement graciously. "It does not rejoice at wrong, but rejoices in the right" (v. 6). Love does not sympathize with evil, but has a concern that others should be established in what is true. "Love bears all things, believes all things. hopes all things, endures all things" (v. 7). Love does not foster an attitude of constant suspicion. It sees what God can do with people.

Let us thank God for His love. Let us pray that we may learn to love as He does.

1 Cor. 13. 1; 1 Cor. 13. 2; 1 Cor. 13. 3; 1 Cor. 13. 4-5; 1 Cor. 13. 6-7

The Fruit of the Spirit

JOY AND PEACE

February 7   Reading: John 14. 27-31; 15. 10-11

In John 15 through the illustration of the vine and the branches our Lord has been speaking of the work of the Spirit pruning and disciplining His people that they may bear the fruit of His character. In v. 10 He speaks of the need of obedience and then says, "These things I have spoken to you that my joy may be in you, and that your joy may be full" (v. 11). Discipline and implicit obedience are not generally looked upon as particularly joyful experiences, but it was in obedience to the will of the Father that Jesus found the triumphant joy that took Him through the experience of the cross.

The joy of Jesus was joy in doing the Father's will. This is the joy He commends to us, and He says it is a joy which is 'full'. It is never doubtful or half-hearted. The history of the church over the past two thousand years is full of examples of men and women of God who have found the joy of doing His will greater by far than their many sufferings. When we submit to God, joy is one of the fruits of the Spirit.

Joy wants to do the will of God. Peace is the confidence that, in doing His will, God's sovereign hand is there working out His purposes. Our Lord bequeathed both His joy and His peace to his disciples. "Peace I leave with you; my peace I give to you" (14. 27). Our Lord said these words as He faced the cross. He not only rejoiced to do what the Father wanted Him to do, He also had the confidence or peace that all would work out right, because God does nothing without purpose. The same was to be true of His disciples. When He left, the Holy Spirit would come (v. 26) to guard God's purpose in His people, and to be their enabling in whatever circumstances they might be called to pass through. God's people would never have any reason to worry. The way ahead might not be easy, but the glorious end would always be sure.

This is the difference between the peace of God and the peace that the world offers. In the world, peace is merely absence of trouble. The peace of God is peace in the midst of trouble, a peace unshakable which the world cannot take away. Let us thank god for His peace and joy.

John 14. 27; John 16. 22; Heb. 12. 2; Phil. 4. 7; Isa. 55. 12

38

The Fruit of the Spirit

PATIENCE AND KINDNESS

February 8   Reading: Colossians 3. 5-17

Paul often draws a contrast between the new life and the old. He never ceases to marvel at the transforming grace of God. He urges the Colossians to 'Put to death therefore' the things of the flesh (v. 5) and to 'put on' the characteristics of Christ (v. 12). The emphasis here is on our human response. The fruit of the Spirit is the gracious gift of God, but it is not given to an unresponsive people unwilling to receive it. In this list of Christian graces Paul includes patience and kindness (v. 12), two of the nine-fold fruit of the Spirit of Gal. 5. 22-23.

All the virtues listed here have to do with relationships between man and man. The world sets great value on qualities like cleverness and efficiency. These may be important, but they bring the deadness of the machine to living if they are not conditioned by the basic spiritual virtues which Paul lists here. Life in Christ brings people into fellowship with God, and offers a solution to the problems of daily relationships.

Patience with one another is a reflexion of the patience of God. We do well to consider not only how patient God has been with us in the past, but how patient He continually has to be with us. Where would any of us be today if God had dealt with us with the impatience we so often display to others? In our waywardness God has never given in to despair or cast us aside.

'Kindness' is an interesting word. It is the word our Lord used when He said to His disciples, "My yoke is easy" (Matt. 11.30). We could as well translate it, "My yoke is kind." In the standard we demand of others in our preaching we can be harsh. The 'goodness' of the Pharisees was like this. It was stern and hard. Our Lord never lowers His standards. He never removes the yoke from us, but it is kind, and so it is easy to bear. Let us pray that the Lord will make us more patient and more kind.

Col. 3. 12; Col. 3. 14; Matt. 11. 30; Rom. 11. 22; Heb. 6. 12

The Fruit of the Spirit

GOODNESS AND FAITHFULNESS

February 9   Reading: 2 Thessalonians 1. 3-12

Paul exhorts the Thessalonian believers in the light of the second coming of Christ. He thanks God for their faith and their love for one another, a testimony to the reality of their relationship with the Lord. Then he prays for them (v. 11-12). Paul's prayers are always important, for they sum up some of the most vital needs of Christian living. In this prayer he prays that God will fulfil in them 'every good resolve and work of faith' (v. 11). These two phrases are translations of the words 'goodness' and 'faithfulness' in Gal. 5. 22.

The phrase 'every good resolve' brings out the full force of the word 'goodness'. It is not something passive, but a concern for what is good which is determined to put it into effect. Yesterday we considered the fruit of the Spirit, kindness. Our Lord's character was not harsh like the character of the Pharisees. It was kind. At the same time our Lord does not lower the demands of goodness. He does not lower His standards in order to make things easier. He has an infinite concern for what is right and holy, and a consuming desire to see it fulfilled in His people. He is kind in all His working, but true kindness never sacrifices goodness for an easier way. This is the goodness that is one of the fruits of the Spirit.

The phrase 'work of faith' brings out the full force of the word 'faith' which has two senses. It means both fidelity and belief. It can, therefore, be translated 'faithfulness' as in Gal. 5. 22. It is not something passive. It means both belief in the Lord Jesus Christ and committal to Him as a person. The person who believes in Jesus in this way is ready both to live for Him and work for Him. The fruit of the Spirit combines the ideas of faith and faithfulness as we use these words today. In Scripture, faith and faithfulness are inseparable. As with all the fruits of the Spirit, the supreme example of faithfulness is our Lord Jesus Christ Himself.

Let us thank God for His goodness and faithfulness to us. Let us pray that we may be faithful to Him, and have a greater concern for goodness both in ourselves and in others.

2 Thess. 1. 11; 1 Peter 1. 7; Deut. 7. 9; 1 Cor. 4. 2; Mark 11. 22

The Fruit of the Spirit

GENTLENESS AND SELF CONTROL

February 10   Reading: 2 Corinthians 10. 1-6

In speaking of the gentleness of Christ Paul lays down a powerful principle. We live in a world where the principle of self-assertion is predominant, but God's people have another standard. In our relationships with one another and with the world around, our guiding principle is the gentleness of Christ. The world looks upon this as weakness, but the reality is that 'the weapons of our warfare are not worldly but have divine power to destroy strongholds' (v. 4).

Paul's point is that Christian gentleness is not weak as the world thinks. It is not easy to express the meaning of Paul's Greek word, but it is closely associated with humility. It means not simply gentleness in action, but a spirit of humility before God which accepts all His dealings without resistance, knowing that they are good. This is the source of the Christian's power. Our Lord was gentle of disposition not because He was unable to help Himself, but because He had all the resources of God at His command. He did not need to bluster and make a pose of power. He could afford to leave all quietly in the hands of the Father, knowing that He was in control. The power of the gentleness of Christ has been demonstrated through two thousand years of the church's history. However violent the persecution, whatever the means employed to destroy the faith of God's children, the gospel still is the power of God unto salvation experienced by countless thousands.

Self-control, the last of the nine fruits of the Spirit, is the personal power and poise which flow from the attitude of gentleness. The gifts and capabilities which God has bestowed upon man can all be abused, but a person who is truly dependent upon the Lord will find in Him the power to use what He has given to His glory. Self-control to the Christian is not an assertion of human will power. It is dependent on the control of God to which he gladly submits. The culminating fruit of the Spirit is, therefore, a God-controlled life.

Let us thank God again for the working of His Spirit, and pray that the fruit of the Spirit will be more and more evident in our daily lives.

2 Cor. 10. 1; 1 Tim. 6. 11; Gal. 6. 1; 1 Peter 3. 15; Matt. 11. 29

The Fruit of the Spirit

EBED MELECH

Ebed Melech is a little known character of the Old Testament who lived in a harsh age and long before the truth of the Holy Spirit was fully revealed. God had His faithful people in such days, not only prophets such as Jeremiah, but humble people like Ebed Melech who evidenced the grace of God and the fruit of the Spirit even though their understanding was limited. Ebed Melech did not make any pretence to great spirituality. His actions were natural and his thoughtfulness quite unconscious. This is a mark of the Spirit's working. Jeremiah certainly saw God's grace in this humble man, and no doubt many others did also.

Ebed Melech means 'servant of a king'. He was an Ethiopian attached to the household of king Zedekiah (v. 7), but he was also servant of a much greater king, the King of kings, God Himself, and for his love of the Lord he was spared when Jerusalem was finally overthrown (Jer. 39. 15-18). His love of the Lord and his confidence in God's ways enabled him to speak for Jeremiah at considerable risk to his own life. It is true that Zedekiah respected Jeremiah, but he was not strong enough to resist the demand for his arrest. He held precarious rule over a corrupt people and was harried by two opposing powers, the Chaldeans and the Egyptians. His actions were unpredictable. Ebed Melech could have no assurance that he would heed his request. The king might just as well have him thrown into the pit beside Jeremiah.

Ebed Melech's relationship with God was worked out in his consideration for others. Not only what he did for Jeremiah was kind, but the way he did it. Pulling Jeremiah out of the pit could have been a very painful experience apart from his rescuer's thoughtfulness. The fruit of the Spirit is seen not only in what we do, but in the way we do it. In the whole incident Ebed Melech showed a measure of self-control which was not his own, but came from his deep faith in God.

Lord help us practically to show forth the fruit of the Spirit in our lives.

Col. 1. 10; 1 Peter 2. 6; Matt. 7. 18; Phil. 1. 11; Jer. 39. 17

Man and Sin

MAN MADE IN THE IMAGE OF GOD

February 12   Reading: Genesis 1. 26-31

"Let us make man in our image, after our likeness" (v. 1). Some christians speak as if man were nothing, of no more value than the dust of the ground. Man has fallen, it is true, and with tragic results, but we must not, therefore, consign man to the rubbish heap. God, in creating man, had a great purpose for him, and that purpose is still going to be worked out. Man was the peak of God's creation and, as this passage specifically shows, was given dominion over all else that God had made. Many of the problems within the church today would be obviated if God's people held the same view of man as God does.

Man has a dignity higher than anything else in creation because God created him in His own image (v. 27). What does this mean? There is a tremendous gap between the highest animal and the lowest man, for god has endued man with some of His own special faculties. Man is moral. He has a sense of the difference between right and wrong, and can make choices on the basis of that understanding. The life of an animal, on the other hand, is controlled not by moral choice, but by an inner sense called instinct, whereby it does what is conducive to its own safety and pleasure.

Secondly, man can think. He is a rational being. He is capable of planning to a set purpose as God is. A third indication of God's image in man is man's creativity. Man can make beautiful things. He can produce works of art, and he can appreciate their beauty just as God appreciated the beauty of the world He made (v. 31).

Man also loves. Love, of course, has been debased by the fall as has every God-like quality in man, but man is capable of a quality of love that is nowhere evident in the animal kingdom. A dog may love and be loyal to its master, but that can never be parallelled to the love of God for the world or the love which is the fruit of the Spirit.

Let us thank God for the way He made us, and let us pray that we may recognize more fully the great purpose He had in creating man in His own image.

Gen. 1. 26; Gen. 1. 27; Gen. 1. 31; Heb. 2. 7; Col. 3. 10

Man and Sin

THE FALL

February 13   Reading: Genesis 3. 1-7

The account of creation abundantly proves the goodness and grace of God. He made man in His own likeness and gave him authority over all other created things. Man, however, was not autonomous. He was dependent upon God, and in that fact lay his greatness. God was the centre of creation and the centre of man's life.

The events which led to the fall began with a temptation to doubt God's truth and love. "Did God say?" (v.1). What He said was construed as a lie (v. 4). In spite of the fact that God had made man in His own image and had given him a privileged position, Satan suggested that God had deprived man of blessings, and pointed to a way whereby man could take these blessings for himself. What he had to do was disobey God and order his living according to his own will.

"Then the eyes of both were opened" (v. 7). Satan had said their eyes would be opened (v. 5), but he had not told the whole truth. Immediately they recognized the evil they had committed, but they recognized something more, "They knew that they were naked" (v. 7). They realized with fear and shame that they had no resources to deal with the evil into which they had fallen.

The central part of the tragedy of the fall is clear. Man ousted God from His position of supremacy and himself took over control. He now lives in a world of which he is the centre. The first sin was not something which today would be considered a crime. It was simply man's asserting his own will over the will of God. The consequences of this act have passed down to the present day. The fall has reduced man to living in his own self-centred world with all its problems. problems with which he has no resources to deal. Not so many years ago man seemed to have boundless confidence in his own ability to progress, but there are few responsible people in the modern world who now have the same confidence. The Bible and our own experience tell us that the fall is a stark reality.

Let us pray that God will help us to realize the terrible reality of the fall, and that without Him we have no resources to meet our needs.

Isa. 53. 6; John 3. 19; Rom. 5. 12; James 4. 1; Ps. 51. 5

Man and Sin

THE EFFECTS OF SIN

February 14   Reading: Romans 1. 18-2. 1

The effects of sin are far reaching. They invade every aspect of living. Paul in his great exposition of the gospel in the letter to the Romans explains the tragedy of sin and the fall. He shows that sin has brought about a great separation. It has separated man from God. It has separated man from nature. It has separated man from his fellow men. It has separated man from himself. The result has been that "God gave them up" (vs. 24, 26, 28). People want to go their own way, so God allows them to do so with the terrible results Paul lists in this chapter (vs. 24-32).

MAN IS SEPARATED FROM GOD. The word 'ungodliness' in v. 18 means disregard for God's person, living as though God did not exist. This separation from God is pointed out very forcibly in the story of the fall where Adam and Eve were driven out of the garden (Gen. 3: 23-24), separated from God both physically and spiritually. This is man's basic problem, his spiritual problem.

MAN IS SEPARATED FROM NATURE. Paul tells us that man 'worshipped and served the creature rather than the Creator' (v. 25). He began to use what God had made without any reference to Him and for his own ends. God made the world for man's good, but man in his selfishness has abused it. We see man's abuse of nature all around us, resulting in natural catastrophes which are an ever increasing source of anxiety to the nations of the world. We call these environmental problems.

MAN IS SEPARATED FROM HIS FELLOW MEN (2. 1-3). The world is rent asunder by disputes from a family level to an international level, the judgement of one man by another. These are social problems.

MAN IS SEPARATED FROM HIMSELF. Paul points out that man's judgement of others is really a reflection of his own conduct (2.1), what we call a guilt complex. Each person is a medley of complexes and fears which give rise to the breakdowns, mental and nervous, which abound today. These are called psychological problems.

All the confusion and evil of the world can be traced back to the fall. Lord help us to realize the terribleness of sin.

Rom. 1. 18; Rom. 1. 25; Rom. 2. 1; Rom. 2. 4; Rom. 6. 23

Man and Sin

THE NATURE OF SIN

February 15   Reading: Romans 3. 9-18

Paul here sums up his exposition of man's fall. What is the nature of sin? Paul's presentation of man's problems should prevent us from adopting a simplistic view of man and sin. Sin is something tremendously complex which affects every part of a man's being, not only his actions, but his thoughts and attitudes, and the realm of the unconscious of which he is so little aware.

We should be on our guard against the idea that sin is something almost material within us which can be removed by some sort of spiritual surgery. In v. 12 Paul uses a very interesting phrase. He says, "Together they have gone wrong." One of the uses of the Greek word translated 'gone wrong' is of milk going sour. Sin is not like dirt in a liquid which can be strained out and thrown away. It is something which affects the very composition of man's nature. So the problem of renewing man's nature which God answers in the gospel is no easy matter. It is something which only the gospel as the power of God can solve.

It is important to have a clear understanding of what sin is, otherwise we will not have a clear understanding of the gospel. A superficial and powerless half-gospel is often preached today because many of God's people have a superficial idea of the nature of sin. Sin is a corruption which is part and parcel of the fabric of human nature. It is bound up with man's self-will and power of choice. In its outworking it consists not only of acts but of omissions. We can sin not only by what we do, but by what we do not do. We can sin by what we say or by remaining silent when we ought to speak. We can sin by doing something good with a wrong motive. Sin exists in our attitudes which can transform right actions into wrong ones.

Let us pray that God will help us to recognize the fearsome complexity of sin, and let us thank Him for the gospel which is the power of God unto salvation.

Rom. 3. 12; James 4. 17; Rom. 1. 16; Matt. 5. 22; Matt. 15. 18

Man and Sin

SIN AND SINS

Reading: Romans 5. 12-21

At ch. 5.12 Paul commences a new part of his argument. Up to this point SIN has been mentioned in Romans only three times. From this pont on SIN is mentioned thirtynine times. This shows up a very important distinction, the difference between SIN and SINS. They are, of course, very much related, but they are two distinct aspects of man's problem.

After explaining the problem of the fall and its terrible effects, Paul sets out from ch. 3.21 to explain God's answer. He shows that there are two things to be dealt with, first the wrong deeds man has actually committed and their consequences, and secondly, the inner spiritual corruption which is the reason why man acts sinfully. The fall began with a wrong attitude to God which resulted in disobedience. The inner corruption of sin led to the outward action of sin which brought contamination to the whole human race. But our Lord has provided an answer in the gospel. Through His unsullied oneness with the Father and His life of practical righteousness, He offers His own victorious life to all who trust Him. This is the sum of Paul's argument in vs. 15-21.

Both SIN and SINS are included in v. 12. Sins are an affront to the holy character of God and require His forgiveness, otherwise our relationship with Him remains broken. But the gospel not only brings us back into a relationship with God, it works in our inner being a transformation whereby the root of all our wrong doing is ultimately dealt with.

John tells us that 'sin is lawlessness' (1 John 3.4) (NOT 'sin is the transgression of the law' as the AV wrongly translates it). This is precisely what Paul tells us in vs. 13-14. Even where there was no system of law, as was the case between Adam and Moses (v. 14), man was still sinful. Man has an inner lawless disposition which will accept no restraints except those of self-interest. The gospel is much more than forgiveness of sins. It is the tranformation of the inner man defiled by the corruption of sin.

Let us thank the Lord for the power of the gospel and ask Him to help us understand our need, not only of forgiveness, but of transformation as well.

Rom. 3. 23; Rom. 5. 15; Rom. 5. 17; Rom. 5. 19; 1 John 3. 4

Man and Sin

GOD'S PURPOSE FOR MAN

February 17   Reading: Romans 8. 28-39

In these verses Paul reaches the peak of his argument. God's ultimate aim could be summed up in one word, 'glory'. What is entailed in this word becomes clearer as we trace God's work in justification and sanctification to its consummation in glory. Justification brings man into a new relationship with God from which God is able to work in him. Sanctification is the continuous work of the Holy Spirit through which man in all his relationships is transformed, and all that was lost in the fall is ultimately restored. The end is glory.

The present passage, however, is concerned not so much with the mezning of glory as with its certainty. Paul emphasises the powerful nature of the Spirit's work in his ringing affirmation, "We know" (v. 28). We know 'that in everything God works for good with those who love him' (v. 28). From v. 29 Paul traces God's providential care from eternity past to future glory. In foreknowledge God made His sovereign choice, and in predestination He decreed that it should be so. Paul does not neglect the importance of human responsibility in his explanation of the gosepl, but he is clear that the believer who looks back beyond the faith which was his response to Christ has finally to admit that his salvation is due from first to last to the sovereign act of God.

The object of predestination is likeness to Christ, not simply on an individual level, but in a community of people, the church, of whom Christ is the Head as 'first born among many brethren' (v. 29). We should see a glimpse of this glory in the life of the church on earth, but its fulness will be revealed in the church in heaven.

"What then shall we say to this?" (v. 31). Is it really possible? Paul's answer is a magnificent hymn of assurance (vs. 31-39) that the humanly inconceivable purpose of a sovereign God for His people is going to be gloriously fulfilled.

Let us thank God for His great purpose for us, and let us pray that we may live more worthy of it.

Rom. 8. 29; Rom. 8. 31; Rom. 8. 32; Rom. 8. 35; Rom. 8. 38-39

Mand and Sin

PETER

Reading: Luke 22. 28-34

Of most of the disciples we know very little, but Peter is one in whose life we can trace the Lord's working not only during our Lord's own lifetime, but beyond.

This passage shows us something of the Lord's purpose for His disciples and His patience with them. In all of them there was so much He had to do, yet He commends them where He can. "You are those who have continued with me in my trials" (v. 28). Peter accepted the commendation as a boost to his own self esteem. When our Lord spoke to him of the trials that were to follow, Peter was full of brave words. He did not seem to feel there was any need of sifting. He had no sense of any instability in his own character. His attitude was that of the natural man full of assurance in his ability to manage his own life.

Peter was soon in for a rude shock. He had imagined himself braving the wrath of the Roman Empire in loyalty to his Lord, but he was unable to be true to Jesus even before a little girl (Matt. 26. 69). No wonder 'He went out and wept bitterly' (Matt. 26. 75). The experience was the beginning of a deep work in Peter's life, a work which went on throughout the years of his service for Christ. The Peter about whom we read in the book of Acts was not suddenly transformed from the impulsive self-assured Peter of the Gospels into a man of spiritual maturity and poise, but he is a man growing in stature through the work of the Holy Spirit, eager to fulfil the commission the Lord had given him, the commission to feed His sheep (John 21. 17).

Scripture does not tell us how Peter died, but tradition has it that he was crucified for his faith. Peter's ultimate transformation was not due to his own strength but to the grace of God. It was the answer to Jesus' prayer. "I have prayed for you that your faith may not fail." Let us thank God for His purpose for us, and let us pray that we may become more dependent upon His grace to see it fulfilled.

Luke 22. 32; John 21. 17; 1 Peter 4. 1; 1 Peter 5. 6; 1 Peter 5.7

The Business World

ASSOCIATIONS IN THE WORLD OF BUSINESS

February 19

Reading: Matthew 6. 19-24

The Bible is a very practical book. In it we find principles to guide us in every aspect of living. Our Lord did not isolate Himself from other people. He was in contact with people from many different walks of life, and He was well aware of the temptations and problems they faced in the workaday world. We know very little of our Lord's life before His baptism, but in the carpenter's shop He was part of the business world. Some of His disciples, the brothers James and John, were part of a family fishing business, so Jesus was not strange to business life.

In His Sermon on the Mount our Lord stresses the importance of right priorities. What things do we really consider most important? What things occupy most of our thought, the things of the Lord, or our daily work? God does not mean us to neglect our daily business any more than He did Himself as Jesus the carpenter, or did James and John. Business, however, can become an obsession. Our desire to get on can crowd out the Lord's interests. We can work and work to become a success and, when we have reached our goal, find that we have really accomplished nothing worth while. The developed countries of our modern world are full of people who have everthing materially, but whose lives are empty and sad.

"The eye is the lamp of the body" (v. 22). Jesus means that what we consider most important brings light or darkness to our lives. If our lives are taken up with material things and we leave God out, we will find ourselves in darkness (v. 23). If we put God first our lives will be full of light (v. 22).

It is impossible to serve two masters (v. 24). We cannot give an equal place to the Lord and our business interests. One or other is bound to predominate. Either Christ has to take control or business interests will crowd Him out.

Let us pray that the Lord will help us to give Him the place of priority in our business lives.

Matt. 6. 19: Matt. 6. 20-21: Matt. 6. 22: Matt. 6. 23: Matt. 6. 24

The Business World

MAINTAINING STANDARDS IN THE WORLD OF BUSINESS

February 20   Reading: 1 Corinthians 8. 1-13

What does the subject of this chapter have to do with modern business life? Most trades and businesses in the Greek world had their patron deities, and worship of these, or presence at feasts held in their honour, played an important part in the business world. Contacts were made at such functions which could mean a substantial increase in profits. Absence from them could result in a boycott, or at least harm the flow of business. The situation was fraught with temptation for the follower of the Lord Jesus Christ.

Paul sets down important guiding principles. He shows how very easy it is to rationalize our conduct in difficult situations (vs. 1-4). The Corinthian Christian who shared meat offered to an idol could say that, after all, an idol is no God, and the meat was no different, so there could be no harm in eating it. In a present day setting a person might similarly excuse himself for accepting an alcoholic drink at a business dinner. He could say that he generally does not drink at all, and never at any time to excess, and in any case there is no specific injunction in Scripture forbidding it. There are many occasions on which we can rationalize conduct which, deep down within our own hearts, we know to be wrong. Let us beware. It usually leads to greater and greater compromise, and eventual spiritual downfall.

Christian conduct must not only be technically right, it must *appear* to be right. It is not enough to be able to give a logical reason for our actions. Our conduct is wrong and our testimony is compromised if a weaker brother, seeing what we do, can be stumbled by it. This is Paul's argument in the second part of the chapter (vs. 7-13). It at once condemns every type of dealing which is not absolutely straightforward. It condemns deception which consists so often, not in what is said but in what is left unsaid. It condemns every type of compromise for business interests.

Let us thank God for the guidance of His Word. Let us pray for help to honour Him in our daily work, and that may not be a means of stumbling to others.

1 Cor. 8. 9; 1 Cor. 8. 12; 1 Cor. 10. 31; Prov. 16. 11; Prov. 22. 1

The Business World

SUFFERING FOR OUR STANDARDS

February 21

Reading: James 5. 1-11

We live in an unjust world. In the society in which James was living there was grinding poverty on the one hand, and the most fabulous wealth on the other. The poor were constantly exploited by the rich. In our twentieth century world it is very often the employee who exploits the employer. He wants wages for doing as little work as he possibly can. Injustice continues to exist, whoever exploits whom.

The extravagance of rich Roman society was almost unimaginable, and a great proportion of people were used merely to satisfy the whims of the wealthy (vs. 4-6). How were those who belonged to the Lord to witness in such a society? James does not suggest that the social evils of his day did not need to be rectified, but he seeks to direct the eyes of the Lord's people to a higher realm which must be their primary concern. His advice is, "Be patient" (v. 7). For how long should their patience be expected to last? "Until the coming of the Lord" (v. 7).

A Christian surrounded by bribery and corruption will certainly be unpopular if he seeks to uphold standards of truth and honesty. He cannot fit comfortably into the pattern which practically everyone else accepts. He may be denied advancement in his job, an advancement he could gain by stooping to dishonest practices. James was writing in the midst of such circumstances. There are countries today where a person who makes a Christian profession is cut off from all hope of material advancement, or even education, and his children are similarly penalized. The Lord calls us to be willing to suffer in loyalty to Him.

Whatever the trials, they are purposeful in the hands of God. The farmer knows that, having sown, he will reap (v. 7). God uses the very injustice of the world to further His glory in the lives of His people.

Let us thank God for the privilege of being a witness for Him in our business, and let us pray that He will give us strength to suffer if need be in our loyalty to Him.

James 5. 7; James 5. 8; James 5. 11; Acts 5. 41; 1 Peter 2. 20

The Business World

CHRIST BEFORE PROSPERITY

February 22   Reading: Matthew 6. 25-34

This is one of the most beautiful passages in the Gospels. One look round the world, as much of it as has been left unspoiled by the hand of man. is sufficient proof of God's concern for beauty, and His providential care over all He has created. If God so cares for the birds of the air, will He not care for His people (v. 26)?

"Do not be anxious about your life, what you shall eat or what you shall drink, nor about your body, what you shall put on" (v. 25). The Lord does not mean that we should be unconcerned about eating healthy food, or that we should be uncouth or dirty in our dress, but if food and clothing become our chief concern they lead to illness and vanity. They make life more empty, not more beautiful.

Much of the business world caters to human vanity. Advertisements make doubtful claims for products which may be of very little real value. People who have money to spend, and many who do not, waste their income to dress and live as other people do. The business world encourages this in its own selfish interest, and sees to it that fashions and the style of living are constantly changing. The result is a world of colossal waste, and a world of man-made goods which are often ugly and vain.

The Lord says that His Father knows all our needs (v. 32), "But seek first his kingdom and his righteousness, and all these things shall be yours as well" (v. 33). There is a vast difference between what a person needs and what, in his greed, he may want. The Christian business man has a responsibility not to make his business a means of satisfying greed and vanity in himself. He also has a responsibility not to play upon the greed and vanity of others.

When we seek first the kingdom we will see our need of material things in its true perspective. We will not become enslaved to the world of commercial interests, and there will be a truer revelation of God's beauty and order in the needs He promises to supply. Let us pray that God will help us to seek first the kingdom.

Matt. 6. 25; Matt. 6. 26-27; Matt. 6. 28-29; Matt. 6. 30; Matt. 6. 31-32

The Business World

BUSINESS AND THE INDIVIDUAL

February 23   Reading: Acts 19. 21-28.

Demetrius was a silversmith of Ephesus who made his money out of the religious credulity of others. He resented Paul's teaching, not because, he had weighed it up and decided that Paul was teaching error, but simply because it interfered with his business. In his concern he gathered together his fellow craftsmen, and it is at once obvious what was uppermost in all their minds. Demetrius mentions first what touches them most deeply, "Men, you know from this business we have our wealth." Later he mentions 'the great goddess Artemis' (v. 27), but his religious language carries little conviction. He was a business man first and a worshipper of his heathen goddess second, if at all.

His concern for making a profit blinded Demetrius to the truth. Not only was he unable to recognize truth, he did not want to recognize it. He was not ready to give Paul so much as a fair hearing. What Paul said threatened his business, and anything that threatened his business was unwelcome, whether it was truth or a lie.

Demetrius's anxiety that 'the temple of the great goddess Artemis may count for nothing' (v. 27) was little more than a piece of showmanship, but he was willing to invoke religion if it was to his advantage. This was the only use religion had for him. It offered him an excuse to heap abuse upon the servant of God since he had no valid argument against the gospel he preached. Demetrius's consuming interest was his prosperous business.

True, Demetrius was a heathen, but the attitudes to which his obsession with business led him are not altogether unknown among Christians. Devotion to business instead of to the Lord has closed many a believer's mind to the truth of the Word about himself. A child of God too can use his faith as a cloak for selfish interests, and make pretensions to spirituality from which to condemn others, when he himself is the one who stands condemned before God. Let us pray for grace to allow no one or nothing to dominate our lives but Christ Himself.

Matt. 7. 21; Prov. 28. 25; Luke 12. 20; Mark. 8; 36; Mark 8. 37

The Business World

BUSINESS AND THE CHURCH

February 24   Reading: 1 Corinthians 11. 17-22

Corinth was a great business centre and seaport which attracted people from all over the known world. Like most cities of a similar character to-day, it was a hot-bed of vice and sharp practices. Mistrust, trickery and scheming were facts of every day life in Corinth. This was the background of the people who composed the first Corinthian church.

It is not surprising that the Corinthians should have brought many of their business attitudes over into the life of the local church. In fact, Paul's letter is an indication of the struggle there was to establish truly Christian standards among people who had, up to the time they trusted Christ, known nothing but the standards of a self-seeking world. Justification is the work of a moment in the heart of someone who trusts Christ, but the practical implication of faith in Christ are only gradually recognized as a person faces the circumstances of daily living.

Paul chides the Corinthians that 'when you come together it is not for the better but for the worse' (v. 17). The Corinthians were going through the motions of church fellowship, but they brought with them the attitude they employed in their worldly dealings with the result that fellowship was destroyed. They had not learned that the association of the Lord's people in the church cannot be treated like a worldly business meeting or club. More basic still, they had not yet been freed from the old rivalries and class distinctions of their business associations.

The believer who tries to conduct his worldly affairs in the way the godless world does will certainly bring something of his self-seeking attitudes into the fellowship of the church. There were divisions in the Corinthian church (v. 18) and senses of superiority and inferiority such as were so common in the city of Corinth. There was selfishness, each man concern-ed with his own pleasure and interests (v. 21). The Corinthian attitude to business had destroyed both the fellowship of the Lord's people, and the witness of the church to others. Let us pray that the Lord will keep us faithful to Him in our daily business so that we may be a strength to the church and to its witness.

Col. 3. 1; Col. 3. 2; Col. 3. 17; Rom. 14. 12; Eccl. 3. 17

55

The Business World

JACOB

February 25   Reading: Genesis 31. 1-9

Jacob was a fairly typical business man, hard-headed and self-confident. How much havoc his obsession with business caused in his own spiritual life and in his family before he allowed God to deal with it.

Jacob's business acumen seems to have come from his mother's side. Laban, his mother's brother, had similar business interests, and for over fifteen years Jacob and he made every effort to get the better of the other. Jacob appears to have made the more profit, but at a great cost to himself, a cost he is not yet willing to recognize.

No wonder Jacob was unpopular with Laban and his sons. Yet though Jacob complains about their unfriendliness, he does not admit that it is mainly due to his own selfih scheming. He attributes his material prosperity to the blessing of God (v. 9). In this he was more than a little self-deluded. God was certainly with him, though not in the particular way Jacob assumed. God certainly did not set His seal of approval upon Jacob's years of trickery.

There is something tremendously tragic about this period of Jacob's experience, all the more so because Jacob himself did not recognize the tragedy. He had given full play to his business instincts, setting God aside, and what was the result? He was rich, but not happy. He was without friends, even the friendship of some of his closest relatives. He dealt with people only for personal gain, with the result that no one trusted him. But a much more terrible result was the effect of his attitude upon his own children, many of whom had been brought up in an atmosphere of cunning where God was not given His place. Consequently they became like their father who in later years had to suffer through the deceitfulness of his own children just as he had made others suffer.

Let us thank God for the lessons He wants to teach us through Jacob's experience, and let us pray that we may learn them well.

Prov. 11. 5; Prov. 12. 22; Rom. 14. 7; Eph. 6. 4; Gen. 35. 1

Law and Grace

THE LAW OF MOSES

February 26   Reading: Exodous 20. 1-17

The ten commandments are the most familiar part of the law of Moses. Very often they are neglected on the pretext that God's people are now not living under law but under grace. It is true that we are no longer under the Mosaic law as a system, but that does not mean that there is nothing of value to learn from it. The moral law was given through Moses in order to help people understand the holy character of God, and something of His purpose for them. It still serves that purpose for us today.

The first four commandments deal with man's relation to God. The remaining six deal with man's relation to his fellow men. The first of these relationships is the foundation of the second. How a person relates to God will determine how he treats other people. The person who has been drawn nigh to a holy God and has learned something of His ways will have no desire to sin against others. Our Lord Himself emphasises this in this answer to the lawyer's question, "Which is the greatest commandment in the law?" Jesus replied, "You shall love the Lord your God with all your heart, and with your soul and with all your mind. This is the great and first commandment. And a second is like it. You shall love your neighbour as yourself. On these two commandments depend all the law and the prophets" (Matt. 22. 37-40). He sums up the standard of the law as a right relationship to God which leads to a right relationship with other people.

The tenth commandment, "You shall not covet", is unique in that it deal not with an act, but with an attitude. Only as far as the tenth commandment is obeyed can the others be obeyed as well, yet the tenth commandment cannot be enforced. It shows how impossible it is for a system of law to produce righteousness. It also shows that true righteousness is a matter of the heart as well as of the outward act.

Let us thank God for the revelation of His righteousness, and let us pray that we may be kept right with Him and with others.

Ex. 20. 1-3; Ex. 20. 12; Ex. 20. 13-16; Ex. 20. 17; Matt. 22. 37-38

57

Law and Grace

THE PURPOSE OF THE LAW OF MOSES

February 27   Reading: Galatians 3. 19-29.

"Why then the law?" If, as Paul has been explaining, salvation is through faith, why did God need to give the law at all? Paul has no doubt whatever that the law itself could not give life (v. 21). "It was added because of transgressions," he tells us. In other words, the purpose of the law was not to bestow salvation, but to make man recognize his need of it. The law shows us how impossible it is of ourselves to live according to God's standards. It shows us that we are not rightly related to Him or to others, and that our motives are at fault. Only when we realize this will we appreciate our so great salvation and begin to understand what God wants us to be.

We would like a gospel which does not condemn us too harshly, or does not make too heavy demands upon us, a gospel which does not require too much change in the way we live. This is why so many people who profess to have experienced the gospel take it so lightly. The law shows us ourselves completely condemned before a holy God, and it helps us to understand the standard God requires of His children, a standard the law itself is powerless to produce, but a standard that is possible through grace.

In the second part of our reading Paul uses an interesting word to describe the law. He says it is 'our custodian' (v. 24). In the society in which Paul lived the 'custodian' was usually a slave employed by a rich family as guardian to the son of the house. His job was to oversee the boy's conduct, and to accompany him to and from school. Paul says, "The law was our custodian till Christ came, that we might be justified by faith." His meaning is clear. The law was given to teach us God's standards, to show us our need of Christ and prepare us to be led to Him, for only through faith in Christ can God conform us to the image of His Son (Rom. 8. 29).

Let us thank God for the reason He gave the law, and pray that from it we may learn more of His holiness and our need of Christ.

Gal. 3. 24; Gal. 3. 25-26; Rom. 7. 7; Rom. 3. 20; Rom. 3. 21

Law and Grace

THE FAILURE OF THE LAW

February 28   Reading: Romans 7. 7-12

God gave the law for a specific purpose, and it has served its purpose well. As a means of salvation, however, the law is a failure. Of course, God never intended the law to be a means of salvation. It was man who, failing to understand God's purpose in the law, tried to use it in that way. All his efforts only showed the law's inability to save. Paul's language is very graphic. He says the law 'proved to be death to me' (v. 10).

"The law is holy, and the commandment is holy and just and good" (v. 12), but it is limited in what it can do. There are two main reasons why the law is unable to save. Paul illustrates them both in quoting the tenth commandment, "You shall not covet" (v. 7).

Sin exists apart from any law. Man was sinful before God ever gave the law through Moses, but it was the law that clearly brought sin to light. This is Paul's meaning in v. 7. The tenth commandment made him conscious of his covetousness. But Paul goes still further, "Sin, finding opportunity in the commandment, wrought in me all kinds of covetousness" (v. 8). He actually says the law was responsible for making him more covetous. There is something perverse within man which is stimulated by the existence of a law, to disobey it. The driver who sees a sign '30 k.p.h.' wants to go faster. The little boy who sees a sign, 'No writing on this wall', wants to do that every thing. So the law actually encourages people to do what it forbids.

But the law has another grave weakness. It cannot deal with a person's heart and attitudes. It can deal only with outward acts. The law can say, "You shall not steal" (Exod. 20.15), and because of fear of the penalty imposed, people may be prevented from stealing, which is good and necessary. The law, however, cannot say, "You must not *want* to steal". That is a realm where the law is powerless, yet unless our desires and motives are touched there can be no salvation. Our 'inner man' can be changed not by law, but only through a relationship with Jesus Christ. Let us thank the Lord that He has made this gloriously possible.

Rom. 7. 4; Rom. 7. 12; Ps. 51. 6; Matt. 5. 17; Rom. 13. 8

Law and Grace

GRACE IS MORE POWERFUL THAN LAW

February 29   Reading: Romans 6. 12-16

The tenses in vs. 12-13 urge a continuous repudiation of sin and a decisive yielding to the will of God. Sin is tremendouly complex. Sin exists in the misuse or perversion of what God has given. It is not to be viewed as an independent entity, but as a product of man's misdirected will. As the natural man's will is inclined to self-pleasing and so to sin, the will of the man who is alive to God is inclined to God and righteousness. Nevertheless, the believer's free will has not been abrogated. He can still choose good or evil.

But spiritual victory is not finally a question of man's exercising his will in his own meagre strength. This is Paul's point in v. 14. Man under law as the only hope of righteousness found himself powerless. Law told him the difference between right and wrong, but could not help him yield to the right and repudiate the wrong. The result was that sin had dominion over him. Under grace all is changed. Grace has brought us into a new relationship with God through Christ. That relationship itself is powerful, but it has also meant that the believer's very heredity has been changed. The will to 'yield.....to God as men who have been brought from death to life' is no longer empowered by mere human strength, but by all the power that flows from the grace of God.

In vs. 15-16 Paul approaches the position of the Christian from another standpoint, using the analogy of slavery. Man cannot live independent of the forces of good and evil. He is not free in an absolute sense. Either he is enslaved to his own desires, or to the will of God. The restraints of law in the past may have meant that a person was unable to give free rein to his own carnal wishes, but now that he is free from a rigid system of law and lives under the grace of God, he cannot do as he pleases (v. 15). Christian freedom never means licence. It is freedom from sin, and the only freedom from sin is to be found in the grace of God, living under Christ's absolute control.

Let us thank God for His triumphant grace and pray for His help to yield ourselves constantly to His control.

Rom. 6. 12; Rom. 6. 13; Rom. 6. 14; Rom. 6. 16; Rom. 6. 19

Law and Grace

THE LAW OF CHRIST

March 1   Reading: Romans 8. 1-8

Paul draws a contrast between two laws, 'the law of the Spirit of life in Christ Jesus' and 'the law of sin and death' (v. 2). The 'law of sin and death' is the old attitude of legalism which leads only to sin and death. The 'law of the Spirit of life in Christ Jesus' refers to the whole operation of the Spirit as He imparts the life of Christ and works to maintain its standards in the believer.

It is significant that the work of the Spirit, or the 'law of Christ' as we may call it, radically affects a person's attitude. When we are brought into a new relationship with God through the work of Christ (v. 3), and thus 'live according to the Spirit' (v. 5) (The phrase would be better translated 'ARE according to the Spirit'), we begin to set our minds on the things of the Spirit (vs. 5-6). This could never happen unaided under the old law. The law of Moses was good as far as it went, but man's attitude made it into a stumbling block instead of a means of redemption. The law of Christ supplies the essential missing element, a right attitude to God which makes possible the fulfilment of 'the just requirements of the law' (v. 4), not only in letter but in spirit.

The person who is after the Spirit sets his mind on the things of the Spirit (v. 5), and the result is a WALK according to the Spirit (v. 5). What we ARE determines what we THINK, and what we THINK determines what we DO.

The word translated 'set the mind on' in v. 5 is an apt word. It means to set one's heart upon something. It is a clear demonstration of the transforming effects of a personal relationship with Jesus Christ. To be thus related to God brings an inevitable change of attitude. It determines our priorities. Whereas the person whose life is centred in himself sets his heart upon the things of self, the person whose life is centred in Christ has Christ as his object. A person's priorities, spiritual or earthly, determine the quality of his day to day living.

Let us pray that we may more and more show forth the law of Christ in our daily lives.

Rom. 8. 1; Rom. 8. 2; Rom. 8. 3; Rom. 8. 5; Rom. 8. 6

Law and Grace

JESUS AND THE LAW

March 2   Reading: Matthew 5. 17-22.

Our Lord quite clearly shows His respect for the law. Both the law as it was given to Moses and the preaching of the prophets were expressions of the mind and standard of God. Jesus had come not to abolish these, but to fulfil them (v. 17), a fact which He goes on to emphasise (vs. 18-19). But what exactly does our Lord mean by 'fulfilling the law'?

First of all it is perfectly clear that if our Lord had not come, the law could never be fulfilled. To fulfil the law is something not possible in human strength alone. It is not merely a matter of the legalistic observance of certain commandments. The all important factor which our Lord stresses is that of motive (vs. 20-22). This comes out with particular force in His mention of the Pharisees (v. 20). He does not say that the Pharisees were unrighteous, but that there was something missing in their conception of righteousness. They thought that they were obeying the law exactly, but in reality they were not. The Pharisees' error was that they thought righteousness consisted merely in doing good acts. They did not realize that the right act has to be done in the right spirit.

For example, giving to the poor is a good act. But a person may give to the poor from a purely selfish motive, so that other people might think highly of him, while in his heart he despises the poor. Our Lord shows that if a person were to do this, his act would be one of unrighteousness. Righteousness is right action from a right spirit and with a right motive.

In vs. 21-22 Jesus emphasises the fact again. It is certainly wrong to kill, but righteousness is not only in abstaining from murder, but in victory over the attitude of hatred which is the cause of murder (v. 22). More than that, true virtue exists in the basic positive attitude of love from which alone right conduct flows. This is what our Lord demonstrated in His own life. He loved and, therefore, completely fulfilled the law. Let us pray that we too may learn to love and live in righteousness.

Matt. 5. 18; Matt. 5. 20; Rom. 8. 4; Matt. 22. 39-40; Matt. 5. 19

Law and Grace

GRACE DELIVERS FROM LEGALISM

March 3   Reading: Galatians 1. 1-9

One of Paul's main emphases in writing to the Galatians is that grace delivers from legalism. Yet this is something which the Galatians, in common with many other people, found it very difficult to learn. There was a constant tendency to turn away from the grace of God they had received in Christ and to return to the legalistic attitude from which they had been saved. Personal experience shows how very easy it is for a once vital faith to descend into legalism.

Paul tells us that the gospel is a deliverance. Christ 'gave himself for our sins to deliver us from the present evil age' (v. 4). The word for 'deliver' is a strong word, and the way it is used indicates purposefulness. It is used of Joseph's being released from his affliction to fulfil God's purpose for him as governor of Egypt (Acts 7.10). It is used of Peter's being rescued from the hand of Herod (Acts 12.11).

The 'present evil age' (v. 4) from which our Lord died to deliver us is the world that is dominated by human wisdom and self-sufficiency, an age initiated at the fall by the great deceiver himself. Elsewhere Paul calls him the 'god of this world' (2 Cor. 4.4). How insidiously the spirit of selfsufficiency invades our Christian thinking, contaminating spiritual life till it becomes a cold legalism void of all warmth and vitality. We come to believe that if we pray so much, read the Bible so much, witness so much and go to so many meetings, God is automatically happy with us. This is the attitude from which grace delivers us. Grace may well mean that we will pray more, read more of the Word, witness still more consistently, be still more zealous in assembling ourselves together, but we will do these things not in the proud belief that we are thereby winning God's favour, but as an outflow of His love and grace.

Paul pronounces the direst condemnation on anyone, be he an apostle or an angel from heaven, who would preach a gospel which does not magnify the grace of God in its vitory over legalism (vs. 8-9). Let us thank God for the gospel of deliverance, and pray that we may be saved from legalism.

Gal. 1. 3-4; Gal. 1. 8; 2 Cor. 4. 4; 1 John 5. 18; 1 Cor. 1. 12

Law and Grace

MOSES

Reading: Exodus 33. 7-11.

The failure of the law of Moses as a system was demonstrated in a most dramatic way. Before Moses had delivered the tables of the commandments to the people, the commandments had been broken. At the instigation of the people Aaron had made the golden calf for them to worship. True, they had not as yet received the commandment against idolatry, but they had been made very much aware of the sovereignty and power of God in their deliverance from Egypt. In bowing down to the golden calf they were denying God Himself, a denial which would inevitably lead to further disobedience. They lacked the heart relationship with God through which alone they could fulfil the law.

Moses took the tent of meeting, a structure which preceded the tabernacle, and pitched it outside the camp. Those who sought the Lord had to come out of the camp to it (v. 7). They thus disassociated themselves from the sin of the people and indicated their need of a personal relationship with God, a relationship of which Moses himself was the example.

When Moses entered the tent, the cloud, the symbol of God's presence, descended. Moses' relation to the law, God had given him was conditioned by his relationship to God Himself. This is confirmed as Moses pleads for the people. He well knew they had sinned and that, on the basis of law alone, there was no hope for them. His faith, however, was not in human ability to keep the law, but in a gracious God.

The depth of Moses' relationship with God is strikingly brought out in v. 11, "Thus the Lord used to speak to Moses face to face, as a man speaks to his friend." Jesus also speaks of His disciples as His friends. "You are my friends if you do what I command you." (John 15.14). The disciples obeyed the Lord out of their relationship of love towards Him, as did Moses.

Let us thank the Lord for the wonderful privilege of being counted His friends, and let us pray for a greater love and spirit of obedience.

Ex. 33. 7; Ex. 33. 11; Ex. 33. 13; John 15. 14; John 15. 15

Truth and Honesty

THE LORD IS THE TRUTH

March 5   Reading: John 8. 31-40

"What is truth?" Pilate asked Jesus (John 18.38). Many people ask the same question today. They, like Pilate, have no fixed standard by which to judge truth from error. The result is that they consider truth to vary from one set of circumstances to another, or to be something of little or no consequence. The Bible provides us with a fixed standard whereby we can know the truth, and that standard is the Lord Jesus Christ Himself. In fact Christian discipleship is based upon Jesus as the Truth. To be a disciple of the Lord Jesus Christ begins with a person's believing that what He says is truth (v. 31). To the believer there are not two or more standards of truth. There is only one, and that one is Jesus. What He says cannot be the subject of debate or doubt. It is wholly true and demands our acceptance.

Discipleship, of course, means still more than that. It means continuing in His Word. (v. 31). To continue in the Word of the Lord involves listening to His Word. The Greek word for disciple means a 'learner', and to learn from the Lord Jesus is to learn the truth.

Truth brings freedom (v. 32). The Jews were annoyed at our Lord's talk of freedom, for they prided themselves that they were not the slaves of any man. In reality, however, they were slaves to many inner complexes, because they were not willing to face up to the truth of our Lord's words. Acceptance of the truth brings freedom from self and from the fear of what others may think. It also brings freedom from sin, because not only does the Word of truth judge and cleanse us, but it frees us from the hypocrisy and dissembling to which self and fear of others lead.

The truth which our Lord spoke brought a strong reaction from those who listened, a reaction of acceptance, or from some, of rejection and hatred (v. 37). The truth will never make us universally popular. Let us thank God for His Son who is the Truth, and let us pray that we may understand more clearly what the truth demands of us in our practical living.

John 14. 6; John 8. 31-32; John 8. 36; John 3. 21; John 1. 17

Truth and Honesty

HAVING A CONCERN FOR TRUTH

March 6   Reading: 2 Samuel 21. 1-6

Scripture contains many object lessons on the importance of having a concern for truth. This is one of them. The story goes back to the time of Joshua who had made a covenant with the Gibeonites (Josh. 9. 3-27). The covenant was extracted from Israel through trickery. Joshua ought to have been more discerning, and the agreement he made with the Gibeonites was in violation of God's explicit command. Nevertheless, a word once given was sacred and on no account should it have been broken.

The promise made to the Gibeonites was made on behalf of the nation, so it was permanently valid. No ruler of Israel had a right to set it aside. He could not plead the Gibeonites' deceit, or Joshua's lack of insight. A promise given was much greater than any of these considerations. To violate such a promise was to deny the importance of truth and to deny the God of truth.

King Saul, however, in his zeal for the defeat of the enemies of the Lord felt that the promise given could be set aside. It was a terrible mistake and led to terrible consequences. The first was a famine which ravaged the land for three years (v. 1). The second was the execution of seven members of Saul's family (v. 6). God not only permitted this judgement, but directed it (vs. 3-6).

We see here the great concern God has for truth. Truth cannot be lightly set aside on some pretext or other. We must never think that we can abandon truth because others resort to falsehood. The fact that we live in a world of untruth and deceit should be the greater incentive to testify to the God who is Truth in our daily dealings. We can never advance the cause of the Lord by sacrificing truth.

Let us pray that God will give us a deep concern for truth in all that we do and say.

Deut. 32. 4; Ps. 45. 4; Prov. 3. 3; Jer. 5. 1; Zech. 8. 16

Truth and Honesty

TRUTH IN THE INWARD PARTS

March 7   Reading: Psalm 51. 1-9

This is a psalm of mourning, not of praise. David's song of praise had been silenced by his sin. Through Nathan the prophet God had brought his sin before him in all its sordid evil. David saw the sin not only of his adultery with Bathsheba, but of his scheming hypocrisy which had resulted in the death of Uriah, the Hittite. The sin he had committed in his heart and mind was no less evil than the sin he had committed in the body. David realized as he never had before that God desired truth in the 'inward being' (v. 6)

It is significant that when Nathan confronted David he accused him directly of murdering Uriah "You have smitten Uriah, the Hittite with the sword.... and have slain him with the sword of the Ammonites" (2 Sam. 12.9). David, of course, would have given plausible reasons for his conduct. He had not killed Uriah with his own hands. He was king and Uriah was a soldier. He had a right to allot Uriah to a position in the battle, and there can be no warfare without casualties. Someone had to be in the forefront of the fighting, and if Uriah had not been killed someone else would have been. Technically, David had done nothing wrong. He had acted in his capacity as king and Uriah was a casualty of war.

But God did not look upon the incident in this light. David had lied and deceived in his own heart. He might try to justify his conduct before men, but he could never justify it before God.

There are many believers guilty of David's sin. We can do everything in a techically correct fashion, yet be terribly guilty in the sight of God. We can destroy a person's character by silence. When we should say a word in his favour we say nothing, and thus allow others to harbour an impression we know is false. At the same time we can blandly say, "I never said anything against so-and-so." Truth depends not only on what we say but on our attitudes.

Let us pray that God will preserve us from hypocrisy, and give us a deep concern for truth in the 'inward parts'.

Ps. 51. 1; Ps. 51. 2; Ps. 51. 3; Ps. 51. 4; Ps. 51. 10

Truth and Honesty

SPEAKING TRUTH IN LOVE

March 8   Reading: 2 John

We do not know who the 'elect lady' was to whom John wrote this letter, but she was apparently someone who had a zeal for the truth and whose children (v. 4), no doubt spiritual children, had been inspired through her ministry. John, however, had one particular request to make, "I beg you, lady .... that we love one another" (v. 5). It seems that zeal for the truth was not sufficiently balanced by a loving attitude.

The words 'truth' and 'love' are both mentioned in this letter a number of times. In fact John so unites truth and love as to make them inseparable (v. 6). We must never isolate truth from love or love from truth. John shows us that truth becomes something less than truth if it is not held in love, and love is not real love unless it also has a concern for truth.

It is very easy to pride ourselves in our understanding of the truth, and to use it as a means of judging others or showing our superiority over them. Truth without love can lead to contention and division among God's people. It can shatter people instead of building them up. It can lead to spiritual deadness and pride.

Truth is very important as John shows especially in the second half of his letter where he speaks of the attitude we should adopt to those who deny the truth. We must be concerned about holding the truth ourselves and also about communicating it to others, but truth must edify and build up. If we do not have a heart of love and concern for others, we are in no position to proclaim the truth to them.

When we see a fellow believer doing what is wrong, it is our duty to present him with the truth of the Word, but we must first be sure that we have a real concern for his restoration. When truth is spoken in the spirit of love, it will bring light and life.

Let us thank God for the truth of His Word, and let us pray that He will give us a concern to further the truth in love.

2 John 5; 2 John 6; 2 John 8; 2 John 3; Eph. 4. 15

Truth and Honesty

RECEIVING TRUTH IN LOVE

March 9   Reading: John 3. 16-21

If it is necessary to speak the truth in love, it is necessary also to receive the truth in love. This is something which many people find difficult to do. When first the Holy Spirit shows us our need of salvation, we respond in love and gratefulness to God that He so loved the world. However, as we progress along the Christian pathway God keeps shedding the light of His Word into our lives, and too soon our attitude tends to change. Instead of accepting the light of His truth with thankfulness, we begin to resent what He says. When God uses another believer to bring the truth to us, instead of receiving it with humility, we criticize the one who spoke in love to us and justify ourselves.

The words of our Lord here have an important application to every believer. Our old relationship with fallen Adam always tries to intrude and make us accept our own selfish way instead of accepting the light of God (v. 19). Constantly and consciously we have to choose the light however much its truth may hurt our feelings and self-esteem.

A refusal to accept the truth in love is one of the greatest hindrances to spiritual progress among the people of God. Even when truth is not spoken in love, God can still use it to our blessing if we accept it in love. When someone criticizes us, how do we react? Do we try to justify ourselves and adopt the self-righteous attitude, "How dare he criticize me?" If we do, we will be of litle use to God. The spiritual attitude is to accept the most cutting criticism in humility and love, to take it to the Lord and ask Him, "Lord, is this really true of me?" When we do so the bitterest criticism will become redemptive.

Let us thank God for those who speak to us the truth in love, and let us pray that we may learn to accept the truth in love that we might grow more in Him.

John 3. 20; James 1. 21; 1 Cor. 10. 12; 1 Peter 2. 1-2; Luke 7. 23

TRUTH AND LEGALISM

March 10   Reading: Mark 7. 5-13

A certain course of action may be morally wrong yet legally right. Some lawyers are experts at finding loopholes in the law of the land so that the law becomes ineffective, and a person who is actually guilty of a crime is released because he is technically innocent. Believers not infrequently do the same thing. They find a way round the Word of God so that they can do as they please and at the same time justify themselves. Technically they obey the Word, but in their hearts they are disobedient, and their action is sinful in the sight of God.

The Pharisees were experts at this type of conduct, and our Lord roundly condemns them as hypocrites. Their first question showed the tenor of their thinking, "Why do your disciples... eat with hands defiled?" (v. 5). They were quick to condemn as a sinner someone who had not observed the ceremonial law, while their own hearts were full of jealousy and selfishness. Many of the Pharisees had reduced truth to a mere form and thought that their attitudes did not matter.

Jesus faces them up with one of the ways they got around the law. The law of Moses commanded respect towards one's parents, and that obviously included providing them with needed assistance. A Pharisee might be quite able to give his parents the help they required, but if he could say that his property had been 'given to God' (v. 11) and could not, therefore, be used for a common purpose, he would refuse to help his parents and use his property for his own personal benefit as a priest. He would plead that he was doing as the law commanded, but in fact he was simply fulfilling his own selfish desires. In God's eyes, instead of obeying the truth, he was disobeying it.

Let us pray that God will make us people whose hearts are true to Him.

Mark 7. 6; Luke 6. 42; Isa. 1. 16; Matt. 6. 5; Matt. 6. 16

Truth and Honesty

DOEG

We have already seen from John's second letter how truth and love should always go together, that truth becomes something less than truth if it is not spoken in love. Doeg's tale-bearing to king Saul is an example of the terrible results of a malicious use of the truth. Eighty-five priests were slain, and their city, Nob, with everything in it, was put to the sword (1 Sam. 22. 18-19).

It cannot be said that Doeg lied to Saul. What he said was the truth, but he knew that although Ahimelech was innocent Saul would view his helping David as disloyalty to himself. Doeg used the truth to betray an innocent man.

Doeg had no real sense of loyalty to anyone. He was anxious only to ingratiate himself with the king, and he did not care how many other people suffered in the process, so he took to tale-bearing. He did not have to invent any lies to carry out his purpose. It was to his advantage that the facts he narrated to Saul were true, though he well knew that Saul would misconstrue the truth. So although Doeg spoke the truth, it led Saul to believe a lie, the lie that Ahimelech and the priests were disloyal to the kingdom.

Doeg did not stop at mischievous tale-bearing. He went the length of murdering the priests at the king's command. People who will use truth to further their own selfish ends can seldom be trusted. People who do not have a respect for truth will not have much respect for others. If they use truth as a tool to advance their personal plans, they are equally capable of using people in the same way. Nothing and nobody is safe from them.

Let us pray that God will give us a deep respect for truth so that we may never use truth for wrong ends.

Ps. 52. 1; Ps. 25. 5; John 17. 17; Isa. 61. 8; Ps. 119. 43

71

GOD'S REVELATION OF HIMSELF

March 12   Reading: Psalm 119. 89-105

Psalm 119 is a psalm of praise for the Word of God. The Psalmist, of course, did not possess the full revelation which we have today in the Old and New Testaments, but he realized the truth and importance of the fact that God has revealed Himself to man.

V. 89 tells us that God's Word is not variable. His standards do not change. "For ever, O Lord, thy word is firmly fixed in the heavens." In our passage there are two important words which explain the nature of the revelation God has given us. The first of these words is 'precepts', and it occurs in vs. 93, 94, 100, 104. The second is the word 'understand', which is found in vs. 99, 100, 104.

The Hebrew word for 'precepts' occurs only twenty-four times in the Bible. It is found only in the book of Psalm, and twenty-one out of the twenty-four times it is used are in Psalm 119. It could equally well be translated 'charge'. It is an authoritative word of guidance from God which carries with it an obligation of obedience from those who hear. The Psalmist here speaks a number of times of keeping God's Word (vs. 100, 101, 102).

The word 'understand' is used in vs. 99, 100, 104, and the Psalmist uses other words also to emphasise the importance of understanding God's precepts. This shows us that God has given us His revelation in a way that we can understand with our minds provided we use our minds and meditate in His law (v. 97). God has not given us a jumble of texts to provide guidance in different circumstances, nor has He given us a book of allegories to which we have to give a 'spiritual' meaning from our own imaginations. He has given us His Word in such a way that from it we can understand clearly what He is like and the principles on which He lives and wants us His people to live. Having understood these principles, we are responsible to apply them to our daily living.

Let us thank God for His revelation of Himself and pray that He will help us to understand and keep His precepts.

Ps. 119. 89; Ps. 119. 93; Ps. 119. 97; Ps. 119. 104; Ps. 119. 105

The Scripture

THE INSPIRATION OF SCRIPTURE

March 13   Reading: 2 Peter 1. 16-21

Nearly two thousand years ago, as today, there were people who denied the facts of the gospel. Peter writes strongly in the gospel's defence, "We did not follow cleverly devised myths" (v. 16). What he writes is based on actual happenings which he and others witnessed (v. 16). He, along with James and John, had witnessed the transfiguration where the person and ministry of our Lord Jesus Christ were authenticated by the voice of God Himself. The life and ministry of the Lord were also a fulfilment of Old Testament Scriptures (Matt. 1. 22; 2.5; John 5. 39). All went to show that the God whose voice Peter had heard had spoken through the prophets and was behind the authors of all Scripture (v. 21).

When Peter speaks of men 'moved' by the Holy Spirit, he uses a very significant word which means to be 'borne along'. The same word is used in Acts 27. 15,17 of a ship being driven. As sailors hoist the sails of their ship and the wind carries them in the desired direction, so the prophets were receptive to the direction of the Holy Spirit who bore them along in their writing.

The inspiration of the Scriptures, therefore, resulted from co-operation between man and God. God did not set aside the personalities of the writers, but used them and their literary talents in such a way that the words of every part of the Bible are His revelation to mankind, a revelation free from all error and of divine authority.

From the inspired writings of the original authors the Bible has been translated into all the major languages of the world. The first English version was the work of John Wycliffe. The New Testament appeared in 1380 and the Old Testament two years later. The greatly respected King James or Authorized Version was but one in a long line of translations which extend right up to the present day and all of which contribute to our understanding of the inspired Word.

Let us thank the Lord for His inspired Word.

2 Pet. 1. 19; 2 Pet. 1. 20; 2 Pet. 1. 21; John 5. 39; Luke 24. 44.

The Scriptures

THE OLD TESTAMENT

March 14   Reading: Luke 24. 13-27

The two disciples on the road to Emmaus were sad and dispirited. They had hoped Jesus would be the one to redeem Israel, and they had heard of a prophecy that the Messiah would rise on the third day (v. 21). However, they had not heard of anyone having seen Jesus after His burial, and they could not understand how the religious rulers could have rejected Him if He were the Messiah (vs. 19-20).

Jesus chides them for their lack of understanding in the Scriptures, showing them that Christ had to suffer before entering into His glory (v. 26). Then 'beginning with Moses and all the prophets, he interpreted to them in all the scriptures the things concerning himself' (v. 27). In this way Jesus testifies, as He had done many times previously, to the inspiration of the Old Testament.

We do not possess any of the original manuscripts of the Old Testament. This is not surprising when we remember the turbulent history of the children of Israel and the fact that there were no such things in those days as printing presses. Every piece of writing had to be copied out by hand.

The inspiration of the Old Testament is not based on the decision of any group of people that it should be considered holy writ. The spiritual insight of godly men over the centuries recognized the work of the divine hand in the various Old Testament books. Malachi, the last of the Old Testament books, was written about 400 B.C. and by the second century B.C. the complete Old Testament as we know it today was accepted by the Jews as the Word of God.

The oldest manuscripts of the Old Testament we posess are the famous Dead Sea Scrolls which were discovered in 1947. They contain whole books or fragments of every book in the Old Testament except Esther, and they have confirmed again the confidence we can have in the inspiration of the Old Testament.

Let us thank God for the way He has preserved His Word for us and ask His help to appreciate it more.

Luke 24. 25; Luke 24. 27; Acts 10. 43; 2 Cor. 1. 20; John 5. 46-47.

The Scriptures

THE NEW TESTAMENT

March 15   Reading: Luke 1. 1-4

Luke wrote two of the books of the New Testament, the gospel which bears his name and the book of Acts. In these introductory verses to his gospel he sheds some interesting light on the meaning of inspiration. From a careful reading of them it is clear that writing the gospel involved Luke in a great deal of hard work.

Inspiration did not mean that God dictated the gospel to Luke and all he had to do was write it down. Others before him had apparently written down accounts of what they had heard and seen of our Lord's ministry and work (v. 1). Still others told of their experiences (v. 2). So Luke collected his material from many sources as well as from his own personal experiences. Editing all of this material, he produced the 'orderly account' (v. 3) which is Luke's Gospel. God used the personality and gifts of Luke, and the circumstances of the moment, in this case a concern to acqaint a person called Theophilus with the facts of the gospel (vs. 3-4), to produce His inspired Word. The same is true of the rest of the New Testament.

About four thousand seven hundred manuscripts of the New Testament or parts of it are available to us. In fact there is far more evidence for the text of the New Testament than for any other work of ancient literature. The oldest manuscript is a fragment of John's Gospel from about A.D. 125. From these different sources scholars have worked to determine the text of the original writings, and translations have been made into the languages of today.

The books of the New Testament were all written during the latter half of the first century. Over the following hundred years they were collected and read in the churches. Their authenticity was perceived by spiritual men, and between 300 and 400 A.D. the New Testament as we know it today was generally accepted, through the witness of the Holy Spirit, as the Word of God.

Let us thank God for the way He has preserved the New Testament writings for us, and let us ask His help to live by them.

2 Thess. 2. 15; 1 Tim. 6. 20; 2 Tim. 1. 13; 2 Pet. 3. 18; Matt. 24. 35

The Scriptures

THEIR RELIABILITY AND SUFFICIENCY

March 16   Reading: 2 Timothy 3. 10-17

Not only does Paul state the reliability and sufficiency of Scripture, he demonstrates it in his own living. What Timothy heard in Paul's teaching (v. 10) he saw worked out in his conduct. Paul was saturated in the Old Testament Scriptures, and his God-given spiritual perception saw their fulfilment in Christ, a fulfilment of which a permanent and complete record has been left for us in the New Testament. This revelation was Paul's rule of life. It transformed him. It was evident in his 'aim in life' (v. 10), his character, and his readiness to suffer for the sake of the gospel.

It was Paul's conviction that anyone who was ready to accept a set of standards so different from the standards of the world was bound to suffer persecution (v. 12). But the Word of God so transforms a person's life and thinking that he sees the gospel as something abundantly worth suffering for.

Paul appeals to Timothy to remain loyal to the teachings he had received because 'they are able to instruct you for salvation through faith in Christ Jesus' (v. 15). If this claim can be made for the Old Testament, it is just as valid for the fuller revelation of the New Testament Scriptures.

While there will always be need for further growth, the Scriptures contain everything 'that the man of God may be complete' (v. 17). They are valuable for reproof and correction (v. 16). That is they show up our errors and are the standard by which every idea or doctrine has to be measured. They are valuable also for 'teaching' and 'training in righteousness' (v. 16). We must be ready to accept the corrections of the Word if we are to be built up by the Word. The Word corrects in order to train in righteousness. It trains in righteousness in order to equip for every good work (v. 17). This is the essential conclusion. Our study of the Scriptures should lead us to more effective service for God and for other people.

Let us pray that the Word may work still more deeply in our hearts.

2 Tim. 3. 10; 2 Tim. 3. 12; 2 Tim. 3. 14; 2 Tim. 3. 16-17; 2 Tim. 3. 1-2

The Scriptures

READING REGULARLY

March 17   Reading: Psalm 1. 1-6

If the Bible is as important as we have said, then reading and studying the Bible should be a regular part of our daily living. The Psalmist tells us that God's Word is like water to a tree (v. 3). Without water the tree would wither and die. Without God's Word man is equally lifeless.

The contrast between the man of God and the man of the world is vividly brought out in v. 4, "The wicked are ...like chaff which the wind drives away." This is an apt picture of many people in our modern world. They are rootless. They have no foundation on which to build their lives. They have no standards outside themselves, with the result that they have no clear distinction between right and wrong. They are unstable and liable to be driven away by the least wind of adversity. Sometimes these are the people who make the loudest professions of being able to guide others. They talk spaciously of being free, of not being under bondage to any system of rules, but their freedom is like the freedom of the chaff. Chaff is free in a way that a tree is not, but it is lifeless and useless.

Blessing does not come from denying all standards and scoffing at those who do have solid standards (v. 1), but in a life which is firmly anchored in the 'law of the Lord' (v. 2). When the Psalmist speaks of meditating in the law day and night, he means that the Word of God should be so familiar to us that we automatically refer all our thoughts and actions to it. If we are tempted to do something that is contrary to God's standards, at once our knowledge of the Word checks us. This can only be so if we are constanly reading and studying our Bibles.

Let us thank God again for His Word. Let us pray that we may so learn to understand it that it will be our constant standard of reference for all we think, say and do.

Ps. 1. 1-2; Ps. 1. 3; Ps. 119. 1; Ps. 119. 2; Ps. 119. 66

The Scriptures

THE BEREANS

March 18   Reading: Acts 17. 10-15

The Bereans' acceptance of the Word was a great encouragemnet to Paul and Silas after the persecution they had experienced at Thessalonica. Paul's custom on visiting a city was to go to the synagogue if there was one, and explain the gospel from the Scriptures. This he had done in Thessalonica, and he did the same at Berea. Although he was an apostle, he did not speak on his own authority, but he emphasized the authority of the Word rather than the authority of himself as its bearer.

It is interesting to notice the Bereans' attitude both to Paul and to the Scriptures. They obviously treated Paul with respect as a minister of the Word, but Paul directed them beyond himself to the Word, and it is clear that they looked first and foremost for the pronouncement of Scripture, not for the pronouncement of Paul. This is something of great importance, because it is very easy for our faith to become man-centred instead of God-centred, and it can only be God-centred when we give prime respect to His Word.

Paul was in no way offended that the Bereans searched the Scriptures for confirmation of his message instead of accepting automatically what he taught them. He realized that whatever authority he possessed was derived from the Lord through His Word, and his teaching was subject to the judgement of the Scriptures as was the teaching of anyone else. When the Bereans were convinced of the truth through what God's Word said, they had found a faith securely anchored in the Lord. Had their faith been anchored in Paul, it could have lasted only as long as Paul was with them. Paul might be taken away, but the Lord whose Word they accepted would always remain.

Let us thank the Lord for His messengers through whom He brings to us His Word, but let us pray that He will help us to see beyond His messengers and to anchor our faith in Him.

Acts 17. 11; Acts 17. 2; Matt. 4. 4; Isa. 55. 11; Rev. 3. 11

Guidance

GUIDANCE THROUGH THE WORD

March 19   Reading: John 6. 60-71

The life of the child of God is a guided life, yet to many believers guidance poses a constant problem. Many of the disciples found it very difficult to accept what Jesus was saying. They realized that He was claiming to be God, and claiming that no one could know true life without being guided by Him. For this reason many left Him (v. 66). The twelve, however, stood with Him. This does not mean that they had no doubts or fears, but Peter voiced the feeling that was common to them all when he said, "Lord, to whom shall we go? You have the words of eternal life" (v. 68). This is the basis of all guidance, submission to Jesus Christ. The truth of His claim to deity was to be abundantly confirmed in His resurrection and ascension (v. 64).

Jesus said, "It is the Spirit that gives life, the flesh is of no avail; the words that I have spoken to you are spirit and life" (v. 63). He meant by this that His Word, rightly understood and responded to, was sufficient to guide His disciples. If we approach the Word in the attitude of the flesh, that is, bent on having our own way, not truly submitting to the will of God, we will misinterpret the Word to fit into our own selfish and mistaken ideas.

Two things are, therefore, necessary before the Word of God can be our guide. The first is that we understand it properly. God has not given us a jumble of isolated texts, but a book which by precept and example sets down clear spiritual principles. We are responsible to understand them and then apply them intelligently to our circumstances. Some people try to find guidance from an isolated text which seems to speak to their immediate need. This can be a dangerous practice, for it often neglects the true meaning of a passage and interprets it according to a person's individual liking. The second thing that is necessary is a true submission to the will of God. The guidance of the Scriptures will always be what is best for us, but not always what we would naturally like. If we do not want the will of God more than our own way, the Bible will be a means of frustration instead of God's leading.

Let us thank God for the guidance of His Word, and seek His help to understand it and be truly submissive to His will.

John 6. 63; John 6. 68-69; John 6. 27; John 6. 58; Ps. 119. 112.

Guidance

GUIDANCE THROUGH THE SPIRIT

March 20   Reading: Exodus 13.17-22

God guides His people gently. He understood the limitations of the Children of Israel. God did not hide from them that there was warfare ahead, so they were equipped for battle (v. 18), but He did not allow them to be subjected to the strains of battle before they were able to bear them (v. 17). When God guides us into difficult circumstances He supplies the spiritual strength to overcome.

Many different symbols of the Holy Spirit are used both in the Old and New Testaments. Here there are two, the pillar of cloud and the pillar of fire (vs. 21-22). God had a means of leading His people both by day and by night, in the light and in the darkness. It was assumed, of course, that the people were always attentive to any movement of the cloud or the fire, and that they were always ready to follow. They did not possess the revelation of the Holy Spirit as we do today, but the Spirit guided them nevertheless.

The guidance of the Holy Spirit can be a wonderful reality for all of God's people, but we need to be careful not to claim as the Spirit's guidance what is, in reality, our own will and not the will of God. If we keep close to the Word of God, however, we will not be misled. In our reading, the guidance of the Spirit was not a matter only formulated in the people's minds. The Holy Spirit's leading was expressed in very tangible symbols which the people could both see and understand. There was a pillar of cloud and a pillar of fire whose movements could be clearly discerned.

Today the touchstone of the Holy Spirit's working is the Bible. The Spirit always guides in accordance with the Word, and we can only expect Him to guide us to the extent that we honour and know the Word. The Spirit's guidance is not merely a flash of inner light. It is a light which can be verified through recourse to the Scriptures. Let us pray that the Lord will prevent us from attributing our own ways to the Holy Spirit.

Ex. 13. 21; 1 Cor. 2. 11; 1 Cor. 2. 12; 1 Cor. 2. 14; Neh. 9. 19

Guidance

GUIDANCE THROUGH CIRCUMSTANCES

March 21   Reading: Acts 16. 6-12

Paul, Silas and Timothy obviously had an ear open to the direction of the Spirit. There was an inner witness which gave them the confidence to move forward or held them back (v. 6). We must always remember, however, that behind all God's dealings with Paul and his fellow workers there was a sound knowledge of the Scriptures and submission to them. The Spirit also used circumstances to guide the apostles. This will not surprise us if we believe that God guides all the ways of His children. He has given us the faculties of understanding and what we call 'common sense', and provided we use them consistently with the standards of the Word, God works through them to lead us in His ways.

Luke tells us that Paul and his party 'attempted to go into Bythinia, but the Spirit of Jesus did not allow them' (v. 7). Apparently not having clear guidance of the direction in which they should go, they journeyed towards Bythinia. The Spirit, however, in some manner which we are not told, barred the way. Paul and his companions did not wait in idleness till a clear word came from God. They moved in the direction their experience and interest indicated, ready for the Spirit to open up the way clearly, or to direct them elsewhere.

When children grow up to years of responsibility, parents do not expect to direct their every step. They expect their children to use their own judgement while remaining faithful to the principles they have been taught. God deals with His children in a similar way, and graciously checks them if they move off His path for them.

We do not read that the Spirit specifically told Paul, Silas and Timothy to go to Troas, but it must have seemed to them the obvious direction in which to go. Their decision to make for Troas was confirmed as God's leading by subsequent events. Through a vision Paul received his commission to Macedonia, and so the gospel was carried over on to the continent of Europe.

Let us thank the Lord for the way He orders our circumstances, and pray that we may be kept open to the directions and checks of the Spirit.

Acts 16. 6; Acts 16. 7; Acts 16. 9; Acts 16. 10; Gen. 24. 27

Guidance

THROUGH THE FELLOWSHIP OF GOD'S PEOPLE

March 22   Reading: Acts 15. 6-21

Some men had come from Judea to Antioch claiming that circumcision was necessary to salvation (15.1). Their claim necessitated a decisive and authoritative word on the subject. Paul and Barnabas were in no doubt as to where they themselves stood, but they did not insist that their own apostolic word was sufficient. A matter of such grave importance required a confirming word of guidance from a wider representation of God's people, so the question was taken to Jerusalem and placed beforethe elders.

The subject was given detailed examination and was the occasion of 'much debate' (v. 7). Then Peter spoke, affirming that God had given to Gentiles, though uncircumcised, the assurance of salvation through the witness of the Holy Spirit (v. 8). Paul and Barnabas added their testimony of circumstances in which God had worked miraculously among the Gentiles. James adds further weight to both Peter's, and Paul and Barnabas' statements by quoting the Old Testament prophet Amos (vs. 16-18).

In coming to a conclusion three factors were involved, the witness of the Word, the witness of the Spirit, and the witness of confirming circumstances. As well as these there was the discernment, not of one man, but of the company of apostles and elders. The matter was one which implicated all believers, and guidance, therefore, was the responsibility of a representative and responsible company of the Lord's people.

Guidance can never be free from the human element. The Word and the Spirit may speak clearly, but a fallible person has to hear and discern, so there is always the possibility of error. God has given the blessing of fellowship so that the error of one person may be checked through the spiritual discernment of another. In seeking the guidance of God we should always consider with prayer and respect the insights of other spiritual people.

Let us thank God for the blessing of fellowship, and pray that we may learn to respect what He shows us through our fellow believers.

Acts 1. 14; Acts 15. 25; Phil. 2. 2; Eph. 3. 18-19; Eph. 4. 25

Guidance

THE NEED OF COMMITMENT

March 23   Reading: Psalm 37. 1-9

So far we have seen how God guides through His Word, through His Spirit, through circumstances, and through the fellowship of His people, but always in accordance with the principles of inspired Scripture. There is, however, another important aspect of guidance, and that is the need of personal commitment to God in accepting His will.

The greatest enemy of guidance is the lack of willingness to commit oneself, an attitude which often follows doubt. How do I know my guidance is right? The doubt comes to all of us, and since all of us are fallible human beings, there is always the possibility of error, a possibility we must honestly face. We should give serious consideration to the advice of others, to circumstances, to the witness of the Spirit and the principles of the Word, but when the time comes to commit ourselves to God in a course of action we should do it decisively, and not allow even the conflicting advice of godly men to leave us in a confusion of indefiniteness and indecision. If we are sincere in our desire to do God's will, God knows our hearts, and will not condemn us if, in our sincerity, we make a mistake. It is much more to the glory of God to commit ourselves clearly to what we sincerely believe is His will, even if we do make a mistake, than to remain indecisive and do nothing, afraid of committing ourselves on the pretext that we are seeking His will.

This is the message of the Psalmist. Do not be turned aside by the circumstances around you (vs. 1-2). Commit yourself to what you believe God wants and 'do good', that is, move forward to do His will (v. 3) If you are sincere in your desire to follow the Lord, He will keep His hand on you (vs. 4-6). And always keep your ear open to anything else the Lord may want to say (v. 7). Do not blame circumstances, and do not worry (v. 8). The Lord's sovereignty is over all, working out His own plans (v. 9).

It is significant that the exhortations to be still and to wait (v. 7) come after the exhortations to 'do good' and 'commit your way to the Lord' (vs. 4-5). Waiting on the Lord does not mean inaction. It means an open ear while we are following Him. Let us afresh commit ourselves decisively to the Lord to follow Him in the way He wants us to go.

Ps. 37. 1-2; Ps. 37. 3; Ps. 37. 4; Ps. 37. 8; Ps. 37. 9

THE CHRISTIAN LIFE A GUIDED LIFE

March 24   Reading: Philippians 1. 12-21

Although Paul was in prison awaiting trial in Rome, uncertain whether he would be executed or released, he was full of rejoicing. Not for a moment did he doubt that his circumstances were directed by God. Since the time when he had committed himself to the will of God on the Damascus road, he knew that his life in all its details was divinely guided. This did not mean that the way was always smooth. It was much more often hard than easy, but through it all God was working.

It made a tremendous difference to Paul to realize that every circumstance, however distasteful, was meaningful in the hands of God. Circumstances were not to be an object of complaint, but a means of learning and of developing his spiritual character.

Paul rejoices that God had allowed his imprisonment because, through it, the gospel went forth to many who would not otherwise have heard (vs. 12-13), and through it other believers were encouraged (v. 14). But if he could rejoice in the opportunities of witness, what of the criticism and resentment displayed by some believers who ought to have been supporting him by their prayers? Could he rejoice in this also? Such circumstances could well have embittered him against his detractors, but he rejoices in them also (vs. 15-18). He does not lash out critically in return against those who were seeking to discredit him, but accepts this painful experience also as a means whereby God is trying to mould his character. He believes that all is for his deliverance (v. 19), that is, certainly for his spiritual betterment, even if not a means of physical deliverance (v. 20). For Paul to live, whether in ease or in hardship, was to be in the hands of Christ (v. 21). His was a guided life.

Let us thank God for His hand upon us in all our circumstances, and pray that we may learn from the ways in which He guides us.

Phil. 1. 12-13; Phil. 1. 14; Phil. 1. 18; Phil. 1. 19; Phil. 1. 21

Guidance

BALAAM

Reading: Numbers 22. 15-35

Was Balaam a true prophet or was he an imposter? It is quite possible to be a true prophet at one time and not at another. Balaam's attitude was one that is fairly common. He wanted the blessings of the God of Israel, but he was also very much concerned with his own interests. Part of his reply to Balak had a very spiritual sound (v. 18). Another part did not (v. 19).

Balaam's profession of devotion to the God of Israel is unmistakable, as is his professed desire for God's guidance. But God had already told Balaam what to do. He had refused to allow him to accept Balak's request (v. 13). Had Balaam been single minded to do the will of God, there was no need for him to ask again. However, Balak's offer of 'great honour' (v. 17) was a strong temptation. Clearly, Balaam wanted to go, and seeing his determination God allowed him (v. 20).

God's anger at Balaam's going (v. 22) is not inconsistent with God's allowing him to visit Balak. When a person is determined to go his own way, God will allow him to do so. We, like Balaam, can often rationalize what we do as the will of God when, in reality, God is simply letting us go our own selfish way. To say, "God told me," is not always a proof that we are doing what God wants of us. Balaam did not curse the people of Israel as Balak had desired (v. 17). God did not allow him to do so, and all along Balaam insisted that he would not say anything but what God wanted him to speak. Nevertheless, at heart he was more concerned with himself than with the will of God, and Peter uses his name as a symbol of avarice (2 Peter 2. 15). In guidance, as in so many other aspects of the Christian life, our heart attitude of submission to the will of God is so important.

Let us thank God for the warning from the experience of Balaam, and let us pray that we may not seek His guidance for our own interests.

Ps. 106. 15; 2 Pet. 2. 15; Jude 11; Num. 23. 19; Gal. 6. 7-8

Obedience and Faithfulness

EXCUSES FOR DISOBEDIENCE

March 26   Reading: Haggai 1. 1-6

Some of the captive Jews had returned to their homeland, and the rebuilding of the temple had been commenced under Zerubbabel, governor of Judah, and Joshua the high priest. Difficulties had arisen, however, and the work was discontinued for a number of years. Now it had been restarted, and through Haggai His prophet the Lord encourages His people to be busy about building His house.

Sadly enough, when permission to continue the work had been received, the people were not all too keen to start. The initial enthusiasm had died down, and there were other things engaging their attention. The reason they gave made a pretence at spirituality, "The time has not yet come to rebuild the house of the Lord" (v. 2). It is true that God has a time and a way for His work to be done. We need to be concerned not to run before Him, but we must also beware lest our profession of awaiting God's time is not an excuse for our own disobedience.

The people in Haggai's day were obviously prosperous. They had both the money and time to spend on their own houses. Haggai asks them, "Is it a time for you yourselves to dwell in you panelled houses, while this house lies in ruins?" (v. 4). Stone was cheap and plentiful, but timber was expensive and scarce. People had the means to panel their houses with costly wood, yet they felt they could afford neither the time nor the money for the work of the Lord. Their priorities were wrong.

Many believers do the same today. They neglect obedience to the Word on the pretext that the time or the opportunity is not yet ripe. Meanwhile the time always seems opportune to work for themselves, but their labour brings them no true satisfaction (v. 6).

God has given us opportunities to work for Him. Let us thank Him for them and pray that we may not neglect them. Let us pray that we may learn to set right priorities in our living.

Hag. 1. 4; Hag. 1. 5; Hag. 1. 6; Hag. 1. 9; Hag. 1. 14

Obedience and Faithfulness

FAITHFULNESS AND DISOBEDIENCE

March 27   Reading: Haggai 2. 10-15.

This is a very humbling passage. It demonstrates, like many other passages of Scripture, the subtlety of the heart of man. There is a relentless temptation to use our service for God as a means of serving ourselves. In the New testament the source of this temptation is called 'the flesh'. The tragedy is that we well know when we succumb to this temptation, even though we may not admit it. As believers we live lives which are a mixture of faithfulness and disobedience. It is this mixture that God is working to correct in His work of sanctification.

There is such a thing as unconscious sin, but disobedience is not unconscious. Disobedience entails a deliberate act of the will. It is a choosing of what pleases ourselves instead of what pleases God. We have a tendency to think that the good we do should outweigh our disobedience. This was the attitude of many of the people to whom God spoke through Haggai, and it is against this attitude that Haggai warns them in our reading.

Haggai puts two questions to the priests, questions based on the Levitical law. If consecrated meat touches what is unconsecrated, is the unconsecrated food thereby made holy? (v. 12). The answer is 'No'. Then he asks if something unclean touches what is clean, whether the clean thing is polluted. The answer in this case is 'Yes' (v. 13). The conclusion is, "So is it with this people" (v. 14). The good we think we do cannot sanctify our disobedience. On the other hand, unfaithfulness pollutes and makes of none effect even that which of itself is right.

The lesson is not a difficult one to understand, but it is all too easy to ignore. How often a testimony for the Lord is damaged or irretrievably lost through behaviour inconsistent with a Christian profession. Let us pray that God will help us to face up to the inconsistencies of our living, the mixture of faithfulness and disobedience. Having done so, let us pray that the Lord will deal with it.

Deut. 30. 19; Mark 9. 24; James 1. 7-8; Hag. 2. 12; Hag. 2. 13

THE SIN OF RESENTMENT

March 28   Reading: Jonah 4. 1-11

Jonah was a prophet, but he was far from being perfect. God had a lot of work to do in him. God had to take Jonah through the experience of being swallowed by a great fish before Jonah was finally obedient to his commission as a prophet to Nineveh. But his outward profession of obedience had little depth. He was still more concerned about his own interests than about God's. He was more interested in his reputation as a prophet than in the repentance and salvation of the people to whom he had been sent to minister.

God had a still deeper work to do in the heart of Jonah, and it was marred by the sin of resentment. God showed mercy to the people of Nineveh, but Jonah did not. "It displeased Jonah exceedingly, and he was angry" (v. 1). Jonah even excuses his running away to Tarshish on the ground that, knowing God's graciousness, he was afraid God would not carry out His warning of judgement, and thus make His prophet look like a fool (v. 2).

Jonah still hoped that God would give in to his whim, so he built himself a booth overlooking Nineveh and sat there in a sullen, resentful mood, waiting to see what would become of the city (v. 5). He had just complained against God for changing His mind. Now he was anxious for God to change His mind again, since it was in his own interest. When God provided a plant to shield Jonah from the sun and then took it away, Jonah was swift to object, but he wanted God to destroy a whole race of people on which He had expended much more labour than on the plant (vs. 6-8). Jonah's every attitude mirrored resentment, and resentment is an indication of inner disobedience and pride.

We do not know whether Jonah ever found victory over his resentful spirit. Tragically, many of God's people never do. Let us ask the Lord to save us from the sin of resentment.

Jonah 2. 2; Jonah 2. 7; Jonah 4. 9; Ps. 119. 165; James 4. 7

Obedience and Faithfulness

THE FAITHFULNESS OF GOD

March 29   Reading: Zechariah 13. 7-9

This passage is attested by our Lord as referring prophetically to Himself (Mark 14.27). He is the one who is struck by the sword of the Lord. The result is a sifting of His followers and the emergence of a people to live in fellowship with God. These verses are a testimony to God's faithfulness which does not shrink from personal suffering, nor from allowing His people to suffer if it is to be for their ultimate good.

God Himself has suffered the rejection of men, and He is gathering together a purified people who will inevitably be rejected in a fallen world. He came Himself to be rejected and asks His people to follow only in a way that He trod before them. The cross is a mark of God's faithfulness to us. It is a mark of the Son's faithfulness to the Father and His purposes.

The faithfulness of God extends to His personal dealings with His people. We often tend to resent the Lord's dealings with us as did the prophet Jonah, but whatever the circumstances He may lead us through, or the difficulties He may allow to overtake us, all are part of His faithfulness. They are part of His refining process (v. 9).

The faithfulness of God does not include only what we normally think of as blessings. It also includes the judgement of everything that is unworthy of Him. It was to be true of the nation Israel in general. Those who were unworthy of the Lord and did not want to follow Him would be left to their own way, to be cut off and to perish (v. 8). It is true also of the character of the individual. God's faithfulness wants to deal with everything in us that is dishonouring to His name. If we refuse His dealings, to that extent our joy, our fellowship and our usefulness to Him will be marred.

Let us thank God for His faithfulness, and let us pray for grace to allow Him to do all that He wants to do in us.

Zech. 13. 9; Mal. 3. 1; Mal. 3. 2; Mal. 4. 2; Heb. 12. 3.

Obedience and Faithfulness

FAITHFULNESS TO ONE ANOTHER

March 30   Reading: Ruth 1. 15-22

The books of Judges and Samuel tell of God's dealings with the nation Israel. Inserted between them is the little book of Ruth which tells the story of one poor, obscure family. God deals not only with nations and great leaders. He is sovereign too in the personal affairs of the humblest of His people. Ruth 4. 17 tells us that Ruth's son Obed was the grandfather of king David from whom, of course, our Lord Himself, according to the flesh, was descended. God had a purpose for the family of Elimelech and Naomi of which they were completely unaware.

God's purpose for them would never have come to fruition apart from the faithfulness of Ruth to her mother-in-law. Ruth was a Moabitess, a foreigner, married to one of Naomi's sons. Naomi's husband had died, and then her two sons (Ruth 1. 2-5), so both Naomi and her daughters-in-law Ruth and Orpah were left widows. When Naomi wanted to return to her home-land Ruth and Orpah insisted on going with her. Naomi tried to persuade them to remain with their own kinsfolk, pointing out the difficulties and lack of prospects for them in a foreign land. Orpah went back, but Ruth chose to remain.

God had so worked in Ruth's heart that she was not attracted by the security she had previously known. She chose the pathway of loyalty to God and His people in spite of the hardship that lay ahead. Whatever the future might hold for Naomi, she was prepared to share it. In her heart she knew that Naomi's God was the true God, and she was ready to follow Him regardless of what happened to herself. God honoured her faithfulness.

Faithfulness to one another as God's people is an indication of the measure of our faithfulness to God. Often it may cost us much hardship to stand by our brethren in their difficulties, but it is the way of blessing. The Lord is faithful to us. Let us pray that He may make us faithful to one another.

Ruth 1. 16; Ruth 1. 17; 2 Tim. 1. 8; 2 Tim. 1. 16; 1 John 3. 16

Obedience and Faithfulness

THE PERILS OF BLESSING

March 31   Reading: Judges 2. 1-5.

The book of Judges covers a period of about four hundred years in the history of the children of Israel. It recounts many victories, but also many defeats. It is a story of frequent declension, of God's judgement, and then His gracious restoration of His people.

In this passage an angel of God reminds the people of the nation's miraculous deliverances from Egypt under God's hand. God had also brought them into the land He had promised them, but they had not obeyed the conditions He had laid down for them. God had forbidden them to enter into any covenant with the inhabitants of the land, but they disobyed and compromised with their heathen neighbours for their own advantage. The result was spiritual tragedy and God's judgement.

The people wept when they heard the angel's message (v. 4). Repentance was followed by a period of spiritual blessing, but the next generation again lapsed into heedlessness of God's ways. The tragedy of Israel's lapses during the rule of the Judges is that the people declined from a position in which they could have gone on from strength to strength. They did not fall because of the hardships of the way. They fell because, in the time of victory, they became self-confident and lost their deep sense of God's purpose and need of God's help.

The dangers of spiritual blessing are a fact of Christian experience. Our faithfulness to the Lord is most severely tested when we can be tempted to think that we have few spiritual needs. We no longer commit our affairs so much to the guidance of God, but order them according to our own self-confident judgement. The end is coldness and spiritual defeat.

Let us thank God for His blessing, but let us pray that in our times of blessing God will protect us from selfconfidence that we may never lose a deep sense of our need of Him.

1 Cor. 10.11; Prov. 23. 17; Prov. 26. 12; Jud. 6. 12; Isa. 40. 29

Obedience and Faithfulness

DANIEL

Reading: Daniel 6. 10-18.

The strength of Daniel's character was in his communion with God. When the test came, and the choice lay between his relationship with God and his life, Daniel did not hesitate. The privilege of prayer was too precious to be bargained away. It was too precious to be kept hidden. Daniel had already proved the faithfulness of God in many trials. As a young man he was taken captive by Nebuchadnezzar into Babylon. There he remained faithful to God (Dan. 1.8) and was ultimately raised to a position of authority in the land. After the death of Nebuchadanezzar, Daniel left public life and only returned from his obscurity to interpret God's words of judgement to king Belshazzar (Dan. 5). When Belshazzar was overthrown by Darius the Mede (Dan. 5. 30-31), Daniel was no longer young, but an experienced and respected statesman whom Darius planned to set over the whole kingdom (6. 3).

Daniel's wisdom and fear of God had, however, provoked the jealousy of other men in authority. Intent on doing him harm, they were sure that his devotion to God was something on which he would never compromise (v. 5), and was the one point of his character they could use to further their evil designs. In this they were right. The document they asked the king to sign prohibited prayer for only thirty days. It would have been easy for Daniel to hide his prayer life for such a short time, but he did not. Throughout his life he had maintained an open testimony to his faith in God and had proved God's faithfulness. He was determined not to be disloyal, or even appear to be disloyal to the One he had served so long, even if it meant death.

Let us thank God for the example of people such as Daniel, and let us pray that He will keep us faithful to Him and to His people.

Dan. 6. 26; Dan. 6. 27; Ps. 36. 5; Lam. 3. 22-23; 2 Chron. 19. 9

The Life of Our Lord

THE TRIUMPHAL ENTRY

April 2   Reading: John 12. 12-19

Jesus' choice of an ass on which to make His entry into Jerusalem was significant. The ass was the beast of kings, but used only on missions of peace and goodwill. Our Lord was giving open testimony as to who He was and was inviting a respnse from the crowd.

Jerusalem was filled with people who had come to observe the feast of the Passover. At such a time and in such circumstances, with the city of Jerusalem under the yoke of the heathen Roman power, thoughts of the Messiah were prominent in people's minds. Our Lord's entry into the city was a clear claim to be the Messiah, and was a fulfilment of the prophecy of Zechariah which John quotes (v. 15). The action of Jesus entering the city riding on an ass was a sign that He was coming in peace, and it was this that the people failed to understand.

The Jewish people had long dreamt of a Messiah who would come as a man of war and lead the nation to victory over the Roman oppressor. In their shout of acclaim the crowd showed that that was what they expected of Jesus. "Hosanna! Blessed is he who comes in the name of Lord, even the King of Israel!" (v. 13). The word Hosanna means, "Save now!" It was an urge to the Messiah to do what the Jews thought was His military duty, but they were expecting Jesus to be something He refused to be. He was not a military conqueror, but the Prince of Peace. There were none who really understood His claim, and the result was that many turned against Him because He did not fulfil their own human expectations.

The Lord has given us a clear revelation of Himself, but so often we fail to understand what He is seeking to do. We interpret His claims in our own way, to fit into our own human standards and personal ambitions. In doing so we miss God's best for us.

Let us thank God for our Lord Jesus Christ's revelation of Himself, and let us pray that we may not be offended by His standards which are often so different from our own.

Zech. 9. 9; Matt. 11. 6; Jer. 9. 24; Matt. 13. 16-17; Matt. 16. 17.

The Life of Our Lord

THE TRIAL

Reading: John 19. 7-16

The trial of Jesus was certainly the most dramatic trial of all history. The frenzied fanaticism of the Jews; the vacillations of Pilate, a man manouvered into a position in which he had not the courage to do what he knew to be right; the real dignity of Jesus; all demonstrate the depravity of human self-will and the greatness of the Lord.

Hatred is a terrible thing. It is a kind of madness that takes away from people all sense of proportion and goodness. The Jews were determined to do away with Jesus. Their charge against Him was one of blasphemy, that He made Himself God (v. 7), but they well knew that Pilate would never proceed against Him on such a charge, so they twisted the charge to one of political insurrection (v. 12). But still more indicative of the way hatred had distored their thinking was the astounding reply of the chief priests to Pilate, "We have no king but Caesar." The Jews who so resented Roman rule, who in the past had braved the most terrible persecution because they insisted that God alone was their king, now, in order to eliminate Jesus deny even God Himself.

All the time they were showing their implacable hatred to God's anointed One they were meticulously carrying out the details of the ceremonial law. They did not enter the praetorium as it would have made them ceremonially unclean (18. 28). Let us beware lest we as believers busy ourselves with the outward forms of the faith, yet break God's law of love and service.

Pilate's standing with the Roman emperor was none too secure. The suggestion that he might be accused of further disloyalty if he released Jesus (v. 12) was too much for him. He did not have the courage to do what he knew to be right.

But beyond the hatred and weakness of those who surrounded Him stands out the regal dignity of the Lord. He was not in the hands of men, but in the hands of the Father (vs. 10-11). It was not the Lord who was on trial, but those who accused Him and condemned Him, in fact the whole world. We too are on trial before Him. May the Lord help us not to deny Him.

John 18. 25; John 18. 37; John 19. 11; John 19. 17; Judg. 8. 23

The Life of Our Lord

THE CRUCIFIXION

April 4   Reading: Mark 15. 21-39

The story of the crucifixion shows, as no other story can, the indifference of the world to Christ. While our Lord was dying in agony for the sins of the world, the soldiers sat gambling for His garments as if it did not matter (v. 24). But we too can at times act perilously like these soldiers. We can be so taken up with selfish interests as to lose sight of the will and work of God.

Those who derided our Lord (vs. 29-32), from the chief priests to one of the criminals who was crucified with Him, little realized the irony of their words. Our Lord could have come down from the cross, but His not doing so was our salvation.

Our Lord's cry of dereliction leads us to the heart of the atonement. We may never fully fathom its depths, but in some way we know that God, who cannot look upon sin, forsook His Son the sin-bearer, that we might never be forsaken. Before the actual crucifixion Jesus was offered wine mingled with myrrh (v. 23). This was an opiate, but our Lord refused it. He bore the pain of the cross with His mental faculties unclouded, and by a voluntary act He gave up His life. His death was not the result of exhaustion or other natural causes. At the end He uttered a loud strong cry (v. 37), and gave up His life at the moment of His own choosing.

The rending of the temple curtain (v. 38) must have made a tremendous impression upon the Jews, whether or not they were willing to accept the momentous implications of this momentous event. The way into the holy of holies which, through centuries of tabernacle and temple worship had been closed to all but the high priest on the Day of Atonement, was now open. The atoning death of our Lord had for ever opened up the way into the presence of God for all those who come through faith in Him.

Let us thank God for the work of the cross, for redemption and for the way opened for us into His presence. Let us pray that we may never live and act as if it were something insignificant.

Mark 15. 31; Mark 15. 38; John 10. 17; Heb. 10. 19-20; Heb. 10. 21

The Life of Our Lord

THE RESURRECTION

April 5   Reading: John 20. 11-18.

Mary was the first person to see Jesus after His resurrection. Her initial thought on seeing that the stone had been rolled away from the tomb was that someone had removed the body (20. 2). She was deeply devoted to the Lord, but like the disciples who did not seem to have understood our Lord's prophecies concerning the resurrection, she was not at first disposed to believe that He had risen from the dead. When Jesus called her by name, the wonderful fact broke in upon her.

The resurrection is one of the cardinal doctrines of the Christian faith. Paul speaks at length of its importance in 1 Cor. 15. In the resurrection God set His seal on the deity of our Lrod Jesus Christ, on the value of the atoning work of the cross, and on the message of the gospel. Death could not hold our Lord. This is a witness to all those who trust in Him that they too will be preserved through death for a much more glorious life beyond.

Mary was not only the first to see the resurrected Lord. She was the first witness of the resurrection to others. On recognizing the Lord her inclination was to cling to Him, but He forbids her to do so and tells her to go and inform the brethren what had happened. The resurrection was not to be merely a matter of personal comfort to a few people who had been close to the Lord during His public ministry. It was to be the motive of a message of hope and salvaton to the world. The fact of the resurrection occupied a prominent place in the preaching of the apostles, because it raised the Christian message to an altogether higher plane than any of the popular philosophies of the day. The resurrection meant that Christian teaching was not a mere matter of philosophic speculation. It was a revelation from God Himself, and an assurance of divine power available to see that revelation fulfilled.

Let us thank God for the resurrection of our Lord Jesus Christ. Let us pray that we may know more of its power in our daily lives, and be zealous to take the message of a risen Christ to others.

Rom. 1. 4; Acts 2. 32; Luke 24. 34; Heb. 13. 20-21; 1 Peter 1. 21

The Life of Our Lord

JESUS AND JUDAS

April 6   Reading: John 13. 21-30.

The presence among the twelve disciples of one who was a traitor is something of a mystery, but the tragedy of Judas Iscariot teaches many pointed lessons. Jesus had a deep affection for all His disciples, and His love for Judas is clearly shown in this incident. For a host to offer one of His guests a tit-bit was a sign of particular friendship. Jesus gave the morsel to Judas (v. 26). From Jesus' words to Judas it also seems possible that Judas was occupying the place to the left of our Lord, the place of honour, another indication of our Lord's love for him. Judas must have been a hardhearted man indeed to remain so unmoved. He was open to the influences of Satan himself (v. 27).

It is a terrible thing for a child of God to be open to the wiles of the devil. The devil can take what is good and so twist it in a person's mind that it is turned into something evil. He can turn holiness into pride, love into weak compromise with evil. Here he took the love of Jesus for Judas and perverted it into a means for Judas to betray his Master. Judas went out into a night that was physically dark, and spiritually dark as well.

The treachery of Judas shows the depths of human depravity. The rest of the disciples were completely unaware of what was taking place. Outwardly Judas must have been a picture of devotion and loyalty. He was the perfect hypocrite. But though he could deceive the rest of the disciples, he did not deceive the Lord. Judas is a grim warning to all of us.

Yet we must believe that when our Lord chose him, He saw in Judas the making of a genuine disciple. Judas had all the privileges of the other disciples, the same revelation of the power and purposes of God that they had received, but he misused it with terrible results. May the Lord grant that we may never so misuse the privileges God has given us.

Let us pray that God will help us to heed the warnings of Judas' tragic life.

John 13. 20; Mal. 1. 6; Rom. 2. 4; Prov. 13. 13; Num. 15. 31

The Life of Our Lord

JESUS IN GETHSEMANE

April 7   Reading: Mark 14. 32-42

The agony in the garden of Gethsemane show us that Jesus had a real humanity which shrank from suffering. What he faced, however, was much more than physical suffering. Many Christian martyrs have faced the most terrible physical suffering with tremendous courage. Jesus faced not only the agony of the cross. His sinless soul faced the agony of being 'made sin' for our sake (2 Cor. 5. 21). All that this means is beyond our understanding, but we know that for our Lord it meant an agony of spirit such as no sinful mortal can possibly suffer.

Jesus' prayer in the garden also shows us that He possessed a real human will, distinct from the will of the Father, though always submissive to it. The point of our Lord's triumph was here in Gethsemane when He prayed "Yet not what I will, but what thou wilt" (v. 36). Our first parents brought about the fall by asserting their wills against the will of God. Our Lord wrought salvation by submitting to the will of God.

The victory of calvary was actually won here in the garden of Gethsemane in prayer. All spiritual victories are won at the same point, in the prayer of submission to the will of God. Self-will, on the other hand, always leads to defeat. The real threat to our spiritual lives comes through our wills, not through the difficulties of our circumstances. Jesus won the battle at the point of His will, so there was never any possibility of defeat, whatever spiritual and physical sufferings the cross might bring.

In sharp contrast to our Lord at prayer there is the picture of the sleeping disciples. Among them was Peter who had insisted that he was ready to die with Jesus (v. 31), but could not watch with Him for one brief hour. How little they realized the need of vigilance and prayer in the face of temptaion. Their failure is a warning to us all.

Let us pray that the lord will preserve us from self-confidence, and help us to surrender our wills to Him, for this alone leads to victory.

Mark 14. 36; Mark 14. 37; Mark 14. 38; Heb. 2. 9; Heb. 5. 7

The Life of Our Lord

THE RESURRECTION APPEARANCES

April 8   Reading: Luke 24. 28-43

One of the proofs of the resurrection was the appearance of our Lord to different individuals or groups of people, one group numbering five hundred (1 Cor. 15. 6). In our present reading Jesus appears to two disciples on the road to Emmaus and ministers to them. Then He appears to the eleven in Jerusalem.

Paul in writing to the Corinthians (1 Cor. 15. 35-44) warns us that our understanding of the nature of the resurrection body is limited. Nevertheless the body is important. Jesus rose and appeared to others with the same body which was placed in the tomb. It was a real body, not a spirit. When He appears to the eleven He particularly emphasises this (v. 40). He asks them to touch Him, and in further indication of His body being real, He eats before them (v. 43).

When Paul speaks of a 'spiritual body' (1 Cor. 15. 44) he does not mean that the body is gone and only spirit is left. This is a mistaken idea which finds no support in the Bible. There is still a body, but it is dominated by the spirit. All that this means we do not know, but it was true of the resurrection body of our Lord, and will be true of our bodies in the heavenly state.

Our Lord's resurrection body possessed characteristics of His human body. As we have already seen, it was the same body as that placed in the tomb, and our Lord partook of food. His body also bore the wounds inflicted through His crucifixion. There were other characteristics, however, such as our human bodies do not possess. The Lord suddenly vanished from the sight of the two on the Emmaus road (v. 31). He suddenly appeared in the midst of the disciples (v. 36). When He rose from the dead it seems He passed through the rock-hewn tomb. He occupied the body in which He suffered, but it was a body no longer beset by the limitations of the body of fallen man.

Through His resurrection appearances our Lord demonstrated the sanctity of the earthly body, and has given to His people an assurance of their one day assuming a glorified body. Let us pray that the Lord will help us to glorify Him in our bodies now.

Luke 24. 32; Luke 24. 39; 1 Cor. 15. 40; 1 Cor. 15. 44; 1 Cor. 15. 48

The Cross and Resurrection

THE CROSS OF SELF-GIVING

April 9   Reading: Philippians 2. 1-13

The cross of our Lord Jesus Christ, besides being a work of atonement, demonstrates principles for every day living. They are principles by which our Lord Himself lived, and He calls us to live by them in following Him.

In Phil. 2 we have just read Paul's great passage on the self-giving of Christ. The cross showed the utter extent to which He was prepared to go in self-giving. We begin in v. 6 with Christ Jesus 'in the form of God'. In v. 8 we end with 'death on a cross'. We move from one extreme of glory to an extreme of shame. Christ Jesus who was in the beginning, one with the glory of the Father, did not hold on to His position, but 'emptied Himself' (v. 7). Having become incarnate He could have been a king, but He became a servant. He the author of life did not need to die, but He died. He could have died the death of a martyr, but He chose instead to die in the manner of a criminal, for crucifixion was the means the Romans used to execute criminals who were the very dregs of society. Christ Jesus emptied Himself of everything but His deity. He could not become less than Himself, the incarnate Son of God.

"Have this mind among yourselves, which you have in Christ Jesus" (v. 5). Paul sets up our Lord as an example to us of self-giving. As He took the way of the cross, the way of death to self, so must we. The life and death of our Lord were the very opposite of selfishness and conceit (v. 3). His concern was not with Himself, but with the interests of the Father and of the world He had come to save.

The passage ends with an appeal for a practical outworking of the submission to God that we profess. On His part, God has done all and is doing all that is necessary to complete His salvation in us (v. 13). We must co-operate with Him in the same way as Christ Jesus gave Himself to do the Father's will.

Let us thank God for the self-giving of our Lord Jesus Christ. Let us pray that we may more diligently work out our own salvation in the spirit of self-giving to Him and to others.

Phil. 2. 3; Phil. 2. 4; Phil. 2. 5; Phil. 2. 8; Phil. 2. 9.

The Cross and Resurrection

THE CROSS OF COMMITMENT

April 10   Reading: Hebrews 10. 1-10

The cross was a demonstration of our Lord's total commitment to the will of the Father. In the garden of Gethsemane, while He prayed that, if possible, the cup of suffering might pass from Him, His overriding concern was for the will of God. "Yet not what I will, but what thou wilt" (Mark 14. 36). Here in the letter to the Hebrews the same total commitment is expressed in v. 7 which is a quotation from Ps. 40. 8 applied directly to our Lord Jesus Christ.

Our Lord's sacrifice was the sacrifice of an obedient will, and that really is the only true sacrifice. This is what the writer to the Hebrews is seeking to point out. At best the sacrifices of Old Testament times were a shadow of Christ's redemptive work. They were not indicative of a totally obedient people. The fact that they had to be repeated over and over again showed their own imperfection and the imperfect obedience of those who offered them (vs. 1-2). Only our Lord's sacrifice of Himself was a sacrifice of perfect obedience, so it alone was effective in cleansing the sin of man.

Basically, sacrifice is something noble. It means that a person takes what is dear to himself and, out of his love for God, offers it to Him. But man's subtle nature easily abuses this noble thing, and man begins to think that sacrifice is a means of buying God's favour. When this happens, sacrifice ceases to be an expression of love for God, and becomes merely an empty ritual. This is why the Old Testament prophets so often condemned the sacrifices and offerings people made, though, technically, they were offered exactly according to the law the prophets knew that there could be no true sacrifice apart from an obedient spirit.

God's people today are often guilty of the same sin as His people in Old Testament times. Prayers, Bible reading, worship, all good things in themselves, can become 'sacrifices' by which people think they earn God's favour while at heart they are disobedient to Him.

Let us pray that the Lord may receive from us the sacrifice of an obedient heart.

Heb. 10. 5; Heb. 10. 7; Heb. 10. 10; 1 Sam. 15. 22; Hos. 6. 6.

101

The Cross and Resurrection

THE CROSS OF REJECTION

April 11   Reading: Hebrews 13. 10-16

"So Jesus also suffered outside the gate" (v. 12). The place of crucifixion was outside the wall of Jerusalem. Crucifixion itself, a death inflicted only on the basest criminals, and the place where the sentence was carried out, emphasised the rejection by society of the one who was executed. The cross of Christ symbolized His rejection by the world.

There were two main reasons why Jesus was crucified. First, of course, He was crucified for the sins of the world. The reason He came to the earth was to accomplish the redemptive work of the cross. That was the divine reason for the crucifixion. There was, however, a more immediate and earthly reason why He was crucified. He was crucified because He was so different from others, and the reason why He was so different was that He was supremely holy.

Our Lord stood out as distinct from all around Him. He mixed with the people of the world, but He was never one of them. He was a friend of sinners, but He was never a sinner Himself. There could be no mistaking His character. He stood out from all others as someone who was absolutely good. Our Lord in His words condemned the sin and hypocrisy of many of the religious leaders of His day, but even more than His words. His life was a condemnation of everything that was evil. The light of His sheer goodness showed up everything that was sinful. This was the reason why He was hated. The world, unwilling to be seen in the light of God's holiness, rejected Him. So He was crucified.

The writer to the Hebrews tells us that Jesus suffered 'in order to sanctify the people through his own blood' (v. 12). He went to the cross in order to make a people who would be like Himself, willing to be different, willing to be rejected as He was rejected. "Therefore let us go forth to him outside the camp, and bear the abuse he endured. For here we have no lasting city" (vs. 13-14).

Let us thank God for His Son who was despised and rejected of men, and let us pray that we too will be strong to identify ourselves with Him in His rejection.

Isa. 53. 3; Heb. 13. 12; Heb. 13. 13-14; Heb. 13. 15; Heb. 13. 16

The Cross and Resurrection

THE CROSS THE GATEWAY TO LIFE

April 12   Reading: Psalm 16. 1-11

On the day of Pentecost Peter preached Jesus crucified and risen from the dead. Then he quotes part of Psalm 16, applyng the words of David directly to our Lord Jesus Christ (Acts 2. 25-28). Psalm 16, though written many years before calvary, is a clear explanation of the principle of the cross. It is one of what we call the Messianic Psalms, those Psalms which speak prophetically of Jesus.

In vs. 1-3 we see the uniqueness of the family of God. Our Lord is identified with the Father (v. 2) and with the 'saints in the land' (v. 3). Here is the unique company that has been called out through the work of the cross. In contrast there are 'those who choose another God' (v. 4), whose lot is the very antithesis of life.

In the second section of the Psalm (vs. 5-11) there are continued expressions of rejoicing, all the more remarkable when we consider the path of suffering our Lord trod. But He saw beyond the suffering of the cross to the resurrection and life that was beyond. To the worldly man it would be inconceivable to associate with the death of the cross such expressions as, "The lines have fallen for me in pleasant places" (v. 6); "My heart is glad, and my soul rejoices" (v. 9); "In thy presence there is fulness of joy" (v. 11). Our Lord, however, saw in the cross a gateway to glory. He knew that through the whole experience the Father was there (v. 8), and He could rejoice in a glory which was so much greater than the suffering involved.

There is no resurrection without death. That was true for our Lord, and the same principle is true of us His people. We will experience the fulness of His life only to the extent that we are prepared to identify ourselves with Him in the experience of the cross, the cross of self-giving, the cross of committal to the will of the Father, the cross of rejection by a world which has rejected Him.

Let us thank God for the cross, the way of death which is the pathway to life, and let us pray that we may be willing to identify ourselves with our Lord in all that His cross means.

Ps. 16. 2; Ps. 16. 5; Ps. 16. 6; Ps. 16. 8; Ps. 16. 11

The Cross and Resurrection

THE HISTORICAL RESURRECTION

Reading: 1 Corinthians 15. 17-26

To Paul the resurrection was not just a spiritual event. It was an event which had happened at a specific place at a specific time not so many years before he wrote this letter. He states quite clearly that if that actual historical event had not taken place, the faith which God's people profess would be futile (v. 17).

Some of the Christians still held to mistaken Greek ideas, that at death the soul escaped from the body and continued a shadowy, disembodied existence, or was absorbed into the divine. To believe this would make nonsense of Christ's resurrection. It would mean that the body did not matter, and make any kind of immoral conduct excusable.

If there was no resurrection, then the preaching of the apostles was a lie, because the resurrection was the basis and dynamic of their message. If the apostle's preaching was based on a lie, then the whole Christian faith means nothing at all.

"But in fact Christ has been raised from the dead" (v. 20). Because of the sin of Adam, unregenerate man exists in an order whose characteristic is death. Now through the work of another Man, those who are 'in Christ' exist in an order whose characteristic is life (v. 21).

The consequences of Christ's resurrection are temporal, universal and eternal. Through His resurrection in the same body as was laid in the tomb, Christ has set His seal on the sanctity of the body. He made it possible for resurrection life to be revealed now through the medium of the earthly body we at present occupy. The resurrection has universal consequences in that the possibility of life is open to all men (v. 22). It has eternal consequences because Christ will never die again (Rom. 6.9). He continues as the risen Lord. He rose from the dead as the 'first fruits' of His glorified people (v. 23). This means that, for God's people, death is not the end. They will rise as He rose to continue to live out His resurrection life in a heavenly body. Let us pray that the Lord will fill us afresh with this glorious hope, and that more of His life might be revealed in us now.

Rom. 6. 9; 1 Cor. 15. 17; 1 Cor. 15. 20; 1 Cor. 15. 21; 1 Cor. 15. 25-26

The Cross and Resurrection

RESURRECTION LIFE IN THE BELIEVER

April 14   Reading: Philippians 3. 1-11

Paul sets the keynote of the resurrection life in the first verse. It is rejoicing, a confidence in God which rises above every trial and knows that He is in control. Paul then sounds a warning (v. 2) against 'dogs', people who are always scrounging around for their own interests; 'evil workers', those who do good for their own benefit; 'those who mutilate the flesh', people who pride themselves in their religious exercises. The warning is as much against the spirit of these things in ourselves as against others.

If any man had a right to boast, Paul had that right. In observance of Jewish custom, lineage, education, zeal for the law and his religion, no one could point a finger at him. But all of these things in which men prided themselves he counted as nothing. He was living now on a completely different level. He had an entirely new set of priorities. These priorites are summed up in the word 'righteousness' (v. 9) and the phrase 'that I may know him' (v. 10).

Righteousness to Paul means two things. It means a right relationship with God, and it also means the type of conduct and attitude to God which God Himself desires. Each of these, relationship and conduct, affect the other. A right relationship with God produces right conduct, and right conduct leads to a deeper relationship with God.

When Paul expresses his longing to know Christ (v. 10), he uses a word which means to know someone in a most intimate and personal way. For Paul this intimate knowledge of the Lord meant 'the power of his resurrection' (v. 10), that is, a dynamic power which operated in his every day living; it meant to 'share his sufferings' (v. 10), that is, to count it a privilege to share the rejection He endured; it meant 'becoming like him in his death, that.... I may attain the resurrection from the dead' (vs. 10-11), that is, so sharing in what the cross meant to our Lord and in its power in daily living that he would continue to share His life in an eternity to come.

Let us pray that we may so know the Lord that we may show forth the power of the resurrection in our daily lives.

Phil. 3. 7; Phil. 3. 8; Phil. 3. 9; Phil. 3. 10; Phil. 3 11.

The Cross and Resurrection

JOHN

This incident throws an interesting light on the character of the apostle John. Mark tells us that Jesus called John and his brother James the 'sons of thunder' (Mark 3. 17), a name, no doubt, which aptly described the easily roused disposition of the two brothers. Their reaction on our Lord's being rebuffed by the people in a Samaritan village was violent. "Lord, do you want us to bid fire come down from heaven and consume them?" they asked the Lord. Nor was this an isolated example of their temper. Mark tells of an occasion when John saw a man casting out demons in Jesus' name. He had been offended and had forbidden the man to continue his ministry of deliverance on the ground that he was not one of the disciples' own company (Mark 9. 38).

All this contrasts rather strangely with our dominant impression of John whom we call the apostle of love. John's Gospel and his epistles are full of the love of God and of the need of love in the lives of God's people. The John of later years was a changed John from the one who wanted to destroy the Samaritans who refused to accept Jesus.

Three of the disciples seemed to be much closer to the Lord than the other nine. The three were Peter, James and John. They alone of the disciples witnessed the transfiguration, and they alone accompanied our Lord on various other occasions. No doubt there were a number of reasons for this, but may it not be that Jesus gave these three hot headed disciples more attention simply because they were more in need of his mellowing, transforming influence?

The change in John is evident at the crucifixion when our Lord commits Mary, His mother, to his care (John 19. 26-27). John, the aggressive, self-confident disciple, was beginning to learn something of the principles of the cross and of life in Christ. May the Lord help us to learn these principles too.

John 19. 27; 1 John 2. 3; 1 John 4. 7-8; 1 John 4. 9; 1 John 4. 10

The Christian and the Nation

HUMAN GOVERNMENT ORDAINED OF GOD

April 16   Reading: Romans 13. 1-7

Paul wrote this passage before the Roman government had begun to persecute the Christians, but later when persecution against the church was raging Peter still writes counselling submission to the powers that be, and much later still Christian leaders continued to say the same thing.

There are certain principles here of great importance. Human government has been ordained by God (v. 1), and as long as the State is fulfilling its God-ordained function, it is the duty of every Christian to be submissive to it. Paul puts the matter very strongly when he says, "He who resists the authorities resists what God has appointed" (v. 2). The extent of the State's legitimate authority is quite clearly outlined (vs. 3-5), and in loyalty to God and his own conscience the believer has a duty to recognize that authority (v. 6).

No one can dissociate himself from the society in which he lives. Each one of us is part of a nation, and because of that we enjoy benefits we could not have as individuals living an isolated existence. We may at times complain about incompetence in official circles, but we still have facilites which would be impossible if the official system did not exist at all. We cannot expect to enjoy all the advantages and escape all the duties involved. Privileges and responsibilities go together. This is true of all life, both spiritual and secular. The Christian is duty bound to fulfil his responsibilities to the State.

Paul brings the matter very much down to earth in v. 7. "Pay all of them their dues, taxes to whom taxes are due, revenue to whom revenue is due, respect to whom respect is due, honour to whom honour is due." We cannot take everything and give nothing. As God's people we receive much, and we should also give much. It is a shame for any Christian to avoid paying legitimate taxes, whether it be a tax on income, on a radio, on a dog, or on anything. The Lord expects us His people to be an example to others in these matters. Let us pray that He will keep us faithful in our duties to our country.

Rom. 13. 1; Rom. 13. 5; Rom. 13. 6; Rom. 13. 7; 1 Tim. 2. 1-2

The Christian and the Nation

THE CHRISTIAN A GOOD CITIZEN

April 17   Reading: Mark 12. 13-17

The questiion of paying tribute to Caesar was hotly debated among the Jews. They resented the Roman rule, and the 'likeness and inscription' on the coinage was offensive to them on account of the tendency to deify the emperor. In asking their question, however, the Pharisees and Saducees were more concerned about scoring a point than knowing the truth. It was so framed that if Jesus had answered, "Yes", He would have lost the support of the crowd. Had He answered, "No", the Jews would have had a clear case against Him to bring before the Roman authority.

In His masterly reply Jesus laid down a principle which is true for all time. His followers should be model citizens. Duty to God and duty to the State are not incompatible unless the State overreaches its authority and demands an allegiance that is due to God alone. The principle is clear, "Render to Caesar the things that are Caesar's, and to God the things that are God's (v.17).

The Jews, in common with others, enjoyed the great benefit of a stable government. It was the stability of Roman government in New Testament times that, under the hand of God, enabled the gospel to spread as it did. Was it right that the Jews should expect to receive the benefits of the administration, yet refuse to contribute anything to its maintenance? Jesus' advice to His Jewish detractors is equally applicable to believing Christians. It is true that we belong to a heavenly kingdom, but we live by the standards of that heavenly kingdom here on earth, and it is part of a Christian's testimony to accept his responsibilities to the government under which he lives.

The time was to come when Christians were to be sorely persecuted, and many stood firm unto death rather than submit to a State which ordered them to deny their God, but Christians won acceptance among ordinary people largely because of their law abiding character, their honesty, and their submission to the State functioning within its God ordained boundaries. Let us thank God for the freedom we enjoy in our land to honour Him, and let us pray that we may be good citizens for His glory.

Mark. 12. 17; 1 Peter 2. 13-14; 1 Peter 2. 17; Tit. 3. 1; Tit. 3. 2

The Christian and the Nation

THE CHRISTIAN AND SOCIAL SERVICE

April 18   Reading: James 2. 8-17

God loved the world, and so should we. Some Christians live and act heedless of anyone outside their community. This is what James call 'partiality' and severely condemns (vs. 8-9). As believing Christians we should learn to identify ourselves with the needs of others. We should have a sense of what today we call 'social concern'.

There is a wrong idea in some sections of the so-called Christian Church that the gospel is little more than meeting the material needs of mankind. Much of the material suffering in the world today has a deep spiritual cause, and the gospel alone can meet that spiritual need. The preaching of the gospel deals with something much more basic than man's material wants. It deals with the root causes of mankind's disease, not merely the symptoms. Nevertheless, that does not mean that we should ignore the suffering all around us on the pretext that we are concerned with the more important spiritual needs.

James says emphatically that true faith will manifest itself in a concern for the practical needs of others (vs. 14-17). Our Lord Jesus Christ identified Himself with the suffering He saw all around Him. We must not close our eyes to the stark realities of the world in which we live. There is a crying need for a greater feeling of Christian compassion. We should not be able to live in a world which suffers as it does, without feeling for it. Our Lord felt for the multitudes around Him, for their spiritual need, and for every need they had. So should we.

It is so easy to settle down in complacency and self-satisfaction amidst the blessings God has bestowed upon us. James turns our attention to basic attitudes out of which our acts must flow. The world is quick to discern whether behind our preaching and our testimony of faith there is a real attitude of love and concern. We will see a response to the gospel we proclaim accordig to the measure of our concern for the glory of God and our burden for others.

Let us thank God for the way our Lord Jesus Christ identified Himself with the needs of a suffering world, and let us pray that we may learn to feel for the need of the world in which we live.

James 2. 8; James 2. 9; James 2. 14; James 2. 17; Acts 20. 35

The Christian and the Nation

WORKING FOR WHAT HE RECEIVES

April 19   Reading: 2 Thessalonians 3. 6-13

The hope of the second coming of Christ was very much alive in the hearts of the Christians of the early church. In Thessalonica, however, some of the believers had given up their daily employment to wait in excited idleness for the coming of the Lord. Paul tells them that it is their Christian duty to work for their livelihood (v. 12).

In our modern world there are many people who want to work but are unable to find employment. Paul does not condemn such. What he does condemn is the refusal to work (v. 10). The full-time Christian worker needs to take note of this also. Writing to Timothy, Paul speaks of the Christian worker as a labourer who deserves his wages (1 Tim. 5. 18). The ministry of the gospel is a worthy labour, but the minister should always keep before him the responsibilty of adequately fulfilling his ministry.

Paul reminds the Thessalonians of the example of Silas, Tiomthy and himself (v. 7). Not only had they laboured in the ministry, but they had also contributed to their maintenance by doing other work (v. 8). Not that they were obliged to do this, but they felt it necessary as a tesimony to other Christians.

Paul was a trained Rabbi, but the Jewish law required that every Rabbi follow a trade. Paul's trade was that of a tentmaker (Acts 18.3). Rabbis engaged in many different practical skills. All Jews believed in the dignity of manual labour. In fact the Jews felt that a scholar lost something if his intellectual pursuits made him forget how to work with his hands. There are many people, Christians included, who look upon any type of manual labour as beneath their dignity, and who look down upon people who perform the more humble tasks of life. This is an attitude which finds no sympathy in the pages of the Bible. The child of God should always give a fair return of work for the reward he receives, and be his work intellectual or practical, he should recognize that both are equally honourable in the sight of God.

Let us thank God for the privilege of working for Him, and let us pray that whatever our task might be, it might be done to His glory.

2. Thess. 3. 7; 2. Thess. 3. 8; 2. Thess. 3. 10; 2 Thess. 3. 12; 2 Thess. 3. 3

The Christian and the Nation

THE CHRISTIAN AND FAMILY PLANNING

April 20   Reading: 1 Timothy 5. 3-8

Paul's subject here is Christian responsibility within the family. He speaks of the responsibility of the younger for their elders (vs. 3-4). Then he speaks of the responsibility of older people for their own families (v. 8). The way people fulfil their responsibilities towards their own children will determine the way, in later years, the children will fulfil their responsibilities towards their parents.

The 'population explosion' is one of the greatest problems facing our nation and the modern world. The question of family planning brings this problem down into every Christian home. It is a subject which arouses strong emotional feelings, but each believer should face it frankly and recognize the Biblical principles which have a bearing on the matter.

God pronounces His blessing on the family when He says, "Children are a heritage from the Lord" (Psa. 127. 3). The blessing of a gift, however, is closely associated with the measure of the gift. Water is a blessing without which life on earth would be insupportable, but when water comes in a mighty flood, bringing devastation in its wake, its blessing is doubtful. Many of God's blessings cease to be blessings if they are not controlled.

The Bible lays great emphasis on responsible parenthood. This is what Paul stresses in v. 8. The provision which parents owe to their children, however, is not only material. It is emotional and spiritual as well. Poverty is no shame, and the lack of affluence may find more than adequate compensation in emotional and spiritual security. Material, emotional and spiritual provision are all important, and people do not have a Scriptural right to keep on adding to their families when they are unable to provide the barest necessities for their children in the material, emotional and spiritual realm. To cast the responsibility back on God is not the answer. God has placed the responsibility squarely on His people themselves. The Bible's teaching on responsible parenthood is something that must be seriously faced.

Let us thank God for the blessing of the Christian family and pray that we may understand more fully the responsibilities involved.

1 Tim. 5. 8; Ps. 127. 1; Ps. 127. 3; Matt. 5. 29; Prov. 20. 7

The Christian and the Nation

THE CHRISTIAN'S LOYALTY TO GOD

April 21   Reading: Acts 5. 27-42

Peter and John had been thrown into the common prison for their insistence on preaching Christ (5. 17-18). By a miracle they were released, and are found in the temple once again teaching the people about the Lord. The apostles are brought before the council and questioned by the high priest (v. 27). "We strictly charged you not to teach in this name, yet here you have filled Jerusalem with your teaching," he said (v. 28). The apostles' answer was, "We must obey God rather than men" (v. 29).

Palestine was under a Roman governor, but within the jurisdiction of Roman authority the Jews were allowed to administer their own community according to Jewish law. The apostles, therefore, were arraigned before Jewish religious leaders. The charge brought against them was not moral or criminal. It was a charge involving the apostles relationship with God. They had been forbidden to preach in the name of Christ, but had refused to comply. God's authority, they claimed, was above the authority of any human council (v. 29). No human council, therefore, had a right to dictate their relationship to God.

On the council was a greatly loved and highly respected Pharisee named Gamaliel. He advises the rest of the council against hasty action. If the apostles' teaching is of man, he says, it will die a natural death, but if it is of God they can never destroy it (vs. 38-39). He warns the council to beware lest they be 'found opposing God' (v. 39). In doing so he acknowledges the point of the apostles' answer.

The apostles here state the same principle as our Lord when He said, "Render therefore to Caesar the things that are Caesar's, and to God the things that are God's" (Matt. 22. 21). There is a limit to human authority. Just as, in an army, a low ranking officer does not have the authority to dictate a soldier's relationship to a superior officer, so no human government has authority to dictate a person's relationship to God. If we are ever commanded to disobey God, our reply should be the reply of the apostles, "We must obey God rather than men."

Acts 5. 29; Acts 5. 31; Acts 5. 38; Acts 5. 39; Acts 5. 42

The Christian and the Nation

MANOAH

April 22   Reading: Judges 13. 8-20

The age of the Judges was corrupt and lawless. A number of times in the course of the book of Judges we read these words, "Every man did what was right in his own eyes." Yet in the midst of a nation which was living in rebellion against God there were godly people who were concerned for their land and for God's glory. When Jesus said, "You are the salt of the earth," He was speaking of people of quiet godliness and solid piety like Manoah who made this sinful world worth living in.

Manoah was the father of Samson. He and his wife had been chosen by God as the parents of one who was to be Judge over the nation Israel. They preserved their faith and simplicity through years of hardship and oppression, and taught their respect for God to their son Samson whose life, nevertheless, was a strange mixture of devotion to God and devotion to the spirit of the world in which he lived.

Stable families mean a stable nation, and if there had been more households like that of Manoah, the country would have been a better country. The angel of God appeared first to Manoah's wife to announce that she would bear a son. We are not told her name, but the angel's visit to her a second time is an indication that, though little known by other people she was well thought of by God. Manoah listens attentively to his wife. There is an obvious spirit of love and unity between them.

Manoah never doubted the promise of God (v. 12), but knowing that what was said would come to pass, he was eager to receive as explicit instructions as God would give for the upbringing of the son who would be born to them. And having received instructions, Manoah offered a sacrifice (v. 19). It was a sacrifice which symbolized the giving of himself, his life and his devotion to do the will of God. A nation is exalted by righteousness like that of Manoah and his wife. Let us pray that God will help us to honour our country by honouring Him.

Prov. 14. 34; Jud. 13. 12; Jud. 13. 19; Prov. 3. 9; Prov. 11. 11

Salvation

THE SCOPE OF SALVATION

April 23   Reading: Romans 1. 1-16

In v. 16 Paul says the gospel 'is the power of God for salvation'. Salvation is one of the great words of the New Testaments, and its meaning is the subject of the epistle to the Romans. It sums up all the blessings bestowed by God on men through the redemptive work of Christ and the work of the Holy Spirit.

Paul's introduction to his letter is important because, in these verse, he sets down spiritual principles which He goes on to elaborate later in the epistle. He does not do this in a formal manner. They emerge from the way he speaks of his relationship with the Lord and with all his fellow believers. This is precisely what the gospel is, first a new personal relationship with God, and secondly a new relationship with other believers.

The gospel as a personal relationship with God is expressed in various ways. Paul calls himself a "slave of Jesus Christ' (v. 1), and he tells of 'belonging' to Jesus Christ (v. 6). This is a truly dynamic concept. We all know how important relationships with other people are. A relationship can make or mar a person's character. If a relationship with another person can be so powerful, what can we say of a relationship with the personal, all holy, all powerful God. A person who enters a relationship with this God just cannot be the same again.

In v. 3 Jesus is described as descended from David. In v. 4 He is 'designated Son of God'. Jesus was both man and God. He lived a life on earth as we do, and in divine power His human life was an example of the life of the gospel. The gospel brings divine power into daily living.

In. vs. 8-15 Paul speaks of his deep relationship with the believers in Rome. The gospel is a relationship with others who have been reconciled to God through grace. The gospel relationship can be pictured as a triangle, our link with other believers forming the base, and our individual links with God forming the apex. A marred relationship with God affects our relationship with others, and a marred relationship with others affects our relationship with God. The gospel is the power of God to maintain the triangle unbroken. Let us thank God for the gospel, and let us pray that we may know more of its power practically in our daily living.

Rom. 1. 3; Rom. 1. 5; Rom. 1. 8; Rom. 1. 11-12; Rom. 1. 17

Salvation

THE NEED OF PERSONAL SALVATION

April 24   Reading: John 3. 1-15

Nicodemus was a Pharisee. The Pharisees were a small company of elite Jews who had taken a vow to spend their lives in observing every detail of the law of Moses. the law consists of great moral principles which each person has to work out for himself. The Jews, however, reduced these priciples to hundreds of by-laws and regulations. We cannot doubt the sincerity of the Pharisees' or Nicodemus' devotion to the law, but Nicodemus must have felt that the task he had set himself was an impossible one. It left him with a great spiritual lack, and in his sense of need he came to Jesus.

Jesus tells Nicodemus he must be born anew (v. 3). The word translated 'anew' has two other meanings. It can mean 'from above', or it can mean 'for a second time'. To be born anew is such a radical change that it can only be described as a second birth, and it is 'from above', not the result of human effort, but of the power and grace of God. Nicodemus well knew his need of such a radical change, but it seemed so impossible, like demanding that someone be re-born physically (v. 4).

The new birth brings a person into the kingdom of God (vs. 3,5). The kingdom of God is not something only to do with the life to come. It is the rulership of God here on the earth in the lives of His people. The person who is born again lives a life of response to the will of God. No man can do this in his own power, though it does require the response of man to God's power. Jesus put it this way, "Unless one is born of water and the Spirit, he cannot enter the kingdom of God" (v. 3). Water means cleansing. It is also a symbol of the Word of God and, therefore, of obedience to it. The Spirit denotes power. When the Lord saves us and takes possession of our lives, He empowers us to be what we could never be of ourselves.

Being born again is an intensely practical experience. We can never fully understand how God does His work, but its effects will be obvious to all, like the invisible wind whose effects nevertheless, we see and feel (v. 8).

Let us thank God for His salvation, and let us pray that its effects may be more and more clearly seen in our lives.

John 3. 3; John 3. 5; John 3. 6; John 3. 8; 1 Peter 1. 23

Salvation

JUSTIFICATION

April 25   Reading: Romans 3. 21-26.

The gospel provides an answer to two questions, the legal question of a man's standing before God as a sinner, and the practical question of his state as a sinner in need of transformation. Sanctification begins in and flows from justification. Strictly speaking, justification belongs to the beginning of the Christian's career, and sanctification follows on to its end in final glory (8. 30).

Justification by faith, Paul tells us, leads to a manifestation of the righteousness of God. Justification has a decisive, practical effect upon a person's character. This does not mean that there is a sudden transition to moral perfection, but it does mean that justification leads to a demonstrable result in the life of the person who has true faith in Christ.

We will never fully understand the depths of vs. 24-26, but they do show us clearly that God, while maintaining His own righteousness, has, through the sacrifice of the cross, 'passed over former sins' (v. 25). Justification owes absolutely nothing to man's efforts, and all to the grace of God. Justification is itself a legal term, a final pronouncement of innocence. Let us suppose a person has been arraigned before a court on a criminal charge, found guilty and sentenced to death. In such circumstances it would be meaningless to talk about his reformation. If he is to be reformed he first needs a pardon which will make him legally innocent. By being pronounced innocent, or 'justified' to use the Biblical terminology, a person is not automatically made a good character. Transformation may be a long and difficult process, but the pardon enables the process to be begun. This illustration shows the basic meaning of justication. The sinner is accounted innocent before God and brought into a new relationship with Him which is a prelude to God's deeper work.

A gospel which stops at forgiveness and justification is incomplete. The gospel is the power of God unto salvation, which means justification, leading on through the work of sanctification to glory.

Let us thank God for His work of justification, and let us pray that we may allow Him to continue in us the work He has begun.

Rom. 3. 20; Rom. 3. 21; Rom. 3. 24; Rom. 3. 27; Rom. 3. 31

Salvation

JUSTIFICATION BY GRACE THROUGH FAITH

April 26   Reading: Romans 4. 1-6

In Rom. 4 Paul uses Abraham as an illustration of justification. He shows that the principle on which God deals with man has always been the same, the principle of faith. He goes back over six hundred years before Moses to Abraham who was the father of the Jewish race. This chapter is a decisive repudiation of the poupular idea of two covenants, an old covenant of law through which God dealt with men in a past age, and a new covenant of grace which was instituted through Christ, and through which God deals with men today.

"For by grace you have been saved through faith" (Eph. 2. 8), has always been true. God gave the law to Moses not as a means of bringing salvation, but to demonstrate the inadequacy of law and human effort to save. Paul deals at greater length with this question in his letter to the Galatians.

Abraham, though revered as the founder of Israel, did not fit into the common conception that a person finds favour with God through meticulous observance of a law or, still more important to the Jew, because of the rite of circumcision. God's promise of blessing to Abraham was obviously not due to his obedience of any system of law. In substantiation of this Paul quotes Gen. 15. 6, "Abraham believed God, and it was reckoned to him as righteousness" (v. 3). Similarly, Abraham's circumcision was not the basis of his favour with God (v. 10) for the simple reason that the promise was given to him before he was circumcised. Circumcision was, in fact, a sign of the relationship already esatblished (v. 11).

Law, which is an elaborate machinery calculated to produce righteousness, is the only way man knows of trying to establish morality, but it has been a signal failure. Faith accomplishes what law cannot do, because faith deals with attitudes which are the basis of our actions.

Let us thank God for His free gift of justification, and let us pray for a faith like that of Abraham.

Rom. 4. 3; Rom. 4. 7; Rom. 4. 8; Rom. 4. 11; Rom. 4. 13

117

Salvation

THE RESULTS OF JUSTIFICATION IN EXPERIENCE

April 27   Reading: Romans 5. 1-5

Certain practical results follow from justification. Man suffers from a guilt complex which can paralyse initiative, distort relationships, and give rise to an inner turmoil which works havoc with every thought of progress and constructive living. Justification replaces this chaos with peace (v. 1). The person who is justified is at peace with God.

Justification also produces an attitude in man which is conducive to God's working. Man is now ready to co-operate with God. God is now able to do something in him. This is what Paul means when he says that 'we have obtained access to this grace in which we stand' (v. 2).

The attitude of a justified person is supremely positive. Vs. 2-5 show a faith that is both positive and active. It was the faith of Paul's own experience. The hope of the glory of God (v. 2) was to Paul no mere wishful thinking. It was an assurance which demanded his total involvement and which transformed his view of even the most painful circumstances, for he realized that in them God was moulding his character and working out His own purposes (v. 5).

In v. 5 we have the first explicit mention of the Holy Spirit in Romans. It is significant that He should be introduced in an account of the results of justification. A person cannot belong to Christ at all without having the Spirit (8. 9), but in conforming the believer to the image of the Son, the work of the Holy Spirit belongs principally to the realm of sanctification with which Paul deals in the next section of the letter. The Spirit's being mentioned here confirms that, though justification is a legal pronouncement, the fact that it establishes a personal relationship with none other than the personal God Himself, has a decisive moral effect. In justification the Spirit commences His work of transformation. He lays the groundwork and provides the impetus from which He carries on His work in the life of the believer.

Let us thank God for our new relationship with Him, and let us pray that the Spirit may, unhindered, continue the work of transformation He has begun.

Rom. 5. 1; Rom. 5. 2; Rom. 5. 3-4; Rom. 5. 5; Rom. 5. 11

Salvation

THE RESULTS OF SALVATION

April 28   Reading: Romans 8. 18-27

Paul speaks as a man of divine vision. The world is in a sorry state, but in place of chaos and decay Paul sees a world restored which he calls 'the glory that is to be revealed to us' (v. 18).

The fall led to devastating results, not only in the relationship between man and God, but in the relationships between man and nature, man and man, and man and his own inner self. The basic distortion exists in man's relationship with God, but in his fall man dragged the rest of creation down with him.

The distortion of nature came about not because of any inherent defect in nature itself, but because of man (v. 20). It was man's fault, and because of man's fall God passed sentence on creation (Gen. 3. 17). But in doing so God purposed a restoration, and in man's final restoration the natural creation will be restored with him.

The words of v. 22 are more meaningful today than they have ever been. The world is full of a restless longing for it knows not what. V. 19 tells us what creation is longing for, though it does not know it. It is 'the revealing of the sons of God'. Creation's unconscious longing should be the conscious longing of God's people (v. 23). The believer has every reason to look forward with eagerness to the fulfilment of his redemption. Vs. 18-25 shows the redemption of man in every part of his being and in all his relationships. The 'revealing of the sons of God' is the revelation in eternity of the perfected, united church, the body of Christ. What the complete redemption of man, revealed in the church, will mean to the manifestation of God's glory in the new heavens and the new earth, is beyond human imagination.

Of all this coming glory and liberty, God has, by His Spirit, given His people the first fruits (v. 23). Here and now we could experience so much more of this than we do. Yet, however much of God's purpose we may know, it is but a taste of what is to come, and if we have tasted we will be filled with the hope of what God is yet going to do. Let us pray that here and now we may experience more of our so great salvation.

Rom. 8. 18; Rom. 8. 19; Rom. 8. 21; Rom. 8. 23; Rom. 8. 25

Salvation

BARNABAS

April 29   Reading: Acts 11. 19-26

"He was a good man, full of the Holy Spirit and of faith" (v. 24). This is Luke's simple but beautiful commendation of a man who stands out as a testimony to the grace of God. Barnabas, it would appear, was universally respected among the believers, a person of deep spiritual insight with a warm-hearted love for the brethren. He was a man of sterling character, and a man in whom the Holy Spirit was continuing to do His work.

Barnabas' name means 'son of encouragement', and he lived up to it. He was able to look beyond the limitations of a person or situation and see what God could do. His faith was strong, and because of his faith in the Lord he was ever ready to encourage the Lord's people. It was he who first encouraged Saul of Tarsus. The Jerusalem brethren were, perhaps understandably, afraid of Saul, and were not quick to believe the story of his conversion. Barnabas, however, stood by him.

When the Jerusalem church sent Barnabas to Antioch (v. 22) to follow up reports of spiritual blessing in that city, Barnabas at once recognized the grace of God at work (v. 23). There must have been much immaturity in Antioch, but Barnabas saw the spiritual potential. He also saw at once that Saul was the man who could help these people grow in the things of the Lord. He went to Tarsus in search of Saul who had been lost sight of for nine years, and brought him to Antioch to launch out in the ministry for which God had chosen him.

Later Barnabas withstood Saul, who is now called Paul, in his (Barnabas') desire to encourage John Mark, and his stand was vindicated by Mark's future usefulness as a witness and writer of the second Gospel. But Barnabas' disagreement with Paul in no way detracts from his humble character. Under God, Paul probably owed more to Barnabas than he did to any other man, but Barnabas gladly faded into the background. His life was a true testimony to the salvation he preached. Let us pray that the Lord will make us a tesimony like Barnabas.

Acts 11. 23; Acts 11. 24; Acts 4. 36-37; Acts 9. 27; Acts 15. 39

Marriage and Divorce

MARRIAGE INSTITUTED BY GOD

April 30   Reading: Genesis 2. 18-24

The institution of marriage goes right back to creation, and it was designed by God Himself. This fact alone emphasises the sacredness of the marriage bond. It is not a mere human arrangememnt to be lightly regarded,
to be lightly entered into and easily abandoned as is so often the case today. It is a matter of great solemnity and importance.

God said, "It is not good that the man should be alone. I will make
him a helper fit for him" (v. 18). The arrangement God purposed to make
for Adam was a very special one. In all the rest of creation 'there was not
found a helper fit for him' (v. 20). Man's companion was to be of a much
higher order than anything found in the animal kingdom. The purpose
of marriage was not only to propagate the human race, but to institute
a complementary relationship in which there would be mutual love and
concern.

The prophets frequently use the marriage relationship as a picture of
the relationship between God and His people. The marriage ideal
demonstrates God's care and faithfulness, and the response of love and
faithfulness He receives in return. On the other hand, marital unfaithfulness
is condemned in the strongest terms as an affront to God's character.

God created only one wife for Adam. Monogamy is implicit in the
story of Adam and Eve. Polygamy was practised after the fall, but God's
order is restored in the New Testament. While marriage and family life are
the usual calling, the single life is recognized in the New Testament as the
calling of God to some of His people (Matt. 19. 10-12; 1 Cor. 7. 7-9).
This needs to be remembered as a practical Christian alternative.

Let us thank God for the guidance of His Word, and let us pray that,
in this degenerate age, He may help us ever to uphold the high ideal of
marriage He has ordained.

Gen. 2. 18; Gen. 2. 22; Gen. 2. 23; Gen. 2. 24; 1 Cor. 7. 7

Marriage and Divorce

THE PURPOSE OF MARRIAGE

May 1   Reading: Proverbs 31. 10-31

This is a remarkable picture of the marriage relationship as God has ordained it. There is diligence in ordering the practical affairs of the household for the good of all. There is mutual love and respect between husband and wife (vs. 11-12). The wife has both liberty and responsibility in the management of a wide range of domestic affairs (v. 16). The home is given to hospitality and concern for others in need (v. 20). The children of the family are faithfully taught the ways of the Lord (v. 26). Pride and ostentation have no place. The Lord and His ways have the place of pre-eminence (v. 30). Altogether the household is a testimony to the glory of God.

We have here the physical aspect of marriage, the children of the household; the emotional aspect in mutual confidence and interests; and the spiritual aspect, the fear of the Lord which draws all together in a picture of harmony and witness. All are important, but the spiritual aspect is the basis upon which the other two can develop healthily. The purpose of marriage, as should be the purpose of every aspect of living, is to glorify God. All life is empty if it has no aim, or if its only aim is the gratification of self. Marriage is no exception. It can only find its true fulfilment in the Lord.

The emotional aspect of marriage, however, cannot be neglected. God has made us all different. We have different personalities, different. strengths and different weaknesses. We also have different natural, but God-given interests, interests which flourish only through the encouragement of others. Some people are impulsive and need a restraining hand; others are indecisive and need to be urged on to take initiative. God does not normally put together people who are so alike that they are no challenge to one another, or so different that they cannot appreciate one another. Just as there was harmony in the natural world as God created it, and harmony within the triune God, so God's pupose is a complete harmony within the marriage relationship. Let us pray the Lord may achieve in our own family lives a harmony which will glorify Him.

Prov. 31. 10; Prov. 31. 20; Prov. 31. 26; Prov. 31. 28; Prov. 31. 30

Marriage and Divorce

THE EQUALITY OF MARRIAGE

May 2   Reading: Ephesians 5. 21-33

Much is said today of the equality of the sexes, but the fact is that men and women are not equal in an absolute sense, because God has made them different. This does not mean that one is superior to the other, but that each one has a different function to fulfil. They are equal in respect before God and should be before one another, but they are not equal in function.

In the passage we have just read there are two apparently contradictory factors, subjection (vs. 22, 24) and equality (vs. 28-29). Both of them are brought together in v. 21, "Be subject to one another." It is our mistake to believe that subjection and equality are irreconcilable. When in a marriage partnership one is emphasized to the exclusion of the other, tragedy results. The unconditioned teaching of the wife's subjection to her husband can reduce the wife to a slave and the husband to a tyrant. On the other hand, an emphasis on equality which recognizes no authority can reduce a family to complete chaos. It is obvious that Paul is trying to teach neither of these extremes.

Subjection is necessary in any relationship if it is to prosper. If neither of two partners in a business concern listens to what the other has to say, and each insists on having his own way, the partnership will inevitably break up. Paul states that the subjection of the Son to the Father is eternal (1 Cor. 15. 28), but this does not reduce the Son to an inferior being. "I and the Father are one" (John 10.30). There is a parallel here to the relationship between Christ and the church, and the relationship between a man and his wife.

"Christ loved the church and gave himself up for her" (v. 25). In the love of Christ we have the most potent of all reasons for the subjection of His people to Him. Similarly in the marriage relationship the duty of the wife is subjection, but the responsibility of the husband is to initiate the love and respect which deserves subjection. And, as Paul puts it, "He who loves his wife loves himself" (v. 25) because God has made them one—equal.

Eph. 5. 21; Eph. 5. 23; Eph. 5. 25; Eph. 5. 28; Eph. 5. 31

Marriage and Divorce

THE COMMITTAL OF MARRIAGE

The interpretation of the Mosaic law's permission for divorce (Deut. 24. 1-4) was a matter of dispute among the Pharisees. Jesus, however, takes them back beyond Moses to God's ideal when marriage was first instituted (vs. 6-7). He shows that the Mosaic legislation was a concession made to regulate the order of a fallen society (v. 3). God's ideal was that the marriage bond should be permanent and indissoluble (v. 9).

"For this reason a man shall leave his father and mother and be joined to his wife" (v. 7). Notice that the man takes the initiative in entering upon the married state. When he does, God sets His seal upon the transaction and accepts man and wife as a single unit (v. 9). Marriage is an institution which applies only to life on the earth (Mark 12. 25). God certainly wishes to guide His people in their choice of partners, but the responsibility for that choice rests upon the individuals themselves, not upon God. When two people enter upon a contract of marriage in a manner accepted by the society in which they live, and live together as man and wife, their union is a valid one in the sight of God.

The committal of husband and wife to one another is for life, and every Christian about to enter upon marriage should take serious note of this fact. This is a matter in which God sets His seal of approval upon the individual choice. It does not mean that every marriage is a happy one, but it does mean that when the committal has been made, for better or for worse, there is no going back on it.

In societies in which marriages are generally arranged by parents or relatives, it is not uncommon among Christians to hear excuses brought forward for a marriage which has not worked out happily, "We were joined together by relatives not by God". There is no Biblical justification for such an attitude. Christian parents should never pressurize their sons or daughters into unsuitable marriages, and Christian young people should resist such pressures, for finally the responsibility is theirs. God accepts their committal to one another before Him, and there is no turning back.

Let us pray that we may recognize the seriousness of commital in marriage, to the glory of God.

Mark 10. 9; Mark 12. 25; Mark 10. 11-12; Eph. 5. 29; Rom. 7. 2

Marriage and Divorce

DIVORCE

May 4   Reading: 1 Corinthians 7. 10-16

Marriage ties in Corinthian society were lightly regarded, and the question of divorce was an acute one. Paul here lays down specific guidelines, no doubt based on the teaching of our Lord Himself, Vs. 10-11 deal with those who have been married as believing Christians. Vs. 12-16 deal with marriages in which one partner has subsequently been converted.

The standard for Christians in vs. 10-11 is unequivocal, and Paul reinforces the charge by emphasizing that it is given, not by himself, but by the Lord (v. 10). Divorce is not permitted to a Christian couple. Should a Christian couple for some reason decide to live apart, they have no other option than to remain single or to seek a reconciliation (v. 11). Paul makes no mention of our Lord's accepting, as a one and only ground for divorce, the sin of fornication (Matt. 19.9). If this does give to a Christian a final dread legal alternative of divorce in the case of a partner whose sin is consistent and unrepented, the spiritual alternative is nevertheless on a much higher level, of forgiveness and faithfulness in the face of unfaithfulness. God's attitude to divorce is clear, "For I hate divorce, says the Lord" (Mal. 2. 16). For any believing Christian to do that which God distinctly says He hates is a very serious matter indeed.

In a church like that in Corinth there were bound to be believers who had been converted after marriage, but whose partners had not yet trusted the Lord. The fact that now a believer and an unbeliever were thus united did not invalidate the marriage. The believer was bound to recognize this and should not think of putting way the unbelieving partner (vs. 12-13), but should seek to win the other through prayer and godly living. If, however, the unbeliever refused to live any longer with a believing wife or husband, the believer should not compromise his faith in order to maintain the partnership.

This passage emphasises the sacredness of the marriage tie. Let us pray that God will help us to hold it as sacred as He does Himself.

1 Cor. 7. 10-11; 1 Cor. 7. 12; 1 Cor. 7. 13; Mal. 2. 16; 1 Cor. 7. 14

Marriage and Divorce

MARRIAGE PARTNERS

May 5   Reading: 2 Corinthians 6. 14-18

Paul here lays down a principle which is applicable in many different situations, but nowhere is it more applicable than in the question of marriage. Many spiritual tragedies could be avoided if what God says here in His Word were obeyed.

There can be no mixing of diametrically opposed principles of good and evil (vs. 14-16). Separation unto the Lord (v. 17) is the condition for God's blessing. Where one partner has been converted after marriage there are grounds to plead the grace of God, but there are no grounds to do so when a believer deliberately rejects God's standard.

In some countries marriages are arranged by parents or relatives, in others the individual makes his own choice of a marriage partner. Where the latter is the case, the Christian needs to keep the Scriptural standard clearly before him and not be led astray by emotional or other considerations. Where arranged marriages are the rule, parents are responsible to observe the standard of God's Word and to recognize that this is much more important than worldly respect or security. On the other hand, parents should understand that if it is wrong to marry a believing son or daughter to an unbelieving partner, it is equally wrong to try to marry an unbelieving child to a believing partner in the hope that he may later turn to the Lord.

Young people too have their responsibilities, to resist attempts to ally them with partners who do not share their faith. When obedience to parents clearly conflicts with obedience to God, God must be honoured.

Temperamental, intellectual or other differences may constitute an unequal yoke, and these are matters which also need to be taken into consideration, but the need of spiritual affinity in a personal relationship with God must never be sacrificed for other things. This is God's standard. Let us thank Him for the blessings of a family life which is solidly founded upon faith in Him, and let us pray that we may never be tempted to compromise with darkness.

2 Cor. 6. 14; 2 Cor. 6. 15; 2 Cor. 6. 16; 2. Cor. 6. 17; 2 Cor. 6. 18

Marriage and Divorce

ABSALOM

We look upon David, the slayer of Goliath, the sweet Psalmist of Israel, as one of the greatest of Old Testament characters, a man blessed by God. But there was a tragic side to David's character, and David's tragedy is pointed up in his son Absalom. We may condemn Absalom as a conceited wastrel, disloyal to his father, his country and to God, but though it is true that every man bears responsibiliy for his own sin, it is also true that Absalom was a product of his upbringing.

Absalom was the son of Maachah, one of David's many wives (2 Sam. 3.3). He was a young man full of potential, outstandingly handsome and of a winsome personality. David's family life is a sorry tale of deceit and lust, of jealousies and sin amongst his own children. This is the background of the home in which Absalom was brought up. His tragic life makes an interesting psychological study. Its potential was never realized. He grew up into a man full of strange complexes, haunted by a sense of insecurity.

It is a solemn fact that David, prosperous and full of fervour for the cause of the Lord, was, at the same time, living a life of defeat within his own family circle. His failure to maintain God's standards in his married life was a blot on his character the consequences of which could not be removed. The Bible teaches us not only through the victories of God's servants but through their failures as well. It shows up what happens when God's standards are honoured. It shows also the consequences when His standards are dishonoured.

A sincere Christian who reads the story of Absalom can never doubt the wisdom of God's principle of monogamy, and the importance of marital faithfulness. This is the only foundation for stable homes which can teach a coming generation to live to the glory of God.

Let us thank God for the warnings of His Word, and pray that we might be faithful to His standards in our family life.

2 Sam. 12. 9; 2 Sam. 12. 10; Prov. 10. 17; Deut. 4. 1; Deut. 4. 2

127

Sanctification

THE SCOPE OF SANCTIFICATION

May 7   Reading: Romans 6. 17-23

Paul uses the word 'sanctification' twice in this passage, in v. 19 and again in v. 22. These are actually the only occasions on which the word is used in the letter to the Romans, but sanctification sums up the purpose of the Spirit's working in the people of God, a purpose which ends in 'eternal life' (v. 23). The Greek word Paul uses signifies separation unto God and conduct which is consistent with such a position. It touches, therefore, every aspect of living, the inner life and the outer life in their relationship to God, to others and to the world in general.

Paul puts it another way. Sanctification means being 'slaves of God' (v. 22). Man cannot live independent of the forces of good and evil which determine the course of the world (vs. 17-18). He is not free in an absolute sense. Either he is enslaved to his own desire, or to the will of God. Christian freedom never means licence. It means freedom from sin, and this is to be found only in the absolute control of Christ. Bondage to sin is replaced by slavery to righteousness (v. 18). As in the past we pleased ourselves, so now our wills are decisively subjected to Christ to the end that our lives manifest a progressive likeness to Him. (v. 19). This is the outworking of sanctification.

The contrast between the way of natural, fallen man, and the way opened up through Christ is sharpened by pointing to the result of those two divergent paths. The end of one is death (v. 21), of the other 'eternal life' (v. 22). 'Eternal life' is first and foremost a term of quality. Death is the negation of everything qualitative, the negation of purpose, of goodness, of love of others and of God, of life itself. The death that is the wages of sin is experienced in this life and finds its consummation in the world to come. Eternal life is also to be experienced now and finds its consummation when we go to be with Christ. Sanctification is eternal life being worked out in us.

Let us thank God for the sanctifying work of the Holy Spirit and pray that He may find freedom to do His work within us.

Rom. 6. 15; Rom. 6. 17-18; Rom. 6. 20-21; Rom. 6. 22; 1 Cor. 1. 30

Sanctification

PROBLEMS OF SANCTIFICATION

May 8   Reading: Romans 7. 13-25

Two great problems face the Spirit's work of sanctification in us. They are the problem of law and the problem of the flesh. Paul faces these two problems squarely before he deals with the victorious outworking of sanctification in chapter eight. There can be no victory unless we are willing to face our problems honestly and frankly. The Bible is always realistic.

The problem of law is simply that it can deal only with what is outward, not with man's inner motives and attitudes. Yet there is something within all of us which tends to reduce our faith to no more than a legal system. The law of Moses shows God's standards which is good (vs. 13-14), but it is powerless to enforce them since God's standard depend first of all on the state of man's heart, about which the law can do nothing.

There is another ironic factor in man's relation to the law. The very existence of a law arouses in man a perverse desire to disobey it. The motorist who sees a speed limit sign wants to go still-faster. The child who is forbidden to do something wants to do it just because he was told not to. So law often defeats its own purpose. It can actually encourage someone to do what it forbids. We must appreciate what the law does in showing us God's standard and our need of Him, but we must see beyond it. God wants to do something deeper than the law can do. If we do not see further than law we will miss God's purpose.

Paul uses the word 'flesh' in a technical sense. The flesh is the residue of attitudes and habits left over from our old relationship with Adam. It consists of things we do almost automatically but which we know are wrong (vs. 15-20). The flesh was to Paul the cause of a constant inner warfare (vs. 21-24), but the work of the Holy Spirit is to reshape the attitudes and habits which have been distorted by the fall. Through Jesus Christ our Lord there is victory (v. 28).

Let us ask God to help us face up to our problems, and in doing so to experience His triumph over them.

Rom. 7. 14; Rom. 7. 18; Rom. 7. 21; Rom. 7. 22; Rom. 7. 24-25

Sanctification

THE HOLY SPIRIT'S CONSTANT WORK

May 9   Reading: Romans 8. 9-17

V. 9 is quite conclusive. The work of justification reuslts in the indwelling of the Spirit. A person who is not indwelt by the Spirit is not a child of God. Notice too the permanence of the work of the Spirit (v. 11). The mark of the child of God is that the Holy Spirit is doing a constant work within him through the circumstances of every day living. The extent and constancy of the Spirit's work is reinforced by the mention of all three persons of the trinity in vs. 10-11. It is awe-inspiring to realize that all the power of the God-head, Father, Son and Holy Spirit, is active in the believer to bring to fruition God's purposes.

Vs. 12-17, while continuing to stress the Spirit's work, also emphasise our human obligations. Two facts have already been established, the indwelling of the Holy Spirit (v. 9), and the fact that through His indwelling our spirit have been made alive (v. 10). and, therfore, enabled to walk in the way of victory. "So then, brethren," Paul continues, "We are debtors, not to the flesh, to live according to the flesh—" (v. 12). The apostle does not complete his sentence. If he had completed it he would have said, "But to live according to the Spirit."

The mighty work of God in us through the Spirit calls forth a sense of obligation on our part, a sense of gratitude, supplying a powerful motive to lay hold on the Spirit's power. God has so worked that not only is His grace irresistible, but we WANT to live for Him. This desire to walk in the ways of the Lord is the basis of the believer's self-discipline. It is always possible to respond to the self-satisfying propensities of the flesh. We are never removed from the realm of real choice, but the bent of the believer's desires is towards the Spirit which means life indeed (v. 13). The priority of the Spirit's control in a person's life is a mark of a child of God (v. 14). And as long as the Spirit is in control we have the assurance of all that is entailed in being sons of God (vs. 15-17).

Let us pray that we may always be conscious of our obligations as people indwelt by the Spirit of God.

Rom. 8. 10; Rom. 8. 12; Rom. 8. 13; Rom. 8. 15; Rom. 8. 16-17

Sanctification

IN ATTITUDES AND ACTS

May 10   Reading: Romans 7. 1-6.

The contrast in this passage is between an impersonal legal relationship (vs. 1-3) and a relationship with a person (vs. 4-6). The illustration of the marriage bond which Paul uses in vs. 1-3 undergoes a change of standpoint in the middle of the passage, but the meaning is clear. The unregenerate man is wedded to his association with fallen Adam. Through his identification with the death of Christ, however, he has been absolved from that old relationship, and has been joined in intimate union with Christ Himself (v. 4).

V. 5 looks back to unregenerate experience, when the perversity of human nature seemed to be provoked to disobedience by the very fact that the law said, "Thou shalt not." But this self-defeating relationship with the law has now been replaced through our relationship with Christ by the new life of the Spirit' (v. 6). A new force has become operative, the power of the Holy Spirit.

V. 5 also contains the first mention of 'the flesh' in the more technical sense in which it is used frequently in chapter eight. The Greeek word here denotes human nature in its propensity to self-pleasing and sin. The point Paul wishes to stress is that the law itself brings out this selfish propensity to evil within man. To use more familiar language, the law brings out the worst in a person. The new relationship with Christ, on the other hand, has a completely different effect. It touches a person's heart. It begins by transforming his attitudes and motives, something the law could never do, and these new attitudes and motives, all dominated by a love for Christ, result in transformed practial living. This is what Paul means when he says, "We may bear fruit for God" (v. 4).

Let us thank God for the depth of His sanctifying work. Let us pray that our inner being may be more and more transformed in our relationship with Him, that in our practical living we may bear fruit for God.

Rom. 7. 5; Rom. 7. 6; Isa. 32. 17; Gal. 3. 10; Gal. 3. 11

Sanctification

THROUGH OBEDIENCE TO THE WORD

May 11   Reading: John 17. 14-26

This passage tells us what Jesus prayed for His disciples, and what Jesus wanted for His disciples must be very important indeed. V. 17 sums up His first request, "Sanctify them in the truth; thy word is truth."

Notice first how our Lord specifically states that He does not want His disciples taken out of the world. This tells us something important about sanctification. It tells us that Jesus expects our sanctification to be worked out in the midst of the trials and troubles of ordinary living. Sanctification is not a life lived separately from the world and its problems, but a life lived in the midst of the world in victory over its problems. This was the life our Lord Jesus Christ Himself lived.

We have already seen that sanctification means being set apart for God, and living in a way which is consistent with that high calling. How does God guide us to live in a manner which is pleasing to Him? He guides us through the truth of the Word (v. 17). One of the great problems God faces in doing His work of sanctification in us is the law, because the law breeds self-righteousness, and by its prohibitions even encourages man to break its commands. Since this is so, some people might feel we should dispense with anything that seems like rules. But this would be a mistake. The completed Word as we now possess it, including the law of Moses, teaches us what God is like and the principles on which He works. If we use it rightly and in a humble spirit, it serves as a guide to our practical daily living. It is not a book of rules telling us exactly what to do in every conceivable circumstance, but it does guide us in basic principles which are honouring to God and which, by the help of the Spirit, we are responsible to apply to our day to day lives.

Let us thank God again for His Word, and let us pray that, under its guidance, we may learn to know more and more of His sanctifying power.

John 17. 13; John 17. 14; John 17. 15; John 17. 16; John 17. 18

Sanctification

ADOPTION

Reading: Galatians 4. 1-7

A child may be heir to an estate but reject his inheritance. God sent forth His Son (v. 4) that we might receive adoption as sons (v. 5) and become His heirs (v. 7). His adoption can be refused. Adoption is an aspect of redemption made real through faith in Christ.

Paul alone in the Scriptures uses the word 'adoption' (v. 6). The Roman procedure of adoption had very far-reaching implications, and it is necessary to understand something of this procedure if we are to grasp what Paul is trying to convey. Adoption was rooted in the Roman conception of fatherhood. In Roman law a son never came of age as far as relationship with his father concerned. As long as the father lived, the son was under his absolute authority. Adoption, therefore, meant being freed from the absolute control of one person in order to come under the absolute control of another.

In the Roman procedure of adoption the father of the boy symbolically sold his son to the adopting family, thus renouncing his own rights over him. Then followed a ceremony of acceptance by the adopting father. In the eyes of the law the adopted son was literally the son of his new father. Legally, his previous life was obliterated. He lost all rights in his old family, but gained the full rights of sonship in his new family.

This is the picture Paul draws of the believer, his past cancelled, and made an heir of God. The work of the Holy Spirit has not brought us into a relationship of fearsome slavery, but into a relationship of real sonship. In the truest and most intimate family sense we can call God 'Father' (v. 6). Adoption is a present and blessed fact, but it will be fulfilled when our salvation is completed in our being with Christ (Rom. 8. 23).

Let us thank God for the privilege of being His adopted children, and let us pray that our lives might be worthy of Him.

Gal. 4. 3; Gal. 4. 4-5; Gal. 4. 6; Gal. 4. 7; 1 John 3. 1

Sanctification

PHILEMON

Paul must have written many personal letters, but this little letter to Philemon is the only one of them that has survived. Paul writes on behalf of a slave called Onesimus who had run away from Philemon his master, no doubt having helped himself to his master's money. Onesimus makes the long journey to Rome where, by the grace of God, he is converted through Paul's ministry (v. 10), and remains to serve Paul in his imprisonment (v. 12). Paul, however, feels obliged to send him back to Philemon in Colosse.

In the Roman world a master had power of life and death over his slaves, and runaway slaves were treated harshly. There were six crore slaves in the Roman Empire, and if they could have organized a revolt they would have caused serious trouble, so they were kept under strict control.

The idea of slavery was deeply engrained in the mind of the ancient world, and it is at this point that we can see so clearly the extent of the transformation that had taken place in Philemon's life through his faith in Christ. Onesimus had been a rogue (v. 11), but Paul makes an appeal not only for Philemon to forgive him, but to accept him back as a brother in Christ. Obviously Philemon's character was such that it was possible to make this appeal to him, and the preservation of the letter indicates that he responded to it.

When a person enters into a deep relationship with Christ, questions of community and caste cease to matter. Before he trusted Christ, Philemon was probably as conscious of his position as any other person of similar status, but now things had changed. He was a man whose faith in the Lord resulted in a love for all of God's people (v. 5) and an eagerness to share with others the grace he himself had received. In sharing he himself was blessed (v. 6). Philemon obviously was a man responsive to the Holy Spirit's sanctifying work.

Let us pray that we too may be responsive to the Holy Spirit's work and allow Him to break down in our lives those deeply engrained ideas that are not honouring to Him.

Philem. 4-5; Philem. 6; Philem. 7; Philem. 16; Philem. 20

Trial and Temptation

TRIALS A PART OF LIFE

May 14   Reading: James 1. 1-11

James' letter is one of the most practical of all the books of the Bible. His message is how faith works out in practical living, and he begins with a fact that is part of all life, the fact of suffering. It is extraordinary how many believers seem to be stumbled when God allows them to pass through periods of hardship. At no time did our Lord ever say that following Him would mean exemption from the trials of life. In fact He warned His disciples repeatedly that to follow Him would mean suffering. The same message is repeated by the writers of the other epistles, and the book of Acts tells of the persecution of some of the early believers.

For His disciples our Lord prayed, "I do not pray that thou shouldst take them out of the world, but that thou shouldst keep them from the evil one" (John 17.15). Our testimony is revealed not in being removed from the world's trials, but in being granted victory over them. James urges us not only to recognize the fact of our trials, but to rejoice in them because of their result in moulding our characters (vs. 2-4). He asks us to ask God for wisdom, that is wisdom how to face the trials of life, if we are perplexed. The wonderful thing about this is that the answer to this prayer is right in the asking. The moment we ask God to give us wisdom in our trials we are recognizing His sovereignty in them, and we are recognizing, therefore, that they are not meaningless intrusions, disturbing the peace of our lives, but they are supremely meaningful. When we see our trials in this light, with God in them, we begin to learn through them, and our faith begins to grow.

Trials come to rich and poor alike, and to both they are part of God's sanctifying work. In our trials the Lord levels our differences and brings us to see that we are all equal in Him (vs. 9-11).

Let us thank God for our trials, and let us pray for His wisdom in them, that through them our faith might grow.

James 1. 2; James. 1.4; James. 1. 5; James 1. 6; James 1. 7

Trial and Temptation

TEMPTATIONS A PART OF LIFE

May 15   Reading: James 1. 12-18

The word 'trial' can be used in two senses. In the earlier verses of the chapter James has dealt with trials which do not have a necessary connection with sin, trials such as illness, poverty or persecution. Now he turns to trials which bring with them an incentive to do what we know to be wrong. These trials we usually call temptations.

We live in a fallen world, and temptations come to all of us. Different temptations beset different people, but no one is totally free from temptations of some sort. There are criminal temptations such as theft or bribery, moral temptations such as adultery, spiritual temptations such as that to compromise one's faith, and they can come in a very subtle way.

James warns us against the tendency to pass off responsibility for our temptations to someone else, even to place responsibility for our temptations upon God (v. 13). Many Christian believers do just this. They do what they want themselves and then find 'guidance', most probably from the Scriptures, to substantiate it. They will say, "God told me to do it," though it may be something quite inconsistent with the principles of God's Word. Another tendency, which James does not mention, is to blame the devil for our temptations. James tells us that responsibility for falling into temptation rests squarely upon our own shoulders (vs. 13-14). We cannot blame God, Satan or others. When we are willing to admit and accept our responsibility God will give us victory, but if we refuse to accept our responsibility we are on the road to further defeat.

Vs. 16-18 show us the magnitude of the grace of God. If we read these verses in the context of the chapter, we will realize that the good endowments and perfect gifts (v. 17) of which James writes are nothing less than our trials and temptations. By giving us victory over them God uses them to conform us to His likeness (v. 18).

Let us thank the Lord for our trials and temptations, and let us pray that the Lord will use them to make us more like Him.

James 1. 12; James 1. 13; James 1. 14-15; James 1. 16-17; 1. 18

Trial and Temptation

WHY GOD'S PEOPLE SUFFER

May 16   Reading: 1 Peter 2. 18-25

1 Peter in the New Testament is the counterpart of the book of Job in the Old Testament. Both deal with the problem of suffering. Peter was writing at a time when Christians over a wide area were suffering persecution. The waves of persecution rose and fell. At some times and places it was more violent than at others, often depending on the attitude of local officials. But Christians were also liable to petty persecution as we see from our reading. Prejudiced employers would intimidate those working for them, and even if this was not on account of their faith the question rose of the right Christian attitude in such circumstances.

The Christian is obligated first of all to take stock of his own attitudes and actions, and to be sure that he is not doing anything that merits or invites the harsh treatment he receives. He has also to resist the temptation of returning evil for evil. In all this we have the example of our Lord Himself (vs. 21-23) and the power we need (v. 24).

God allows His people to suffer in order that they might demonstrate the quality of His life in a sinful world. It is easy to preach the superiority of eternal life, but eternal life begins here on the earth, and its superiority has to be demonstrated in the circumstances which all men have to face in an imperfect world. Were God to shield His people from every problem and difficulty, there could be no testimony to the quality of life He gives them. The quality of a thing is only proved when a thing is put to the test. If it cannot be used at all without breaking down, it is totally useless. If it breaks down easily under little strain, its quality is poor indeed. Jesus, under the strain His perfect life must have endured in a sinful world, demonstrated what eternal life really is. He calls upon us to do the same. Let us seek His grace and help to do so.

1 Pet. 2. 18; 1 Pet. 2. 19; 1 Pet. 2. 21; 1 Pet. 2. 22-23; 1 Pet. 2. 24

Trial and Temptation

GOD'S WORKING THROUGH TRIAL

May 17   Reading: 2 Corinthians 6. 1-13

The privilege of 'working together with him' (v. 1) is far greater than any of the trials we may be called to endure, so Paul urges the Corinthians 'not to accept the grace of God in vain' (v. 1), that is, not to make a high sounding profession of faith and then to live merely superficial lives.

The genuineness of Paul and Timothy's service for Christ can be seen in the way they lived (v. 4). They did not tread an easy path. In fact it would have been impossible to do what they did apart from the sense of purpose God had given them. They were servants of an almighty God, and the fruit of their trials could be seen in the quality of their own lives and the lives of others.

The catalogue of trials and spiritual qualities enumerated in vs. 4-10 shows three things. It shows the sheer physical, mental and spiritual hardships they endured (vs. 4-5); the qualities of truth and righteousness they exhibited in their relationship to God and to others; and their readiness to be misunderstood and pay the price of being different in a world which inevitably fails to understand the sacrifice and motivation of the child of God.

At the beginning of this impassioned utterance Paul uses one great word which conditions all he says. It is the word translated 'endurance' (v. 4), a word used also by James (James 1.3, 4). Much is bound up in the meaning of this word. It implies a recognition of God at work in every difficult circumstances. Trials are not mere intrusions. God has ordered them. God is in them. God is working through them. They are all meaningful. Through them God is working our a purpose He could workout in no other way, and teaching what He could teach in no other way.

Paul urges the Corinthians to widen their understanding, to see God at work in their difficulties (vs. 12-13). Let us pray that our vision too may be spiritually enlarged.

2 Cor. 6. 1; 2 Cor. 6. 3; 2 Cor. 6. 4-5; 2 Cor. 6. 6-7; 2 Cor. 6. 12-13

Trial and Temptation

THE EFFECT OF TRIALS

May 18   Reading: 1 Peter 1. 3-9

One of the tragedies of our modern world is the sense of purposelessness that pervades it. Most people have no real aim in living. To belong to Jesus Christ, however, means to have a purpose for this life and a sure hope for the next. Salvation is a past and present as well as a future experience. "We HAVE BEEN born anew" (v. 3). "We ARE guarded" by God's power (v. 5). Salvation is "ready TO BE REVEALED in the last times" (v. 5). If we have a hope for the future, we are being prepared for that hope in the present, and herein lies one of God's purposes in our trials.

Peter puts it this way. "So that the genuineness of your faith...may redound to the praise and glory and honour at the revelation of Jesus Christ" (v. 7). Perhaps it has never occurred to us that faith could be anything other than genuine, but this passage shows us just how mixed faith can be. Peter speaks of a refining process, like gold which is refined through fire (v. 7). Self-seeking is tremendously subtle. Let us never think that we are totally freed from it. Even our prayers which we believe are for the glory of God can be motivated by selfish desires. Often God has to bring us through failure before we realize how much selfish, personal success really means to us. We begin to see that our desire for success, perhaps even spiritual success, was due more to the desire for personal reputation, than to a concern for the will of God to be done.

"As the outcome of your faith you obtain the salvation of your souls" (v. 9). There is no word 'your' before 'souls' in the original language. A faith which is purified through testing has an effect much beyond the individual himself. It is a means of life to others.

Let us thank the Lord for the testing of our faith. Let us admit how much our faith needs to be purified, and let us pray that through our refined faith we might grow and others might be blessed.

1 Pet. 1.4; 1 Pet. 1. 5; 1. Pet. 1.6; 1. Pet. 1.8; 1 Pet. 1.9

Trial and Temptation

RESISTING TEMPTATION

May 19   Reading: 1 Corinthians 10. 1-13

The Corinthian Christians were beset by many temptations, but they were not to think that this was anything unusual. Paul cites the temptations of the Children of Isreal years before. The Children of Israel had known much of God's care and blessing (vs. 1-4), but they became self-confident with the result that when temptation came they succumbed to it. There is always the danger of feeling that we have advanced spiritually to the extent that we are immune from temptation. Apparently the Corinthians were in this danger although they were very young believers. Paul gives them a terse warning, "Let anyone who thinks that he stands take heed lest he fall" (vs. 12).

No believer is beyond temptation, but neither is he at the mercy of temptation. We can never plead that temptation was too strong for us, or that our temptations are unique (v. 13). God does not allow any of His children to be tempted beyond what they are able to bear. He provides the strength to resist or the means to escape.

'Escape' is an important word when it comes to temptation. We should never deliberately put ourselves into circumstances where we know we will be tempted, but if we find ourselves unwittingly in such circumstances, the best thing to do may be to run away. This is what Joseph very wisely did (Gen. 39. 11-12).

In speaking of the Children of Israel's idolatry before the golden calf (v. 9), Paul quotes from Ex. 32. 6; "The people sat down to eat and drink and rose up to play." Eating, drinking and playing were quite incidental to the actual worship of the golden calf, but in this instance they were associated with it. Sometimes we are tempted to do things which in normal circumstances are quite right, but which in other circumstances may lead us into definite evil. Beware! Let us thank God for His warnings, and let us pray, "Lead us not into temptation."

1 Cor. 10. 6; 1 Cor. 10. 7; 1 Cor. 10. 8; 1 Cor. 10. 12; 1 Cor. 10. 13

Trial and Temptation

SAMSON

May 20   Reading: Judges 16. 10-17

Samson was physically strong, but morally weak. It is difficult to draw any spiritual conculsions from his tragic life. God used him as He has used many earthly rulers to the working out of His purposes. Samson was the son of godly parents, but his character mirrored much of the degeneracy of the people of Israel who 'did what was evil in the sight of the Lord'. (13. 1). Samson's life is certainly much more a warning than an example.

Samson's great folly was that he adopted a frivolous attitude to life. Everything and everybody was his plaything. He seemed to feel that his privileges and his great strength were sufficient excuse for him to live as he pleased. No one could withstand him, and he belittled the subtle temptations of life, treating with contempt everything that could not be measured by his standard of physical toughness. Women were Samson's downfall. He seemed to have no sense of the sanctity of marriage. Women were merely more playthings for him, and the type of women he associated with led eventually to his tragic end.

Until the event which culminated in his being captured by the Philistines, it seems that Samson more or less fulfilled the conditions associated with his Nazarite vow, but even this he did not accept with sufficient seriousness. Had he seriously valued his privilege as a Nazarite he could not have trifled with the temptation to give away his secret as he did. He would have made it unmistakably clear that this was a sacred domain into which he could allow no intrusion. Instead of doing so, he started to play a game which resulted in the loss of his stregth, the loss of his sight, the loss of his dignity, and the loss of his life. Never trifle with temptation.

Let us pray that we may learn not to treat temptation frivolously, or to treat lightly the spiritual privileges God has given us.

Jud. 16.18; Jud. 16.19; Jud. 16.20; 1 Cor. 10. 4.5; 1 Cor. 10. 9.10

Spiritual Warfare

OPPOSITION OF SPIRITUAL POWERS

May 21   Reading: Ephesians 6. 10-13

Not so long ago worldly people would ridicule the idea of a devil or satanic powers. More recently, however, there has been a revival of awareness of the existence of demonic forces. The Bible, of course, quite clearly teaches the reality of evil spiritual powers. Paul here shows that the real struggle in which the church is engaged is against these powers, and not against human forces (v.12). In fact evil spiritual forces lie behind the apparently human opposition to the work of God.

Paul describes these forces in some detail. We should not underestimate them. The exact implications of the various descriptive phrases he uses may not be easy to determine, but the general facts are clear. They are 'principalities' and 'powers', they are forces to be reckoned with. They are 'world rulers of this present darkness'; they are the power behind the darkness and the unbelief that encompass the earth. They are 'spiritual hosts of wickedness in the heavenly places'; they are many and subtle, operating not on a superficial level, but on the deepest level of man's being.

As God's people, we need to be thoroughly aware of these forces. We also need to realize that spiritual warfare will not be won by purely natural means, nor will it be won if we are not spiritual people. The reality of our warfare is a powerful plea to 'be strong in the Lord and in the strength of his might' (v.10).

Yet we must never overestimate the strength of demonic forces. While we should be aware of them, we should not concentrate on them. Paul's phrase 'spiritual hosts of wickedness in the heavenly places' in v.12 is significant . Earlier in the letter (1.20-21) he told us that our Lord rules 'in the heavenly places', and that means defeat for all the powers of darkness. Our Lord's victory is our victory if we are clad with His armour.

Let us thank the Lord for His triumph over all the forces of evil, and let us pray that we might learn to be partakers with Him in His victory.

Eph. 6.10; Eph. 6.11; Eph. 6.12; Eph. 6.13; Col. 2.15

Spiritual Warfare

THE ARMOUR OF GOD

May 22   Reading; Ephesians 6. 14-20

The armour of God is nothing less than an identification with the character and purposes of our Lord. The exhortations of this chapter are throughout in the plural. The armour of God is not a means of purely personal victory. It is for the victory of the church. No single Christian is truly victorious as long as his brother remains defeated.

From v. 14 Paul lists the weapons of our warfare, truth, righteousness, the gospel of peace, faith, salvation, the Word of God. Truth is indicative of what we are. It is an unalterable characteristic of a life of which Christ is the centre. Righteouness is the practice of truth, the works that must follow faith. If our profession of faith is bereft of the character of Christ revealed in our daily walk, then we are defenceless indeed. To publish the gospel of peace is the commission the Lord Himself has given us. It should be one of the greatest incentives of our Christian walk in the world. Let us ever be pressing forward to make Christ known. This, our work, is also our defence. Inactivity always leaves a way open for satan to attack.

To these three aspects of Christian testimony Paul adds another three, all of which increase in effectiveness in proportion to our faithfulness in walk and witness; faith, that confidence in the Lord which experience of His grace can increase, but never diminish; salvation, that growing demonstration of victory and power over sin which is an inalienable part of a life lived under His control; the Word of God which the experience of ages has demonstrated as the sure and only weapon to combat sin and the forces of evil. If we but learn to use these weapons of our spiritual warfare, every power that would exalt itself in opposition to the purposes of God must bow in defeat.

Let us thank God for His armour, our complete protection and means of triumph, and let us seek His help to use it aright, to the end that we may 'keep alert with all perseverance, making supplication for all the saints' (v.18).

Eph. 6.14: Eph. 6.15; Eph. 6.16; Eph. 6.17; Eph. 6.18

Spiritual Warfare

WARFARE AGAINST SELF

May 23   Reading: 1 Corinthians 9. 19-27

Probably few are as ready to adjust to other people and circumstances in their witness for Christ as was the apostle Paul. Paul's readiness to adjust is all the more remarkable when we consider his rigid background and the deep prejudices he once had. Yet now, for the sake of the gospel, he is ready to sacrifice any personal consideration, or to accommodate himself to the scruples of a weaker brother, provided no vital principle is at stake (vs. 19-23).

After such an obvious demonstration of zeal for the gospel, it may seem strange to hear Paul speak of disciplining himself as an athlete preparing for a contest lest he be found unfit and disqualified (vs. 24-27). Paul was constantly aware that he was waging a spiritual warfare, but more important still, he realized that his worst enemy was often within. It was himself.

In reading the life and letters of Paul there are many indications that he fought a continuing battle against ingrained attitudes that had carried over from his pre-conversion days; his cry in Rom. 7.24, "Wretched man that I am!"; his dispute with Barnabas over John Mark (Acts 15.36-39); the suggestion of his unpopularity with some other Christian brethren (Phil. 1. 14-17). Paul had been a proud Pharisee. No doubt again and again the old sense of superiority, of pride, the desire to dominate others, would come welling up. Perhaps he was tempted to pride by his very willingness to adjust to others. Had he not been freed from so much of the old Pharasaic bondage? Was not that something to be proud of? The greatness of Paul is seen in his acceptance of his own fallibility.

Paul had no fear that he would be eternally rejected, but he knew it was possible to become useless in the service of Christ. "I pommel my body and subdue it" (v. 27). The body with all its desires is a bad master. It has to be subdued to be the servant of the Spirit.

Let us ask God to help us recognize the subtleness of self, and so to bring ourselves into subjection to Him that He may truly be Lord.

1 Cor. 9.19; 1 Cor. 9.22; 1 Cor. 9.24; 9.25; 9.26-27

Spiritual Warfare

TAKING LIGHTLY THE GRACE OF GOD

May 24   Reading: Hosea 6. 1-6

There are many subtle aspects to our spiritual warfare. We have always to be on our guard against the tendency to treat the grace of God lightly, or to reduce our fellowship with the Lord to a mere formality. That this was an ever present danger in the life of the early church is evident from a reading of the New Testament epistles. Paul's letter to the Galatians is a pertinent example.

Here the prophet Hosea put into words the shallow attitude of the people to their God (vs. 1-3). God exposes the foolishness of their outlook and states His conditions for fellowship with Him. The people seemed to have no true conception of the holiness of God. It was true that He had 'torn' and 'stricken' them, but they complacently expected that He would resstore them to His favour again without any need on their part of a true repentance. God was good, and they were His children. He would not be too hard on them, or be much concerned about their sins. This was what they thought. His mercy was as sure as the dawn and the spring rains (v. 3).

God speaks in sorrow at the inability of His people to grasp the truth (v. 4). He knew that there was no depth in their love. It was as transient as the dew or the morning mist (v. 4). Through His prophets His word had gone forth to them with an unmistakable sound (v. 5), but they were not simply defeated in a battle against their own shallow misconceptions of God's character. They did not realize there was any battle going on.

What God wanted was real devotion, not a formal sacrifice; a deep desire to know Him, not an empty outward profession. The outward motions of faith as against a real heart relationship with God; here is where the battle rages. Let us pray that we may be kept from a shallow conception of the grace of God, and that we may be able to discern the true nature of our spiritual warfare.

Hos. 6.4; Hos. 6.5; Heb. 4.12; Matt. 9. 13; Jer. 31.4

Spiritual Warfare

PRIDE

Today the taking of a census is a common factor in a country's life, and is necessary for the purpose of planning and national development. Why then was it a sin that David should have ordered a census of Israel? Behind the command of David we see the hand of Satan (v. 1). David had won many victories on the battle field, but here was an enemy before whom he crumbled up in ignominious defeat. His strategy was to play upon the success which had brought David to his present place of authority and stability. Had not David won all these victories? Had not David led the nation to its position of power? Was not David justified in being proud of his accomplishments?

But was all this David's doing? Apparently David was not sufficiently aware of the danger of spiritual pride. His own position was due simply to the mercy of God and the prosperity of the nation was the blessing of God. Yet David was set on satisfying his arrogance by numbering the people, just as a miser might count his money and gloat over what belongs to no one but himself.

It is disappointing that in this test of his character David failed, but it is a failure which has been repeated many times over in the lives of others. Many spiritual people have been sadly defeated when, having been used of God to the blessing of others, they have, tacitly perhaps, taken the credit to themselves.

It is interesting that Joab sought to dissuade David from his course (vs. 3, 6). Joab was the son of Zeruiah, David's sister or half-sister (1 Chron. 2.16) and was commander-in-chief of the army. His character was a strange mixture. He certainly was not a man of the spiritual stature of David, but in this instance he discerned quite clearly the folly of what the king proposed. David would have been wise to heed his counsel, but his pride blinded him to the truth.

We wage a constant warfare against the pride of our own hearts. Let us pray that God will grant us victory.

1 Chron. 21. 1; 1 Chron. 21. 3; Job 40. *11; Eccl. 7.8; Prov. 21.4

Spiritual Warfare

THE ARM OF FLESH

May 26   Reading: Ezra 8. 21-23

Ezra with a company of some thousands of Israelites are preparing to start on the long journey from Babylon, the land of their captivity, to Jerusalem. The journey was to take over four months (7.9). Along with them they took the Temple treasure (7. 13-16), to a value of about one and a half crore rupees. Understandably they proclaimed a fast and sought the Lord's protection before they set out at the river Ahava (v. 21).

The journey was a long one beset by the danger of marauding bands. From the human standpoint Ezra would have been perfectly justified in asking the king for an armed escort, and such no doubt would have been granted. The temptation to do so must have been great, but Ezra resisted it. The life of the exiles had been a witness to a heathen king of the power of God. They had told him, "The power of our God is for good upon all that seek him" (v. 22). How could they now make a request for the protection of military might when they had so clearly testified to the keeping power of God?

It is easy to boast of the strength of the Lord. The test comes when we are confronted with circumstances in which our confidence in the Lord can be demonstrated , and in which there is also a human way out. It is not always wrong to use the logical means at our disposal, but it is wrong to use purely fleshly expedients to obtain spiritual ends. The question before Ezra was not merely one of protection on a journey. It was a spiritual question of the reality of their testimony to the faithfulness and power of God.

Many spiritual battles are waged on this level. We face problems in personal relationships or in relationships with the church. How do we deal with them? Do we, as Ezra did, by prayer commit them to the grace of God, and handle them in the Spirit, or do we resort to the arm of flesh? The way we handle our problems is often a measure of our own victory or defeat in the spiritual warfare. Let us pray for grace to trust the Lord in all our needs.

Ezra 8.21; Ezra 8. 22; Ezra 8. 23; Ps. 118. 8; Prov. 3. 26

Spiritual Warfare

JEHOSHAPHAT

May 27   Reading: 2 Chronicles 20. 14-22

Jehoshaphat has shown us a vital principle of spiritual warfare. As he went out into battle he set singers in front to sing praises to the Lord. The way to face a battle is with trust and praise.

The army arrayed against Israel was a formidable one. Well might Jehoshaphat and the people be afraid. Humanly speaking, they were powerless against such a foe. We tend sometimes to criticize the fears of others, but fear is a very natural emotion, and God does not condemn us for it. The fact is that we all have our fears. Even those who can put on a brave front may have inner fears which are hidden from others. What is wrong is if we allow our fears to destroy our trust in the Lord and we trust instead in the arm of flesh. Jehoshaphat feared, but his fear drove him to God in greater dependence, and he called a fast throughout the land that the whole nation too might seek the Lord (20. 3-4).

God honourd them by giving His word of assurance through a Levite called Jahaziel (v. 14), and the confidence of the people gradually increased. No longer were their thoughts centred upon the massive forces arrayed against them, but upon the Lord Himself. He had assured them that the battle was His. It had not to be fought in human strength. There is always a danger that we concentrate too much on the powers of evil which oppose us. Jehoshaphat and his people were thoroughly aware of them, as we should all be, but they were much more aware of the greatness of the Lord who is over all, and their hearts could not but be full of praise.

God's exhortation to His people these many years ago is just as applicable today, "You will not need to fight in this battle; take your position, stand still, and see the victory of the Lord on your behalf" (v. 17). Let us pray that in our spiritual battles the Lord will help us to take the position of faith, and see His triumph.

2 Chron. 20.3; 2 Chron. 20.15; 2 Chron. 20.17; 2 Chron. 20.19; 2 Chron. 20.20

Sickness and Suffering

ITS PURPOSE

Reading: Job 42. 1-10

The book of Job deals with the problem of human suffering. In ch. 1 the reader is privileged to be told the background of God's dealings with Job, something neither Job himself nor the other characters in the book know. This teaches us an important lesson, that many of our problems stem from the fact that our outlook is limited. We do not see the whole picture, and we misinterpret, therefore, what we do see.

Job suffered physically, but his sickness was only part of his trouble. In fact he was probably more concerned with the reaction of others, his wife, his neighbours, his friends, than he was about his bodily pain. Physical suffering is only part of the problem with which the book deals.

Three friends who came to comfort Job had one basic answer to his difficulty. It was that he must be suffering because of sin. This Job vehemently denied, and we know from the first chapter of the book that his denial was justified. Finally the Lord rejects the explanation of Eliphaz and his two friends because 'you have not spoken of me what is right, as my servant Job has' (v. 7). Their view was too narrow, and their understanding of God too small. It is true that sin brings suffering, and that some individuals suffer directly as a result of the sins they commit, but this is certainly not always so. A fourth friend of Job, Elihu, presents a different explanation, that God sends sufferings for a person's own good (33. 29-30). This too is true, but again it is only a partial answer. Beyond all the reasons man may put forward is the fact that God is working out a magnificent purpose which we can but feebly know because 'we see in a mirror dimly' (1 Cor. 13.12).

God's answer to Job was not one that met every question, but it was one that satisfied his heart. Job knew that beyond all his problems God was there, and his sufferings faded into insignificance. Let us pray that God will help us to see Him in and above all our trials.

Job 42. 1-2; Job 42. 3; Job 42.4; Job 42. 5-6; Job 42. 10

Sickness and Suffering

THE WORLD'S REACTION AGAINST THE LORD

May 29   Reading: John 19. 12-21

In His last great discourse to His disciples our Lord said these words, "If they persecuted me, they will persecute you" (John 15. 20). There has probably never been a time down through the history of the church when, in some part of the world or other, the Lord's people have not been persecuted. Even in countries where there is full freedom to practise one's faith, the individual believer may have to suffer the ostracism and disdain of family or friends. Basically, this is all part of the reaction of the world to our Lord Jesus Christ Himself.

Often throughout His three and a half years of public ministry our Lord had to suffer from the reaction of others to His claim to be the Son of God, but this reaction came to its climax at the crucifixion. Here we have Pontius Pilate convinced of the innocence of Jesus and seeking to release Him (v. 12). The Jewish hierarchy would have none of it, and made the one remark that could have unnerved the Roman governor. Pilate had made a number of serious blunders during his term of office. He was none too popular with his Roman masters, and could ill afford to antagonize them further.

We cannot know whether Pilate's presenting Jesus to the Jews as their king (v. 14) was a further feeble attempt to make the religious hierarchy relent, but it brought forth from them the most astounding retort, "We have no king but Caesar" (v. 15). Here were the Jews who hated and resented the Roman rule, pleading their loyalty to the Emperor. At no other time is their reaction against Jesus more flagrantly displayed.

The world always reacts against truth and righteousness. Jesus was the supreme manifestation of these virtures, and to the extent that those who profess His name have His life, they too can expect to suffer the rejection of a godless world. Let us thank God for the privilege of being identified with our rejected Lord, and let us pray for grace to accept the world's rejection for His sake.

John 19. 12; John 19. 15; John 19. 18; John 19. 19; John 16. 1

Sickness and Suffering

IDENTIFICATION

May 30   Reading: Lamentations 3. 1-12.

The Lamentations of Jeremiah were written after the fall of Jerusalem. They are a series of five poems of lament, and chapter three is considered one of the greatest poems in the Old Testament. Jeremiah's prophecies concerning Israel had been fulfilled, but he did not consider this a matter of rejoicing. He mourned for the downfall of his people. The author personalizes the suffering of Jerusalem. He takes it upon himself and feels as though he is the one upon whom the wrath of God has fallen. There is a wonderful aspect to this book. It portrays the identification of our Lord Jesus Christ with the suffering and sin of a fallen world.

There is here an aspect of suffering which is known only to the child of God, but which should find some part in every believer's life. Do we feel for a world that has gone wrong? Have we been able to enter into something of the hopelessness of a world which knows not God? To many people who know not the Lord there seems only distress in the present and darkness in the future (vs. 5-6). It seems that the whole world is against them (vs. 7-9) actively seeking to destroy them (vs. 10-12). It is true that the sufferings of the nation Israel were the result of their own sin (1. 3). It is true that the suffering of the world today is the result of the sin of the fall. It would have been easy for the writer of the Lamentations to criticize the nation, but he recognized instead that he too was part of a fallen race and in spirit suffered with them. At the same time he saw a hope in the Lord, for he himself had experienced it (vs. 22-24).

Paul also suffered in identifying himself with the needs of others. Writing to the Corinthians he speaks of 'the daily pressure upon me of my anxiety for all the churches' (2 Cor. 11.28). He did not hold himself aloof from the churches in their trials and follies. He suffered with them and so was able to minister life to them.

Let us thank God for the unmerited grace we have received, and ask Him to help us identify ourselves with a suffering world and a suffering church that we might be a ministry to them.

Lam. 1. 12; Lam. 1. 18; Lam. 3. 40; Lam. 3. 41; 2 Cor. 11. 28

Sickness and Suffering

THE LORD SUPREME OVER THEM

May 31   Reading: 2 Corinthians 12. 1-10.

Paul does not go into detail about the nature of his extraordinary revelation, but his knowledge of the Lord was balanced by a very real measure of suffering. He says quite frankly that his 'thorn in the flesh' was given him 'to keep me from being too elated by the abundance of revelations' (v. 7). He realized that he was in constant need of some restraint to remind him of his intrinsic weakness and his need of dependence upon the Lord. No man, Paul included, has ever been without his weaknesses. Our weaknesses should prevent us from being self-satisfied in our spiritual understanding.

There has been much speculation as to the nature of Paul's 'thorn in the flesh'. Was it physical or mental suffering? Or did it contain aspects of both? Some physical deformity, chronic malaria, defective eyesight, are suggestions which have been put forward as an answer. God, for His own reasons, has not revealed to us the exact nature of His servant's malady, though a bodily ailment seems to be the most probable.

Whatever it was, Paul's ailment was of sufficient gravity to induce a repeated plea that God would remove it from him. The Lord's answer was, "My grace is sufficient for you, for my power is made perfect in weakness." God rules graciously supreme over our trials, whether they be mental or physical. He can and does heal those who are sick, but always according to His sovereign will. Whatever the nature of Paul's 'thorn in the flesh', God's reply to him quite clearly shows that He allows suffering in the lives of His people for His own purposes. Those who claim that God always wills to heal the sick where there is faith and a confession of sin have no Scriptural support for their idea.

Paul accepted God's answer as a cause of rejoicing, because he knew that through his trial God would be glorified. Let us thank the Lord for our 'thorn in the flesh'. Let us recognize His sovereignty over all our weaknesses and pray that He may be glorified in them.

2 Cor. 12. 7-8; 2 Cor. 12. 9; 2 Cor. 12. 10; Ezek. 34. 16; Job 19. 25-26

Sickness and Suffering

WITNESS IN PERSECUTION

June 1   Reading: Acts 16. 25-33

Philippi was the first great centre in Europe in which the apostle Paul preached the gospel. It was the beginning of a tour which took him and his party
to Thessalonica, Berea, Athens, and then on to Corinth. In Philippi Paul
and Silas were imprisoned. In Thessalonica they were hounded out of the
city. In Berea, there was a disturbance which necessitated Paul's leaving
in a hurry. In Athens he was mocked. Little wonder he looked forward
to his visit to cosmopolitan Corinth 'in much fear and trembling' as he
reminds the Corinthians in writing to them later (1 Cor. 2.3).

Yet everywhere the suffering of the apostles was a means of witness.
There was no shame in their imprisonment at Philippi, for they had done
nothing amiss. They had not been gently treated. The magistrates had
ordered them to be beaten, and when they were eventually thrown into
an inner cell their feet were fastened in the stocks (vs. 23-24). But they
did not spend their time complaining. They prayed and sang praises to
God (v. 25). We are not told the substance of their prayers, but to their
prayers and their hymns the prisoners were listening attentively. Perhaps
too, the jailer was listening attentively, though we are not told this.

Subsequent events leave no doubt as to the witness of the apostles'
conduct. When an earthquake had shaken the prison and the jailer awaken-
ed to find what had happened, he was about to take his own life, for he
would have been liable to execution had any of the prisoners escaped.
But they were all there. Was this also due to the advice and witness of
the apostles? The jailer was deeply impressed; and rushing to Paul and
Silas said, "What must I do to be saved?" (v. 30). It is difficult to know
exactly what he meant by the question, but there is no doubting what he
received, full salvation through faith in Jesus Christ.

We may never be imprisoned for the sake of the gospel, but are we
a witness to Christ in whatever trials and sufferings we are called to pass
through? Let us pray that the Lord will make us a tesimony to which others
will listen attentively.

Acts 16. 25; Acts 16. 29-30; Acts 16. 31; Acts 16. 32; Acts 16. 33

Sickness and Suffering

READINESS TO SUFFER FOR CHRIST

June 2   Reading: 2 Timothy 1. 8-14

Paul can now look back over a life in which he had suffered much for the cause of the gospel. 2 Timothy is his last letter, written from prison in Rome. Paul knew that his end was near, but he had no regrets. He knew too that great trials lay ahead for the Church, but he did not advise Timothy to try to avoid them. He urges him to be willing to suffer for the gospel. The gospel is worth suffering for. He had led the way by his own example, and was calling upon Timothy to follow. The power of God was available to give him the strength he needed.

Vs. 9-10 give a magnificent outline of the gospel. Sometimes in our talk of the 'simple gospel' we lose our sense of its greatness. Often in fact the gospel has been debased to no more than a few glib words of repentance which result in a 'salvation' that leaves people just the same as they were before. This is not the gospel that Paul preached. In these verses we see something of the sheer greatness of the gospel, a gospel which results in a change as marked as a change from death to life (v. 10). This is a gospel worth suffering for. "Therefore I suffer as I do," says Paul (v. 12).

But the gospel is not only great, it is a trust committed to God's children by the Holy Spirit. To the Greek society in which Paul lived, a trust was absolutely sacred, something not to be sacrificed at any cost. So we are reminded not only of the wonder of the gospel in itself, but of the fact that its preservation and proclamation are a sacred trust committed to us by God. God does not demand that we keep this trust in our own strength. He, in the person of His Son, suffered to bring the gospel to us. He asks us also to be ready to suffer to take the gospel to others--in His strength.

Let us thank God for the greatness of the gospel, and pray that we will be true to the sacred trust He has committed to us.

2 Tim. 1. 9-10; 2 Tim. 1. 12; 2 Tim. 1. 14; 1 Tim. 4. 10; 1 Cor. 4. 12

Sickness and Suffering

JEREMIAH

June 3   Reading: Lamentations 3. 22-33

The prophecy of Jeremiah and the book of Lamentations show something of the depth of grief into which Jeremiah was plunged. He suffered intensely within his own soul because of the contradictions of his own character, and he suffered intensely because of the sufferings of others. The suffering of the nation was his suffering also.

Yet the intense feeling of sorrow which Jeremiah experienced did not blot out his vivid hope in God. What we have just read is a cry of confident assurance in the midst of the deepest mourning. There is a prophetic ring in v. 30 which looks forward to the One who suffered for a suffering world in order that the world might have hope in Him. Jeremiah identified himself with his suffering people that he might minister to them of a restoration to come.

The character of Jeremiah is more clearly portrayed in Scripture than that of any other prophet. The book of Jeremiah contains many autobiographical sections, and from these we learn something of his intense suffering. He suffered both mentally and physically. Plots were made to kill him. He was imprisoned. The first scroll containing the words God had given him was promptly destroyed. He suffered at the hands of both enemies and friends. He sounded warnings to a nation that was heedless of them.

While it is true that the people to whom Jeremiah ministered rejected his message, there may well have been many carried into Babylon who remembered his words and met with God in a new way. Jeremiah, however, has had a ministry which has carried on down through the centuries, a ministry which has carried conviction because he not only preached but suffered with his suffering people. He saw hope beyond the judgement of God, but felt with his people in the midst of their judgement and, therefore, preached hope with an assurance that could not be gainsayed. Only when we sorrow for the world as Jeremiah did can we minister effectively to it.

Let us ask God to help us enter into the plight of a lost world that we may minister to it hope and life in Him.

Lam. 3. 24; Lam. 3. 25; Lam. 3. 26; Lam. 3. 31-32; Lam. 3. 33

155

Angels and Evil Powers

SATAN

June 4   Reading: Ezekiel 28. 11-19

This passage is prophetic, a funeral dirge over the coming fall of the king of Tyre (v.12). Throughout it is a mockery of a heathen king who had exalted himself as a god (28 . 2). Ezekiel uses what was probably a common heathen version of the story of the Garden of Eden to emphasise the certainty of the king of Tyre's downfall. There is little warrant to see in this passage, as some people do, a picture primarily of the fall of Satan. However, when men go Satan's way they do, in some measure, reflect the character of Satan himself.

The Bible does not tell us anything of the origin of Satan, and references to him in the Old Testament are few. Most of our information comes from the New Testament. The name Satan means 'adversary'. He is a personal being who stands in constant opposition to God and His people. The Biblical references to him bear this out. In the Old Testament we find him in the first chapter of Job speaking against God's servant. In Zech. 3.1 he stands at the right hand of Joshua the high priest 'to accuse him'. In the New Testament Satan is continually opposed to the gospel. He sought to work through Peter whom our Lord rebuked wih the words, "Get behind me, Satan"(Matt. 16.23). Paul writes of his desire to visit the Thessalonian believers, "But Satan hindered us"(1 Thess. 2.18).

Our Lord referred to Satan as 'the ruler of this world'(John 12.31;14.30; 16.11). His character is one of arrogant self-confidence and self-seeking, a spirit which dominates the godless world. This spirit is aptly portrayed in the king of Tyre. Vs. 11-15 are his estimation of himself. The reality is in v.17, "Your heart was proud". All the evil of Satan has its basis in arrogant pride. This is a solemn fact, for it brings home to us that when we give in to arrogance and pride we are playing Satan's game. Through inducing pride in our first parents Satan engineered the fall. By the same means he has caused many another fall among the people of God.

Let us pray that the Lord will protect us from the devil's sin of pride.

Ezek. 28. 6-7; 1 Pet. 5.8; John 12. 31; Isa. 14. 5; Isa. 14. 11

Angels of Evil Powers

SATAN AND THE BELIEVER

June 5   Reading: James 4. 1-10

A number of times our Lord referred to Satan as 'the ruler of this world'. Here James speaks of friendship with the world as enmity against God (v. 4). In doing so he brings before us the subtleness of Satan's working to destroy the testimony of God's people.

Notice that James does not describe friendship with the world in terms of open or blatant evils, what believers sometimes call 'worldliness'. He describes it in terms of pride, Satan's sin and the basis of all other sins. Pride is first of all an attitude of heart which may be kept well hidden from others, but it is bound to show itself, perhaps in acts of selfishness, and most tragically in the breakdown of personal relationships. It is here where Satan does his most subtle work in the believer.

God's attitude to pride is unrelenting. "God opposes the proud" (v.6). God actively resists the spirit of the world which would drag us down. The terrible lengths to which pride can take us are described in the first three verses. James explains his point by using a very suggestive word translated in vs. 1 and 3 'passions'. Its predominant idea is self-gratification and, of course, self-gratification and pride are practically the same thing. We see this element again and again where the devil is mentioned, whether it be when our Lord rebuked Peter for suggesting that the cross could be avoided (Matt. 16.21-23), or in our Lord's dealings with the Jews (John 8.42-45), or in Satan's entering Judas Iscariot (John 13.27-30).

God's great concern is that His Spirit should triumph in us (v. 5). He resists pride in us not to destroy us, but to bring us in submission to Himself. At the same time He gives a warning. Vs. 8-9 may seem rather strange, but they are a reminder that there is the potential in every one of us to deny the Lord unless moment by moment God grants us the grace of humility whereby we are consciously and totally depended upon Him.

When Satan is resisted he flees (v.7),and we resist him by humbling ourselves before the Lord (v.10). Let us ask God to make us aware of the subtlety of Satan's devices, and pray for grace to see Satan defeated by submitting ourselves totally to the Lord.

Jam. 4. ,4; Jam. 4. 5; Jam. 4. 6; Jam. 4. 8; Luke 14. 11

Angels of Evil Powers

SATAN AND THE LORD

June 6   Reading: John 12. 27-36

This was the last but one of our Lord's public testimonies, and in it He makes constant reference to His impending death. The result of the cross was to be the defeat of the powers of evil once for all, and the overthrow of Satan himself whom Jesus here refers to as 'the ruler of this world' (v. 31). In his first letter John tells us, "The reason the Son of God appeared was to destroy the works of the devil " (1 John 3.8).

Although Satan is not specifically mentioned in the events surrounding our Lord's birth, there can be no doubt that he was active in seeking the destruction of the child Jesus. As the 'ruler of this world' he gained ready access to the mind of Herod the Great who, in his latter years, became obsessed by the thought of others posing a threat to his power. The very rumour of one who was to be born king of the Jews was enough to arouse in him the scheming fear which resulted in his ordering all male children under two years of age in the region of Bethlehem to be slaughtered (Matt. 2.16).

Satan, unable to destroy our Lord in His infancy, appears again at the beginning of His public ministry. Matthew, Mark and Luke all record an account of the temptation. Satan's efforts on this occasion were directed mainly against the realm of our Lord's mind seeking to inculcate wrong and selfish motives as Jesus took up the commision He had come to fulfil. Luke gives an interesting side-light on the temptation. He says, "And when the devil had ended every temptation, he departed from him until an opportune time"(Luke 4. 13). Satan left, but he came back again later. He was always seeking a means of destroying the work our Lord had come to do.

Satan entered into Judas to betray our Lord (John 13.27). At last it seemed that his efforts were successful and that the cross had put an end to Jesus' influence once and for all, but that apparent defeat was the most glorious triumph. Through His death the one who had the power of death has been defeated.

Let us pray that we too may know the power of our Lord's victory over all of Satan's devices.

1 John 3. 8; John 12. 32; John 12. 35; John 12. 36; 2 Cor. 12. 14

Angels of Evil Powers

ANGELS

Reading: Hebrews 2. 1-9

The writer to the Hebrews here and in chapter one shows the superiority of our Lord to angels. Angels, however, are beings of great power and authority. The writer tells us that in His incarnation Jesus 'for a little while was made lower than the angels' (v. 9). This indicates that angels are supernatural beings, though they are inferior to God Himself. Paul, writing to the Colossians, says, "For in him were all things created, in the heavens and upon the earth, things visible and things invisible" (Col. 1. 16). Angels, therefore, have been created by God, and their duty, as Hebrews tells us, is to minister to Him and serve Him (1. 14).

The word angel is used both in the Old and New Testaments of a mortal person sent with a message from God, but it more generally indicates a higher order of being, living in communion with God, acting as the bearer of His message to men or carrying out His will among men. The Bible always portrays angels as holy in their creation. They were personal beings with freedom of choice who, consequently, were not immune from temptation and sin. The Bible gives a number of indications of an angelic fall led by Satan before the fall of man (Job 4. 18; 2 Pet. 2.4).

The Old Testament records many instances of angels appearing to men, to Abraham on Mount Moriah (Gen. 22.11). to Moses in the burning bush (Ex. 3.2), to Daniel (Dan. 8. 16). They carry out the judgement of God as in David's punishment for ordering a census of Israel (1 Chron. 21.15). They are the bearers of God's help to His servants, as to Elijah (1 Kings 19. 7). Heb. 2.2 associates angels with the giving of the law. The part angels played is not mentioned in the Old Testament, but an association with the revelation of the law would be quite in keeping with their ministry.

The New Testament endorses the Old Testament teaching. Angels frequently ministered to our Lord, and they minister also to his people. The existence of angels and their ministry is another indication of the great care of the Lord for His people. Let us thank God for His never ceasing care for His own.

Heb. 2. 1; Heb. 2. 5; Heb. 2. 6; Heb. 2. 7; Heb. 2. 8

Angels of Evil Powers

ANGELS AND THE BELIEVER

Reading: Acts 12. 1-11

We have here a mystery of divine providence which has been repeated countless times down through the centuries. James died (v. 12) while Peter was delivered. No heavenly messenger intervened to save James the brother of John from the hand of Herod, but God used miraculous power to engineer Peter's release from prison. The lesson surely is that it is not always God's will to rescue His people from suffering and even death, but He does have a definite purpose for each one of them. For that purpose, whether it mean life or a seemingly premature death, they are kept in safety, and angelic messengers are ever available to intervene on their behalf.

The sequel to Peter's release gives another interesting insight into the ministry of angels. Peter went to the home of Mary the mother of John Mark and knocked. When the door was opened, those in the house could not believe it was Peter. "It is his angel," they said (v. 15). They believed that each of God's children has a personal guardian angel, and also apparently, that the angel could assume the form of the one he was protecting. Both Old and New Testaments confirm the existence of personal guardian angels. The Psalmist says, "For he will give his angels charge of you in all your ways" (Ps. 91.11), a verse, incidentally, which Satan quotes in tempting our Lord (Matt. 4.6). Our Lord also speaks of guardian angels, "For I tell you that in heaven their angels always behold the face of my Father who is in heaven" (Matt. 18.10). The guardian angel has constant access to the presence of God to report on his charge.

Jacob recognizes the ministry of his guardian angel when he is blessing Joseph and his sons (Gen. 48.16). Nebuchadnezzar, a heathen king, recognizes the protecting power of God's angel over Shadrach, Meshech and Abednego who had been cast into a fiery furnace (Dan. 3.28). Daniel was protected from the lions by an angel (Dan. 6. 22).

Let us thank God for His angelic host and for their ministry of care and protection over His people.

Acts 12. 7; Acts 12. 11; Matt. 18. 10; Heb. 1. 14; Dan. 6. 22.

Angels of Evil Powers

ANGELS AND THE LORD

June 9

Reading: Luke 2. 8-14

We have already seen Satan active at decisive stages of our Lord's life and ministry to thwart the purpose for which He came to earth, but our Lord also received the ministration of angels.

An angel appeared to the shepherds to announce Jesus' birth (v.9), and a multitute of angels then appear to sing the glories of the coming incarnation (v. 13). This was an obvious confirmation not only of the fact of the Lord's coming, but of the Father's pleasure in it and, therefore, His protecting care over His Son.

Following the temptation, Matthew tells us that 'angels came and ministered to him' (Matt. 4.11). Angels were no doubt watching over Him throughout the period of temptation, and when it was over came to sustain Him in His human weakness and exhaustion. If the Lord required the ministrations of God's heavenly messengers, how much more do we.

Luke tells us that after our Lord's prayer, "Father, if thou art willing, remove this cup from me; nevertheless not my will, but thine be done", an angel appeared from heaven strengthening Him (Luke 22.43). This is similar to the angels' ministry to our Lord after the temptation. The Father did not leave His Son alone in human strength to fight spiritual battles, nor does He leave us His people.

There was one occasion on which our Lord resolutely denied the help of angles, at the time of His betrayal. Angels were there to help at any time He should call, but He was at no time prepared to step aside from the pathway of the cross. Angels withheld their protection from Him because 'it pleased the Lord to bruise him' (Isa. 53.10), but they protected and sustained Him right up to the point of the sacrifice of Himself, which was the purpose for which He had come into the world.

Let us thank God for the protecting care ministered to His Son, an assurance of His protection over all His children.

Matt. 4. 11; Matt. 26. 53-54; Luke 2. 9; Luk 2. 10; Luke 2. 13-14

Angels of Evil Powers

ATHALIAH

June 10   Reading: 2 Kings 11.1-4, 12-16

The daughter of Ahab and Jezebel, Athaliah is described in 2 Chron. 24.7 as 'that wicked women'. Her reign of six years and the events that lead up to it show just how wicked a human being can become. Six years was a suggestive length for her reign, for six is the number of man. Her rule was an example of humanity at its lowest, controlled and directed by Satan himself.

Athaliah completely dominated her household, including her son Ahaziah during his short one year reign, although he was a man of over forty years of age (2 Chron. 22. 2). The following verse (2 Chron. 22. 3) says these terrible words, "He also walked in the way of the house of Ahab, for his mother was his counsellor in doing wickedly". Athaliah would use her nearest kin to further her own ends, and would destroy them if they stood in her way. When her son died, in order to maintain her own influence, 'she arose and destroyed all the royal family' (v.1). They were her own grandchildren, but they meant nothing to her. One, however, was saved, Joash.

Jehosheba who was able to rescue Joash was herself a daughter of king Joram, Athaliah's husband, so she was sister or half-sister to Ahaziah. It is not altogether strange to find such contrasting characters within one family, and they show the results of a life given over to God and the terrible results of a life put into the hands of Satan. Jehosheba married Jehoiada, the only recorded instance of a princess of the royal house marrying a high priest. It was a union used by God to bring about for a time a restoration of religic in Judah during the reign of Joash.

There were no doubt angelic forces at work guarding Joash during his infancy while his murderous grandmother reigned supreme in the land. In this whole incident we see a conflict between the forces of evil and the forces of God. Let us be warned of the dire depths to which Satan's influence can reduce a person, but let us be assured that the Lord is always victorious. Let us thank the Lord for His triumph over all the forces of evil.

2 Kings 11. 2; 11. 17; 2 Kings 11. 20; Eph. 4. 27; Rev. 20.10

Prayer

OUR LORD AND PRAYER

June 11   Reading: Luke 6. 12-19

It may be asked why our Lord needed to pray since He Himself was God. The answer is that our Lord was also truly man, and in His humanity He needed to pray just as we do. We should also remember that there is fellowship and communion within the trinity. Our Lord's prayer life was an indication and expression of that fact.

Prayer played a regular and important part in the life of Jesus. Here we are told that He went to a mountain to pray and continued in prayer all night (v. 12). During this time He was alone, indicating the importance for all of us of personal, unhurried communion with God. We are not told specifically what our Lord prayed for on this occasion, but two obvious outcomes of this time of waiting upon God were His choice of the twelve (v. 13), and His spiritual power (v. 19). There can be little doubt that our Lord sought guidance in the choice of those who, more than anyone else, were to be the objects of His care during His three and a half years of public ministry. They were one of the most important choices He made.

While through His life of prayer Jesus did derive enabling for His daily walk, He never specifically prayed for spiritual power. Spiritual power there certainly was (v. 19), but it was the result of His relationship and communion with the Father, not an answer to a specific request. Jesus gave thanks for the simple things of every day life, and in His thanksgiving there was power to multiply what He had received (John. 6.11). Much of His prayer, however, was intercession, the great example being His prayer for His own in John 17. But to Jesus prayer also meant communion with the Father, sometimes along with His disciples (Luke 9.28). It was on such an occasion that He was transfigured and God's glory was revealed.

Throughout our Lord's ministry, prayer was an indication of His dependence upon the Father, of thanksgiving, and of His concern for His disciples and the world. Let us ask God that our prayer lives might also be characterized by these same concerns.

Luke 6. 12; Luke 6. 19; Luke 9. 28; John 6. 11; John 17. 9

Prayer

THE NATURE OF PRAYER

June 12   Reading: Matthew 6. 5-15

What we call the Lord's Prayer gathers in a few words all that is essential in true prayer. Our Lord was here teaching us how to pray. He was not giving us a prayer to be repeated word for word. The Lord's Prayer can be repeated to the glory of God provided it is said with a clear understanding of its meaning, but we need always to heed the warning of v. 7 about 'empty phrases'.

The prayer contains six petitions, three directed towards the fulfilment of God's purposes, and three towards the meeting of our own needs. The interests of God come first.

"Our Father who art in heaven. Hallowed be thy name" (v. 9). Prayer is based upon relationship. God in His grace can and does hear the prayers of those who are far from Him, but just as a child has a right to go only to its own father for its needs, so only God's children have the right to go to Him. Relationship with God leads to worship which is the beginning of all prayer.

"Thy kingdom come" (v. 10). Our first allegiance is to the interests of God, not to our own interests, and that means our concern for the building of His kingdom among men. Later in this same chapter our Lord said, "Seek first his kingdom and his righteousness" (v. 33).

"Thy will be done, on earth as it is in heaven" (v. 10). This is both a prayer for guidance and an undertaking to obey His will as and when He reveals it.

"Give us this day our daily bread" (v. 11). Only after a concern for the will of God comes this request for the supply of daily needs. It includes all our daily requirements, and emphasises our dependence upon the Lord for everything.

"And forgive us our debts, as we also have forgiven our debtors" (v. 12). Implicit in this request is confession and repentance, but we cannot sincerely seek forgiveness for ourselves and our own shortcomings unless we are free from a spirit of hatred and revenge.

"And lead us not into temptation. But deliver us from evil" (v. 13). If we are truly repentant we will long to be free from sin. This is a request that God who orders our circumstances will save us from circumstances in which temptation is severe.

Let us thank the Lord for teaching us how to pray.

Matt. 6.7; Matt. 6. 9; Matt. 6. 10-11; Matt. 6. 12; Matt. 6. 13

Prayer

THE UNITY OF PRAYER

June 13 Reading: Ephesians 3. 14-21

The greatest prayer in the Bible is in John 17 where our Lord prays for the unity of His people; not the unity of one group or sect, but 'for those who believe in me through their word, that they may all be one' (John 17. 20-21). We may acclaim the spiritual oneness of all who truly belong to the Lord, but it is a sad fact that it is dreadfully marred by envies, jealousies and divisions among those who yet acknowledge one another as children of God.

Paul's prayer in Eph. 3 is in some way a counterpart to our Lord's prayer for unity. Two basic requests form the substance of Paul's intercession. The first is for individual spiritual stability (v. 16); the second is that they may be rooted and grounded in love towards all saints (vs. 17-18). This is a prelude to a fuller understanding of God's ways (v. 18), a greater experience of the His fullness (v. 19), and the end to which God is moving, His glory in the church throughout eternity (vs. 20-21).

The logical progression of Paul's prayer is clear. A true strengthening by His Spirit in the inner man will lead to an increasing appreciation of our need of all saints and what we can learn through one another. Yet how often those who profess the greatest spiritual enlightenment shut themselves resolutely off from the fellowship of other believers who do not pronounce their shibboleths.

The very act of praying for other believers has a powerful unifying influence. The prayer life of Paul in this respect is quite remarkable. How many times in his letters he mentions that he is praying for those to whom he is writing. Writing to the Romans he says, "Without ceasing I mention you always in my prayers" (Rom. 1.9). He had met some of the Roman believers in other cities, but he himself had so far never been to Rome, and most of the believers were strangers to him. Yet he has a most profound sense of his oneness with them. Do we pray for believers whom we know, much less for believers whom we do not know?

Let us never sin against God by refusing to pray for any of His children. Let us cultivate the habit of praying for those who, with us, belong to the Lord.

Rom. 1. 9; Eph. 3. 14-15; Eph. 3. 17; Eph. 3. 20-21; 1 Thess. 1. 2

Prayer

INTERCESSORY PRAYER

June 14   Reading: James 5. 13-20

Intercession is one of the greatest privileges God has given to His people, but it is a privilege which carries with it great responsibilities. The final sentence of v. 16 is the central thought of this passage, "The prayer of a righteous man has great power in its effects." Notice James does not say that prayer in itself is powerful. We must never think that we have the right at any time, in any circumstances, to come into the presence of God, ask Him for whatever we want, and believe He will give it to us. God never promises to do so. The ministry of intercession is never independent of our obedience and our concern to walk with the Lord. Effective prayer is dependent upon a right relationship with God.

There can be no true intercession from a life which is still rooted in self, or which does not recognize personal sins, so James emphasises a concern for others, as elders in a church care for the people (v. 14), and confession of sin (v. 16). This section on intercession comes at the end of a letter in which James has been building up a picture of the righteous man. The effectiveness of intercession is dependent upon our accepting the responsibility of living according to the faith we profess.

At the same time, let us not be discouraged by thinking that our intercession is useless apart from an almost impossible standard of perfection. James reminds us of Elijah (vs. 17-18). We tend to look back upon the characters of the Bible as near super-human people, but they were not so. They were not men without faults. Elijah was very fallible. Read his story. He was not beyond discouragement, wondering what God was doing with him, feeling that God had deserted him. He 'was a man of like nature with ourselves' (v. 17). Yet he was a man with a great passion for God, a man of a single goal—the Lord. He prayed and God answered him. This is written for our encouragement.

Let us thank God for the ministry of intercession. Let us pray that we may understand its great responsibilities, and that we may enter into it more fully.

Jam. 5. 13; Jam. 5. 14; Jam. 5. 15; Jam. 5. 16; Jam. 5. 17

Prayer

CORPORATE PRAYER

June 15   Reading: Acts 4. 23-31

This is an account of one of the prayer meetings of the early church. From the very beginning the Lord's people met together for prayer (Acts 2.42). On this particular occasion they were drawn together to pray on the release from detention of Peter and John. Their gathering was an indication of their united concern for the will of God above personal considerations. The result of their prayer together was a new courage and power from the Holy Spirit which sent them forth to preach the gospel with a fresh boldness (v. 31).

Every aspect of our relationship with the Lord should have an out-working in our relationship with one another. This is true also of our prayer life. We may pray privately FOR others, but to pray WITH others unites us in a sense of purpose, obligation and strength such as nothing else can. This is all the more important when we realize the spiritual battle to which we are called.

What Luke records is, of course, but a synopsis of what these early Christians prayed, but the burden of their prayers is most instructive. There is a complete absence of any self-seeking or of any complaint. They did not question their trials or ask God for a relief from them. They recogniz-ed the sovereignty of God in all their circumstances (v. 24) and quoted the opening verses of Psalm 2 (vs. 25-26) to show that the persecution they had experienced was only to be expected, as God had already foretold it in His Word (vs. 27-28). Their one request was not for any personal need, but for boldness and faithfulness in carrying out their witness (v. 29). Little wonder their prayer was answered in such a dramatic way.

In our prayers together it is quite right that we should bring personal needs before the Lord, but much more important than our personal needs are the interests of God Himself and of His kingdom. Let us set right our priorities when we pray together.

Let us thank God for the privilege and strength of praying together as His people, and let us be faithful in it.

Matt. 18. 19; Acts 4. 24; Acts. 4. 27-28; Acts 4. 29; Acts 4. 31

Prayer

PERSONAL PRAYER

What does this passage have to do with personal prayer and devotion? A great deal. It shows us that personal devotion is not just a matter of going through the motions of prayer, but depends first of all on a right attitude of heart.

God condemns His people in the strongest terms. He calls them 'rulers of Sodom' and 'people of Gomorrah' (v. 10). Sodom and Gomorrah were two cities in the time of Lot which God destroyed because of their wickedness. The people of Israel had continued to observe all the offerings and rituals which God had instituted, but they had become meaningless, with the result that God pronounces them iniquitous (vs. 11,13,14). God says He will no longer hear His people's prayer (v. 15), and calls for repentance (v. 18) and practical holiness (vs. 16-17).

The people were living as they pleased, and then pleading the grace of God on the ground that they were diligent in prayers and offerings. Let us always remember that prayer is never a substitute for obedience. Personal prayer must always begin with a penitent heart and an obedient will. The people of Israel had disassociated prayer from their practical living. They had lost sight of the fact that the life they had to live for God has to be lived in the present, and their communion with God should strengthen them to live for Him. They no longer expected God to answer them specifically, but only to keep them in health and happiness. They were not looking for the involvement of God in their personal lives, and this, of course, is what prayer really means.

Personal prayer means a recognition of the supremacy of the Lord in our own lives. It recognizes His right to direct us as He pleases, and thanks Him for it. It is an admission of personal weakness which lays hold on His strength. It is a seeking of His guidance for every day and a willingness to accept it. Personal prayer sets the tenor of our own lives and prepares us to be involved in the lives of others.

Let us pray for obedient hearts, that our prayers may never become a meaningless form.

Isa. 1. 11; Isa. 1. 16; Isa. 1. 17; Isa. 1. 18; Isa. 1. 19

Prayer

SOLOMON

Solomon had just prayed his prayer of dedication of the temple which, incidently, is the first mention in the Bible of a man kneeling to pray (v. 54). Now he stands before the people and offers a prayer of blessing. He thanks God for His faithfulness (v. 56), prays for His continued presence (v. 57), and prays that God may keep them faithful to His ways (v. 58). Solomon prays that the Lord's relationship with His people may be a testimony to'all the peoples of the earth' (v. 60). Then he urges the nation, "Let your heart therefore be wholly true to the Lord our God, walking in his statutes and keeping his commandments, as at this day" (v. 61).

These are fine words, but Solomon's life ended in tragedy and shame. His own life was not a testimony. He himself was not true to the Lord. He himself did not walk in His statutes and keep His commandments. One wonders whether Solomon was as diligent in private prayer as he was in public prayer. His kneeling before the alter was an outward indication of submission, but it would appear there was little submission in his heart. He had begun his reign in humility with a request for the divine wisdom to shoulder his responsibilities as king (1 Kings 5.7-9). God granted his his request and gave him much more than he had asked. Solomon was greatly blessed, but he later turned away from the God who had blessed him (1 Kings 11.1-13).

When did the decline begin? It is difficult to say, but in all of Solomon's wisdom and words there is no sign of a penitent heart. When later he sinned openly and blatantly there is no indication of sorrow. In the days of his greatest power there is no indication that he recognized the subtlety of his own heart. His prayers lacked that quality of humility that is the very foundation of all true prayer. His prayer to God at the beginning of his rule, "I am but a child" (1.Kings 3.7) finds no echo throughout the rest of his reign.

Solomon is a grave warning to us all of the need of penitence and humility in prayer, and the need to pray in private before God as we pray in public before men. Let us pray that God will give us a humble spirit as we seek His face.

1 Kings 8. 56; Kings 8. 57; 1 Kings 8. 58; 1 Kings 8. 60; 1 Kings 8. 61

Calling and Purpose

GOD'S PURPOSE IN CREATION

June 18   Reading: Isaiah 43.1-7

Israel, of course, was but one small part of God's creation, but God's dealings with the nation expressed His concern for the fulfiling of his purposes
in man. These seven verses are an assurance that no power on earth, or
even 'the gates of Hades' as our Lord said (Matt. 16.18) will thwart God's
design. Everything and everybody, under God's sovereign hand, is contributing to the fulfilling of His purposes which are summed up in the word
'glory' (v. 7). Everything was created for His glory.

It is important to understand that God's purpose in creation is an integral part of God's purpose in people. Psalm 19 is a witness to this fact.
It begins, "The heavens are telling the glory of God; and the firmament
proclaim his handiwork" (Ps. 19.1). In the second half of the Psalm the
writer goes on to speak of the glories of God's law and its purpose in His
people (Ps. 19. 7-10), and the Psalm ends with a prayer to be kept from
sin (Ps. 19. 11-14). The significance of this is clear. When people are living
to the glory of God, creation will be to the glory of God also.

Many of God's people tend to denigrate man, but the story of creation in the book of Genesis shows that man was the peak of God's work.
The Psalmist tells us, "Thou hast given him dominion over all the works
of thy hands" (Ps. 8.6), a fact already stated in Gen. 1.26. Creation would
have been incomplete without man. In fact it was through man's co-
operation with God that the garden of Eden continued to be what God
wanted it to be (Gen. 2. 15). When man fell, creation fell with him, and
in man's redemption, creation will be redeemed also.

God's purpose in creation is to reveal His glory, and that glory is the
unity which is part of His own being. It is a creation which compasses His
creation, animate as well as inanimate, and is dependent first on people
finding unity with God and with one another. If God's glory in creation
is marred, it is because His glory in us is marred. Let us pray that He may
restore His glory in us so that He may restore His glory in all that He has
made.

Isa. 43. 1; 43. 2; Isa. 43. 19; Ps. 8. 6; Ps. 19. 7

Calling and Purpose

GOD'S PURPOSE IN THE INDIVIDUAL

June 19   Reading: Galatians 1. 10-17

Paul recounts the dynamic change which God had wrought in him, transforming him from a fanatical persecutor of the church to one who lived and worked for Christ. There were three clear stages in the apostle's experience. First, his being set apart for God before he was born (v. 15). Second, his call through grace (v. 15), his conversion on the road to Damascus. Third, God's revealing His Son in him (v.16), the revelation and spiritual growth which made Paul a witness by word and life to others.

"To reveal his Son in me" (v.16). This phrase sums up God's purpose in His people. It is directed to two ends, as a testimony to others, and as a satisfaction to the heart of God Himself. God wants us not only to be a demonstration of what He is able to do, but people from whom He Himself can receive satisfaction and communion. The satisfaction of God's heart comes first. Only when He is able to receive something from us can we be an effective means of commending Him to others. It is significant that when Paul became aware of his calling he did not set out immediately to preach, but went into Arabia, a desert place, to commune with God (v.17).

There are various aspects of God's revelation of His Son in us. Understanding is involved. Paul was learned in the Old Testament Scriptures and saw their fulfilment in Christ. Revelation is involved. Paul's revelation was not a totally new enlightenment unconnected with his past knowledge and experience. It was God's lighting up to him the Scriptures he already knew so well. Relationship is involved. Through his understanding and revelation, all based in the grace of God, Paul came to know the Lord in a deep and intimate way. And he came to be more and more like Him. The result of his understanding was his ability to preach the gospel. The result of his revelation was his conviction of the Gospel. The result of his relationship was his living of the gospel, a testimony to others, and a pleasure to God.

Let us pray that the Lord will fulfil His purposes in us.

Gal. 1. 10; Gal. 1. 11; Gal. 1. 12; Gal. 1. 13-14; Gal. 1. 15-16

Calling and Purpose

GOD'S PURPOSE IN THE CHURCH

June 20   Reading: Ephesians 3. 1-13

Three times in the present passage Paul uses the word 'mystery' (v. 3,4,9). What does it mean? He tells us in v. 6, "How the Gentiles are fellow heirs, members of the same body, and partakers of the promise in Christ Jesus through the gospel". It was difficult for many with a Jewish background to accept that a Gentile should have access to the grace of God through simple faith alone, but it was more difficult still to accept that Jew and Gentile alike should have an equal place in the body of Christ, the church. Yet this was the 'mystery' revealed to Paul.

The fall not only separated man from God, but man from his fellow men. There is a multltude of things in our world today which separates man from man, caste, colour, race, riches and poverty, education and ignorance, and many more, but there is no greater barrier than that which existed between Jew and Gentile. In the gospel this unbridgable gap has been bridged.

Personal redemption finds its fulfilment in the church. God's purpose is to demonstrate 'to principalities and powers in the heavenly places' (v. 10) as well as to people upon the earth, His manifold wisdom through the church. Just as Paul was set apart before he was born (Gal. 1.15), so the church has been set apart to an 'eternal purpose' (v. 11) to be the outworking of what God has revealed in each one of His people. The spiritual life cannot be lived in isolation from others. Our Lord did not live the life of a recluse. He chose twelve with whom He related in His ministry, and whom he taught to relate to one another. Paul fulfilled his ministry with a band of Christian workers. Their relationship was not without its problems, but through it the principles of the life they had received from Christ were worked out for all to see.

God's purpose for the church is that its life together should be a witness to His life, and that He should find in it what is pleasing to Himself. How far short we fall of God's great purpose for us as His people. Let us pray that He might fulfil His purpose in us together.

Eph. 3. 6; Eph. 3. 7; Eph. 3. 8; Eph. 3. 9; Eph. 3. 10

Calling and Purpose

GOD'S CALL TO HIS SERVICE

June 21   Reading: Luke 1. 11-17

The announcement of God's call to John the Baptist was not made to John himself, but to Zechariah his father before John was born. One of the things the angel told Zechariah was, "He will be filled with the Holy Spirit, even from his mother's womb" (v. 15). John's call was not a matter of his choosing and deciding to do the work of God. It was a matter of God's sovereign choice. Luke tells us in 1.80, "And the child grew and became strong in spirit, and he was in the wilderness till the day of his manifestation to Israel". Then God's call came to him, and he launched out upon his public ministry (Luke 3.2). There may have been nothing dramatic about John's call, but it certainly brought to John a sense of compulsion to give his life to the proclamation of God's Word. This is the principle factor in any call to the service of God.

We are not told what was entaled in John's stay in the wilderness for what must have been a considerable number of years. Some believe that he was attached to a desert community of God-fearing people. Whether or not this was so we cannot be sure, but John's subsequent life indicates that he had been well prepared both in body and in mind for the ministry to which God had called him. As a member of a priestly family he must have received a sound education in the Scriptures. He was also in a position to gain a unique insight into the lives of the religious hierarchy of his day. John's father was a saintly man and there were many like him, but there was also within the priesthood much pride, ostentation and luxury, a temptation to any young man who was himself in the priestly line. John reacted violently against all the pomp and arrogance he saw.

There is no doubt that John the Baptist had to count the cost of following his divine commission. The priesthood offered much in terms of security and honour. The prophetic calling offered physical hardship and possible spiritual rejection. John the Baptist counted the cost and followed the Lord, right to the end.

Let us thank God for the example of servants like John, and let us pray that we too might be ready to pay the price of following the Lord.

Luke 1. 17; Luke 1. 66; Luke 1. 68; Luke 1. 76; Luke 3.2-3

173

Calling and Purpose

GOD'S CALL TO A SECULAR VOCATION

June 22   Reading: Psal 37. 23-31.

God loves justice and righteousness, and honours His people who live their daily lives in justice and righteousness. This is the gist of what the Psalmist says in these verses. The righteous man may suffer hardship, but the Lord will sustain him (v. 24). "The steps of a good man are from the Lord" (v. 23). God orders the steps of His people. This is a most important fact. The life of every child of God should be a divinely guided life in which God shows His standards through their every day living.

God calls but a small number of His people to devote their lives entirely to the ministry of His Word. The majority earn their living in the workaday world, but every one of God's children has a right to an equal assurance that he is called of God to the sphere in which he works. There are certain industries in which a Christian should not take part because they are basically harmful, for example the liquor industry or the gambling industry. A believer who seeks employment in such spheres cannot expect the blessing of God.

In other spheres of legitimate employment, however, the believer has many opportunities of living and working to the glory of God. It is true that in many aspects of business and professional life there is corruption, dishonesty and laziness, but the Christian has the opportunity of doing his work as unto the Lord, and thus being a testimony to those with whom he works. He can find his daily occupation a most fruitful field of evangelism.

The Christian believer should never look upon his job as a necessary evil in order to make a livelihood, but as a means of living and witnessing for his Lord. Young believers should pray seriously about the occupation they are to follow. God has a particular place for each one of His children who sincerely wants to live for Him, and God will order his steps.

Let us thank the Lord for the opportunities He has given us of witnessing for Him in the course of our daily work, and pray that we may be faithful to Him in them.

Ps. 37. 23; Ps. 37. 24; Ps. 37. 27; Ps. 37. 28; Ps. 37. 30-31

Calling and Purpose

GOD'S PURPOSE IN THE FAMILY

June 23   Reading: Genesis 18. 16-21

God had a purpose for Abraham and his family which extended down through the centuries. Just as Jesus called His disciples His friends (John 15. 15), Abraham too was called a friend of God (2 Chron. 20. 7; James 2. 23), and God confided to him His plans. Here He tells Abraham of the judgement about to befall Sodom and Gomorrah.

God's favour towards Abraham was due in large measure to the way Abraham ordered his household. He had at this time one son, Ishmael. Isaac had not as yet been born. Later on God led him in strange paths with respect to his sons, but Abraham remained faithful and walked consistently in God's ways. Abraham's family life was not without its problems, but when a problem arose, it was God's word that decided what should be done about it.

In some ways the family is a church in miniature, and the relationship together of the members of a family is a means of spiritual growth and testimony. We see people as they really are within the family. It is comparatively easy to put on a false front with people with whom we are in infrequent contact, but it is almost impossible to do this with those with whom we live all the time. Life within the family really brings out the character of a person. The family, therefore, can be a great means of witness, or it can be a means of bringing discredit to the name of the Lord.

God's purpose for Abraham's family extended down through the generations. Every Christian family has the opportunity of ministering to generations to come. Where God is truly honoured within a household, the family influence can mould the lives of many in succeeding years. It is also sadly true, however, that where God is not honoured there can be generations of spiritual tragedy. God's purpose for Abraham's family was fulfilled. It led to blessing which is still being experienced today.

Let us thank God for the potential of the Christian family and pray that we may play our part to make our family a testimony for Him.

John 15. 16; James 2. 23; Gen. 18. 17-18; 18. 19; 2 Chron. 20. 7

Calling and Purpose

ANDREW

June 24   Reading: John 1. 35-42

This is an account of the Lord's call to some of His disciples. One of them was Andrew the brother of Simon Peter (v. 40). We know so much more about Simon Peter than we do about his brother. In fact Peter was one of the three disciples who seemed to be closest to the Lord, while Andrew remained much more in the background. Yet it was Andrew who first answered the call of the Lord, and who brought Peter to Jesus.

Throughtout his experience as one of the twelve, Andrew was bringing people to Jesus. He first brought his brother. On another occasion he brought to Jesus a little boy with five chappaties and two fish (John 6. 8-9). Then he took to Jesus some Greeks who wanted to see Him (John 12. 20-22). No doubt there were many other times, not recorded in the Gospels, when Andrew took people to His Lord, and we have every reason to believe that he continued to do this throughout his life of service for the risen Christ.

What is notable about Andrew is that, having responded to the Lord's call himself, he recognized God's call and purpose in others. We may have a deep assurance of God's call and purpose for ourselves, but at the same time have scant respect for what He is doing in and through other people. Always let us remember that if God uses us, He uses others as well; if he speaks through us He also speaks through others, and it is our duty to give respect and to listen.

When faced with five thousand hungry people who needed to be fed, Andrew did not despise the little boy with his lunch pack. He saw that Jesus could do much with little things, so he brought the lad to Jesus. Andrew always saw the potential in people or in a situation, and he was never jealous or resentful that the Lord should use others, however humble they might be. Throughout his experience as one of the twelve he lived in the shadow of his brother Peter, because he recognized God's call to his brother, and was happy in God's call to himself.

Let us pray that the Lord will help us to recognize His calling and purpose in others, and save us from the sin of jealousy. Let us be like Andrew, bringing others to Jesus that He might develop the potential He has given them.

John 1. 40; John 1. 41; John 1. 42; John 6. 8-9; John 12. 21-22

The Christian and the World

WHAT IS THE WORLD?

June 25   Reading: 1 John 2. 15-17

The word 'world' is used in the New Testament in a number of different ways. It is used of the planet earth on which we live. It is used of the human race as in John 3. 16, "For God so loved the world." It also means the system of human fallen society controlled by the powers of evil in opposition to God. This is the way John uses the word here, and the command is uncompromising, "Do not love the world or the things in the world" (v. 15).

Two reasons are given for this injunction. First, to love the world in this sense is incompatible with the love of the Father (v. 15). Second, the whole human system opposed to God is transient. One day it is going to pass away (v. 17). Only God's standards are going to rmain. If we build our lives on anything else, one day we will find that all has been in vain.

John describes the world as 'the lust of the flesh and the lust of the eyes and the pride of life'. Notice the words 'lust' and 'pride'. They are inner attitudes. The world is a spirit which pervades the heart of a person. It is easy to condemn a person as 'worldly' because of certain habits or things he does, but we forget that we can be equally worldly because of inner desires and pride which may not show themselves so obviously.

Love of the world is expressed in a carnal desire for things one does not have. The lust of the flesh is a desire for base pleasures whether the desire is satisfied or not. The lust of the eyes is a desire for the superficial, for outward show and respect. It indicates a false sense of values. The pride of life is human arrogance and egoism.

Pleasures and occupations not necessarily wrong of themselves can absorb a person's interests. The material things of the world, pride of place and position, can usurp the place of God or detract from a loyalty that is rightly His. This is the essence of worldliness. How much worldliness there is in the hearts of people who belong to the Lord.

Let us pray that we may know more of the victory of the Lord over the spirit of the world, and that our love may be directed to the Lord alone.

1 John 2. 15; 1 John 2. 16; 1 John 2. 17; Col. 3. 5; Gal. 4. 9

The Christian and the World

THE CHRISTIAN AND FASHION

June 26   Reading: Isaiah 3. 16-26

Fashion is no mere twentieth century temptation. It is an aspect of the world which has existed since the fall. Pride and triviality are the keynotes of Isaiah's words. All the items of finery mentioned in vs. 18-23 are a pitiful proof of human conceit which is maintained at what human cost to countless others (v. 15). Nowhere else in the Bible is this spirit of the world so mercilessly exposed. Fashion is here the symbol of Israel's decay.

What is fashion? Fashion is not something wrong of itself. Fashions vary. They change from one year to the next, and to some extent we all conform to them. Rarely will one see an elderly person wearing the fashions of forty or sixty years ago, however conservative he may appear in the eyes of a young modern. In affluent countries, or among the rich, fashion extends not only to what people wear or the style of their hair, but to the model of their cars, the decor of their homes and a multitude of other things. The temptation of fashion is the temptation to conceit, to be different just to draw attention to oneself. This is only possible when a fashion is new. Once it becomes commonplace there is no distinctiveness in adopting it.

The Bible lays down no specific rules regarding dress or fashion in general, but the principles of Christian humility and stewardship should have their affect in this as in every other aspect of living. The New Testament comments only on women's dress, and enjoins modesty (1 Tim. 2.9-10). Dress or style are, however, not totally unimportant. If the fall has debased man's taste for the modest and the beautiful, it should be restored through life in Christ. Many believers make the mistake of rejecting beauty altogether. God's crowning act was the creation of man, and what God has made should be treated with the respect due to something that is His craftsmanship.

Fashions come and go. As Christians we must never be ruled by them. Let us ask the Lord to guide us in our attitude to the fashions of the day that we might be kept from stumbling and being a stumbling-block to others, that in this too we might glorify Him.

Isa. 3. 15; Isa. 3. 16; Isa. 3. 24; 1 Tim. 2. 9-10; Eccl. 5. 11

The Christian and the World

THE CHRISTIAN AND PLEASURE

June 27   Reading: Ecclesiastes 2. 1-11

"Come now, I will make a test of pleasure; enjoy yourself" (v.1). These words enshrine an attitude which has been common in all ages. There are many millions of people to whom life is just an unremitting drudgery, to whom the word 'pleasure' is almost meaningless. There are others who spend the best years of their lives looking for enjoyment, and in the end come to the same concluion as the writer of Ecclesiates, that all is 'vanity' (vs.1,11).

Solomon had found that pleasure pursued for its own sake led to frustration (v.1), so he tries now to pursue a more moderate path. We might call it pleasure in moderation (v.3). He possessed the money to indulge his fancies, so he used it to build beautiful buildings (v.4), lay out oranate gardens (v.5), collect works of art and listen to music (vs.8). This is a picture of a cultured individual, though Solomon also indulged in the baser side of his nature as well(vs.7-8). He worked to make his life rich and varied in its experiences, and enjoyed doing so (v.10). But his pleasure lay mainly in anticipation. When he finally reached the end to which he had been working, he found that his pleasure had vanished (v.11).

God has given us the capacity to enjoy the world He has made for us, and the believing Christian should, above everyone else, be able to appreciate what is true and what is beautiful. Much of the so-called pleasure of the modern world, however, depicts a distorted creation, and parries to the baser side of fallen human nature. This is largely true of the modern entertainment industry, of popular magazines and novels, of sport and games where people indulge in gambling.

The believer should always remember that his enjoyment of the world that God has created for us can never be separated from considerations of Christian stewardship and personal devotion to the Lord. When it is, the enjoyment ceases. We never find pleasure by pursuing it for its own sake. Everything in the world, even the good things, sought without a concern for the God who gave them, end up in vanity. If we truly seek first the kingdom of God and His righteousness, we will not be allured by the doubtful pleasures of the world, and we will find joy in the Lord. Let us pray that we might find our joy fulfilled in Him.

1 Tim. 6. 17; Eccl. 2.1; Eccl. 2. 11; Isa. 43. 7; Ps. 148. 13

The Christian and the World

THE CHRISTIAN AND FAME

June 28   Reading: 1 Thessalonians 2. 1-12

The sincere Christian worker may sometimes have to suffer slander from those who seek only their own interests and think that everyone else must be like themselves. Paul is here answering charges brought against him in an attempt to discredit him in the eyes of the Thessalonians to whom he had ministered. He was accused of trying to please men rather than God (v. 4), of preaching the gospel for material gain (v. 5), of seeking personal prestige (v. 6). These three charges all have to do with the desire for acclaim, something which is the ambition of many people who do not know the Lord.

The way Paul answers his critics is a demonstration of his humility. His imprisonment at Philippi (v. 2), his concern for the welfare of the Thessalonians (vs. 7-8), his readiness to maintain himself by labour rather than be a burden to them (v. 9), are not marks of a self-seeking man.

What Paul says carries all the more weight when we consider his background as a Pharisee, a man of Greek learning, and a Roman citizen. It is probable that he came from a wealthy background. On a purely worldly level, Paul was a great man. The world lay at his feet. He could have been a man of distinction among the Jews, the Romans or the Greeks, a figure of note in the religious, cultural or political realms. Fame of the kind that men acclaim was awaiting him, but in trusting Christ he put it all behind his back. He lived to please God (v. 4). He was unconcerned about material gain (v. 5). He had no ambition for fame and status, though as an apostle he had a right to respect for his labours (v. 6). His life was in the hands of God.

God did grant Paul fame, though not in the eyes of the world in which he lived, nor because he sought it. None of us may ever be world renowned figures, yet how many believers have a hankering after status or position within some social circle or within the church, a hankering which is self-seeking, not God-seeking. Let us follow the Lord and put ourselves into His hands afresh to be what He wants us to be.

1 Thess. 2. 3; 1 Thess. 2. 4; 1Thess. 2. 5; 1 Thess. 2. 6; Jer. 45. 5

The Christian and the World

THE CHRISTIAN AS A STUMBLING TO OTHERS

June 29   Reading: Romans 14. 1-13

Our lives and our thinking are shaped to a much greater extent than we often realize by our backgrounds. We do have a new source of life in Christ Jesus, but old habits and customs die very hard. Many of them cling to us throughtout our lifetime. We are not, of course, speaking of habits and customs which are basically evil, but of other things which, of themselves, are neither good nor bad, eating or abstaining from certain foods, observing certain days. The Jews, for example, had very strict food laws, and those who trusted Jesus Christ tended to carry them over into their new life. Paul was completely free from such things, but he recognized the problems they could be in the consciences of others.

It is very easy to pass judgement on others who do not see exactly as we do on such matters. The vegetarian may accuse his meat eating brother of being a worldly man (vs. 2-3). A person who feels there is no particular sanctity in observing Christmas may condemn his brother who does observe the day (vs. 5-6). In such matters, where morality is not involved, we have no right to judge others as we ourselves are men under judgement, and our understanding is partial (vs. 4, 10).

In v. 7 Paul sets down a very important principle, "None of us lives to himself." We may disagree with one another, but we cannot, therefore, decide to live in isolation from our fellow believers. This would be the spirit of the world. All that we do vitally affects one another. Our characters are shaped to some extent by our past. In the present our influence affects others for good or bad, and our lives influence generations to come. We must never refuse to face up to our relationship and responsibility to our brethren.

The spirit of the world is to assert our own rights. The spirit of Christ is gladly to relinquish our rights in order that our fellow believers may not be stumbled. It is better to refrain from eating than to stumble our brother by what we eat, or to let go the observance of a day if it is an offence to others.

Let us pray that the Lord will save us from the spirit of the world which insists on our own rights and freedom, and give us a concern to do nothing that will be a means of stumbling to our brethren.

Rom. 14. 3; Rom. 14. 4; Rom. 14. 5; Rom. 14. 6; Rom. 14. 13

The Christian and the World

WORLDLINESS IN RELIGION

June 30   Reading: Galatians 6. 11-18

Paul is here giving a summary of what he has written in this letter. The spirit of the world can be equally evident in religious matters. It takes the form of pride in some outward ritual or observance. In this case it was circumcision, something tremendously important to the Jews, but emphasized out of all proportion to its true value. Christians from a Jewish background were insisting that without circumcision a person could not be saved. Paul bluntly shows this to be absurd. He says the emphasis on circumcision is just a matter of pride (v. 13), or a desire to be like other Jews and thus avoid persecution for the name of Christ (v. 12). This whole attitude of conceit over an outward form and exaggerated claims for it Paul calls the 'world' (v. 14) which has ceased to have any attraction for him whatever.

The same error is made by many Christians today, not with regard to circumcision, but with regard to other matters of the faith. We can just as easily take pride in baptism or the Lord's supper, good and important things in themselves. We can be proud of the number of baptisms on a certain occasion, or the fact that we observe the Lord's supper weekly or monthly while others do not. We can be proud of a pattern of church government which we consider the only Scriptural one. We forget that all of us have but a partial revelation of divine truth, and if we have understood things which many other believers have not, they too have insights which we lack. A sense of superiority in any of these realms is the spirit of the world.

Paul gloried in one thing only, "in the cross of our Lord Jesus Christ" (v. 14), his desire to give himself to the Lord and to His people. Because of this he says, "The world has been crucified to me and I to the world." Pride of place, position or possessions had no attraction for him whatever, whether in secular or in religious affairs. These things did not dominate him, nor did he seek after what they might offer.

Let us beware of the world invading our spiritual lives, and pray that we may learn to glory only in the cross of our Lord Jesus Christ.

Gal. 6. 12; Gal. 6. 13; Gal. 6. 14; Gal. 6. 15; Rom. 12. 2

The Christian and the World

LABAN

July 1   Reading: Genesis 31. 36-49

This is a confrontation between two worldly-minded men. Laban's duplicity seems to have been a family characteristic. We see it in Rebekah his sister and again in Jacob her son. Jacob, however, was to come through into a place of fellowship with God which, as far as we know, Laban did not. The words of the covenant in v. 49 are very beautiful, but to Laban and Jacob they were probably little more than fine words to cover up a stalemate between them. They both recognized that their business association was at an end. Neither was able to outdo the other any more.

When Jacob, having run away from his brother Esau, arrived at his uncle's house, Laban at once saw the opportunity to extract a profit from him. His own life was one of selfishness and greed. The spirit of the world dominated him. Jacob was in desperate need of help, spiritual help, but Laban was not the type of man who could help him in this way. His only thought was to use his nephew to his own selfih ends. Jacob's love for Rachel offered a further opportunity to his greedy uncle who extracted fourteen years of work from him for the right to marry her.

Laban counted everything in terms of financial profit and loss. Jacob was perfectly right in accusing him of unscrupulous dealings, but his claim to God's favour (v. 42) was a bit of hypocrisy. While Laban had been getting all he could out of his nephew, Jacob had been busy with his own schemes in return. God was in no way party to his deceitfulness. Laban's call for a covenant (v. 44) showed that he felt the exposure had gone far enough, but Jacob's accepting it so readily showed uneasiness on his part lest the tables be turned. Two men of the world.

But God did use Laban. He used him as a mirror in which Jacob saw a reflection of his own character. Sometimes the faults we see in others are a reflection of our own. Jacob was helped to recognize the spirit of the world in himself through his relationship with Laban, and eventually he yielded himself to the Lord.

Let us ask the Lord that we might learn to recognize the spirit of the world in ourselves as well as in others whom we so easily condemn.

Gen. 31. 49; Eccl. 5. 10; Matt. 16. 26; 1 Pet. 1. 24-25; Luke 12. 34

Sovereignty and Free Will

THE SOVEREIGNTY OF GOD

July 2   Reading: Romans 9. 14-21

The relationship between divine sovereignty and human freewill is a matter which Christians have discussed almost since the church's beginning. Two apparently opposing emphases have taken their names from two great Christian teachers. Calvinism takes its name from John Calvin (1509 - 1564) the great Reformation leader. Arminianism takes its name from the Dutch theologian Jacobus Arminius (1560 - 1609). Calvinists usually start in their thinking with God's sovereignty and work down to His relationship with man. Arminians tend to start with man's viewpoint and work up to his relationship with God.

The human mind cannot reconcile these two outlooks, but we should not abandon one or the other on that account. The Bible does teach that God is sovereign as this passage clearly shows, and in the final analysis, a sovereign God cannot be controlled or limited by man whom He has created. Paul says quite bluntly that God has the right to do what He pleases with those whom He has made (vs. 26-31). Yet Paul recoils from any suggestion that there might be injustice on God's part (v. 14). We are in the hands of a loving God who has a purpose in all His creation. God can do as He pleases, but what He pleases is always good.

Paul uses two illustrations of God's sovereign choice or election. The first occurred after the judgement occasioned by the worship of the golden calf. Moses sought an assurance of God's presence with His people (Exod. 33. 5-16). God's answer was that He would have mercy on whom He willed (v. 15). The other instance is from the children of Israel's encounter with Pharaoh in Egypt. God raised up Pharaoh expressly to show His power in the face of men who oppose Him (vs. 17-18).

God's sovereignty teaches us that in His dealings with us the essential factors are His purpose and mercy, not any claim we think we can make upon Him. We are not living in a purposeless world. Behind every circumstance is the hand of a sovereign God. Let us thank God for the fTact that He reigns.

Rom. 8. 15-16; 9. 20-21; 2 Thess. 2. 13; 1 Peter 1. 20; Acts 2. 23

Sovereignty and Free Will

THE FREE WILL OF MAN

July 3   Reading: John 5. 33-43

There was something in the ministry of John the Baptist that commanded attention. He was obviously sincere. The mark of divine unction was upon him. Yet of the people who flocked to him many eventually turned away from him, because what he said was too uncomfortable. Jesus had a greater testimony than John (vs. 36-37), but He too was rejected (v. 38). Yet other men who came preaching their own ideas were accepted (v. 43). There had been many so-called prophets in Israel, and most received a following because they promised people the fulfilment of their own desires.

This passage demonstrates very clearly the free will of man and his personal responsibility to choose God's way. There are two parallel truths in Scripture. The first is that God is sovereign and His gracious purposes will be worked out independent of the will of man. The second is that man has a free will whereby he can accept or reject what God offers. A complete reconciliation of these two truths may be impossible, but both are nevertheless true. Bernard of Clairvaux, a great twelfth century Christian said, "Remove free will and there will be nothing to save; remove grace and there will be nothing to save with." He saw the need of both.

The doctrine of free will naturally appeals to men as it makes them believe that they are masters of their own destiny, that everything is in their own hands and they can do as they please. It parries to man's inborn pride. We need to remember that none of us are free in an absolute sense. The decisions we make are all determined by the limitations of our own nature. Our background, our prejudice and a host of other things intrude into our thinking and consciously or unconciously affect the choices we make.

When we realize this we begin to understand our need of the sovereign grace of God to help us exercise our free will aright. Because of the fall we are in bondage to ourselves, inclined to self-pleasing. It is the work of God's grace to incline our wills to please Him. Let us ask God to make our wills more inclined to do His will.

John 5. 24; John 5. 36; John 7. 37; Rev. 3. 20; Acts 7. 39

185

Sovereignty and Free Will

THE BLESSING OF GOD'S SOVEREIGNTY

Reading: Isaish 55. 6-11

Isaiah pleads for people to return to the Lord. In seeking the Lord the whole of man's personality is involved. With his mind he seeks; with his will he returns. There is a decisive repudiation of the old ways; there is a positive cleaving to the ways of the Lord. Old habits, implied in the word 'ways'(v. 7) give place to new. Human plans, which is the significance of the Hebrew word translated 'thoughts' (v. 7), are subjected to the mind of God. 'The motive for this complete surrender is the immeasurable superiority of the purposes of God. Vs. 8-11 portrays the Lord's plans as so much greater than the small expectations of men, plans absolutely certain of fulfilment. Few passages provide a greater incentive to commit ourselves into the hands of a sovereign God.

We make our own plans, but God too has plans for us, and seldom are they the same as ours (v. 8). He works in a manner so different to us in His superior knowledge as Creator and Lord, of us, of circumstances, and of the end to which He is moving. In fact His ways are as high above our ways as the heavens are above the earth (v. 9). Isaiah compares the working of God to the rain and the snow which water the earth and bring fertility (vs. 10-11). The sovereign God works consistently and silently in His people through His Word and the circumstances of daily living.

The sovereignty of God is one of the greatest strengths and blessings to the Lord's people, because it assures us that no circumstances are without meaning, no trial without a purpose. In every experience through which we are called to pass God is working to a positive plan which will inevitably be accomplished. The superiority of God's ways may often mean that we fail to understand them, but we need never doubt that He is working in them for His glory and the good of His people.

Let us thank the Lord for his sovereign hand upon our lives, and let us pray for discernment to recognize His working in the ways He leads us.

Isa. 55. 6; Isa. 55. 7; Isa. 55. 8; Isa. 55. 9; Isa. 55. 10

Sovereignty and Free Will

HUMAN RESPONSIBILITY

Reading: Isaiah 52. 7-12

The gospel of redeeming grace is more clearly revealed in Isaiah than in any of the other Old Testament prophets. Isaiah's prophecy had, of course, a definite local application, but it also had an application fuller and greater than he himself could have understood. Isaiah is quoted frequently in the New Testament, and Paul quotes v. 7 in writing to the Romans (Rom. 10. 15) speaking specifically of the gospel of the Lord Jesus Christ.

God works through men. This is obvious from the very existence of the prophets. The prophets were marked by a sense of divine unction to proclaim the message they had been given, but they responded voluntarily to the call of God. Isaiah's experience in this regard is recounted in ch. 6. God's sending Isaiah forth was in response to Isaiah's own willingness (Isa. 6. 8-9). The same could be said of all the prophets. They served God through the exercise of their own individual personalities willingly subjected to the One who had called them.

At no time in His working does God set aside the need for His people to accept a sense of responsibility in following Him. The proclamation of the gospel is dependent upon the willingness of those who accept the responsibility to announce it. In fact part of the appeal of the gospel is in the fact that God's people want to proclaim it. They recognize the sovereignty of God and choose to make this blessed truth known to others (v. 17). They proclaim the Word not through dire compulsion or for ulterior motive, but because, having tasted the grace of God, they want to proclaim it.

The gospel comes with power to those who look for redemption, the 'watchmen' of v. 8. Here again is human responsibility. God does not thrust His blessings upon anyone unwanted. He does not compel people to receive His Word, though He longs to comfort and to redeem (vs. 9-10).

The separation enjoined in vs. 11-12 had a direct application to a people in bodage in Babylon, but it foreshadows a deeper spiritual responsibility to repudiate all evil in a life given over to the Lord. We are personally responsible to accept or reject the gospel. As God's people we are responsible to proclaim it and to live lives worthy of it. Let us pray that God will make us more alive to our spiritual responsibilities.

Isa. 52. 7; Isa. 52. 8; Isa. 52. 9; Isa. 52. 10; Rev. 18. 4

Sovereignty and Free Will

CO-OPERATION

July 6   Reading: Philippians 3. 12-21

Many times in the New Testament we have the picture of God and man working together. It is here in v. 12, "I press on to make it my own, because Christ Jesus has made me his own." Paul had a deep sense of having been apprehended by Christ. He discerned it in his Damascus Road experience when the Lord had captured his heart but he discerned it also much farther back in his experience. He states quite clearly to the Galatians that God had apprehended him before he was born (Gal. 1. 15).

So Paul looked back throughout his life, at his religious upbringing, his training as a Pharisee, his secular education, at everything, and in it all he saw the hand of God. It was something he may not have recognized at the time, but now that he had come into a new relationship with God through Jesus Christ, he saw it clearly. God's working in Paul to His own sure ends did not in any way diminish Paul's feeling of personal responsibility. On the contrary, it heightened it. Earlier in this letter to the Philippians he has exhorted them, "Work out your own salvation with fear and trembling; for God is at work in you, both to will and to work for his good pleasure" (Phil. 2. 12-13).

Paul had no problem in reconciling God's sovereignty with his own free will. One did not cancel out the other. God worked, and he had to work also. Vs. 12-14 leave no doubt as to the energy with which Paul co-operated with God in the quest for spiritual fulness. His words are emphatic, "I press on" (v. 12), "Straining forward" (v. 13), "I press on" (v. 14).

This attitude of vigorous co-operation with God, Paul says, is a mark of spiritual maturity (v. 15). The word Paul used for maturity does not mean a final perfection which leaves nothing more to be gained. It means rather an adult sense of responsibility which includes a frank recognition of how much we have yet to learn. Vs. 17-21 draw a vivid contrast between the mature and the immature man, are a reminder of our glorious hope, and a call to press on, as mature people, with the Lord. Let us thank God for His working in us, and pray that we may learn to co-operate more diligently with Him.

Phil. 3. 12; Phil. 3. 13-14; Phil. 3. 15-16; Phil. 3. 17; Phil. 3. 21

Sovereignty and Free Will

THE PARADOX OF GOD AND MAN

July 7   Reading: Job 40. 6-14

A paradox is a well founded fact which, nevertheless, contains elements of apparent contradiction. There is much in the Bible that is paradoxical. This is not at all surprising, because the Bible has to do with the relationship between an infinite God and finite man. We have already seen how God's ways and thoughts are so much higher than man's (Isa. 55. 10-11). In our limited understanding, God's ways often seem strange to us. He does not do things the way we would do them.

The paradox of God's ways is clearly brought out in the book of Job. Job was a righteous man beset by the most devastating calamities. It all seemed so unjust, and there was no answer forthcoming from those who sought to help him. His three 'comforters' give the best answer religious thinking can offer to Job's plight. Their conclusion was that Job's suffering must be the result of personal sin. This, Job rightly and vehemently denies, thougth he is unable to give any other explanation. As a child of his age, he had equated righteousness with prosperity, but this idea is now shattered by his own experience. The book of Job shows us that it is impossible to plumb the depths of God's wisdom and ways through our normal experience.

Our reading is part of God's answer to Job. It is not an answer to Job's questions and charges, an answer which satisfies Job's mind, but it is an answer which satisfies Job's heart. Job's problem, and that of his friends, was that their idea of God was far too small. Their horizons were far too limited. When Job realizes this, he may be no nearer understanding God's ways, but he can accept them with thanksgiving.

The question is not that if Job is right in maintaining his innocence, God must be wrong in allowing him to suffer (v. 8). The root of the problem is that our grasp of God's ways is so limited. Is Job in a position to don the garments of God's majesty (v. 10), and to sit in judgement over the world? (vs. 11-12). Of course he is not. God is sovereign, and though we may not understand His ways, and see them even as contrary to what we do understand, we can still trust Him. Let us pray that God will give us Job's acceptance of His majesty.

Job 40; 8; Job. 5. 8-9; Job. 11. 7; Ps. 145. 3; Rom. 11. 33

Sovereignty and Free Will

ELIJAH

July 8   Reading: 1 Kings 19. 1-8

Elijah is the picture of dejection. Elijah who had so recently seen God vindicate His sovereignty before the prophets of Baal throws himself down under a broom tree and wishes he were dead (v. 4). What a change from the man who had stood undaunted before four hundred and fifty heathen prophets (1 Kings 18. 22). Here he is fleeing in terror from the threats of one woman. Jezebel was a formidable character who would stop at nothing to carry out her threats, but the God who had protected Elijah so far could surely protect him still.

God could have led Elijah on in triumph from the victory on Mount Carmel and saved him from the despair into which he fell, but he did not. It may well be that Elijah's fear had a deeper cause than Jezebel's threats. The encounter with the priests of Baal had drained him of all his spiritual energy, and the cry of vengeance from the evil queen was the final strain which drove him to breaking point. Whatever may be the reasons for Elijah's collapse, we see here a very human Elijah, so different from the almost super-human figure we tend to imagine him to be. His thoughts are upon himself and his own safety. No longer is he filled with a sense of the power of a sovereign God. He is intent upon flight, adopting the most obvious human means to ensure his escape from danger. Here we see free will, not in co-operation with God, but in the service of Elijah's own misdirected desires.

But the Lord did not leave him. An angel encouraged him and provided him food (v.6-7), food that sustained him for a further forty days (v.8). This was not the end of Elijah's despondency, nor of the Lord's encouragement as we can read later in the same chapter. God's sovereignty triumphed over the despair into which Elijah's own will had led him.

Very much later Elijah was to be privileged to appear with Moses and our Lord at His transfiguration. What an indication of the sovereign grace of God. God will not allow His purpose for His people to be thwarted by their own misdirected wills. Let us thank God again for His sovereign grace and pray that our wills might be more directed in His ways, not our own.

Kings 19.11; 1 Kings 19. 12; 1 Kings 19. 13; 1 Kings 19. 18; 1 Kings 17.22

Morality

RELATIONS WITH THE OPPOSITE SEX

July 9   Reading: Song of Solomon 6.4-13; Timothy 5.1-2

There is a very marked difference between the passage from the Song of Solomon and Paul's exhortations to Timothy. With all Solomon's wealth and wisdom, his life ended in tragedy. His fatal flaw was his attitude to women, a flaw which destroyed not only his own moral character, but led him into compromise with heathenism. The dire results of his downfall came to fruition in the reign of his son Rehoboam, results which were to have their effects down through the generations.

The Song of Solomon is the story of a beautiful Shulammite girl, already promised to a fine shepherd lad. She is captured to swell the numbers of Solomon's large harem, but in spite of his blandishments and attempts to win her affection, she remains true to her betrothed shepherd lover. The Song of Solomon is a condemnation of all sensuality and a tribute to a love which is pure and wholesome.

Vs. 4-9 are an account of Solomon's empty flatteries, but they are rightly repulsed, a fact which he recognizes in calling the Shulammite 'terrible as an army with banners' (v. 10). The village girl despises his approaches, and he is powerless against such purity and faithfulness as against an overwhelming army. In vs. 11-12 the Shulammite reminisces on the circumstances of her capture and shows her rejection of the king's intentions (v. 13).

In contrast to this picture of permissiveness, Paul reminds Timothy of the Christian attitude to people of the opposite sex (1 Tim. 5.2).This can be summed up in two words, 'respect' and 'purity'. Customs governing the association of men and women, especially among the young, may differ from one culture to another, but the Bible lays down principles which are applicable to every society. We are living in a world in which virtues such as respect and purity are given scant regard. Believers need to take a firm stand on Biblical standards against the encroachment of a godless world.

It is signficant that Paul here links respect for elders with a right attitude to those of the opposite sex. Young people should give due credence to the wisdom and experience of older spiritual people. Let us pray for God's constant hand upon us in this very important area of relationships.

1 Tim. 5.1-2; S. of S. 8.6; Prov. 23. 16; Prov. 23. 22; Prov. 28. 18

THE DISCIPLINE OF DESIRE

July 10   Reading: 1 Corinthians 7. 1-9

Part of the human make-up as God created us is our natural appetites or desires. There is the desire for food, the desire for drink, the sexual desire, and many others. All these desires are legitimate but have to be disciplined and directed into proper channels. Any desire which is debased or perverted will lead to sin. An undisciplined desire for food will lead to gluttony and illness. A wrongly directed desire for drink may lead to drunkenness. Similarly the strong sexual desire has to be maintained within the bounds which God has laid down for it. This is Paul's subject in 1 Corinthians 7.

The temptation to sexual immorality in Corinth was a strong one, and it is the same in our modern world, but God has given the sexual desire for a specific purpose, and He has ordained marriage as the relationship within which alone it should be fulfilled (vs. 2-4). Notice carefully the principle laid down in v.2 which clearly forbids polygamy or polyandry. This is the Christian standard. A man has one wife and a woman has one husband.

Paul also makes clear, however, that the unmarried state is a viable Christian alternative (vs. 1, 8). We should take note of this and realize that it may be the will of God for a person to remain unmarried. On the other hand, it would be folly for a person to take a vow of celibacy if he does not have the capacity to live the single life in purity (v. 9).

Vs. 4-5 have a very pertinent application to family life. God has ordained husband and wife to be one, and within that union alone to fulfil their sexual needs. It follows that husband and wife should avoid prolonged periods of separation. The practice, common in India, of husband and wife being employed in different places is a bad one. The Christian family, to fulfil the purpose for which God has ordained it, should be together if at all possible.

God has given adequate means whereby our desires might be disciplined to His glory. Let us also remember that in temptation there is always grace sufficient to overcome (1 Cor. 10.13). Let us pray for grace to live disciplined lives which will be a testimony to the Lord.

1 Cor. 7. 2; 1 Cor. 7. 5; 2 Cor. 10. 5; 1 Cor. 7. 39; Heb. 13. 4

Morality

WHY ADULTERY IS WRONG

July 11   Reading: 2 Samuel 11. 26-12. 7

The breaking of the seventh commandment, "Thou shalt not commit adultery" was regarded among the Jews with the utmost horror. The sin of adultery carried the severest penalty. Adulterer and adulteress were both condemned to death (Lev. 20.10). Yet the warnings and rebukes of the prophets indicate that no sin was more common, and the legal punishment was seldom carried out. Here we have the great king David caught in a shameless act of adultery with Bathsheba the wife of Uriah the Hittite, and guilty of murder in order to cover up his sin.

The basic principle of human life is a person's relationship to God. Then comes man's relation with his fellow men, and within this relationship is the family from which all other relationships originate. The family is the basis of society. The sacredness of the family is well stated at the beginning of the Bible, "God created man in his own image, in the image of God he created him; male and female He created them". The unity of husband and wife is an expression of the unity of the Godhead, and anything which violates this unity is a sin against God, against the individuals concerned, against the family, and against society. All unchaste conduct, before or after marriage, is a repudiation of the family and violation of the responsibilities which family ties entail.

Modern thinking tells us that the family unit is breaking down because it is outmoded. This is absolutely contrary to every Biblical standard. History shows us that the collapse of the family heralds the collapse of civilization. The downfall of the Assyrian, Greek and Roman Empires are cases in point.

David's fall is an indication of the reason for the tragedy of his own family life marred by instability and sin which was to have its effects down through the generations. The same weakness from which David suffered appeared in his son Solomon. David's sin affected himself, his family, and the whole nation which was eventually led away into captivity. Let us pray that God will give us a sense of horror and shame at the sin of adultery.

Prov. 6. 32; Matt. 5. 28; 2 Sam. 12. 4; Jer. 7. 9; Mk. 7. 21

193

Morality

THE DISCIPLINE OF IMMORALITY

July 12   Reading: 1 Corinthians 5. 1-8

The state of Roman and Greek society in the days of the early church was sensual and depraved. It provided a constant assault on the purity of the church's testimony. The same is true today, and immorality is a problem that has to be firmly dealt with. It is plain that the church in apostolic times was organized in such a manner that discipline could be effectively carried out.

Within the Corinthian assembly was a flagrant case of wilful immorality, apparently known to all. It was such that the Corinthians ought to have been reduced to a state of humility and shame, but instead they were carrying on in their own arrogant way, concerned with petty quarrels and divisions, and unconcerned about a matter which threatened the very life of the church. We need to take very seriously the question of discipline within the church.

The judgement was a drastic one. The guilty person was to be removed from the fellowship of God's people (v.2) by the assembly acting in the authority of the Lord (v. 3-5). "You are to deliver this man to Satan for the destruction of the flesh", Paul says (v.5). Satan is described as the 'god of this world' (2. Cor. 4.4). The evil-doer was to be removed from a company who lived under the authority of God in the faith that his deprivation would be a discipline which would bring about his spiritual restoration. However drastic this measure may have been, it was to be taken in a spirit of humility and love, not with a vindictive desire for retribution, but with a desire for the sinner's repentance and return to the ways of the Lord.

The word 'immorality' in v. 1 is a word used generally of any sexual sin. Vs. 6-8 show the contaminating effect of such evil and the need that it should be strictly dealt with. It is like leaven. A little, if left to do its work, will spread throughout the fellowship to work havoc in the whole moral and spiritual life of the church, "Cleanse out the old leaven" (v. 7). All sin must be purged from the church, for Christ died to cleanse from sin and make the church pure.

Let us pray that the Lord will give us a concern for holiness in His church and the grace to exercise discipline in love.

1 Cor. 5. 6; 1 Cor. 5. 7; 1 Cor. 5. 8; 1 Peter 1. 18; Ex. 13. 7

Morality

MORALITY IN ART

The fall has reached down into every aspect of living. God made man with wonderful potential and the capacity to appreciate the world He created, but that potential has been debased. Art, music, writing all reflect a fallen creation and often parry to the baser instincts of fallen human nature. God has given artistic gifts such as painting, writing and music to different people, and they can be used either to His glory or to depict the despair, emptiness and sin of a godless world.

The world today is flooded with tawdry novels and films which appeal to man's depraved instincts, and make light of such things as love, the sanctity of the family and truth. Many of these books and films major in violence and crime, or in immoral behaviour. The same can be true of painting. Much of what is called 'modern art' is a meaningless jumble, a picture of man's inner confusion and hopelessness. Music too reflects the spirit of the age, though in a much more subtle way. The hard rock of today has its origin in the exciting, stimulating rhythms of non-Christian culture, yet in some Christian circles it is an accepted musical expression. Young believers need to be very careful about the insidious inroads of this type of music into their spiritual lives. It can encourage a superficial attitude to spiritual things and become such an obsession that true devotion to Christ is lost altogether.

Paul here lays down a spiritual principle which is supremely applicable in our relationship to forms of art. So often people judge their involvement in these things by saying, "There is nothing wrong with it". The principle here, however, is a positive one. Our judgement should be based on the presence of what is good and beneficial, rather than on the absence of anything we consider harmful.

Read v. 8 again and again. If you apply honestly the standard of this word to books, films, music and other things, you will seldom have difficulty in deciding whether or not they should have a place in a believer's life.

Our over-riding concern should be for God's interests and God's people (vs. 10-14). When this is so, doubtful things will cease to be attractive. Let us ask the Lord for discernment and for grace to reject what is decadent and evil.

Phil. 4. 8; Phil. 4. 9; Phil. 4. 10; Phil. 4. 11; Phil. 4. 12-13

Morality

SPIRITUAL IMMORALITY

July 14   Reading: Malachi 2. 10-16

Again and again the prophets condemn unfaithfulness to God as spiritual adultery. Considering the Jews horror of adultery, the use of this comparison shows what a terrible thing unfaithfulness to God is. Usually the two sins went together. Part of the 'covenant of our fathers' (v. 10) was a prohibition of marriage with foreign women (Deut. 7.3-4). Forbidden alliances inevitably led to the worship of heathen deities, though one cannot always say which evil came first. Unfaithfulness to God led the people into impermissible relationships, and sinful relationships resulted in unfaithfulness to God. The spiritual and the physical go together. As believers we cannot compartmentalize our lives, owing allegiance to God and living as we please.

Malachi pleads the fatherhood of God who had cared for His people and watched over them (v. 10). This surely should have been a compelling incentive to unity and faithfulness. But no! Israel wanted their Father's blessings but not His standards. When God's favour was withheld they covered the Lord's altar with tears (v. 13), but true repentance was far from their thoughts. God is a God of holiness who must have holiness in His people. Unfaithfulness is abhorrent to Him. Divorce is something He hates (v. 16), whether it be the divorce of husband and wife or the spiritual abandonment by people of their God.

"And what does he desire? Godly offspring" (v. 15). Unfaithfulness pollutes all we produce. One of the tragedies of material unfaithfulness is the havoc it works in succeeding generations. The emotional and psychological instability not only of individuals, but of whole societies, is the terrible price the world today is paying for an abandonment of moral standards. In the spiritual realm, unfaithfulness to God is equally devastating, breeding emptiness and hopelessness to add to the world's confusion. But what glory results from a faithful union between God and His people. A faithful Christian family is a reflexion of what God wants to produce through the relationship with those whom He has drawn to Himself.

Let us ask God to give us a godly horror of unfaithfulness and pray that we may be kept true to Him.

Mal. 2. 10; Mal. 2. 15; Isa. 63. 16; Isa. 64. 8; Ex. 19. 5

Morality

JOSEPH

July 15   Reading: Genesis 39. 6-12

Joseph is confronted with a terrible moral temptation. Nor was it only a fleeting temptation. It was posed to him day after day (v. 10) in a subtle attempt to break down his inner control. He said a resolute 'No' to it because his life was ordered by a clear standard which had its foundation in his devotion to God. This is the first and basic strength against immorality. Joseph realized that the sin presented to him was a sin against God, and because he was loyal to God, he was loyal also to his master, and loyal to the woman who tried to seduce him, although it cost him his freedom.

Joseph had a positive aim in life, to serve God, and he was not, therefore, attracted by things which would destroy that aim. This should always be the Christian's attitude. If we are filled with a sense of God's purpose for us, we will not be so easily allured by temptation to sin.

In the household of Potiphar, Joseph was a slave. Potiphar had brought him from the Ishmaelites to whom Joseph's brothers had sold him (39.1). Although Joseph had risen to a position of authority within the household, he was nevertheless under the absolute authority of his master. From a natural point of view, he was a slave with no future, in a foreign country, circumstances which would have sapped the spiritual energy of many men. It is obvious, however, that Joseph maintained his close touch with God all through his trials. When we are healthy in body we have a strong resistence to disease. When we are healthy in spirit we have a strong resistence to temptation.

When temptation continued to be thrust in his way, Joseph wisely took to flight (v. 12). Joseph's love for God and hatred of immorality not only kept him pure, but helped mould him into the man for whom God had a very special task in the years ahead.

Let us thank God for the example of Joseph who resisted temptation, and let us pray that we may learn well the lessons his experience teaches us.

Gen. 39. 9; Prov. 6. 27; Jer. 21. 6; 1 Cor. 6. 18; Eph. 5. 3

Heaven and Hell

HE FACT OF HEAVEN

Reading: Isaiah 66. 18-23

In the Bible heaven is the dwelling place of God (Deut. 26.15; Matt. 5.45). It is also the dwelling place of angels (Neh. 9.6;Matt. 24.36). It is the ultimate dwelling place of God's people (1 Peter 1.4). Isaiah's prophecy concludes with a statement of God's purpose for the world (v. 18). Its climax is 'the new heavens and the new earth which I will make' (v. 22) in which people from all nations will be brought together into God's family (v.22).

Death is the separation of soul from body, but man's essential being has a permanence which survives death and is not influenced by the physical disintegration which follows death. The emphasis of the New Testament is that at death the believer goes to be with Christ, enjoying the consciousness of His presence in Paradise until the events of the Second Coming. Scripture uses the word heaven to denote the dwelling place of the righteous after the judgement.

The Bible uses highly metaphorical language in describing heaven (e.g. Rev. 21). This is quite understandable, for we can only conceive of heaven in terms we have already experienced. The human terms in which heaven is described can be but a dim reflection of its true glory. We need to avoid two extremes in our thinking, the extreme of a too materialistic view, and the extreme of an excessively spiritualized view which reduces heaven to little more than a dream.

Any consideration of the final state has to take into account the resurrection which was an important aspect of our Lord's teaching (John 5. 28-29). We are to have a resurrection body which will inhabit a real heaven. The resurrection body will be glorified like our Lord's glorified body, and it will be incorruptible. It will have a relation and likeness to our present bodies, but will have powers beyond what man possesses in his present state. God has a glorious destiny for His people in a real and glorious heaven. Let us thank Him for it.

Isa. 66. 22; Neh. 9. 6; Rev. 22.1; John 5. 28-29; 1 Cor. 15. 54

Heaven and Hell

THE FACT OF HELL

In the authorized Version of the Bible the word hell is used to denote three words, sheol, hades and gehenna. Sheol is an Old Testament word and is the name for the place of departed souls. Its counterpart in the New Testament is hades. Gehenna was originally the Valley of Hinnon outside Jerusalem, a place where refuse was dumped and burned. Jeremiah refers to some of the idolatrous barbarities practised in the valley of Hinnon, and prophesies a great judgement of God in the same place (Jer. 7.30-34). Because of these associations Gehenna came to mean the place of final judgement of the wicked.

The book of Revelation pictures hell in vivid language. In our reading it is referred to as 'the lake of fire' (vs. 14, 15). Our Lord also uses the symbol of fire (Matt. 13.42, 50; 25.41). Another symbol He uses is that of darkness (Matt. 8.12; 25.30). Taken literally, these symbols are the opposite of one another, because where there is fire there is brightness, but we have to remember again that the Bible is portraying something which is quite outside our experience, and has to use earthly terms befitting the terribleness of banishment from the presence and blessing of God.

The obvious implication of the 'lake of fire' in vs. 14-15 is destruction. Darkness clearly refers to exclusion from the presence of God who is light. It is unwise to speculate on the nature of hell beyond what the Bible actually says. We may feel that the Scriptures give us very little precise information, but there are certain things which are unmistakably clear. The fact of hell is clearly taught in the Bible as the end of those who reject Christ. Hell is the negation of everything that is meant by life.

No one need go to hell, and its existence should make us who have the light of the gospel of Christ alive to our responsibility to share the light with others. Let us pray for a greater zeal to share the message of salvation.

Rev. 20. 12; Rev. 20. 14; Rev. 20. 15; 2 Thess. 1.9; Ps. 9.17

Heaven and Hell

CHARACTER AND DESTINY

July 18   Reading: 1 John 2. 3-11

"By this we may be sure" (v. 3) is a characteristic phrase of John's first epistle. John uses it to introduce three marks of a true Christian, right character, right relationship and right belief. He deals briefly with the first two of these in our present passage. In doing so he draws a contrast between spiritual darkness and spiritual light (vs. 9-11) showing that a person's character determines not only the quality of his life here and now, but the quality of his life in eternity. Yesterday we saw how our Lord describes hell in terms of darkness, a darkness which will envelop eternity for those who do not accept the light that is offered in Christ.

The first test of the believing Christian is character or obedience. John says quite plainly that a profession of a relationship with Christ should result in a 'walk in the same way in which he walked' (v.6). John's language is strong and unmistakably clear, "He who says 'I know him' but disobeys his commandments is a liar, and the truth is not in him" (v. 4). John shows that obedience to God affects a person's destiny, because obedience to God is the inevitable result of a true faith.

The second test of the believing Christian is the test of fellowship. John does not say specifically what the new commandment is which he brings (v. 8), but it is obvious from the context that the new commandment is our Lord's commandment of love. Again John's language is strong and unequivocal. "He who says he is in the light and hates his brother is in the darkness still" (v. 9). A person who is brought into fellowship with God is brought into fellowship with God's people. To hate a brother in Christ is to deny the relationship with God that we profess.

Later John deals with right belief as a test of the true Christian. Right belief or orthodoxy in itself is not the determining factor in a person's destiny. The profession of orthodoxy must be real, a fact which God alone can determine, but which does show itself in practical obedience to His ways, and in fellowship. Let us ask the Lord to deepen our fellowship with all of His people and to make us more obedient to His ways.

1 John 2.4; 1 John 2. 5; 1 John 2.6; 1 John 2. 9; 1 John 2.11

Heaven and Hell

THE DESTINY OF THE HEATHEN

July 19   Reading: Romans 2.12-16

What is the destiny of the many millions of people who have never had an opportunity of hearing the gospel of the Lord Jesus Christ? The New Testament makes it plain that the possibility of salvation exists only because of the redemptive work of our Lord (Acts 4.12), and acceptance or rejection of Christ is the determining factor in the case of those who have heard and understood the gospel. God is just and will not hold men accountable for truth which has not been accessible to them. They will be judged, however, according to the measure of their obedience to the light they have received. This is the substance of Paul's argument.

Man's great dilemma is that, although God's standard has been revealed to him, he is unable to obey it. The Jews received the law through Moses but could not keep it. There is, however, another factor, what Paul calls 'the obedience of faith' (1.5). When we realize how miserably we fail to obey God's standards in our own strength, it should drive us to cast ourselves upon God in faith to receive His salvation and His strength. Behind every revelation of God's standard is a plain but unspoken commandment, "Have faith in God" (cf. Mark 11.22), and it is obedience to this commandment which brings salvation and victory over sin.

The heathen have a revelation of God's standards though it is much more limited than the revelation given to the Jews. The created world is a revelation of the greatness and power of God (1.20). Man also has an innate sense of right and wrong reinforced by conscience (v. 15). Conscience, of course, is not an absolute, like a clock which always indicates the correct time. It is influenced by our background, by people and circumstances. It can be debased (1 Tim.4.2), but in the believer it should be moulded by his relationship with Christ and be acutely sensitive to God's standards. Conscience is a means whereby God can speak to man and lead him towards the obedience of faith. God judges man in righteousness. Let us thank the Lord for His righteous judgements and pray for a deeper obedience of faith.

Rom. 2. 12; Rom. 2. 14; Rom. 2. 15; Jer. 32. 19; 1 Tim. 1. 19

201

Heaven and Hell

MEASURES OF REWARD

In this parable of the talents the Lord teaches us that we will be rewarded according to our faithfulness in living for Him. The picture is a simple one, of a man who leaves for a journey, entrusting his property to his servants. There is a marked contrast between the words 'master' and 'servants' used throughout the parable. The word master is a word of great authority, used to refer to a king. The servant is a bond-slave, the name by which the apostle Paul so often referred to himself. The point is that we are living in God's world. We are His servants, and He has made us custodians of what belongs to Him during the period till He comes again.

What is the 'property' He has entrusted to us (v.14)? It is all that makes up the life of a believer, the revelation of the gospel and its outworking in our day to day living. Of this we are stewards, and God gives opportunities to each one of us according to our ability, to use our lives for Him. Notice how God takes each individual into account. Each one is given what he has the capacity to use (v.15), and his capacity will increase as he uses what he has received.

The servants entrusted with five and two talents had both used what was given to them and gained one hundred per cent (vs. 20, 22). They are both invited to enter into the joy of their master (vs.21,23). The servants entrusted with one talent, which the master knew he was able to use, preferred to do nothing. He harboured a wrong idea of his master's character and used this as an excuse for his laziness (vs.24, 25). The talent was taken from him and given to one who would use it faithfully (v. 28).

The principle the parable teaches is summed up in v. 29. God rewards His people according to their faithfulness, with greater opportunities of service, opportunities probably in the world to come as well as in life here. Let us ask the Lord to make us more faithful stewards of His property in using the talents He has entrusted to us.

Matt. 25. 15; Matt. 25. 21; Matt. 25. 29; 1 Pet. 4. 10; 1 Cor. 4. 1

Heaven and Hell

THE FINALITY OF JUDGEMENT

July 21   Reading: Hebrews 9. 23-28

The whole of the letter to the Hebrews is a commentary on the completeness and finality of the work of our Lord. In the present passage the writer shows how the eternal destiny of all has been settled through the one sacrifice of the perfect Son of God. Men live once, and die once, so final judgement is made according to the obedience of faith or the disobedience of one lifetime. The work of the cross has accomplished all that is necessary to make final and eternal redemption possible.

Hebrews takes us back to the Old Testament sacrifices which were symbols of the one true sacrifice of our Lord. The means of worship in Old Testament times, the tabernacle and all it contained as well as the people and the priests themselves had to be cleansed through sacrifice (Lev. 16). But Christ has not entered any earthly tabernacle or temple, but heaven itself. His sacrifice has a sanctifying effect upon heaven itself (v. 23). Such is its worth.

The entrance of our Lord into the presence of God was to bring us too into God's presence (v.24). Faith in Jesus does not merely bring us into a relationship with some earthly organization or system, but into a relationship with God Himself, a relationship which can never be broken. A rejection of the saving work of Christ, on the other hand, is a rejection of a relationship with God which can never be retrieved.

The High Priest in Old Testament times had to enter yearly into the holy place to offer the blood of the sacrifice (v.25). To the ritual of the tabernacle there was no end, but something which is really effective does not need to be done over again. The very repetition of the levitical sacrifices and offerings was proof of their ineffectiveness. But Christ was offered once to bear the sins of many (v. 28). His was a sacrifice which needs no repetition, a sacrifice which demands a response from all men of acceptance or final rejection.

Let us thank God for the perfect finished work of the cross of Calvary, and let us pray for others to accept that work for themselves.

Heb. 9. 24; Heb. 9. 25; Heb. 9. 26; Heb. 9. 27; Heb. 9. 28

Heaven and Hell

DAN

July 22   Reading: Gen. 49. 16-18

The word Dan means judgement, and Dan with the tribe that took his name were, like all men, subject to the judgement of God. Dan was one of Jacob's twelve sons, the elder of the two born to Bilhah, Rachel's maidservant (Gen. 30. 5-6). Gen. 49 records the final words of Jacob to his sons before he died. His words to Dan could hardly be called a blessing. He calls him a serpent and a viper (v.17). Later on Moses, in blessing the tribes of Israel, speaks of Dan as 'a lion's whelp, that leaps forth from Bashan' (Deut. 33.22). Apparently both Dan and his progeny were noted for their aggressiveness.

The book of the Revelation speaks of these sealed by God out of the tribes of Israel (Rev. 7. 7-8), but the tribe of Dan is not mentioned. We do not know why the name of Dan is omitted, but one of the early church leaders, a man called Irenaeus, believed it was because the antichrist would come from the tribe of Dan. He based his belief on the words of Jeremiah 8.16.

The one great man who emerged from the tribe of Dan was Samson, the judge of Israel (Jud. 13. 2, 24). Samson's character, however, was hardly a credit to the tribe to which he belonged. The aggression which marked the tribe was very obvious in Samson himself, and the Danites reputation as it appears from the book of Judges is an unsavoury one (Jud. 18).

There were godly individuals within Dan such as Manoah and his wife, Samson's parents, but it is difficult to find much good to say about Dan himself or the tribe as a whole. Whether they were total failures or not we do not know. But one thing we do know is that God the Judge of all the earth will do right, and He will judge them in justice and mercy.

Let us not judge others, but remember that we ourselves,as believers, will one day stand before the judgement seat of Christ.

Gen. 18. 25; Job 10. 14; Ps. 50. 6; Ps. 75. 7; Heb. 12. 22-23

Christian Witness

THE WITNESS OF PERSONAL LIFE

July 23   Reading: Colossians 1. 1-14

Paul had never visited Colosse when he wrote this letter, but he took a deep interest in all of God's people, and had a deep sense of his oneness with them. This introductory passage falls into two main sections, vs. 1-8 is a thanksgiving, and vs. 9-14 is a prayer. It is plain throughout that the Colossians commended their Lord not only by the faith they professed, but by the lives they lived. We see this at the very beginning of the chapter where Paul thanks God 'because we have heard of your faith in Christ Jesus and of the love which you have for all the saints' (v.4).

The Christian life means loyalty to Christ and love to men. It is not enough to say that we have faith. True faith makes our hearts go out to others and should impart a quality of life that is a testimony to the reality of the gospel. Vs. 5-8 are a summary of what the gospel is and does. It is truth (v. 5). It deals in certainities, and the Christian should know what he believes. The gospel gives a hope (v. 5), a sense of aim and purpose, something so lacking in our world today, but something which is vital to real life. The gospel bears fruit (v.6). No man can truly have faith in Christ and understand the gospel, and remain exactly as he was before. The gospel has a transforming power which changes self-centered living to Christ-centered living. The gospel is also a life of constant learning (v.7). The child of God should always be entering into a deeper understanding and appreciation of his faith, as the Colossians were through Epaphras and other servants of God.

Paul's prayer for the Colossians (vs. 9-14) could be summed up as a prayer that they might know God's will, and a prayer that they might have a power to perform it. The phrase 'spiritual wisdom' and the word 'understanding' in v.9 are very important. Spiritual wisdom means a grasp of basic spiritual principles. Understanding means knowledge how to apply these principles to daily living. This leads to right conduct (v. 10) which is an indispensable part of the Christian witness to the world around.

Let us pray that we 'may be filled with the knowledge of his will in all spiritual wisdom and understanding' that our lives might be a testimony to God's glory.

Col. 1. 3-4; Col. 1. 5-6; Col. 1.11; Col. 1. 12; Col. 1. 13-14

205

THE WITNESS OF WORDS

July 24   Reading: James 3. 1-12

James is here concerned to show us that an essential witness to our Christian faith is the way we discipline our words. James 3 is so straightforwaded that it hardly needs any comment. James uses simple illustrations which graphically illustrate the tremendous power of words to edify or to destroy. A horse's bit (v.3); a ship's rudder (v.4); a little flame or spark (v. 5). All are small apparently insignificant things which can be used to great effect.

"The tongue is a fire" (v.6). We can bring discredit to the name of the Lord by a word. Or the character of a person can be destroyed by a word used in an apparently innocent way. How often do people cloak a piece of malicious gossip as a pious request for prayer? "I want to tell you this in confidence, just that you might pray about it." How dangerous words can be. No wonder James takes so much pain to explain their devastating effects, and show that the way we discipline our words is such an important and essential part of our spiritual witness. What we say is really an indication of what is within.

There is a sense in which none of us can, in our own strength, discipline our words as we ought. "No human being can tame the tongue" (v. 8). Yet, as we have just said, our words give expression to what is within us. "Does a spring pour forth from the same opening fresh water and brackish? Can a fig tree, my brethren, yield olives, or a grapevine figs? No more can salt water yield fresh" (vs. 11-12). When the source of our life has been changed the words which emerge from the new source will be changed words.

The need for our faith to be revealed in the words we use means a constant committing of our thoughts and attitudes to God. To the extent we do this our words will truly manifest the faith we profess. The world around us discerns our faith more clearly by the words we use than by any other means. May the Lord help us to glorify Him in what we say.

James 3. 1; James 3. 5; James 3. 6; James 3. 11; James 3. 12

Christian Witness

THE WITNESS OF RELATIONSHIPS

July 25   Reading: Colossians 3. 18 4.6

Christian character can be seen in the way we relate to other people. We cannot live our individual lives in total isolation. Even were we able to cut ourselves off from all unbelivers, we would still face the problems of relationships within our own families and households.

Paul here shows how a Christian witness should be revealed on different levels of relationship, between husbands and wives (3.18-19), parents and children (3. 20-21), masters and servants (3. 22-4. 1), among fellow believers (4. 2-4), with unbelievers (4. 5-6). These five areas of relationship cover every aspect of fellowship and contact with our fellow men.

Paul stresses the fact of mutual obligation in all Christian relationships. A Christian relationship is never the domination of one person over another. It is true that people have duties towards one another, but they also have obligations. Children should obey their parents (v. 26), but parents have a duty not to make unreasonable demands upon their children (v.21). It is so easy to demand that others should fulfil what we imagine to be their obligations to us, and at the same time have no concern about fulfilling our own obligations to them. When this happens relationships breaks down, and the result is disgrace to the name of the Lord.

A believer should be a conscientious workman (v. 23). This is an important aspect of a Christian testimony. In our modern world so many people try to evade their duty rather than fulfil it. A Christian's master is the Lord, and everything he does should be done as unto Him.

Believers should pray for one another, not that they be released from the difficulties that are common to life, but that they should be a witness in them (4. 2-4). Finally, we have an obligation to be gracious and humble in our relationship with outsiders (vs.5-6). All our contact with unbelievers is an opportunity to show them Christ by the way we live. Let us pray that our relationships will be a testimony which the Lord will use to bring others to Himself.

Col. 3. 18-19; Col. 3. 20.21; Col. 3.23-24; Col. 4. 2-3; Col. 4. 5-6

Christian Witness

CORPORATE WITNESS

July 26   Reading: Colossians 1. 15-29

The most wonderful of all Christian relationships is the relationship between members of the family of God in the church. Paul sees the purposes
of God all culminating in the church (v. 18). The church is the work of
our Lord's reconciling ministry on the cross (vs. 21-22) in which people
who were estranged from one another have been brought together. How
sad it is to find a practical denial of our Lord's reconciling work in enmity
and jealousy among those who profess to know and love Christ. How often
traditional prejudices linger on in the lives of believers to destroy their witness
to Christ as a church.

The reconcilation of men and women in the church is a foretaste of
a much wider reconciliation still. Paul says that through Christ God is going 'to reconcile to himself all things, whether on earth or in heaven, making peace by the blood of his cross' (v. 20). We cannot comprehend fully
all that is meant by this, but it must mean at least that the work of the cross
touches all creation and God is moving ultimately to a redeemed world.
The wonderful possibility of this should be seen in the witness of the church.
How tragic it is when the church presents before the world a picture of
jealousy and strife instead of this picture of glorious hope through Christ.
The world should be able to see in the church a 'hope of glory' (v. 27),
something that it sees nowhere else.

The church is the body of Christ (v. 24). Christ is the Head (v. 18).
As the body expresses the thoughts and dictates of the mind, so the church
is the organism through which Christ acts and demonstrates His character
and will to the world. He is the guide without which the church cannot
know the truth or act aright. If the church is truly the body of Christ it will
have a witness of holiness (v. 22), so Paul couples the glory of the church's
witness and privilges with a warning, "Provided that you continue in the
faith, stable and steadfast" (v. 23).

Let us ask the Lord to make us more aware of our privilege and responsibility to be a witness to Him as a church.

Col. 1. 18; Col. 1. 19-20; Col. 1. 21-22; Col. 1. 23; Col. 1. 27

Christian Witness

THE RESPONSIBILITY OF WITNESS

July 27   Reading: Matthew 13. 51-52

This is the last of a series of eight parables the first four of which were spoken to a great crowd (vs. 2-3), and the latter four to the disciples alone (v. 36). We call them the parables of the kingdom because they all deal with the same subject, the kingdom of God, the purpose which a sovereign God is working out on the earth in the age in which we are at present living.

It was a great privilege for the disciples to be made the confidants of our Lord, but every privilege brings its responsibilities, and the point of the parable of the householder is to emphasise to the disciples and to us the responsibilities that devolve upon us in the light of the revelation of the gospel we have received.

The parables contains two words of great authority, 'scribe' and 'householder'. The order of the Scribes dates back probably to the time of Ezra. The Scribes were the interpreters of the Word of God. They mediated God's Word to the world just as Moses mediated His law to the children of Israel (Matt. 23. 2). In the same way God has made His people today mediators of His gospel to a world in need. We are His scribes who 'have been trained for the kingdom of heaven' (v. 52), and He has given to us the responsibility of being a witness to the gospel. God has chosen no other way for the spreading of His Word.

A householder in the society of our Lord's time was a much more powerful figure than he is in most societies today. He was a king in his own right. Under his control were the resources to meet the needs of an extensive household, and he had the responsibility to use these resources wisely. It is a staggering thought, but it is true, that God's people alone have the resources to meet the needs of the world. The modern world is confronted with problems with which it does not know how to cope. Basically these problems are spiritual, and they can be solved only through the gospel of the Lord Jesus Christ. If we do not share what we have with the world around us its needs will never be met. May the Lord make us more alive to our responsibility to witness for Him.

Matt. 13. 52; Ezra 7. 10; Matt. 23. 34; Luke 10. 2-3; Luke 12. 32

Christian Witness

THE COMPULSION OF WITNESS

July 28   Reading: 1 Corinthians 9. 15-18

When we read the writings of the Old Testament prophets or the experiences of the New Testament apostles, we cannot but be struck by the sense of compulsion they had to proclaim the Word God had entrusted to them. Nowhere is this more clear than in the life of the apostle Paul. We do not know much about the early life of Paul, but he was obviously a man of much natural gift and education. He was probably from a wealthy background and could have made a name for himself in the world of his day, but he rejected the security this would have provided to become a preacher of the gospel.

What did Paul get out of preaching the gospel? What was his 'ground for boasting' (v. 16). Simply this, that he received no material benefit whatever. The motive of his ministery was not a material one. A sense of necessity was laid upon him which he could not resist (v. 16). He simply had to preach the gospel. "Woe to me if I do not preach the gospel", he says (v.16). This does not mean that he feared the punishment of God if he denied his calling. He was not driven on by fear of dire consequences. In fact he knew full well that his following Christ was likely to lead him into difficulties and hardships which he could avoid by being less zealous in his testimony. Paul was driven to preach the gospel by the compulsion of his love for the Lord Jesus Christ. The way would have been open for him to make a living from his preaching, but he shuns the very thought (v. 17). He was not in a business looking for pecuniary reward. He was a man entrusted with a commission who was bound to fulfil it whatever the consequences might be.

Right up to the present time there have been people who have aspired to preach the gospel for material gain. Their ministry has never carried, nor ever can carry conviction, because they lack the spirit of compulsion which comes from a deep sense of love and loyalty to Christ. This was what made Paul's preaching so vital and effective. Let us ask the Lord for a greater sense of urgency in our witness for Him.

1 Cor. 9. 15; 1 Cor. 9. 16; 1 Cor. 9. 17; 1 Cor. 9. 18; Jer. 20.9

210

Christian Witness

AMOS

Reading: Amos 3.1-8

The kingdom established by David was divided after the death of his son Solomon into the kingdom of Israel in the north, and the kingdom of Judah in the south. Amos belonged to Tekoa, a town about six miles south of Bethlehem in Judah. He was a 'herdsman, and a dresser of sycamore trees' (7.14). He did not come from a class of people from which many prophets came, but he knew it was the Lord who had called him from tending the flocks to take His message to the northern kingdom in the reign of Jeroboam II.

Amos provoked the jealousy of Amaziah the priest who looked upon him as an upstart and a trouble maker. Amaziah accuses him before the king of subversion, and in contemptuous words orders him back to Judah from where he had come (7. 10-13). Let Amos go back to his own country where people will pay him for his prophecies, but let him not think he will make any headway in Israel. Little did Amaziah realize the type of man to whom he was speaking. Amos was no professional seer playing upon the credulity of the people for his own livelihood. He was a man living and speaking under the authority of God with a message that could not be silenced.

Our reading is Amos' authentification of his message. It begins with a plea to 'hear this word that the Lord has spoken' (v. 1), and its ends with a final affirmation that 'the Lord God has spoken' (v. 8). Although Amos is prophesying within the northern kingdom, his message is for all the people of God (v. 1). God's people are uniquely privileged (v.3) and, therefore, they have unique responsibilities to live in a way which is honouring to the Lord (v.3). Let them never think that their privileges are permission to live as they please. Because they are His people, God punishes them for their iniquities.

Then follows a series of illustrations showing the inevitable law of cause and effect in God's dealings. It applies even to Amos' sense of divine unction to proclaim God's message faithfully to His people (v.8). Let us ask God for a sense of unction like Amos, and a like faithfulness in sounding forth His word.

Amos 3. 2; Amos 3. 8; Amos 5. 14; Amos 5. 6; Col. 1. 28

The Church

THE CHURCH UNIVERSAL

July 30   Reading: Ephesians 1. 11-23

The letter to the Ephesians emphasises the pre-eminence of the risen and glorified Lord (vs. 20,21). The church is always subordinate to Him. However important the church may be, we must always remember this fact, because we can only see the church in its true perspective when we view it in its relation to Christ. If we lose sight of the supremacy of the Lord of the church, the danger is that we deify the church itself, or our conception of the church.

The church can be viewed from two main aspects, the church universal and the church local. We are at present concerned with the first of these. The Greek word for church is 'ecclesia' which means a 'called out people'. In its broadest sense, the church is the company of all true believers in Christ, including those who have passed on and those who are still living, all past, present and future who are 'in Christ'.

The epistle to the Ephesians was probably a circular letter sent to many of the churches in Paul's day. It does not deal with local circumstances, but emphasises the unique relationship into which all of God's people are drawn with Him and with one another. The church is an organism rather than an organization (vs. 22-23). This is true of both the universal and local church, and is the reason why the New Testament lays down principles but not detailed instructions for the church's practical living.

It is important that all believers should recognise that they belong to a universal church, and be willing to accept the practical implications of this fact. 1. We are one with all saints (v. 15) and must strive to express that oneness. 2. The church is called to holiness (v. 13) which we are bound to express in our relationship with all who truly love the Lord. 3. The Lord has 'a glorious inheritance in the saints' (v.18) without distinctions of race or background. 4. The life of the church is based on 'the word of truth' (v. 13) in which we must always be growing (v. 17-18). Let us ask the Lord to give us a greater sense of our need of ALL his people.

Eph. 1. 12; Eph. 1. 13-14; Eph. 1. 16-17; Eph. 1. 18; Eph. 1. 19-20

The Church

THE CHURCH LOCAL

July 31   Reading: Matthew 18. 15-20

The word 'church' is used only twice in the Gospels, first in Matt. 16. 18, and again in Matt. 18. 17. On both occasions it was used by our Lord Himself, and evidently looks to the future when the church as it is later revealed in the New Testament should actually come into being.

In His mention of the church the Lord lays down a very important principle. We could say that every consideration of the church must go back to the words of v. 20,"Where two or three are gathered in my name, there am I in the midst of them". The authority of the previous verses depends on this fact, the presence of the Lord in the midst of His people and their subjection to Him. The local church is the church universal in miniature. The New Testament never loses sight of this fact. It deals with the greatness of the universal church, but also brings it down to practical terms in the local assembly. And where the local church is the main subject for consideration, the fact that it is representative of something much greater is never lost sight of.

The character of the universal church is dependent on the character of the local church. The fall has separated man from man, but the risen victorious Lord has enabled His people to live together in harmony. The influence of His holiness provides the great incentive for holiness in His people. He who humbled Himself to the death of the cross destroys the pride which would bind the fellowship of the church to social, racial or other distinctions. He who is the truth is able to establish His people in the truth and lead them on into deeper depths of truth.

The all sufficiency of the ever present Lord amongst His people wherever they are gathered in His name has far reaching implications. One of the most important of these is the independence of each local congregation. While the local church should always value the fellowship of other believers and recognise its need of them, there is within each local congregation of believers the potential to meet its needs, because the risen Lord, the all sufficient One, is in the midst. Let us pray that we may learn to know more of the power of His presence in the fellowship of the local church.

Matt. 16. 18; Matt. 18. 20; Zeph. 3. 5; Zeph. 3. 9; Acts 13. 2

The Church

RELATIONSHIPS WITHIN THE CHURCH

August 1   Reading: 2 Peter 1. 1-11

Peter does not actually mention the church in this passage, but much of what he has to say has to do with relationships among the people of God, and this, of course, finds its fullest expression within the church.

God's purpose for His people is that they might 'become partakers of the divine nature' (v. 4). Notice that the Bible nowhere tells us that we have already received the divine nature. We have received the divine life, but 'nature' is a word which denotes a settled disposition, and when used of God that means life at its fullest and maturest, devoid of the limitations we as human beings now possess. To the end that we might become partakers of the divine nature, God is working in us through the relationships of the church.

What exactly this means Peter explains in the picture of vs. 5-7. There are eight characteristics mentioned in these verses, and they can be divided into three. 1. Faith. 2. Virtue, knowledge, stedfastness, self-control, godliness. 3. Brotherly affection and love. Faith is the foundation of all else. In faith we go back to a personal relationship of total dependence upon God and subjection to His ways. We recognise Him as Lord of our individual lives and Lord of the church.

The next five characteristics are concerned with personal spiritual character. The spirituality of the church can be no greater than the spirituality of the individuals who compose it. A person lacking in virtue, ignorant, unstable, undisciplined, godless, can have little to contribute to the revelation of our Lord's character in the church. We must be personally anxious to grow in the knowledge of Christ and to live under His control. This, however, cannot be done in isolation. No virtue can be expressed or seen to exist at all apart from our relationship with other people, so in the last two characteristics Peter mentions he brings us into the realm of fellowship.

Here lies the importance of relations in the church. It is through 'brotherly affection' (v. 7) concern for and unity with the Lord's people, and love (v. 7) a concern for a lost world, that we grow and move towards an expression of the divine nature. Let us ask the Lord to teach us through our relationships with others, that we may become more like Him.

2 Pet. 1. 3; 2 Pet. 1. 4; 2 Pet. 1. 5-7; 2 Pet. 1. 8; 2 Pet. 1. 10

The Church

ONE NEW MAN

August 2   Reading: Ephesians 2. 11-12

The New Testament uses a number of different figures to describe the nature of the church. Each one of them highlights a particular facet of truth. In v. 15 Paul speaks of the church as 'one new man', a figure which he uses again in his letter to the Colossians.

To the Jewish mind the world was divided into two classes of people, the Jews and the Gentiles. Between Jew and Gentile there was a 'great gulf fixed'. Paul describes it in v. 14 a 'dividing wall of hostility'. Of all the things which separate man from man, none is as decisive as that which separated Jew from Gentile.

In Christ Jesus the Gentile has been drawn nigh to God (v. 13) as has the Jew. The result is peace where there was enmity, and the breaking down of the dividing wall (v. 14). This itself is a remarkable achievement, the bringing of an unbridgable gap, but the work of the cross has gone still further. God has created 'in himself one new man in place of the two, so making peace' (v. 15). God has, in the church, created one great new personality. Neither Jew nor Gentile any longer exists. They have been fused into something entirely new. This is the wonder of the new man, the church. No human prejudices can survive the work of the cross, if the cross is allowed to do its work. That is why the existence within the church of caste or social distinctions of the past is a denial of the very work of redemption.

A man, of course, is not merely body, but the life also to which the body gives expression. The new man, the church, is not just an outward form. It is dependent upon the vitality of the Spirit within. It can never be too strongly emphasized that the imposition of a pattern, or the mere gathering of people together, does not bring the church into being. A church cannot be organized, it has to be born by the work of the Spirit of God and then grow into an ever increasing likeness of its heavenly Creator.

Let us thank the Lord for making us part of the new man, and let us pray that, in our life together as His people, we may grow more and more into His likeness.

Eph. 2. 15-16; Eph. 2. 17; Eph. 2. 18; Eph. 2. 19; Eph. 2.20

The Church

THE BODY OF CHRIST

August 3   Reading: 1 Corinthians 12. 12-26

The figures used of the church in the New Testament have an application both to the universal and the local church. Paul says to the Corinthians, "The body is one" (v. 12). Obviously he is referring not to one single congregation, but to all who, by the work of the Spirit, have been united to Christ (v. 13). We must never forget this even though we are living in an age of ecclesiastical confusion. Every true child of God is part of the body of Christ, and to say or do anything which denies our need of him is to do despite to the church and to Christ its Head.

A body, however, is a practical, functioning organism, and it is on the level of the local church that we should first see and experience its outworking. The main lessons to be learned from the figure of the body are its unity in diversity, and the dependence of the members one upon the other. It is significant that Paul does not emphasize the nourishment of the body. Natural man is concerned to nourish himself, even at the expense of others. The believer is concerned for the nourishment of the body as a whole under the control of Christ the Head.

The body is a wonderful picture of unity in diversity. All Christians are not equally gifted, nor are all able to fulfil the same function, but everyone has a function chosen for him by God (v. 18) which contributes to the common good. Paul carefully stresses the importance of the 'less honourable' members (v. 22-24). They not only contribute humble service to the church, but have a vital ministry in the realm of relationships. In the church the rich learn to relate to the poor, the poor to the rich; the intellectual to the little educated, the high-born to the humble and vice versa. All are vitally dependent upon one another.

Mutual dependence means mutual responsibility to develop the function God has given, and to fulfil it so that the expression of the church with which we are linked locally should demonstrate the concern of the Lord for His people and their concern for one another. We also have the responsibility of concern that the body today suffers so much through division and dissension (vs. 25-26). Only when we are concerned will the Lord be able to use us to bring healing. Let us pray that we may more worthily fulfil our part in the church which is His body.

1 Cor. 12. 17; 1 Cor. 12. 18; 1 Cor. 12. 19-20; 1 Cor. 12. 21; 1 Cor. 12. 22-23

The Church

THE HOUSE OF GOD

Reading: 1 Peter 2. 1-10

The first obvious fact about the House of God is that it consists of people, not of bricks and mortar. The importance of buildings in the life of the church is often over-emphasized. There may be practical advantages and even a necessity to have a permanent meeting place, but if there are no people imbued with the life of the Spirit of God, there can be no church, however beautiful a building may be, or however many people gather within its walls.

When Peter wrote this letter he was almost certainly thinking of his conversation with the Lord recorded in Matt. 16. Peter's name means a little piece of rock, and our Lord uses a play upon words in speaking to him. What He says is this, "You are a little piece of rock, and on this rock (referring to Himself, and using a slightly different word which means a great rock), I will build my church" (Matt. 16.18). The significance of our Lord's words was that Peter and Himself were the same material, hewn, as it were, from the same quarry. The church is composed only of people who are of the same material, that is, have the same life as Christ. Christ the living stone is rejected by men (v. 4, 8). The standards of our Lord are strange and unacceptable to a fallen world, but these standards should be seen in practical operation in the House of God with Christ as its Head (v. 9).

The House of God should be a demonstration of the unity of the Lord's people. A scattered pile of bricks is not a house though one brick looks very much like another. Similarly, a scattered company of regenerated individuals, all claiming that they are one in Christ, is not a church. They must be 'fitly framed together', each conrtibuting his part in the spiritual building, and conscious of the bond of life and mutual responsibility which binds all of them together.

The church grows in its capacity to express divine life. It is being 'built into a spiritual house' (v. 5). There is nothing automatic about God's expressing Himself through the church. It is conditioned upon the church's spiritual development and growth in understanding of divine things. Let us seek the Lord that, in knowing Him more fully we may contribute worthily to His house.

1 Pet. 2. 5; 1 Pet. 2. 7; 1 Pet. 2. 8; 1 Pet. 2. 9; 1 Pet. 2. 10

The Church

ANANIAS AND SAPPHIRA

August 5   Reading: Acts 5. 1-11

The judgement of Ananias and Sapphira has seemed to some to be excessively severe, but we must remember that the church was in its infancy, and it was important that standards of holiness should be established at the outset. The sin of Ananias was the sin of hypocrisy, something that could have been fatal to the church's very existence. If God's people are not judged today with physical death for the same sin, it does not mean that hypocrisy is any less a sin against God. It shows only that the church is or should be sufficiently mature to deal with its own affairs in the fear of God without demanding God's direct intervention.

We are not passing an opinion on the eternal destiny of Ananias and Sapphira. It may well be that many of their modern counterparts are in spiritual darkness though their bodies live on. The incident serves to show that the church, even in its earliest days, was not a company of perfect people. The fact that Luke includes the story in his narrative is a proof of the honesty of the Bible. He refuses to idealize the church. Writing to the Corinthians Paul shows the human involvement in the building of the church. "We are God's fellow workers... Like a skilled master builder I laid a foundation, and another man is building upon it. Let each man take care how he builds upon it" (1 Cor. 3. 9-10). Wherever there is the hand of man there is imperfection and the possibility of failure. We must recognize this and be prepared to admit failure and deal with it when it arises.

The incident of Ananias and Sapphira also illustrates the reality and practical implications of the Spirit's presence within the church. The Spirit's presence demands a holy respect for the Lord and His standards. It is a very serious matter to make light of the things of God, or to try to manipulate His standards to our own ends. The church is meant to be a revelation to the world of what God is like. When man makes it a spectacle to the world of His own perfidity, the only end he can expect is judgement.

Let us ask the Lord to help us learn the lessons He wants to teach us from His judgement of Ananias and Sapphira.

Acts 5. 3; Acts 5. 4; Acts 5. 11; Ps. 93. 5; Heb. 10. 31

Money and Giving

CONTENTMENT

Reading: 1 Timothy 6. 3-10

A common feature of the Greek world of Paul's day was the wandering philosopher who attracted great crowds to his lectures and made a lucrative income. It is not surprising that their religious counterparts should be found in the early days of the church, self-styled teachers and preachers who made the gospel their means of livelihood. Paul refers to such in vs. 3-5. The motive of these people was money, and in contrast to their attitude Paul sets forth the Christian view.

"There is great gain in godliness with contentment" (v. 6). The word Paul uses for 'contentment' means an internal sense of sufficiency which is not dependent on external things and outward circumstances. This does not mean a fatalistic type of resignation to impoverished circumstances which paralyzes all initiative and is content to live in squalor. It is a Christian duty for a believer to seek to provide adequately for his family. Paul, however, is pointing to certain basic and important factors.

The first is that material plenty does not have the power to bring happiness. There is no special virtue in having insufficient money even for food and clothing, but the desire for money is something much deeper than the concern to supply basic needs. It has its origin in the false idea, which some people would not dare to express, that if only we acquire things we will be happy. This is completely against the teaching of the Bible. The rich countries of the world are a clear warning of the emptiness of purely material standards. Some of the richest people in the world are some of the unhappiest. Many of the modern young people who roam the world with practically nothing have run away from rich homes because life was empty and meaningless.

A second factor to which Paul points is the need to concentrate on what is of lasting value. Whatever we have in this world will be left behind when we die (v. 7). Real life comes only from a personal relationship with God which is eternal, and which alone is the foundation of true personal relationships with others. Let us ask the Lord to help us seek those things which are above.

1 Tim. 6. 6; 1 Tim. 6. 7; 1 Tim. 6. 8; 1 Tim. 6. 9; 1 Tim. 6. 10.

Money and Giving

THE LOVE OF MONEY

August 7   Reading: Luke 12. 13-21

How many disputes there are over money, even amongst those who profess to be the Lord's people. It is a sad pointer to the power of money and the amount of love of money which exists among those who should know so much better. This parable shows the meaning of life to a world which thinks almost wholly in terms of material possessions. There is no suggestion that the rich man used fraudulent means to advance his business. He was diligent, successful and worldly-wise, but God did not enter his thinking. The tragedy was he was completely obsessed by self and selfish gain, "My crops... my barns... my grain... my goods... my soul" (vs. 17-19). The stark fact is that he was, as God told him, a fool (v. 20).

The Bible does not say that money is the root of all evil, but, "The LOVE of money is the root of all evils" (1 Tim. 6. 10). This applies equally to rich and poor. The person who has little can love money just as greedily as the person who has much. The love of money is something which can never be satisfied. The only aim the rich fool had was to eat, drink and be merry (v. 19), but he postponed it for another day. For the present he was too busy making money or making plans to conserve what he had. He was under the illusion that the more wealth he amassed, the more secure he would be, but money cannot buy the important things of life. It cannot buy love, and it cannot save from death, either by prolonging life in this world or securing a place in the next.

The love of money fixes a man's thoughts and concerns upon himself. Others may suffer that he might become rich, but it matters nothing to him. Very often the love of money propels people into sin, thievery, deceit, gambling, or it drives people to a frenzy of effort which ruins their health both mental and physical. Worst of all, it drives people to seek their own ways instead of the ways of God. Paul says, "Through this craving... some have wandered away from the faith and pierced their hearts with many pangs" (1 Tim. 6.10).

Let us pray that the Lord will save us from the love of money.

Luke 12. 15; Luke 12. 22; Luke 12.23; Luke 12.24; Heb. 13.3

Money and Giving

THE SPIRIT OF GIVING

August 8 Reading: Philippians 4. 14-20

A special bond of affection existed between Paul and the believers in Philippi, and it seems that from the very beginning the Philippian church entered into the privilege of Christian giving. Paul speaks of gifts he had received from them in Thessalonica (v. 16) which was the city he had visited immediately after being in Philippi (Acts 17.1). That was about fifteen years before Paul wrote this letter. Now from his imprisonment in Rome he has further occasion to thank the Philippians for their concern for him (v. 18).

Giving and receiving go together (v. 15). Paul had apparently not only received from the Philippians, but had given to them as well. The phrase used is a common one referring solely to pecuniary transactions. Paul, though an apostle and receiving from others, felt that he too had the privilege and responsibility to give. There is, however, something much more to Christian giving than human generosity. Paul calls it a 'fragrant offering, a sacrifice acceptable and pleasing to God' (v. 18). The Philippians were giving not in the hope of receiving something in return, but in their devotion to God and to His servant.

The Philippians did, of course, receive something in return. Giving in material things as unto the Lord is always a spiritual blessing to the giver and to the receiver alike. Paul was thankful for the Philippians' concern for him (v. 14), but more than in the value of the material gift he rejoiced in the love that prompted it, and in the indication it was of the Philippians' spiritual health (v. 17).

The spirit of giving is part of the life in Christ. The spirit of grasping after whatever we can get is the spirit of the world. Earlier in this same letter Paul speaks of the extent to which our Lord gave Himself (2.5-8). He is the eternal example of the spirit that should characterize His people. Because He gave all, we too have the privilege and responsibility of giving. Let us ask God to impart to us a greater spirit of giving.

Phil 4. 14-15; Phil. 4. 16-17; Phil. 4. 18; Phil. 4. 19; Phil. 4. 20

Money and Giving

THE RESPONSIBILITY OF SHARING

August 9   Reading: 2 Corinthians 9.1-15

The believers in Judea were in considerable material need. One of Paul's missions among the churches elsewhere was to receive an offering for their needy Judean brethren. Paul mentions the offering in this chapter (v.1). At the same time he takes the opportunity of setting down some principles of Christian giving. The responsibility of sharing what God has given us extends to the whole spiritual family. Some churches are much more prosperous financially than others, and it is their duty to share what they have with churches which are poorer. Rich city congregations should share with poorer country congregations.

Paul likens giving to sowing seed. The person who gives little will receive little in return. Not that giving should be motivated by material gain. That would be the very denial of Christian giving. The reward of giving is the blessing of others and the glory of God. Giving should not be done sparingly (v. 6). The believer should not calculate how little he can give, but how much he can give. Giving should be 'not reluctantly' (v.7). If we grudge every paisa we give, it means that we have not learned the spirit of Christian giving. Giving should be not 'under compulsion' (v.7). We do not give merely because of a compelling need which demands attention. Christian giving recognizes needs which do not clamour for publicity. Giving should be with liberality and with cheerfulness (v. 6-7).

God is able to multiply the resources of the giver (v. 8) not for his own selfish use, but in order that he may give the more. The potential of a seed is out of all propotion to its size. Many churches have discovered that when they give to God He enables them to give still more. Giving results in spiritual blessing to ourselves and to those to whom we give. Giving is a proof of Christian grace which binds God's people together (vs. 11-14).

Paul concludes by thanking God for His 'inexpressible gift'. This gift can only be the gift of His Son. It is only through Christ that men can really learn to give selflessly. Natural man's whole inclination is to get what he can for himself. It is the grace of God alone which changes this inclination. Let us ask the Lord to increase our sense of responsibility to give.

2 Cor. 9. 6; 2 Cor. 9. 7; 2 Cor. 9. 8; 2 Cor. 9. 9; 2 Cor. 9. 10

Money and Giving

GIVING TO THE WORK OF GOD

August 10   Reading: 3 John 1-8

The subject of the first part of this short letter is the responsibility of giving to the work of God. John is writing to a brother called Gaius who apparently occupied a position of authority in a local church. Gaius was well known for his love and his concern for the truth. He was a man of mature and balanced Christian character. John commends him for his spirit of hospitality and for his zeal in supporting the work of God (v. 5).

There were many false teachers abroad during the early years of the church's history, but those of whom John here speaks as worthy of support are clearly men with a genuine call from God to preach the Word. The word translated 'set out'(v.7) means a deliberate moving out on a mission, not the aimless wandering of someone trying to make merchandize of the gospel. The motive is expressed as 'for his sake', a genuine concern for the glory of the Lord. Another characteristic of these preachers was their refusal to seek help from unbelievers. What John says is literally 'taking nothing from the Gentiles' (v. 7). They regarded it as a matter of principle not to be supported by the heathen.

John presents the support of the work of the gospel as an obligation upon God's people. There are many causes to which a Christian MAY give, but the furtherance of the gospel is one to which he OUGHT to give. The principle which John sets forth is clear. The onus in spreading the Word of God lies squarely upon the Lord's people. The world will not and should not be asked to give financial support to spiritual work. The sincere preacher of the Word is engaged in a task which demands all his physical and mental energy. Believers should consider it a privilege to support the ministry he brings as themselves benefitting from it, and they should consider it an equal privilege to support those who take the word of life to a world in need.

In supporting the work of God we become sharers in the ministry, or as John puts it 'fellow workers in the truth' (v. 8). Let us not neglect giving to the work of God. As God's children it is our obligation and our privilege to further the spread of the gospel.

3 John 3-4; 3 John 5-6; 3 John 7-8; 2 Cor. 2. 17; Gal. 6. 6

Money and Giving

GIVING OURSELVES

The spirit of the church in Macedonia (v. 1) must have rejoiced the heart of Paul. Though they were passing through 'a severe test of affliction' (v. 2), and suffered from 'extreme poverty' (v. 2), they overflowed in a wealth of liberality' (v. 2). They did not need to be urged to give. They gave to the point of real sacrifice (v. 3), with joy (v. 2), and pleaded for the opportunity of doing so (v. 4). The apostles had apparently suggested that they were too poor to give so much, but the believers would not hear of such a thing, so concerned were they to give to the Lord.

What lay behind this unostentatious giving where people, unmindful of their own poverty, were concerned about the poverty of their fellow believers? Paul tells us in v. 5, "First they gave themselves to the Lord and to us by the will of God". This was the secret. Unbelievers often find it impossible to understand why believers give to God's work and to God's people. They do not do it in the expectation that they will gain merit. They do not do it for some other material reward. They do not do it in the expectation of receiving respect or position. They gain nothing. Why should they give at all? The answer is that the motive of Christian giving lies in deep heart devotion to the Lord.

Sometimes it is sad to find even believers questioning the motives of their own brethren in giving. Very often this is an indication of the meagre spiritual devotion of those who doubt. There are people who give for selfish reasons. They imagine God will bless them for their giving as if God could be bribed. Or they give in an attempt to salve their own consciences for lack of personal obedience. Giving can never be used as a substitute for obeying the Lord.

Behind all truly Christian giving must lie the desire to give ourselves to the Lord and to one another. Paul trusted that the example of the churches in Macedonia in this respect would inspire the Corinthians to give themselves also afresh to the Lord. Let it inspire us to do the same.

2 Cor. 8. 1; 2 Cor. 8. 2; 2 Cor. 8. 3-4; 2 Cor. 8. 5; 2 Cor. 8.7

Money and Giving

BARZILLAI

Reading: 2 Samuel 19. 31-40

Fleeing from the rebellion of his son Absalom, David travelled across the Jordan river. He was in need of help which many would have feared to give lest the wrath of the unscrupulous Absalom descend upon them. Barzillai was one of the few who remained loyal and helped David and his men in their time of need (17. 27-29). Materially he had much to lose, for he was a rich man, but he was unconcerned about himself. He was concerned to use what he had in the service of God.

Here we see a wealthy man who held his wealth very lightly. He was not obsessed by his riches. He was more concerned to do what he knew to be right, and was content to leave what he had in the hands of God. This is the spirit of a true man of God. We should never be concerned what will happen if we are faithful to the Lord. We should be guided by what the Lord clearly shows to be right, and all else can be left confidently in His hands. God has called us to give ourselves and our means to Him. The consequences of doing so are his affair. Our responsibility is to be like Barzillai, faithful.

Absalom was defeated, and David naturally wished to honour the old man who had stood by him in his hour of trial. He wanted to take Barzillai back with him to Jerusalem where he could live in luxury for the rest of his days. Barzillai, however, refused the offer. He had not provided for David out of the hope of reward. It was reward enough for him that he had done his duty. He was incredulous at the thought that David should wish to honour him in such a way (v. 36). Nevertheless, he recommended Chimham to David's care (v. 37). We do not know who Chimham was, but he was a symbol of Barzillai's concern for others.

Later, David commends the sons of Barzillai to Solomon who was to occupy the throne after him (1 Kings 2.7). He had not forgotten his old friend's loyalty in his time of rejection. We too serve a rejected Lord and His cause. Let us give ourselves and of what we have to Him and to His people. We can safely leave the consequences in His hands. Let us ask the Lord to keep us faithful to Him.

Ps. 23. 1-2; Ps. 23. 3; Ps. 23. 4; Ps. 23. 5; Ps. 23. 6

The Ministry

THE MINISTRY OF CHRIST

August 13   Reading: Mark 9. 33-41

We cannot understand the Christian ministry unless we understand the ministry of Christ. All other ministry is subsidiary to His and derives its authority from Him. The real minister is always Christ, and men are but the channels through which He works. The New Testament applies to our Lord titles which we normally associate with the ministry of men. He is the Apostle (Heb. 3.1), a term used specifically of our Lord only once, but whose meaning, 'one who is sent', is applied to Him over and over again (v. 39). He is the 'Shepherd and Guardian of your souls' (1 Peter 2.25). He is the Teacher (Mark 5.35). Clearly the ministry of our Lord is the foundation of all other ministry.

Of special significance is the term 'servant'. Our Lord said to his disciples, "I am among you as one who serves" (Luke 22.27). This is the aspect of the ministry particularly illustrated in our reading, and it is basic. It separates the true Christian ministry from the power of human personality and the high-power methods with which it is often associated in these days. Whenever there is an emphasis on man and his methods there is a debasement of New Testament teaching. It may produce what is successful in the eyes of the world, but it will be a failure in building up the spiritual life of the churches and the people of God.

The disciples were very concerned with the human criteria of success, though their silence when our Lord questioned them seems to show that in their hearts they knew they were wrong (vs. 33-34). Jesus turns their thoughts in the opposite direction. He shows them that the criterion of a true ministry is lowly service (v.36), not authority. The greatest Christian privilege is to serve others, not to lord it over them.

The disciples' opposition to the man who was casting out demons in the Lord's name (v. 38) shows a common tendency. Servants of the Lord sometimes think they are a special elite with authority to command others. Jesus rebukes the disciples' intolerance. We must never discourage service done sincerely in the name of the Lord. Let us ask the Lord to give us a true spirit of subjection to Him.

Mark 9. 35; Mark 9. 36-37; Mark 9. 39-40; Mark 9. 41; 1 Peter 2. 25

226

The Ministry

THE PRIESTHOOD OF ALL BELIEVERS

August 14   Reading: Hebrews 10. 11-18

One of the most important titles given to our Lord Jesus Christ is the title Priest. The main work of a priest is to offer sacrifice, and Christ as our Great High Priest has offered the sacrifice of Himself. The writer to the Hebrews has a great deal to say about the worth of this sacrifice. His sacrifice is efficacious 'for all time' (v. 12). "By a single offering he has perfected for all time those who are sanctified" (v.14). No further offering can possibly be required (v. 18). The sacrifice of our Lord is so exalted that His priesthood must be considered the final priesthood.

Since our Lord's priesthood is unique and final, it follows that there can be no priestly class within the community of believers. The sacrifice of the cross was perfect, and nothing can be added to it. The New Testament never uses the word 'priest' of a Christian minister. No man or elite group of men stand between man and God.

Peter writes of God's people as a 'holy priesthood' and a 'royal priesthood'(1 Peter 2.5, 9). The writer to the Hebrews does not use the term 'priesthood' of believers, but he indicates the truth clearly in other ways. In 10.19 he says, "We have confidence to enter the sanctuary by the blood of Jesus". This means that the Lord's people have a privilege which only priests can know, the privilege of entering the immediate presence of God, and this is possible because of the priesthood of our Lord Jesus Christ Himself. Notice carefully that priesthood here refers not to the believer as an individual, but to the church as a whole. This is a further barrier against any man's exalting himself to an elite position among believers. The responsibilities of fellowship and priesthood go together. They are to be exercised within the church.

The priesthood of all believers means the privilege of unhindered access to the presence of God (Heb. 10.19). It means the responsibility of intercession (1 Tim. 2.1). It means the responsibility of proclaiming the gospel of reconciliation (2 Cor. 5.20). It means the responsibility of offering ourselves to God as a living sacrifice (Rom. 12.1). All of these privileges and responsibilities are fulfilled in the fellowship of the church. Let us ask the Lord to make us more aware of our privileges and responsibilities as priests unto Him.

Heb. 10. 12-13; Heb. 10. 14; Heb. 10. 15-16; Heb. 10. 17-18; Heb. 4. 16

The Ministry

APOSTLES

Reading: 2 Corinthians 10. 7-12

Paul here defends his apostleship and substantiates his claim by the evidence of ministry which built up the believers (v. 8). His letters were not sent to frighten them (v. 9). The authority was not in himself, but in the Word he proclaimed, so his weak bodily presence did not weaken the message (v.10). Let the Corinthians neither exalt him nor despise him, but seek the Lord through his ministry.

What is the significance and function of an apostle? In Eph. 4.11 Paul says, "And his gifts were that some should be apostles, some prophets, some pastors and teachers". These were gifts given to the church by the risen Lord. Earlier in Ephesians Paul says that the apostles and prophets have a special foundational ministry (2.20). Their function was to preach and to witness particularly to the resurrection of our Lord and the historical foundation of the gospel. Not all the Lord's disciples were apostles (Luke 6.13), and the implication everywhere is that a person was an apostle because he was appointed by the Lord Himself. So the apostles consisted of the twelve, Paul, and certain others, Barnabas for example (Acts 14.14) and Silas (1 Thess. 2.6). One qualification common to them all was that they had seen the risen Lord (1 Cor. 9.1). The New Testament has very little to say about the apostles as ruling the church, but as a body they provided the norm of doctrine and fellowship in the early church. Their witness has been maintained, not through a succesion of men, but in the abiding Word which the Lord formulated through their ministry.

The apostles of the New Testament were a special gift of God to meet the needs of an infant church. Their position and authority were foundational and unique, based upon their personal contact with the Lord. They were the channels through whom God formulated His Word, the standard by which all later preaching must be measured. There is no evidence that they had a position of authoritative rulership over the church. Today, as then, the Head of the church is Christ.

Let us thank the Lord for the ministry of the apostles in the past, and the continuing ministry of His Word. Let us acclaim Him afresh as Head of the church.

Luke 6. 13; Mark 3. 14-15; John 13. 16; 2 Cor. 10. 8; 2 Cor. 10. 12

228

The Ministry

PROPHETS

August 16   Reading: 1 Peter 1. 10.17

The ministry of the prophet is the second foundational ministry which Paul mentions in writing to the Ephesians (Eph. 2.20). There was a continuing line of prophets from Old Testament times, and Peter's reference here is almost certainly to the Old Testament prophets through whose message God prepared the way for the coming Messiah. Two of the prophets' main emphases were the grace of God to man (v. 10), and 'the sufferings of Christ and subsequent glory' (v. 11).

In the New Testament, prophecy is the gift of God or of the Holy Spirit (Eph. 4.11; 1 Cor. 12. 8-10). The function of the prophet was to proclaim the Word rather than foretell the future, though the foretelling of coming events was an aspect of prophecy as the example of Agabus shows (Acts 11. 27-28). He was not free, however, to add anything he wished to the revelation already given, and his word was not automatically accepted because he was a prophet. Two tests were applied to what the prophet said. Others were to judge what he said by their own knowledge of the truth of God (1 Cor. 14.29). What he said had also to be in line with apostolic truth (1 Cor. 14.37). We have already seen how the Word in its permanent written form has come through the apostles. The word of the prophets had to be in harmony with this authoritative revelation. Prophets were not the source of new truth, but expounders of truth already revealed.

It is evident that the Old Testament prophets, and the prophets of apostolic times, had a function which has been at least partially fulfilled by the coming of the Messiah and the completion of the written Word. The prophetic function in another sense, however, is still an important part of the life of the church. We all know when the Word is proclaimed with a sense of spiritual unction and carries with it a clear 'Thus saith the Lord'. This is the prophetic function so necessary among the people of God today. Nevertheless it is always subservient to the great Prophet Himself, our Lord Jesus Christ, and fails if the word draws people to a man instead of to the Lord.

Let us pray for the Word of God to go forth among His people and in the world with a fresh spirit of prophetic unction.

1 Cor. 14. 29; 1 Cor. 14. 37; 1 Pet. 1. 11; 1 Pet. 1. 12; 1 Pet. 1. 13

The Ministry

EVANGELISTS

Reading: Acts 8. 26-35

The well-known story of the Philip and the Ethiopian Eunuch is one of the early examples of the work of an evangelist. The word 'evangelist' means one who announces the good news, and the gift of evangelism is one of the permanent gifts of ministry the risen Lord has given to the church (Eph. 4.11). Philip is called 'the evangelist' in Acts 21. 8. It is obvious from his ministry to one foreign official in the desert of Judea that evangelism is not only a public ministry to great crowds. It is any ministry of effectively communicating the gospel of reconciliation to those who do not know it. It is the ministry through which the church reaches out to the world around.

There is a sense in which every believer should be engaged in evangelism, for each one is responsible to witness to his faith, but God has also given to some a special ability to reach others with the gospel of redemption and a particular burden to labour for God in the God-rejecting world. The apostle Paul was an evangelist, though he had other gifts as well. He was always concerned to reach out with the good news of salvation through Christ, to Rome, to Spain, wherever the Word had not yet been proclaimed, and he urges upon the churches not to neglect the ministry of evangelism.

Our Lord announced the good news of the kingdom and committed the same message to His disciples. It is summed up in the great commission, "Go therefore and make disciples of all nations" (Matt. 28.19). This is the impetus for the ministry of evangelism which obviously is meant to occupy a very important place in the life of the church. The church must always be going out to the world with the message of salvation. Tomorrow we will look at the ministry of pasters and teachers which is concerned with the upbuilding of the church. It is important to note that the New Testament always balances the upbuilding ministry with the ministry of evangelism. Both are vitally necessary to the life of the church.

Let us pray for a greater burden for those outside the church, that through the ministry of evangelism many may be brought to the Lord.

Acts 8. 35; 2 Tim. 4. 5; Matt. 28. 19; John 4. 35; John 4.36

The Ministry

PASTORS AND TEACHERS

The ministry of pastors and teachers has to do with the upbuilding of the church. Both are closely connected. The word 'pastor' literally means a 'shepherd'. It emphasises the caring heart and attitude of concern which should characterize the ministry. Peter in his first letter urges, "tend the flock of God that is your charge... not as domineering over your charge but being examples to the flock" (1 Pet. 5. 2-3). The pastor should be an example to those to whom he ministers, should see that they are led, protected and fed well. If one should go astray, he is concerned for his recovery. In New Testament times a pastor was not a church official in the sense in which the term pastor is used today. He was a man gifted by God to take his part in the life of the church as were other believers.

Paul urges Timothy to 'preach the word'. The word translated 'preach' is a very important word. It signifies not merely the fact of preaching, but the content of the preaching and its application to practical living. The ministery here referred to is the ministry of the teacher, but in the last phrase of v. 2, "Be unfailing in patience and in teaching", we have the spirit of a true pastor. Then in v. 4 the ministry of the evangelist is mentioned, and in v.6-8 we again see the pastoral spirit in the example of devotion to the Lord and His people which Paul had set throughout his life. So in these verses we have all three ministries of evangelist, pastor and teacher. Whether Timothy was equally gifted in all three directions we do not know, but his ministry was not rigidly confined to one of them.

The gift of teaching is of great importance to the life and health of the church. The person who really knows the Lord will want to know more of His ways and His standards. The ministry of teaching is provided that he might grow in knowledge. Every gift of ministry, however, is given 'to equip the saints for the work of ministry' (Eph. 4.12). God teaches us that we might be able to minister to others, and our ministries should produce themselves in those to whom we minister.

Every gift of ministry is based on the ministry of our Lord Himself. He ministered to us that we might know Him and minister to others. He expects us to do the same. Let us ask God to help us do it.

2 Tim. 4. 1-2; 2 Tim. 4. 3-4; 2 Tim. 4. 6; 2 Tim. 4. 7; 2 Tim. 4. 8

The Ministry

ELISHA

Here we see Elisha, a man weak in body but strong in spirit. Right to the end his zeal for the Lord never flagged. Even after his death there was a life-giving potency in his bones, which a burial party proved to their astonishment (v. 20-21).

Elisha was a very different type of man from Elijah his predecessor. Elijah was a man of rough exterior and dynamic character. Elisha was a man of more gentle and fatherly disposition, though he could also boil up in indignation at anything which infringed God's standards. High and low alike came to him for help. He had a prophet's message and a pastor's heart in a ministry which extended throughout the reigns of six kings of Israel and lasted over fifty years.

When Elijah was taken away, Elisha requested a double portion of his spirit, a request which was granted (2 Kings 2. 9-12), but he did not become a copy of Elijah. He was always himself. There is a simple but important lesson here. God does not cast all His servants in one mould. We do not become useful to God by imitating another spiritual man. God has made us with our own particular personalities, and He fulfils the ministries He gives us through us as we are. He does not expect us to adopt an artificial pose, but to give ourselves as we are to Him.

Right at the end of his life Elisha was still giving forth the word of God. He was concerned that the Lord should have His rightful place among the people. The inclination of weakness in Joash angered him (v. 19), though Elisha's anger and jealousy for the Lord may also have been a means of God's speaking to the king, for his sixteen year reign was a humanly successful one.

Elisha lived some eight hundred years before the time of our Lord, but he had the characteristics of a true minister, a shepherd's heart, a zeal to preach the message God had given him, and a prophet's unction. Let us pray that God will give us something of the spirit of Elisha in fulfilling our ministry.

2 Kings 2. 9; 2 Kings 2. 14; Col. 4. 17; Acts 20. 24; Acts 6.4

Home and Family

THE SANCTITY OF THE FAMILY

August 20   Reading:Luke 2. 40-45

Luke is the only writer who records an incident in our Lord's life between the events which surrounded His birth and the taking up of His public ministry. Our Lord spent His childhood within the security of a family, and in doing so for all time sanctified the place of the family in society.

The feast of the Passover was the one festival which was strictly observed, and many thousands of Jewish families packed Jerusalem for the celebration. Jesus was twelve years old, the age at which a Jewish boy took his place as an adult in the religious community, so although he had no doubt been in Jerusalem before, this was something of a special occasion for the family. Large groups of people generally travelled together for companionship and safety, so it is not surprising that on the return journey it was some time before Jesus was missed.

Mary and Joseph were naturally filled with anxiety, a concern which Mary expressed in her rebuke when Jesus was found (v.48). The whole picture is one of a godly, happy family with a concern for one another and a concern for their duty to God. Mary and Joseph were clearly anxious to bring up their family in the nurture of the faith, and while they had a deep love and concern for their children, they were careful that they did not come between their children and God.

Jesus, of course, was the perfect son. There could not have been any family problems as far as He was concerned. Of His earlier childhood, v. 40 says, "And the child grew and became strong, filled with wisdom: and the favour of God was upon him". Of the period after the incident in Jerusalem, v. 52 says, "And Jesus increased in wisdom and in stature, and in favour with God and man". Through His relationships in a human family Jesus was prepared for the task He had come to fulfil. It was a high honour that God gave not only to Mary who was Jesus' mother, but to the whole household, and what He did through one humble family nearly two thousand years ago is an indication of how He can use any family that is truly devoted to Him.

Let us pray that the Lord may have first place in our family life.

Luke 2. 40; Luke 2. 52; Luke 2. 47; Luke 2. 48; Luke 2. 49

Home and Family

THE CHURCH IN MINIATURE

August 21   Reading: Titus 2. 1-15

Paul here focuses attention on the Christian home. The Christian home, in a sense, is the church in miniature. Our most intimate relations with others are found within the family circle. There as nowhere else do we get to know one another. The way we maintain or refuse to maintain Christian standards within the family shows our spiritual strength and weaknesses. The principles we learn through the fellowship and ministry of the church should be taught and lived out in the home, so the life of a Christian home can be a testimony to the glory of God, or it can bring reproach to His name.

The exhortations of vs. 1-10 are conditioned by the statement of the gospel in vs. 11-14. Few passages in the New Testament so graphically present in the power of the incarnation in daily living. When it is applied to the life of the home and the family as is the case in this chapter, it is at once obvious that the Christian home occupies a place of tremendous importance and potential in the witness of the gospel. How necessary it is to recognize the power of the gospel to transform and give meaning to our homes.

In reading Paul's pleas to the different members of the household (vs. 2-10) we see him by implication drawing a contrast between what conditions ought to be through God's grace, and what they actually were in Crete where Titus was when Paul wrote this letter to him. We catch a glimpse into the chaotic state of Cretan family life, disrespect, self-seeking, irresponsibility. In the Christian family each one should be respected for the place he occupies. Bonds of love unite them together. The family is marked by a spirit of dedication to be what God wants it to be. This does not preclude difficulties such as we face in all human relationships, but these very trials are God's means of training us to discharge our responsibilities more efficiently through the power of the gospel.

It is a sad fact that very often the problems of local churches are the problems of Christian homes. Our homes should be examples to the world around of what the gospel really means. Let us pray that our homes may be a testimony for the Lord.

Titus 2. 1; Titus 2. 4-6; Titus 2. 7-8; Titus 2. 11-12; Titus 2. 14

234

Home and Family

REJOICING AND SUFFERING WITH ONE ANOTHER

August 22   Reading: Galatians 6. 1-10

Christian responsibilities apply in every area of life, and their most immediate application is within the family. This is true of Paul's words here. Within the family there are circumstances which bring sorrow, and circumstances which are a cause of rejoicing, circumstances where correction and restoration are required (v. 1), burdens which ought to be shared (v. 2). Nowhere is it more clearly seen than within the family that according to what we sow in attitudes and relationships we reap (vs. 7-8). In the family there is a constant call for patience (v. 9), a constant opportunity of doing good (v. 10).

The word 'restore' in v. 1 is used in Mark 1.19 of James and John mending their nets. When a member of a family goes astray, we do not consider it none of our business. We feel a responsibility to mend the breach where possible. The same should be true in the family of God.

There are two statements, one in v. 2, "Bear one another's burdens", the other in v. 5, "For each man will have to bear his own load", which appear contradictory. Different words are used for 'burden' and 'load'. They point out an important Christian principle. It is this. We are called to share the burdens of one another when these burdens are too heavy, but each person also has responsibilities which he himself must shoulder. Within a family even the younger members have responsibilities, and to refuse to allow them to fulfil them is not a kindness, but hinders them from growing up into responsible people. There is another aspect to these two verses. We should always be concerned to help others (v. 2), but we should also be concerned to fulfil our own responsibilities and not expect others to be coming to our aid (v.5).

A person's conduct has an inevitable effect upon others. Nowhere is this more true than within the family. The principle of sowing and reaping (vs. 7-8) should make us more alive to our responsibilities one to another. What we sow in personal conduct affects the testimony of the family as a witness for the lord.

Let us pray that the Lord may help us to show forth His life in our family relationships.

Gal. 6. 3; Gal. 6. 4-5; Gal. 6. 6; Gal. 6. 9; Gal. 6. 10

Home and Family

AUTHORITY WITHIN THE FAMILY

August 23   Reading:1 Peter 3. 1-12

In the ancient world, and still in some societies today, the woman is considered an inferior being. In the Bible, however, man and woman are 'joint heirs of the grace of life' (v. 7). They have different functions to fulfil within the family, but both are equal before God.

Within any community of people, be it a family, a local church or anything else, there has to be a recognition of authority if the community is to function properly. Otherwise it will degenerate into a group of individuals each one doing as he pleases. Each member of a family has to recognize authority within the family circle if harmony is to be maintained, and the Bible recognizes the man as the head of the house. The Bible, of course, never teaches unlimited authority, or authority without responsibility, and Peter is very careful to hold the balance. Vs. 1-6 deal with the responsibilities of the wife, v. 7 with the responsibilities of the husband, and vs. 8-10 the responsibilities of the family as a whole.

Humility and modesty are two clear emphases of the first six verses. The quality of life must be such as commends the gospel. There are many homes in which the wife alone has come to know the Lord, and there may be little freedom to speak for Him. But there can never be a hindrance to living for Him, and Christian character is one of the surest ways of breaking down barriers to the gospel (vs. 1-2).

The exhortation of v. 7 is to the believing husband who is enjoined to remember that he and his wife are equal in the Lord. The Christian attitude is always the attitude of service. The husband should be concerned to serve his wife and his family. He should not consider it his right to be served by others. This verse also shows the place prayer should have within the family circle, and particularly the prayers of husband and wife together.

Vs. 8-10 are addressed to all members of the family, but they are vitally important to the one who is head of the house. He should be an example of all that these verses contain. If he is not, his authority will be eroded and the testimony of the family damaged. Let us give ourselves afresh to the Lord that our families might be ordered according to His Word.

1 Pet. 3. 1; 1 Pet. 3. 7; 1 Pet. 3.8; 1 Pet. 3. 9; 1 Pet. 3.10

Discipline Within The Family

HOME AND FAMILY

"Bring them up in the discipline and instruction of the Lord" (v. 4). Christian discipline requires the recognition of mutual responsibilities. Children should learn to obey their parents in the Lord' (v. 1), that is, in all things which are not a dishonour to the Lord. Parents should learn to live before their children in such a manner that they are worthy of their children's obedience (v.4).

What is discipline? Some people have the idea that discipline and punishment are the same thing. That, of course, is not true. Discipline may necessitate punishment, but punishment is the consequence of indiscipline. Punishment is not itself discipline.The words discipline and disciple have a common origin. Both are derived from a Latin word which means 'to learn'. This shows how important the concept of discipline is in the life of the family. We are called to be disciples; that is disciplined people. Since discipline means learning, it also means order and consistency. Personal discipline is an essential basis to discipline in the home.

Discipline must always start with ME, and that is usually the place where we see least need of it. Discipline has to do with attitude rather than words, our practice rather than our preaching. It is the witness of our lives which should stem from our faith. It is of vital importance for the stability of our homes. If parents are not personally disciplined, they cannot teach their children to be disciplined. Discipline implies a specific purpose, and the purpose of Christian discipline is the likeness of Christ. Discipline must always keep this in view or it will become hard and domineering.

The supreme test of a person's self-discipline is how his influence counts for Christ in his own home. Discipline is always actively helpful as well as corrective (v. 4). It not only tells what to do; it shows how to do it. Our Lord not only TAUGHT righteousness, He WAS righteousness. Discipline is the combination of precept and practice which seeks the development of the character of Christ in others. As believers, the Lord holds us responsible for the discipline of ourselves and the godly discipline of our homes. Let us ask the Lord to make us more self-disciplined people that we may establish godly discipline in our homes.

Eph. 6. 1; Eph. 6. 2-3; 1 Pet. 3. 11; 1 Pet. 3. 12; 2 Tim 3. 15

Home and Family

WORSHIP WITHIN THE FAMILY

August 25   Reading: Acts 21. 7-9

By the time Paul made this visit to Caesarea, Philip had a family of four grown daughters, all of whom were prophetesses. No details are given of Philip's home life, but it is clear that the Lord was honoured in his household. We are not told where his daughters exercised their prophetic gift, but it would be reasonable to suppose that Philip and his family devoted time together in their own home to worshipping the Lord and to prayer.

The New Testament has much to say about corporate prayer. The church derives strength and direction from praying and worshipping together, and so should the family. Every Christian family should set apart a time each day when they honour the Lord together. The best time for this is in the morning before the day's work is begun, and again, if possible, in the evening when the duties of the day are over. The family need not spend a prolonged time together, and it should be such that all can benefit from it. It is good to have a song of praise, something in which all can particate, then a short reading from the Scriptures with perhaps a comment on it from some daily reading notes. Then the needs of the family and others can be brought before the Lord in prayer. Different members of the family should be encouraged to take part. The Lord hears the simple prayer of a child. Nothing is too mundane to bring before the Lord. His guidance should be sought in all the different aspects of living, schooling, family problems, work and business, relationships with others.

The family should not confine its requests to its own needs. It should pray for the needs of others, for their spiritual blessing, for the needs of the church. This is of great importance, for it helps us to remember that, as believers, we live not for ourselves but for the Lord and for His interests in others. As we pray we will be encouraged by answers to our prayers, and for these we should thank the Lord together.

Worshipping and praying together as a family is a source of blessing not only to the family, but to many others as well. Let us pray that it might be so in our family as we honour the Lord together.

Ps. 34. 3; Eph. 5. 19; Acts 16.34; Ps. 105. 21; Ps. 147. 11

Home and Family

ELI

August 26   Reading: 1 Samuel 2. 22-31

Eli was priest in the house of the Lord at Shiloh (1.9). He had two sons, Hophni and Phinehas whose scandalous conduct brought reproach to his family and to the name of the Lord. Because Eli refused to correct his sons, God sent a messenger who pronounced divine judgment upon the family (2. 27-31). The judgment was repeated through God's revelation to the boy Samuel (3. 11-14). Hophni and Phinehas were slain by the Philistines (4. 10-11).

Eli judged Israel forty years (4. 18) which is an indication of his devotion to the Lord's people, but he was woefully weak in dealing with his own children. It is a sad fact that the witness of many believers is marred by their inability to rule their own households. Even if Eli is not to be held responsible for the conduct of his sons, he could have removed them from their sacred office as priests, but this he did not do. The messenger of God accuses him of honouring his sons before God, and of complicity in their sin since he apparently was willing to accept part of their ill gotten gains (v.29).

We may partly excuse Eli on account of his age. He was too old and weak to command the respect of his rascally children, but there was a gentleness in his rebuke which was not merited by the seriousness of their conduct (vs. 22-24). Was the character of Hophni and Phinehas in fact the result of their father's negligence in bringing them up? God does not hold parents totally innocent of the misdeeds of their children in later years. We need to give serious heed to the principle of Prov. 22.6, "Train up a child in the way he should go, and when he is old he will not depart from it".

The condemnation of Eli's sons is strong, "Now the sons of Eli were worthless men; they had no regard for the Lord" (2. 12). It is difficult to reconcile this with a home in which the fear of God is consistently lived and taught. Let us take warning from Eli's tragic family life. Let us pray that the Lord will help us by our lives to commend Him to our families.

Prov. 22. 6; 1 Sam. 2. 2; 1 Sam. 2. 30; 1 Sam. 2. 35; Prov. 19. 18

Old Testament Types

THE ALTAR OF INCENSE

August 27   Reading: Exodus 30. 1-10

The writer to the Hebrews says about the Old Testament priesthood, "They serve a copy and shadow of the heavenly sanctuary" (Heb. 8. 5). By this he means that the Jewish rituals of Old Testament times were all pictures of the work our Lord Jesus Christ was to accomplish. They were given to Israel to teach them something of God's character and principles of working. We too can learn from them, and since we know their fulfilment in Christ, we can understand what they mean much more clearly than did the Israelites.

We should always be careful against drawing fanciful interpretations from Old Testament symbols. They are meant to illustrate spiritual principles, and we should not distort them by allowing our imagination to run riot in trying to extract detailed meanings from them.

The altar of incense was part of the tabernacle furniture. It was situated in front of the veil which separated the holy place from the holy of holies (v. 6), the two divisions of the interior of the tabernacle. Morning and evening Aaron burnt incense upon it. Incense in the Old Testament is symbolic of worship, and it was offered only by the priests. True worship is possible only to those who are related to God. The altar itself symbolizes how such a relationship can come about. An altar is a place of sacrifice. The altar of incense was made of acacia wood (v.1) overlaid with gold (v.3). Acacia was one of the commonest of woods, a picture of ordinary humanity clothed with the righteousness of God offered as a sacrifice. It is a picture of our Lord Jesus Christ who became man and offered Himself on the cross that we might be drawn nigh to God.

The symbolism of the altar of incense shows that there is no other approach to God except through Jesus Christ. Any other approach is 'unholy incense' against which we are warned (v. 9). Let us thank God for the way He has opened for us to approach Him through the sacrifice of His Son. Let us pray for others to approach Him in this way also.

Heb. 8. 5; Ex. 30. 37; Col. 2. 17; Heb. 6. 1; Heb. 8. 12

THE DAY OF THE ATONEMENT

August 28   Reading: Leviticus 16. 29-34

The most solemn holy day in the life of Israel was the tenth day of the seventh month (v. 29), the Day of Atonement. The writer to the Hebrews (chs. 9-10) interprets the ceremonies of the Day of Atonement as symbols of the atoning work of Christ. Each of the Old Testament sacrifices pictures a particular aspect of the work of our Lord. The Day of Atonement emphasises not only the putting away of sin, but also the fact of drawing near unto God.

The Day of Atonement was the one time when the high priest entered the holy of holies. It was observed each year, an indication that the perfect atonement had not yet been provided. A sin offering was made for the sins of the priesthood, and a further offering was made for the sins of the people. Then the priest confessed the sins of Israel, laying his hands upon the head of a goat which was subsequently driven into the desert, symbolically carrying the sins of the people away. The carcasses of the two sin offerings were taken outside the city and burned.

Jesus is our Great High Priest, He has entered the presence of God with the sacrifice of Himself on behalf of His people (Heb. 9. 11-12). The Old Testament sacrifice could effect no more than a ceremonial cleansing, but the sacrifice of our Lord has done a deep work in the heart of man (Heb. 9. 13-14). Those who come to God through faith in Christ have no need to stand afar off as did the Israelites of old. They can boldly approach the throne of grace.

The Old Testament sacrifices are symbolic of something much greater and deeper than human language can convey, and it is something supremely positive. Christ by His perfect sacrifice has put away our sins, but that is only the beginning. He has put away our sins that we might lead a new life of power and victory in Him. Let us pray that the Lord will help us to understand and experience more of the great positive purpose of the atonement.

Lev. 16. 30; Lev. 16. 33; Heb. 9. 11; Heb. 9. 12; Heb. 9. 15

Old Testament Types

THE READ HEIFER

August 29   Reading: Numbers 19. 1-9

The Day of Atonement points to the perfect sacrifice of Christ which once for all cleanses sin and brings man into relationship with a holy God. The sacrifice of the red heifer symbolizes another aspect of human need. It has to do with the enjoyment of our relationship with God and with the reality of defilement which, wittingly or unwittingly, we contract in a sinful world. God wants a people who are clean as regards their daily living, and He has made provision for this to be so.

The red heifer was killed outside the camp in the presence of the priest (v. 2-3). The carcass was then completely burned, and the ashes mixed with 'cedarwood and hyssop and scarlet stuff' (vs. 5-6). If a person contracted defilement, the ashes were mixed with running water and sprinkled upon the person on the third and seventh days (v.19). Thus he was cleansed.

The need for this ceremony shows us the insidiousness of sin. We should be constantly aware of our propensity to sin in thought, attitude or silence, as well as in word or deed. It has to be recognized before it can be cleansed. Just as a sacrifice had to be made before the water of cleansing was procured, so daily cleansing is possible only because Christ has already sacrificed Himself for us.

Water was the final means of cleansing, and water signifies the Word of God. Writing to the Ephesians Paul says, "Christ loved the church and gave Himself up for her, that he might sanctify her, having cleansed her by the washing of water with the word" (Eph. 5. 25-26). Through the sacrifice of Christ there is a judicial cleansing once for all which a person receives the moment he exercises true faith in the Lord, but this leads to another practical experience of constant cleansing in the life of the believer. The Word has been given to us that we might subject our thoughts, words and actions to its scrutiny day by day. When we accept the judgement of the Word upon us, the Word cleanses, and our fellowship with God and His people remains unsullied.

•Let us pray that the Lord will help us to know the constant cleansing power of His Word.

Num. 19. 19; Num. 19. 20; John. 15. 3; Heb. 12. 1; Isa. 35. 8

Old Testament Types

THE BLOOD

August 30   Reading: Leviticus 17. 10-14

The shedding of blood its ceremonial use is a familiar part of the Old Testament offerings. Here in Leviticus the eating of blood is strictly prohibited because of its sacred significance. "For the life of the flesh is in the blood" (v. 11). The writer to the Hebrews sums up the purpose of the Old Testament sacrificial rituals when he says, "Without the shedding of blood there is no forgiveness of sins" (Heb. 9.22). In the New Testament the phrase 'The blood of Christ' is used much more frequently than 'the cross of christ' or 'the death of Christ'.

What is meant by the blood? Many believers use the term without any thought of its meaning, as though there were some magical quality in the blood which flowed from our Lord's body in His crucifixion. This, of course, is a completely unbiblical idea. 'The blood' is a phrase used to express something of the most profound spiritual significance. As it applies to our Lord Jesus Christ it means the pouring out of His life in His atoning death.

Some feel that the blood refers basically to life, while others believe it points basically to death. V. 11 indicates that the blood is the life giving principle yielded up in death through an atoning sacrifice. The great majority of references to blood in the Old Testament are associated with violent death. In the New Testament there are passages which unquestionably associate the blood of Christ with His death. Paul, for example, makes two parallel statements in Romans 5, "We are now justified by his blood" (v. 9). "We were reconciled to God by the death of His Son" (v. 10).

When we witness to others of the saving power of our Lord Jesus Christ, let us tell them clearly that He gave His life as a sacrifice for them. This is the meaning of the blood. Not only did He live His matchless life for us; He gave it up for us. He reconciles and makes peace 'by the blood of his cross' (Col. 1. 20). The love manifest in His death should be our greatest incentive to holy living. He gave Himself for us. Let us afresh give ourselves to Him.

Lev. 17. 11; Heb. 9. 22; Rom. 5. 9; John 15. 13; 1 John 5. 6

Old Testament Types

THE TABERNACLE

August 31   Reading: Hebrews 8. 1-7

In the words of the first two verses the writer to the Hebrews shows that the Tabernacle of Old Testament times was but a pattern of the 'true tent', the house of God founded on Christ and composed of His people (3.6). The tabernacle was constructed according to a pattern given by God directly to Moses as a copy and shadow of the heavenly sanctuary' (v. 5). It was a symbol given to teach spiritual truth. We must not allow our imagination to run riot, and draw meanings from the tabernacle and its furniture which were never meant to be there, but the tabernacle shows some clear spiritual principles which are of great importance.

The presence of God in the midst of His people is one of the obvious lessons the tabernacle teaches us. This is substantiated by our Lord's own words, "For where two or three are gathered in my name, there am I in the midst of them" (Matt. 18. 20), also by much of the New Testament teaching regarding the church. In a graphic way the construction of the tabernacle stresses the holiness of God, and sacrificial system emphasises the seriousness of sin as well as the way of deliverance from it. God's holiness conditions all His dealings with His people. It should characterize the life of the local church. Sin of any kind should be abhorrent to the believer, and should be decisively though graciously dealt with in the fellowship of the church. A church which is not ordered to allow for spiritual discipline is a church not built according to the pattern and standard of God.

Another significant factor about the tabernacle was its impermanence. It demonstrated God's presence in the midst of a pilgrim people, a people who have no permanent spiritual home in this world, and who live their lives according to standards which are higher than and different from the standards of the world. There are indications in Scripture that the subsequent building of the temple was not according to the mind of God, the reason being that the tabernacle more clearly portrayed the other-worldly character of the people and the church of God.

Let us ask the Lord to make these truths from the tabernacle practical in our daily living.

Heb. 3.6; Heb. 8. 10; Acts 7. 48; Acts 7.49; Heb. 7.26

Old Testament Types

THE PASSOVER

September 1   Reading: Exodus 12. 1-13

The Passover sacrifice symbolized redemption. It was the point at which God freed the children of Israel from four hundred years of slavery in the land of Egypt. The Passover was the foundation of the whole sacrifical system which God later gave to Moses in the Sinai desert. Those who observed the Passover had the privilege and obligation of sharing in all the other great offerings of the law, but the Israelite who refused to observe the Passover was cut off from his people (Num. 9. 13). As was true of all the levitical offerings, the Passover looked forward to the sacrifice of our Lord Jesus Christ. The lamb, which had to be 'without blemish', prefigured Jesus, the sinless Son of God. The blood which was shed looked forward to the laying down of His perfect life on the cross of Calvary. The result was that the wrath of God passed over those for whom the sacrifice was offered, and they were set free from the slavery into which they had been born.

The Passover was not a meaningless rite. Time was given from the tenth day to the fourteenth day of the month (vs. 3,6) for the Israelites to meditate upon its meaning. The meat of the sacrifice was eaten with unleavened bread and bitter herbs (v. 8), and the people were to eat it prepared for the journey ahead (v. 11). Leaven is a fairly familiar symbol in the Scriptures, and it is invariably used of what is evil. Broadly speaking, it symbolizes the spirit of self-seeking which is destructive of true faith. We cannot seek God for selfish ends. There can be no true faith and, therefore, no salvation where there is an ulterior motive. The meaning of the bitter herbs is not so plain, but it probably indicates repentance, the bitter memory of past waywardness and sin.

The Passover marked the beginning of a long journey, and for this all had to be prepared. Similarly, the assurance of redemption through faith in Christ is not an end but a beginning, the beginning of a walk of faith in which we learn to appropriate more and more of our inheritance in Christ, and in which He is conforming us to His own image.

Let us thank God afresh for our redemption, and pray that we may move forward to see Him accomplish more and more of his purposes in us.

Ex. 12. 8; Ex. 12. 11; Ex. 12. 13; 1 Peter 3. 18; Eph. 4. 1

Old Testament Types

CHRIST THE FULFILMENT

September 2   Reading: Hebrews 3. 1-15

The writer to the Hebrews urges us to give careful thought to our apostle and High Priest, Jesus. An apostle is one who is sent forth on a special mission as was Moses. Jesus, however, was greater than Moses. Moses was a member of the house of Israel built by God, but Christ Himself has built the house over which He is appointed to rule. Our Lord as High Priest came not from the priestly tribe of Levi, but from the tribe of Judah, showing that the Levitical priesthood had been set aside for one which is higher.

The position of Moses, the priesthood of the Levites, and all the God-given ceremonies connected with the life of Israel were but shadows of what was to come, and all found their fulfilment in our Lord. Our Lord Jesus Christ was superior to all of them, because He was the reality to which they all pointed.

Over the past six days we have looked at six Old Testament types. Each one has symbolized either an aspect of the character of our Lord, or an aspect of the work He came to do. The children of Israel understood these types but dimly, but they were able to some extent to grasp the principles God was trying to teach them. The altar of incense showed them the perfection of God's character and the need of personal righteousness before they could approach Him. The sacrifices of the Day of Atonement showed the depths of man's sin and need. The blood showed the efficacy of God's plan of redemption. The Passover showed that God brought His people into a new relationship with Him to walk the way of faith through which He would be able to make them a people to His glory. The red heifer showed the need of constant cleansing through obedience to God's Word. The tabernacle showed the pilgrim nature of God's people in this world and the glorious fact of God's presence in their midst.

In Christ we see these truths not in shadow but in full reality. Heb. 3. 7-15 reminds us that not all who followed Moses were faithful, but ours is the greater sin if we are unfaithful to the greater Messenger, the Lord Jesus Christ through whom all God's plans have been so clearly fulfilled. Let us pray for grace to follow faithfully the 'Apostle and High Priest of our confession'.

Heb. 3. 1: Heb. 3. 12; Heb. 3. 13; Heb. 3. 14; Heb. 10. 1

Baptism and The Lord's Table

THE ORDINANCES INSTITUTED BY OUR LORD

September 3   Reading: Matthew 26. 26-29; 28. 16-20

Our Lord Jesus Christ instituted two symbolic acts to be observed by the disciples. The first of these is what we have come to know as the Lord's Supper, the second is baptism. They were practised by the early church as we read in the book of Acts, and their significance is taught in the epistles. Thus there are three lines of confirming evidence regarding their importance and meaning.

Jesus gave the command concerning His table during the final Passover feast with His disciples. The command to baptize was given during His resurrection appearance to the eleven in Galilee. Our Lord took elements which were already familiar to the disciples and vested them with a new significance. The Lord's table was derived from the Passover, and baptism was already practised by the Jews. The table basically symbolizes our relationship with the Lord and with one another as His people, while baptism has to do rather with our public testimony in relation to the world around us.

Why did our Lord institute these two ordinances? Baptism and the Lord's table are visible, material signs of the grace of God. They are tangible tokens of what God through grace is going to accomplish in us. On our part, they are a pledge to yield to God's working. Baptism and the Lord's table show us that what we have received in Christ has to be worked out in a practical way in a material world in our relations with other people.

There are two tendencies away from the true meaning of baptism and the Lord's table against which we must be on our guard. The first is the idea that in the mere observance of them there is blessing. This is not true. We must be quite sure that unless they are observed worthily and in faith, they bring spiritual weakness, not blessing. The second tendency is to undervalue the ordinances, to look upon them as a routine with little practical significance. This too cuts us off from the blessing God intends them to be. Let us thank God for the ordinances He has given us, and pray that through them we may drink more deeply of His grace.

Matt. 26. 26; Matt. 26. 27-28; Matt. 28. 18; Matt. 28. 20; Heb. 4. 2

Baptism and The Lord's Table

FOR WHOM ARE THE ORDINANCES?

September 4   Reading: Acts 10. 44-48; 20. 4-7

The commands to remember the Lord in the breaking of bread and to baptize were given to the disciples alone, for only those who knew the Lord in a personal way could understand their significance. Here in the book of Acts it is clear that followers of Christ alone were baptized, and they alone met together in the breaking of bread. In Acts 10 we have the first account of converts from among the Gentiles. The Holy Spirit had been poured out upon them as he had earlier been poured out upon Peter and the believers who accompanied him. Seeing this, Peter says, "Can anyone forbid water for baptizing these people?" (v. 47). The criterion was that a divine work had been wrought within their hearts. Through His Holy Spirit God does His work of regeneration (Titus 3. 5; Rom. 8. 9). Through the work of the Holy Spirit a person is brought into a new relationship with Christ. Baptism is a public testimony to a work already done.

Acts 20. 4-7 tells of Paul's one week stay in Troas along with the believers mentioned in v.4. Practically all the names are familiar and are found elsewhere in the New Testament. All of them were people with a genuine testimony to faith in Christ. In v. 7 Luke says that on the first day of the week they gathered to break bread. Here we see that the observance of the Lord's table was confined to people who had entered into a personal relationship with the Lord.

In the days of the early church those who accepted baptism and the Lord's table were identifying themselves with a despised, often persecuted community. The fact that they were willing to do this was itself an indication of the reality of their faith. Their faith was no mere profession. It was a deep dependence upon the Lord for a new life which was borne out by holy living. When this is so, baptism and our gathering round the Lord's table will be a real means of spiritual growth. Let us ask God to keep us from taking these things lightly.

Acts 10. 47; Acts 20. 7; Acts 8. 36-37; Acts. 2. 42; 1 Cor. 10. 16

Baptism and The Lord's Table

BAPTISM—THE PERSONAL SYMBOLISM

September 5   Reading: Romans 6. 1-11

When the word baptism is used in the Bible it does not always refer to baptism in water. When our Lord said to His disciples, "Are you able... to be baptized with the baptism with which I am baptized?" (Mark 10.38), He was obviously referring to His coming suffering on the cross. He used the word baptism to denote identification.

It is open to question whether Paul is here referring to the rite of water baptism, but certainly the experience of which He is speaking is symbolized by water baptism. The point he makes is that the believer is identified with our Lord in His death and redeeming acts. This means not only that we are justified, but that we are heirs to a life of victory which was demonstrated in our Lord's resurrection. "For if we have been united with him in a death like his, we shall certainly be united with him in a resurrection like his" (v. 5). If we have been related with Christ in justification, it will have an inevitable effect upon our daily living. Resurrection is a striking figure, but not too striking to depict the radical nature of the redemptive work of the cross through which God justifies and sanctifies His people.

In contrast to the observance of the Lord's table, baptism is a testimony which is given only once. It is also an individual testimony, whereas the Lord's table is a corporate testimony. Baptism, as far as the individual himself is concerned, is a witness to what has already taken place, to his new relationship with God. It is a witness to a person's identification with Christ not only in the justifying work of His death, but in His resurrection which brings daily victory over sin. Baptism is a personal witness to a change that God has wrought within. At the same time it is a personal dedication to 'walk in newness of life'(v.4). It is an open recognition of the fact that our lives are lived under the powerful influence of our risen Lord (v. 11).

Let us thank our Lord for His death and glorious resurrection, and let us pray that we may live worthily of the testimony we have given in our baptism.

Rom. 6. 1; Rom. 6. 2; Rom. 6. 3; Rom. 6. 4; Rom. 6. 5

Baptism and The Lord's Table

BAPTISM—PUBLIC TESTIMONY OF UNITY IN THE CHURCH

September 6   Reading: Acts 2. 41-47

On the day of Pentecost, following Peter's sermon, many believed and were baptized. Most of these people would have had a background of God's Old Testament revelation. They were looking for the Messiah, and in our Lord Jesus Christ found the fulfilment of their hopes and longings.

V. 42 shows us the essential marks of a local church. As a result of their baptism the believers were drawn into a fellowship. V.47 tells us that they had 'favour with all the people'. What happened at their baptism related them to the company of believers and also made them a witness to the world around. Baptism is not only a testimony to our personal relationship to Christ as we saw yesterday. It is a public committal to the family of God, and it is an open testimony to the world around of whose we are and whom we seek to serve.

It is important to view baptism in relation to the local church, for it is the outward sign that we accept both the obligations and the privileges of the fellowship of God's people wherever we happen to be living. It is true that most of the believers who were baptized on the day of Pentecost must eventually have scattered to the different corners of the Roman Empire, yet it is significant that, following their baptism, those who remained formed themselves into a distinct, witnessing community who 'devoted themselves to the apostles' teaching and fellowship, to the breaking of bread and the prayers' (v. 42).

Baptism should, if at all possible, be conducted in the place where a person lives and is known, not in some far off convention. Pentecost was a unique occasion and the founding of the church. Though the annual feast of Pentecost continued to be observed by the Jews, there is no suggestion in the New Testament that subsequent feasts of Pentecost were of special Christian significance or were times of Christian baptism.

Baptism is a personal committal to the visible testimony of the local church. It is also an open testimony before the world that we are followers of the Lord Jesus Christ and are one with all His people. Let us pray that we may live worthily of the profession we make in our baptism.

Acts 2. 41; Acts 2. 44-45; Acts 2. 46; Acts 2. 47; Mark 10. 38

Baptism and the Lord's Table

THE LORD'S TABLE—UNITY WITH CHRIST

September 7   Reading: 1 Corinthians 11. 23-32

Wherever we read of the Lord's table in the New Testament it was observed among a group of the Lord's people. It was instituted at Passover time when the Lord and His disciples were together. For a person alone to observe the Lord's table is to lose a great deal of its significance, for it symbolizes a unity with Christ which joins together all who are united with Him. In writing to the Corinthians, Paul links their rememberance of the Lord (vs. 23-25) with the need of 'discerning the body' (v. 29). The distinctive Greek plural for 'you' is always used in these verses. This is obscured in some English translations as 'you' can be either singular or plural.

The Lord's table is a remembrance of Him (vs. 24-25) and of a new covenant or relationship (v. 25) into which we have been brought by His death. It is a relationship upon which we remain dependent 'until he comes' (v. 26). The constant need of submission to and dependence upon the Lord is symbolized in the continuous experience of breaking bread. Baptism is observed once, but the early churches observed the table of the Lord week by week.

The table reminds us that we owe everything to the grace of God revealed on Calvary, that we are dependent upon the Lord constantly if His will is to be fulfilled and His name glorified through us. To partake of the table 'in an unworthy manner' (v. 27), to do so in a spirit of self-sufficiency, is to be 'guilty of profaning the body and blood of the Lord', because self-sufficiency leads not to godliness and fellowship, but to self-righteousness and contention which bring discredit to the Lord's name. This was the case in Corinth. The Corinthians were full of self-importance and self-assurance. They looked lightly upon the divisions which existed in their midst, thus denying the importance of the body of Christ. The Lord's table had become an empty ritual to them, and instead of being a means of blessing, it made them spiritually weak and sickly (vs. 29-32).

Let us ask the Lord to make the meaning of His table real to us, and a testimony which will lead to true-dependence upon Him, and a deeper fellowship with His people.

1 Cor. 11. 23-24; 1 Cor. 11.25; 1 Cor. 11.26; 1 Cor. 11. 27-28, 1 Cor. 11.29

Baptism and the Lord's Table

THE LORD'S TABLE—UNITY WITH HIS PEOPLE

September 8   **Reading: 1 Corinthians 10. 16-24**

Here we see very clearly the corporate significance of the Lord's table. When Paul speaks of the cup and the bread being a participation in the blood and body of Christ (v. 16), he uses a word which means a 'sharing together'. He reinforces the thought of unity in v. 17 by saying that though we are many individuals, we are all partakers of one bread.

In v. 18 Paul goes back to an Old Testament illustration and applies it to the Corinthians' present situation. Participation in the Old Testament sacrifices symbolized a total allegiance to God (v. 18). Similarly, a participation in the Lord's table is a testimony to an exclusive allegiance to Christ. We are surrounded by temptations to compromise with the world, the flesh and the devil, but a person who partakes worthily of the table of the Lord shows openly that he belongs to a spiritual fellowship of people who follow Christ and Christ alone (vs. 10-21).

This testimony has very practical implications. It is easy to say, "We owe complete allegiance to Jesus Christ. We are one with all the people of God". The proof of this profession is how we act towards our brethren in Christ, and in gathering round the Lord's table we are really making a promise that we will so live and act together as God's people, that our fellowship will be a testimony to the heathen of the reality of the gospel.

The mention of the Lord's table in ch. 10 is set in the midst of a discussion of practical details of every-day living. Fellowship means a concern for one another, a readiness to lay aside things which might not be helpful to the spiritual growth of our brethren (v. 23), a readiness to put the interests of others before our own interests (v. 24). When we partake of the Lord's table we recognize that God has put us together, and we take upon ourselves these obligations of fellowship.

The Lord's table is a solemn reminder of our unity with all the people of God, and of our responsibility to demonstrate that unity before an unbelieving world. Let us pray for the Lord's help to do so.

1 Cor. 10. 16; 1 Cor. 10. 17; 1 Cor. 10. 21; 1 Cor.10. 23; 1 Cor. 10. 32

Baptism and the Lord's Table

THE EARLY CHRISTIANS

Peter's sermon on the Day of Pentecost contained the very essence of the thought of the early disciples. Responding to the message, about three thousand people were baptized (v. 41) and continued in the breaking of bread (v. 42).

The emphasis of Peter's message is Christ crucified and risen. The risen Christ has been exalted as Lord (v. 36), and His Lordship is to be worked out in the lives of those who receive Him through the indwelling presence of the Holy Spirit (v. 38). This is the message which so many people accepted, recognizing Jesus as the Messiah. Their committal to Jesus as Lord, and their submission to His transforming work through the Holy Spirit were testified to in baptism. Through their baptism they took a public stand as a people separated unto God, different from 'this crooked generation' (v. 40).

These new believers gathered themselves into a witnessing community and 'devoted themselves to the apostles' teaching and fellowship, to the breaking of bread and the prayers' (v. 42). The breaking of bread symbolized their commitment to the Lord and to one another in the other three aspects of their life together. The believers were committed to the Lord in learning His ways. The early church was always eager to know more. Their faith was not static. They were pressing on to enter into more of the unsearchable riches of Christ. In doing so they grew in fellowship, learning through their relationship with one another and helping one another. The early church was also a praying church. The believers knew that they could not face life in their own strength, but they prayed not only for themselves, they prayed also for those who did not know the Lord, as a further reading of Acts and the epistles clearly shows. Breaking bread together was no empty ritual.

Let us pray that we may follow worthily in the footsteps of the early believers.

Acts. 2. 33; Acts 2. 36; Acts 4. 32; Acts 4. 33; Acts 4. 34-35

The Meaning of Prophecy

CAUSE AND EFFECT IN GOD'S ORDER

September 10   Reading: Hosea 5. 1-7

Many believers find the Old Testament prophets difficult to understand, and prophecy is often looked upon as merely a matter of curiosity. The prophets prayed a very important part in God's revealing His ways to His people. Hosea belonged to the northern kingdom of Israel and prophesied during the unstable period before the kingdom was overthrown. His message is characteristic of the prophets of Old Testament times.

The prophets were concerned both with the present and the future. Hosea foretells God's judgment upon His people Israel, but his prediction is based upon their present unfaithfulness. The prophet was first and foremost a man of the Word of God. He knew God and His character in a way which gave him a unique insight into His purposes. All the prophets lament the sin of the people. God has created a moral world, and when His standards are rejected judgement is the inevitable result.

Hosea mourns for the sin of the nation and likens their spiritual unfaithfulness to harlotry (vs. 3-4), a figure so often and so aptly used in the Old Testament. "They shall go to seek the Lord, but they will not find him" (v. 6). Hosea probes behind the religious veneer, showing that outward form is of no avail if people do not have a right heart relationship with God. He points to future judgment on account of present sin. Beyond the judgement, however, the prophets looked to salvation for those who returned to God in humble repentance, so their message finds its fulfilment in Jesus Christ our Lord, the Messiah.

Prophecy, therefore, is directly relevant to our daily walk with the Lord. It shows us divine principles in action. We are warned of the certain consequences of spiritual unfaithfulness. God is holy, and His purposes in His people must conform to His standard of righteousness. Otherwise there will be judgement. We cannot trifle with God. We cannot receive His blessings on our own terms.

Let us ask God to give us a greater sense of His holiness and of His holy purposes for us His children.

Hos. 5. 3; Hos. 5. 4; Hos. 5. 5; Hos. 5. 6; Hos. 5. 7

The Meaning of Prophecy

THE MESSIANIC PROPHECIES

September 11   Reading: Micah 5. 2-4

The Old Testament prophets were men of great spiritual insight, but their prophecies also contained a depth which went beyond what they themselves understood. Their knowledge of the character of God, His holiness, His grace, His purpose, led them into an understanding of the Messiah as one who would come to do away with sin and establish the rule of God in the hearts of His people.

Isaiah's remarkable prophecies see the coming Messiah as the suffering servant. Micah, however, goes further than Isaiah in prophesying the birth of the Messiah at Bethlehem (V. 2). The literal fulfilment of this prophecy was of unmistakable significance to those who lived at the time our Lord was born. It is plain that this coming king is to be no ordinary man. His 'origin is from of old, from ancient of days' (v. 2). At the same time it is clearly shown that He is to be born of a woman (v. 3). So the passage contains an expression both of His divinity and His humanity. The Messiah was to be God incarnate.

There is no doubt that the Jews looked for a Messiah who would rule on earth over a reconstituted Jewish nation. The twelve disciples themselves clung to this idea, failing to understand the true nature of our Lord's mission. Yet there is something in Micah's prophecy which sees beyond an earthly, temporal rule. Israel is the covenent name of God's people. It denotes not merely a racial group, but a spiritual people called together by the grace of God. The Messiah is to rule, but He will also 'feed his flock in the strength of the Lord' (v. 4). There is here the idea of teaching a gathered out company and building them up in the ways of the Lord. This is being fulfilled today in the church.

The Old Testament prophets contain a wealth of understanding of God's ways, and a confirmation of the work of our Lord Jesus Christ to whom they looked forward. God gave them an insight into His character and purposes which made them mighty instruments in His hands. Let us pray that God will give us a measure of their spiritual discernment.

Mic. 5. 2; Mic. 5. 4; Isa. 40. 11; Ezek. 34. 15; Ezek. 34. 23

The Meaning of Prophecy

GOD'S WORKING IN HISTORY

September 12   Reading: Esther 9. 23-28

It may seem strange that the book of Esther should form part of the canon of Scripture, for the name of God is not mentioned once throughout. The sovereignty of God, however, overshadows the whole story, and at least in the mention of fasting in 4. 16 prayer to God is implied.

The book of Esther is historical narrative, not prophecy, but prophecy sets down the working out of divine principles in every day life, and Esther is a demonstration of this. Our reading is a summary of the main events of the book. It shows us how God's sovereignty in the affairs of the Jews did not eliminate human responsibility. Mordecai made prudent use of his position, and Esther had to put into action the plan she felt urged to pursue. Yet had they and other people failed in their responsibility, God's purpose would not have been thwarted. Deliverance would have risen 'from another quarter' (4. 14).

Haman's action shows the futility of superstition. Haman had cast a lot (v. 24) to decide on a 'lucky' day on which to stage the persecution of the Jews, but it was to no avail. The ways of God are far higher than the superstitions of men. Superstition should have no place whatsoever in the life of believing Christians. The massacre which Haman planned is a fearful warning against the consequences of wounded pride. How much evil has been committed because of personal vanity or resentment. There was no fear of God in Haman's heart, but we who profess to fear God need all the more to flee the type of personal pride and hatred that was his downfall.

If Haman's pride was his downfall, the Jews had no reason for pride in being the objects of God's protecting care. They were no better than most others, and the book of Esther does not justify them for seeking to destroy their enemies. Esther is an example of the principles of God's righteousness and His sovereign hand in the affairs of men, principles which underlie all prophetic Scripture. Let us pray that we may take these principles to heart.

Esther 4. 14; Dan. 4. 17; Jer. 27. 5; Ps. 83. 18; Ps. 22. 28

256

The Meaning of Prophecy

THE WARNING OF PROPHECY

September 13   Reading: Obadiah 1-10

Obadiah's name means 'servant of the Lord'. It is a fairly common name, but we cannot identify the writer of the prophecy for certain with any who bear the same name elsewhere in the Old Testament. He may have been a contemporary of Jeremiah. His book, the shortest in the Old Testament, is a prophecy against Edom, and sounds a dire warning against human arrogance.

Edom was descended from Esau. Their country was a wild, inaccessible land to the south of the Dead Sea. In spite of their kinship with Israel, their conduct towards them on the fall of Jerusalem was cruel and treacherous. The Edomites had an intolerable conceit, and boasted in their impregnable fortress of a country. Obadiah assures them that they are not secure against the judgment of God (vs. 3-4), a judgment which will be complete. When thieves break into a house by night, they do not take everything. Grape gatherers at least leave the gleanings behind (v. 5), but the destruction of Edom will be total. This prophecy was remarkably fulfilled not long after.

Obadiah demonstrates the certainty of God's judgment upon all human pride and self-sufficiency. The Bible and experience are full of examples of the principle, "As you have done, it shall be done to you, your deeds shall return on your own head" (v. 15). This does not suggest the punishment of a vindicative God, but is a simple statement of the fact that life returns to us what we put into it. Let us never gloat over the suffering of others as Edom did (v. 10).

It is important to remember that judgment did not immediately fall upon Edom. The farmer does not at once reap the fruit of his sowing, but the harvest day will surely come. The same is true of us. We will reap the fruit of our wilful follies, whether as individuals, as a church, or as a nation. The prophets sound a salutary warning that whatever is built on pride, however well hidden it may be, will be brought to nought.

Let us pray that the Lord will keep us from arrogance and gloating over the misfortune of others, the sins of Edom.

Obad. 3; Obad. 4; Obad. 15; Obad 21; 1 Pet. 5. 5

The Meaning of Prophecy

THE ASSURANCE OF PROPHECY

September 14   Reading: Zephaniah 3. 14-20

Zephaniah prophesied during a period of spiritual darkness and apostasy when the kingdom of Judah was subservient to the Assyrian Empire. He was the grandson of king Hezekiah (1.1) and was, therefore, related to Josiah in whose reign he prophesied. Later in Josiah's reign there was a great revival, but prior to that period the land was full of idolatry, immorality and unbelief which Zephaniah denounces in the strongest terms. No evil will escape the scrutiny of the Lord who is pictured searching Jerusalem with lamps (1. 12).

God's judgement will cover the nations. It is not confined to one people, but is passed upon all who dishonour His name. Zephaniah's vision goes far beyond the limited confines of his own nation to the purposes of God in the world, but it does not stop at a realization of judgement. His insight sees judgement as a means to a glorious end, the manifestation of God's righteousness through a people purified and redeemed. Zephaniah's message is one of hope.

Ch. 3. 9-20 is in some ways so different from the rest of the book that some people have suggested that it cannot be part of Zephaniah's prophecy. This, however, cannot be true. Often those who most clearly recognize God's judgements are those who most clearly see His grace and mercy. This is the case with Zephaniah. He knew that God's love cannot overlook sin, but he also knew that God's judgment cannot destroy His love. In these final verses of the chapter we see God as king over His people (v. 15) freeing them from reproach and removing judgement (v. 18). He is also a warrior encouraging His people to victory over evil (v. 17) and transforming their shame to praise (v. 19). He is the one who loves His people (v. 17) and will gather them together to Himself (v. 20). This is the great hope which Zephaniah's prophecy holds out to the people of God.

Let us thank God for the great hope set before us in Christ, and pray that we may move forward to enter into more of our inheritance.

Zeph. 1. 12; Zeph. 2. 3; Zeph. 3. 12; Zeph. 3. 17; Zeph. 3. 20

The Meaning of Prophecy

THE PRINCIPLES OF PROPHECY

September 15   Reading: Deuteronomy 34. 5-12

We do not normally think of Moses as a prophet, but we are told here specifically that he was. "And there has not arisen a prophet since in Israel like Moses, whom the Lord knew face to face" (v. 10). Moses had a wonderfully intimate relationship with God. We might say that he was drawn into God's counsels. He had a spiritual discernment which saw the implications and relevance of what God said, and he ministered this to the people.

Earlier in Moses' experience when God called him to stand before Pharaoh, Moses pleaded his inability. God said, "See, I make you as God to Pharaoh; and Aaron your brother shall be your prophet" (Ex. 7. 1). Moses spoke the word to Aaron and Aaron communicated it to the king. This is a clear example of the prophet's function. He mediates God's Word to the people. The writer to the Hebrews tells us that the ministry of the prophets found its consummation in our Lord Jesus Christ (Heb.1. 1). Our Lord was much more than a prophet, but Paul says that He is the one Mediator between God and men (1 Tim. 2. 5), and this is the essence of the prophetic ministry.

With the coming of our Lord we are ushered into a new era of the prophetic ministry. Prophecy can no longer be vested solely in man since the Lord Himself dwells in our midst and has given to us a full revelation of Himself in the written Word. In the Acts we occasionally come across a type of prophecy which characterized the transition period between the Old Testament revelation and the completion of the revelation of God's Word. The ministry of prophecy is now based upon the written Word. It is very important to understand that there can be no prophecy which is inconsistent with or extra to the revelation of the Scriptures. Prophecy exists wherever there is a ministry of God-given insight into the Word applied to practical living.

Let us ask God to give us a greater insight into the Word of Truth.

Deut. 34. 10; Col. 1. 25; Acts 15. 32; Luke 16. 16; Rom. 15. 8

The Meaning of Prophecy

September 16   Reading: Joel 2. 23-29

Nothing is known of Joel's background apart from the information in 1.1 that he was the son of Pethuel. From his prophecy itself it would appear that he was a native of Judah and lived in Jerusalem. From his concern over the discontinuation of the temple offerings (1.9) it is clear that he placed great value on the regular services of worship. He was a man who lived close to God and had that insight into the ways of the Lord which is the hallmark of true prophecy.

The book of Joel emphasizes all the aspects of prophecy we have already considered. The holy character of God is much in evidence. He has created a moral world in which violation of His ways will be followed by retribution as night follows day. The first part of the book describes a plague of locusts which devastated the land (1.4). Joel sees this as a judgment from God and a portent of universal judgment to come. This does not mean that every experience of suffering is a direct judgment upon those who suffer, but all natural calamities are a result of the distortion of the relationship between man and nature brought about by the fall. Every natural disaster is a sign of the violation of God's order and is a warning to seek a restoration of the relationship with God that is now possible through Christ.

Vs. 23-29 is a passage of assurance. God judges in order that He might purify and restore. The damage done by the locusts will all be made good (v. 25). In fact there is something much greater ahead for God's people than the restoration of what has been lost. V. 28 is quoted by Peter on the Day of Pentecost when he sees in the advent of the Spirit the fulfilment of Joel's prophecy. So Joel looks beyond the immediate working of a holy God. He sees God judging in order to purify a people unto Himself. He sees right into the age of the Messiah to a people indwelt by God through His Spirit (v. 27). Let us thank God for His workings in judgement and in grace, and for His holy presence in our midst.

Joel 2. 13; Joel 2. 21; Joel 2. 25; Joel 2. 26; Joel 2. 27

Studying the Bible

TO HEAR WHAT GOD HAS TO SAY

September 17   Reading: James 1. 19-25

The way we use the Bible is one of the most important things in our spiritual lives, because the Bible is God's word to us. As a basis of right living, James emphasises the need to have an attitude of learning. We must be ready always to learn from others, from our circumstances, and most of all from the Word of God.

V. 19 is an apparently simple piece of advice, "Let every man be quick to hear, slow to speak", but it is something which does not come naturally to any of us. We are usually much more ready to speak than we are to listen. Even people of few words may not be 'quick to hear'. They may not say very much, but they may not listen very much either. Only when there is a readiness to listen can there be a readiness to learn.

God speaks to us through others, and if we cannot listen to others we may miss what God has to say. Make no mistake about it, if we cannot learn to listen to one another we will never really learn to listen to the Word of God (v. 21). When we are so self-opinionated that we cannot bear what God says through others, we will almost certainly read our own desires into what He tries to say to us through His Word.

Having learned to listen to God's Word we must be ready to obey it (v.22). James presses home this point with a very simple illustration. The Word, he says, is like a mirror (vs. 22-23). In a mirror we see ourselves as we really are. It shows up our blemishes so that we have an opportunity of dealing with them. There is no point in becoming offended if the Word of God shows something in us which has to be put right, yet how often offence is the reaction of God's people. They do not like what God says, so they reject it, not because it is untrue, but because the truth is unpalatable.

Let us thank God for His Word. Let us pray for a readiness to hear what He has to say through it and to obey it.

James 1. 19-20; James 1. 21; James 1. 22; James 1. 23-24; James 1. 25

Studying the Bible

TO LEARN FROM GOD'S DEALINGS WITH OTHERS

September 18   Reading: Romans 15. 1-6

It is significant that about one third of the total content of the Bible is made up of historical narrative. Why are the stories of events which took place thousands of years ago of such great importance? They are important because they show us the principles according to which God deals with His people, principles which are the same today as they were in Biblical times.

Paul tells us, "For whatever was written in former days was written for our instruction, that by steadfastness and by the encouragement of the Scriptures we might have hope" (v. 4). The Bible is a story not only of victories, but of defeats as well. It shows us people as they really are, with their strengths and their weaknesses. Even a man like Paul is not presented to us as a perfect man. The Bible recounts his mistakes as well as his insights. In the Bible we see what happens when people follow God's ways. We also see what happens when people violate God's principles.

If we read our Bible with a readiness to learn from God's dealings with others, we will have no room for pride. The greatest men of God in the Scriptures had their short-comings. One of the most important lessons we can learn from God's dealing with others is the lesson of humility. We will then be in a better position to minister to the needs of our brethren (vs. 1-2). Our own character is mirrored in the character of men and women of the Bible, and God's dealings with them shows us how He needs to deal with us.

Vs. 5-6 is a prayer for harmony among God's people. One of the reasons why fellowship is so important is that fellowship is really a willingness to learn from God's dealings with one another. Fellowship is not just happiness in the company of God's people. It is something much deeper, and it cannot really be said to exist in a Biblical sense unless we can learn from one another.

Let us thank the Lord for what He can teach us through His people past and present, and let us pray again for a willingness to learn.

Rom. 15. 1; Rom. 15. 2; Rom. 15. 3; Rom. 15. 4; Rom. 15. 5-6

Studying the Bible

TO BE LIKE CHRIST

September 19   Reading: 2 Corinthians 3. 1-6

God's purpose for us and the reason He has given us His Word is that we might 'be conformed to the image of his Son' (Rom. 8.29). Paul in writing here to the Corinthians uses an interesting illustration. He calls them a letter 'written on your hearts, to be known and read by all men' (v.2), and a letter 'from Christ delivered by us, written not with ink but with the Spirit of the living God... on tablets of human hearts' (v. 3). Paul means that the gospel which he and others had preached and demonstrated in Corinth is now manifested in the lives of those Corinthians who accepted Christ.

A little later Paul speaks of a written code which kills (v. 6). It is sadly possible for us to use the Word of God merely to establish our own self-righteousness. We read it and refuse to allow God to speak through it, but because we read it we congratulate ourselves that we are not like other people, as the Pharisees used to do.

God's Word is an expression of the life of our Lord Jesus Christ. In the gospels we read how He lived and what He taught. In the epistles His teaching is explained to us so that we might be able to face up to the practical demands of His standards in our own lives. When we do this our lives become a living expression of God's Word in the measure that we obey it. Remember, we proclaim the gospel not only by what we say, but by the type of people we are. When the gospel was preached to the Corinthians, they not only heard it from the lips of Paul but they saw it being lived out through his conduct in their midst. The same was true in the visit of Paul and his company to Thessalonica (1 Thess. 1.5).

Our attitude to the Scriptures can lead to our becoming more like our Lord, or it can lead to our becoming more self-sufficient and self-righteous. As God's children we have a solemn responsibility so to respond to God's Word that it transforms us more into the likeness of His Son. Otherwise, however much we may think we understand the gospel, we will never be able to minister it adequately to others.

Let us pray that we may so respond to God's Word that we will be letters 'known and read by all men'.

2 Cor. 3. 2; 2 Cor. 3. 3; 2 Cor. 3. 4-5; 2 Cor. 3. 6; 2 Cor. 3. 7-8

Studying the Bible

TO BE ABLE TO SERVE HIM

September 20   Reading: 2 Timothy 2. 1-10

Paul sums up the gospel in a few brief words when he says in v. 8, 'Remember Jesus Christ, risen from the dead, descended from David". Our Lord's descent from David points to His manhood, His resurrection from the dead points to His divinity. The gospel is divine life worked out in human circumstances, and the fact of the resurrection is our assurance that this is actually possible. All that this means is revealed through the Word which we are responsible to understand and communicate to others as Paul did even in his imprisonment.

The first seven verses show something of what is implied in our service for God. Whatever we have received from Christ we are responsible to hand on to others (v. 2). This initially means evangelism, a witness to the gospel of God. It is in the realm of Christian leadership, however, that this verse finds its greatest application. Here is where many fail. How many people in positions of responsibility within the local church will work their fingers to the bone in the service of others, but are unable or unwilling to encourage others to fulfil the same ministry? The reasons may vary, pride of place, authoritarianism, fear of being outshone by someone else, fear that the work will not be done efficiently; but unless we learn to encourage responsibility in others, we are failing sadly in our service for the Lord.

The task of entrusting the gospel to others will entail difficulties, some of which are evident from the three illustrations of vs. 4-6. We must be ready to pursue an aim through many trials like a soldier; to be whole-hearted, personally disciplined and mindful of the rules of Christ, like an athlete; to be patient, diligent, ready to work all hours like a farmer. The end is worth all the trials.

Let us ask the Lord to help us serve Him faithfully in obedience to His Word, and to make us ready to encourage others to accept responsibility in His service.

2 Tim. 2. 1-2; 2 Tim. 2. 3; 2 Tim. 2. 4; 2 Tim. 2. 5; 2 Tim. 2. 6

Studying the Bible

TOPICAL STUDY

September 21   Reading: Joshua 1. 1-9

When Moses died and the leadership of the children of Israel passed over into the hands of Joshua, God emphasized the importance of the book of the law as a guide for daily living (v. 8). The people were urged to meditate upon it and to be careful to do according to what was written.

We today possess not only the book of the law, but the fulness of God's counsels in the Old and New Testament Scriptures, and these provide a completely adequate guide in all matters. We need to know how to use the Scriptures so that we can avail ourselves of their teaching on any particular subject.

The Bible does not deal with various subjects in an ordered manner. It deals with them in the context of human experience. This has the advantage that nothing of what the Bible says is only theory. The Bible always relates the great questions of doctrine and ethics to practical living. In studying the Bible topically we take a subject, perhaps a doctrinal subject such as grace or redemption, or a practical subject such as the home, anger or temptation, and follow it right through the Scriptures. In doing so we will learn how it relates to our conduct, our relationship with God and with others. We will learn the difficulties and responsibilities involved in a subject such as the home, the dangers involved in ignoring God's principles, the blessings in following them, and the way to victory in our trials.

The topical method is only one way of studying the Bible, but it is a very rewarding one, and a way in which we will find the guidance of the Bible becoming relevant to the problems we face day by day. An invaluable aid to studying the Bible in this way is a concordance. With the aid of a concordance we can follow any subject consecutively through the Scriptures. Let us set some time aside to search out what the Bible has to say on matters of every day importance.

Josh. 1. 5; Josh. 1. 6; Josh. 1. 7; Josh. 1. 8; Josh. 1. 9

Studying the Bible

BOOK BY BOOK

September 22 Reading:Revelation 1. 9-16

John, a prisoner on the island of Patmos, heard a voice from behind him (v. 10). Turning to see who was speaking, he had a vision of the all glorious, all sovereign God. God commands him to write in a book messages to be taken to the seven churches (v. 11). In the second and third chapters we have these messages in detail.

God has seen fit to give us His revelation in the form of the sixty-six books of the Old and New Testaments. These were written by different people at different times and in different circumstances. Some books are historical such as the books of Moses, the Gospels and the Acts. Others are letters such as the New Testament epistles. Whatever form they take, each book was written for a specific reason. One of the most profitable ways of studying the Bible is to do so book by book. We may find some of the books difficult to understand, but let us remember that they are all part of God's Word to us. If we are faithful and diligent in our study of them, we have the Holy Spirit to help us understand them.

In studying a book of the Bible it is very important that we should try to understand the message as a whole. Be careful not to take a text out of its context and give it a meaning it could not possibly have when viewed in the light of the whole book. It is important also to consider who wrote the book and when, to find out why it was written and the circumstances of the people to whom it was written. When we find ourselves in the same type of circumstance, then the message of the book will be of particular assistance in guiding us aright. We move in constantly changing circumstances, but none of them are strange to God's Word. Somewhere in the Bible we will find a passage written to people facing the same problems as we do ourselves, and laying down principles which apply to our own needs as they did to theirs.

Let us thank God again for His Word, and let us begin now to make a close study of some particular book of the Bible.

Rev. 5. 3; Rev. 5. 9; Rev. 3. 7; Rev. 3. 14; Rev. 1. 12-13

Studying the Bible

JOSIAH

September 23   Reading: 2 Chronicles 34. 29-33

Before Josiah's reign over Judah there had been nearly sixty years of spiritual compromise and idoltary under his grandfather Manasseh and his father Amon. The country had been brought to the verge of ruin. Manasseh was in terror of his powerful northern neighbour Assyria, and in an attempt to appease his enemy, adopted many Assyrian heathen practices and spread them throughout the land. His son Amon followed the same evil ways till he was assassinated after a reign of only two years.

Josiah was only eight years of age when he came to the throne. 2 Chron. 39 gives an account of the reforms of his reign. When he was sixteen 'he began to seek the Lord of David his father' (v. 3), and four years later he started to purge the land of the idolatrous practices that had been established in the two previous reigns (vs. 3-4).

But it was six years later still that the most important aspect of his return to the Lord took place. In that year 'Hilkiah the priest found the book of the law of the Lord given through Moses' (v. 14). Vs. 29-33 tell the effects of this great discovery. When Josiah heard the word of the law he was convicted of the terrible sin of his people and of the dire need of repentance (v. 21). All the elders of Judah and Jerusalem were gathered together, and the law of God was read out before a great company of people (vs. 29-30). The king himself made a public 'covenant before the Lord, to walk after the Lord and to keep his commandments and his testimonies and his statutes, with all his heart and all his soul, to perform the words of the covenant that were written in the book' (v. 31).

The Word of God was restored to its rightful place among the people. The result was a putting away of evil and a transformation of daily living. God wants His Word to have its rightful place in each one of our lives, and through it to guide our daily living that it may glorify Him. Let us pray that this may be so in each one of us.

2 Chron. 34. 1-2; 2 Chron. 34. 30; 2 Chron. 34. 31; 2 Chron. 34. 32; 2 Chron. 34. 33

Repentance and Forgiveness

THE NEED OF REPENTANCE

September 24   Readng: Joel. 2. 12-17

The message of John the Baptist, who was sent to prepare the way for the coming of the Lord, was, "Repent, for the kingdom of heaven is at hand"(Matt. 3. 1-2). When our Lord took up His public ministry He proclaimed the same message (Matt. 4.17). The need of repentance is a fundamental aspect of salvation.

Repentance figures prominently in the message of the Old Testament, as in our reading in the prophecy of Joel. There could be no blessing from God as long as people did not recognize their own need and turn from their self-sufficient ways.

Joel emphasizes that repentance is a matter of the heart. It is only too easy to make an outward show of contrition without any real change of attitude (vs. 12-13). The call to a fast for the whole community further stresses the importance of repentance. To the Hebrews it was unthinkable that a bridal party should fast (v. 16), but repentance is more important than wedding festivities.

When Scripture uses the word 'heart' as in v. 12, it does not mean a person's emotions, but his powers of thought and will. Repentance is a deliberate act of the will in turning to God, and it is based on a revelation God has already given. The revelation of His holy character which the prophets always clearly depict. Only when people are willing to accept this revelation is there a true basis for repentance.

God takes the initiative by His Spirit in revealing man's need and giving the call to repentance (John 16. 8). This results in a repudiation of sin and a humble approach to God in the dependance of faith which leads to a change of conduct (Luke 3. 8). it is true that initially a person's sense of sin may be limited. A consciousness of the depths of sin develops as we grow in our knowledge of the Lord, but repentance begins in a will which denies self and chooses Christ. Let us ask the Lord to show us what repentance means.

Joel 2. 12; Joel 2. 17; Joel 3. 17; Joel 3. 18; Luke 3. 8

Repentance and Forgiveness

REPENTANCE—A TURNING TOWARDS GOD

September 25   Reading: Matthew 21. 28-32

Our Lord frequently used a parable to get over some spiritual truth. Here it is the story of the two sons whom their father asked to work in his vineyard. The first refused to obey while the other assented. The second son, however, did not honour his promise, while the first, thinking the matter over, 'repented and went' (v. 29).

The point of repentance is clearly brought out in this little story. It was a complete reversal of attitude which resulted in a change of action. The son who at first refused to do his father's bidding could conceivably have expressed his sorrow to his father for disobeying, yet still have left the work undone. There are many who treat God in this way. They recognize the truth of God's revelation and of man's sin. They admit that it applies personally to them but having admitted their need they continue to live in exactly the same way as they did before.

True repentance not only repudiates what is wrong, but bows in submission to God with a readiness to live a life transformed by His grace. As we said yesterday, our sense of sin may initially be limited. To a great degree our initial sense of sin will depend upon our background. A person who, from childhood has been brought up to know the Bible will most likely have a much greater sense of sin than the person to whom the Bible is a strange book. Nevertheless, the working of the Spirit of God will bring a sense of need and human failure even though a person may not be able to explain it as a sense of sin. The person who repents will turn his back upon the failures of the past and cast himself upon God. As his faith becomes more mature he will become more and more aware of the depth and sutlety of sin. Repentance will become a more and more real experience.

Let us not imagine that repentance is a once for all experience which precedes faith in Christ. There are depths of repentance which we can experience only as we grow in the Lord. Let us ask the Lord to lead us into more of these depths.

Matt. 3.2; Matt. 4. 17; Acts 17. 30; Rom. 2. 4; 2 Cor. 7. 10

Repentance and Forgiveness

THE ASSURANCE OF FORGIVENESS

September 26   Reading: Psalm 103. 6-14

Some people have tried to contrast what they say is an Old Testament stern God of justice, with a New Testament God of love revealed in the Lord Jesus Christ. Both Old and New Testaments, however, show a God of both justice and love. God's very judgement of His people is a mark of His love towards them, for real love for others cannot accept what would destroy them.

The Psalmist was very conscious of the holiness of God, and many of the Psalms ring with pronouncements of judgement upon evil. Yet the Psalms are also full of expressions of God's love and forgiveness. V. 6 stresses the universality of God's justice, but behind all lies His mercy and His grace (v. 8). The nature of God is wonderfully expressed in v. 7, "He made known His ways to Moses." This is no vindicative God. No other than a God of the deepest concern for man could so draw man into His own counsels. V. 7 is the language of fellowship, and fellowship means reconcilation and care.

The Psalmist had a deep, personal experience of the forgiveness of God. He had been severely rebuked (v. 9), but he had to admit that God 'does not deal with us according to our sins, nor requite us according to our iniquities' (v. 10). David was not to see the supreme manifestation of God's steadfast love, yet he experienced what was ultimately demonstrated before the whole world on the cross of Calvary. Anyone who truly comes to God through faith in Chirst and sees in some little measure what Calvary means in terms of God's love to man, can never doubt the reality of forgiveness. Its completeness and finality are wonderfully expressed in v. 12, "As far as the east is from the west, so far does he remove our transgressions from us."

Yet forgiveness is but a prelude to a new relationship, a transforming relationship with God who is our Father (v. 13). Let us thank God for the assurance of forgiveness, and for the assurance of His fatherly care and His purpose for His children.

Ps. 103. 8; Ps. 103. 9-10; Ps. 103. 11; Ps. 103. 12; Ps. 103. 13-14

Repentance and Forgiveness

ACCEPTING THE STANDARD OF THE WORD

The character of Ezra is well summed up in 7. 10. "For Ezra had set his heart to study the law of the Lord, and to do it, and to teach his statutes and ordinances in Israel." In this spirit of devotion to the Lord he views the terrible situation he finds on his arrival in Jerusalem. On every hand there was compromise with heathenism, even on the part of the priests and Levites who should have been an example to the people There had been widespread inter-marriage with the surrounding nation resulting in a divided allegiance, which was in fact a denial of the Lord altogether. The first of the commandments was, "You shall have no other gods before (or 'besides') me" (Ex. 20. 3).

Ezra himself was not implicated in this terrible compromise, but he does not separate himself from his people. He identifies himself with their sin, and himself comes before the Lord in repentance (vs. 5-6). There was, however, a faithful remnant 'who trembled at the words of the God of Israel' (v. 4). They gathered round Ezra, one with him in his sorrow. The basis of their repentance was their acceptance of the standard of the 'words of the God of Israel'. God brought conviction through His Word, and the immensity of their evil began to grip the hearts of the people. The result was a turning back to the ways of the Lord.

Repentance is no mere emotional experience. It has its emotional overtones in sorrow and contrition, but it affects the mind and the will. Repentance is an acceptance of the truth of what God says about ourselves, a longing to trun away from sin and be built up in the truth. The initial experience of repentance should lead to a concern to know what God's standards are, a concern which can be satisfied through the Word. Where there is no such concern there is no real repentance.

Let us thank God for His standards revealed to us in His Word, and let us pray for a greater concern to understand them more fully.

Ezra 9. 6; Ezra 9. 8; Ezra 9. 15; Luke 15. 10; Luke 11. 32

Repentance and Forgiveness

FORGIVING OTHERS

September 28

Reading: Matthew 18. 23-35

The parable pictures a servant who, through fraud and corruption, owed his master an immense sum of money. He pled for mercy and promised to repay the debt, given time (v. 26). His master, however, went far beyond what the servant asked. He cancelled the debt completely. Then the man who had been forgiven found one of his companions who owed him a trifling sum. This fellow servant pleaded for time to pay, but his plea was rejected and he was cast into prison (v. 30)

The Lord has forgiven us much, but how ready are we to forgive others? This is the obvious point of the parable. Our Lord says that the extent to which we will experience God's mercy will be the extent to which we have mercy on others (v. 35). There are few sins more disastrous to personal spiritual life and to the testimony of the Lord than an unforgiving spirit. Money may not be involved, and, of course, money was not involved in our relationship with the Lord. It was something far more serious. God has forgiven us not a mere cash debt, but a spirit of rebellion and enmity against Him. In comparison with this, how little are the slights and insults, real or imagined, that we suffer at the hands of others. Yet it is in this realm of personal relationships, usually with our fellow believers, that we have so much need to learn the grace of forgiveness.

On the cross our Lord prayed for the forgiveness of His persecutors, even though they were far from repentant (Luke 23. 34). Stephen too prayed for the forgiveness of those who caused his death (Acts 7. 60). The tragedy with many of God's people is that forgiveness is refused even to those who come in a repentant spirit. If we have a true appreciation of the qualities of God's forgiveness towards us, we will not be slow to forgive others, even when repentance is lacking: We will not harbour resentment and spite but will, even while being wronged, show the grace the Lord has shown to us.

Let us ask the Lord to fill us with a spirit of forgiveness.

Matt. 6. 15; Mark. 11. 26; Luke. 6. 37; 2 Cor. 2. 7; Luke 17. 3-4

Repentance and Forgiveness

CONFESSING OUR FAULTS

September 29

Reading: 1 John 1. 5-10

"God is light and in him is no darkness at all" (v. 5). Light shows things as they really are, and when we come into the presence of God we see ourselves in our true state. If we walk in darkness, that is refuse to face up to ourselves, there will be no incentive to seek cleansing. The result will be a break in fellowship with God and with our fellow believers. To say there is nothing in our past which requires confession is to 'make him a liar' (v. 10). To say there is nothing in the present which requires confession is equally untrue (v. 8). Confession is an essential prerequisite to fellowship.

This is John's message. It shows the importance of confession in maintaining our relationship with God unclouded and in maintaining our relationship with one another. Confession requires a spirit of honesty with God, with His Word and with ourselves. The more we face up honestly to the teaching of His Word, the more we come to recognize how prone we are to failure, conscious and unconscious. So often we see circumstances and people through the eyes of human prejudice, instead of the way God sees them. The result is misjudgement and misunderstanding which breaks fellowship.

Do we recognize that this does take place? Do we recognize when it takes place that the fault is ours, that the confession should come from us, not from others? All wrong is against God, so wrong should be confessed to Him, but confession has also to be made to those whom our actions and attitudes have wronged. A sin committed in public requires a confession in public. A sin committed against an individual requires a confession to that individual.

Practically everything in the spiritual realm can be counterfeited, and confession is no exception. Many people are quick to make general confessions of unworthiness, "Lord we have many times failed Thee," but will seldom confess to a specific fault. Confession which is not specific has little if any value.

Let us ask the Lord to help us face up to our own faults, and to make us quick to confess, so that fellowship with Him and His people may be full and unhindered.

1 John 1. 5; 1 John 1. 6; 1 John 1. 8; 1 John 1. 9; 1 John 1. 10

Repentance and Forgiveness

HEZEKIAH

September 30   Reading: 2 Chronicles 30. 13-22

Hezekiah was one of the most outstanding of Judah's kings. He was a man of deep devotion to God, and his reign was marked by a return to true worship. Under his predecessor Ahaz, the spiritual life of the nation had been contaminated by heathen influences, so Hezekiah was faced with the widespread worship of false gods, and heathen shrines had been constructed all over the country.

God's Word had commanded that the people gather year by year, so Hezekiah sent invitations to observe the Passover in Jerusalem. Some made a laughing stock of the couriers who went from city to city, but others humbled themselves 'and many people came together in Jerusalem' (v. 13). Hezekiah led the way in his concern to follow the Lord, and God used him to bring many to a true experience of repentance and blessing. The reality of their repentance showed itself in their desire to rid Jerusalem of the marks of heathenism which had disfigured it (v. 14), and the positive desire to seek God's pardon through the blood of the Passover sacrifice.

There were irregularities as might be expected among a people who has strayed so far from their faith, but God forgave them in answer to Hezekiah's prayer (vs. 18-20). God looked for a heart that was sincere towards Him, and that was far more important than the details of the rituals He had instituted. It is right to be concerned to do things in the proper way, but it is possible to do things according to the right form with a heart that is far from surrendered to God's will. God looks upon the heart. He can overlook a form, but He cannot overlook a self-seeking heart and attitude. This is the one thing that cannot experience forgiveness for it sees no need of forgiveness.

Hezekiah and his people met with God in repentance. God met with them in forgiveness, and there was blessing. Let us pray for a heart to follow the Lord, a readiness to cast aside all that is dishonouring to Him, and a spirit of rejoicing in His forgiveness.

2 Chron. 30. 14; 2 Chron. 30. 20; 2 Chron. 30. 21; 2 Chron. 30. 22; 2 Chron. 30. 27

Contention and Lawsuits

CONTENTION A MARK OF CARNALITY

October 1   Reading: 1 Corinthians 3. 1-15

Paul's first letter to the Corinthians is full of very practical instructions on how the principles of Christ should work out in every day living. Paul wrote the letter some three or four years after the Corinthian church was established. He says in v. 1, "But I, brethren, could not address you as spiritual men, but as men of the flesh, as babes in Christ." The Corinthian believers were learning the implications for daily living of their new found faith. They had come from a background of moral evil and corruption. Things like loyalty, honesty, truth, chastity, were strange to them. On coming to Christ they found themselves in an entirely new world, and they had their problems in adjusting to it.

In the Corinthian world they had always done things in the ways of the flesh. They tended to bring the same attitude over into the life of the church and to treat the church like some business club. They had to learn that life in Christ meant a change in their way of dealing with one another. Whereas their old attitude had been based on self, their new attitude should be based on the supremacy of Christ.

One of the evils which plagued the early life of the Corinthian church was rivalry. Some championed one leader, others another leader. Paul shows that all are equally servants of God (v. 9). All are instruments whom God uses, and our loyalty must be firmly anchored not first in men, but in the Lord who uses men. There can be no true foundation apart from Christ (v. 11). When our faith is not built on Him we inevitably lapse into contention and strife.

Notice what Paul says in v.3. "For while there is jealousy and strife among you, are you not in the flesh, and behaving like ordinary men?" Contention itself is a mark of carnality whether a person is right or wrong. When Christ has His rightful place a person will not be a party to contention.

Let us ask the Lord to help us see beyond His servants to Himself, so that we might be kept from being a party to contention.

1 Cor. 3. 3; 1 Cor. 3. 5-6; 1 Cor. 3. 8-9; 1 Cor. 3. 11; 1 Cor. 3. 14

275

Contention and Lawsuits

OUR PARTIAL UNDERSTANDING

October 2   Reading: 1 Corinthians 1. 26-31

Corinth was a centre of trade and commerce, so most of the Corinthian believers were probably engaged in business. Not many of them came from the upper classes of Greek society, or belonged to the elite of Greek philosophers (v. 26). Even so, they had complete confidence in their own powers of judgement. This, of course, is a trait of natural man, whether he is highly educated or poorly educated. How unwilling we are to try to see things from the point of view of another person. In Corinth this attitude fostered the spirit of contention which was dividing the assembly. The followers of Paul or Apollos or Peter all thought that their man was right and the other two were wrong.

Paul emphasises to the Corinthians their own limitations. Only to the extent that we are subject to the Lord can we hope to be able to discern aright in matters relating to one another. Even in our claims of Spirit-guided discernment we need to exercise great care. We must always remember that the human element is never absent, and it is liable to err. Whatever the Lord may show me has to be discerned by ME, and it is always possible that I am wrong, that I misunderstand what God is trying to show me.

This is a humbling thought. Our understanding of any situation is always partial, and paradoxically, I will be more liable to discern aright when I am fully aware just how easy it is for me to be wrong. We can never have any reason to boast in our discerment (v. 29). We can boast in the Lord (v. 31). He does reveal His ways clearly to us, but we do not discern His ways with the same clearness. To say, "We are absolutely certain of God's will," is a fleshly boast. By God's grace we can discern His will with sufficient clearness to act with confidence, but simply because we are fallible beings we should always be ready to say, "We may be wrong." If we view our problems with others in this spirit, we will be saved from much contention.

Let us ask the Lord to help us realize our limitations so that we may be the more able to discern aright.

1 Cor. 1. 26; 1 Cor. 1. 27; 1 Cor. 1. 28; 1 Cor. 1. 29; 1 Cor. 1. 31

Contention and Lawsuits

LAWSUITS FORBIDDEN FOR BELIEVERS

October 3   Reading: 1 Corinthians 6. 1-11

Litigation was a part of every day life in Corinth. When some of the Corinthian believers trusted Christ and came into the family of the church, they found that fellowship with other believers did not maintain itself automatically. They had their differences, and as they had done when they were living in the godless world, their first thought was to take their differences to the law courts.

Paul shows the total inconsistency of such action with the way of Christ. The believer, by his faith in Christ, professes to have the answer to the very deepest problems of mankind, and yet he is unable to find an answer to problems which are trivial in comparison (v. 2). It is perfectly clear from what Paul says here that for believers to go to law with one another is wrong and sinful.

In the first place, to do so is a denial of the power of the gospel. In Christ we are united with the Lord and with one another. Writing to the Romans Paul tells us that the gospel 'is the power of God for salvation' (Rom. 1. 16), meeting the needs, as Romans clearly shows, not only of an eternity to come, but of a life of fellowship here on earth. To take a dispute before godless men is an admission that our gospel has failed.

Secondly, it is a denial of our own faith. The recourse of the believer is always to the Lord. If I take my needs to men of the world, it shows that I have more confidence in them than in the Lord, or that I prefer their judgement to what God says about the matter.

Thirdly, it is destructive to the testimony of the church. Can we expect the world to listen to our witness when our lives deny the power and love and grace that we profess?

Fourthly, it is a denial of the grace of God. To engage in litigation with a fellow believer shows a concern for our own rights above the good of others and the rights of the Lord. God's Word is perfectly plain. "Why not suffer wrong? Why not rather be defrauded?" (v. 7).

Let us pray for grace to seek the Lord's interests rather than our own.

1 Cor. 6. 1; 1 Cor. 6. 2; 1 Cor. 6. 3; 1 Cor. 6. 5-6; 1 Cor. 6. 7

Contention and Lawsuits

CONTENTION A DISGRACE TO THE LORD

October 4   Reading: James 3. 13-18

In this short third chapter of his letter James shows us that a true faith is manifested in the way we discipline what we say. A discipline of our speech will lead to harmony (vs. 17-18). A lack of discipline in speech will lead to contention (v. 16). These are the conclusions James draws from his dissertation on the power of words in vs. 1-12.

True wisdom and understanding produce a meek character (v. 13). This is the witness of the believer. Believers who feel they are the recipients of some special spiritual light are tempted to be arrogant and impatient. They are often intolerant of anyone who does not voice agreement with them, and jealous of others whose lives have the ring of truth about them. Selfish ambition then pushes its way into the forefront. The result is 'disorder' (vs. 14-16).

This is the road which leads to contention. It begins with attitudes which are not surrendered to the Lord. These attitudes burst out in undisciplined words, and the result is strife. In contrast to this James says, "The harvest of righteousness is sown in peace by those who make peace" (v. 18). He means that words of peace diffuse an attitude of peace in others, and the result is righteousness. One is the way of fallen man, the other is the way of man transformed by the grace of God. One is a disgrace to the name of the Lord, the other is a testimony to the reality of the gospel.

Jude calls us to 'contend for the faith' (Jude 3). The word 'contend' literally means to 'strive together'. It implies the unity of God's people against godlessness. When, however, the contention is within the church itself, it is always tragic, leading to spiritual weakness in the individuals concerned and in the testimony as a whole. Our Lord prayed for His disciples 'that they all may be one....so that the world may believe that thou has sent me' (John 17. 21). He knew that when oneness is broken by contention, the testimony is broken also.

Let us ask the Lord to save us from contention.

James 3. 13; James 3. 14; James 3. 16; James 3. 18; Jude 3

Contention and Lawsuits

RESOLVING OUR DIFFERENCES

October 5   Reading: 1 Corinthians 1. 18-25

Dissention was the main problem in the Corinthian church, and party disputes blinded the eyes of the Corinthian believers to other evils in their midst. Basically, all their differences and problems were due to their self-will, wills which had not been surrendered to Christ. Paul sums this up in these verses by showing that the life of the believer and of the church must be based on the cross. Unless this is so, differences can never really be resolved, and the life of the church will be a continuing crisis, moving on from one crisis of relationship to another.

The cross was an affront to the Jews and foolishness to the Gentiles (v. 23). Natural man tries to deal with his problems through a show of superior understanding, through defeating his opponents or ignoring them, or through manipulation. And how many believers try these same methods? The cross is something quite contrary to man's natural thinking.

What does Paul mean when he says the cross 'is the power of God' (v. 18)? The cross is a symbol of our union with Christ and, therefore, of our seeking His way, not our own. The cross is also a symbol of rejection. Isaiah, speaking prophetically of our Lord, says, "He was despised and rejected by men" (Isa. 53.3). He did not stand on His own rights or dignity. Very often disputes among the Lord's people cannot be solved because the people concerned are unwilling to lose face. They insist on holding by their position even when they know they are wrong. The experience of the cross is unknown to them.

The cross signifies the spirit of self-giving. It was on calvary that our Lord 'emptied' Himself (Phil. 2.7), giving Himself completely for those He had come to redeem. When we have a difference with a brother let us ask ourselves how far we are willing to give ourselves for him.

Above all, the cross is the symbol of reconciliation. There we were reconciled with God and with one another. If we know something of the spirit of the cross we will be deeply concerned to be reconciled with our brethren. Let us pray for a deeper working of the cross in our lives.

1 Cor. 1. 18; 1 Cor. 1. 20; 1 Cor. 1. 21; 1 Cor. 1. 22-24; 1 Cor. 1. 25

Contention and Lawsuits

THE ATTITUDE OF CONTENTION IS SELF

October 6   Reading: James 4. 11-17

Contention is almost always accompanied by defamation of character. With our limited understanding of spiritual matters there will always be differences of opinion among the Lord's people, and we should be able to hold these with grace. Contention arises when we begin to hold these differences in a fleshly spirit and allow them to breed distrust and evil speaking.

James strongly condemns the sin of evil speaking. He leaves no doubt that it is a sin against God. God has given us the responsibility of judging actions as we see clearly, for example, in 1 Corinthians, but He has not given us the responsibility of judging the hearts of our fellow believers. This He alone can do. When we presume to cast aspersions on the character of others because of disagreements, James tells us that we are making our own law which goes beyond the law of God (vs. 11-12).

The root cause of this spirit of contention he goes on to explain in greater detail in the subsequent verses. It is self, self which takes over the place the Lord alone should occupy in our lives. The attitude James describes in v. 13 is the attitude of 'who can stop me doing as I please?'. It is the attitide of a person who arrogates to himself a place above God, though he may not admit it. He may make the profession of a believer, but acts as though he were master of his own destiny. He fails to take into account the God he professes to honour. In reality he cannot foresee even one day ahead.

Before we start condemning others who measure up to James' picture, let us ask how far it is applicable to ourselves. There are many people who profess to know the Lord but who act or refrain from acting, as James points out in v. 17, as if God and the standards of His Word did not exist. They live for themselves and live in contention with others.

Let us ask the Lord to deal with anything in us that fosters contention.

James 4. 11; James 4. 12; James 4. 13-14; James 4. 15; James 4. 16

Contention and Lawsuits

ABNER AND JOAB

October 7   Reading: 2 Samuel 3. 31-39

David was an anointed ruler over Israel, but the men he gathered round him were a strange mixture of loyalty, bravery, self-seeking and treachery.

Abner was 'captain of the host' under Saul and supported the line of Saul on the king's death. Later, however, he left Ishobosheth, Saul's son, and worked for a reconciliation of the two sides under David. The reconciliation was effected, but Abner was never to enjoy it. He was murdered by Joab.

Jaob was commander of David's armies. His character was a peculiar mixture of loyalty and devotion on the one hand, and of selfish cunning and treachery on the other. He was a skilful general who worked untiringly for David to establish the monarchy. He adopted the role of peacemaker in an attempt to reconcile David and his son Absalom. Yet in his loyalty Joab could be unscrupulous and cruel as is all too clear from the way he carried out David's plan to kill Uriah the Hittite.

One could almost say there were two Joabs. His attempt to dissuade David from numbering the people (2 Sam. 24. 2-4) showed a certain spiritual insight, yet he did not seem to have sufficient faith in God to deliver him from his own self-seeking. Joab was jealous, and he would go to any lengths to get his own way. He nursed an old grievance against Abner, he also saw in Abner a threat to his own position, so he eliminated him.

The story of Abner and Joab is a sad commentary on the evil of contention. It destroyed both men involved and brought loss to the whole kingdom. David, though an anointed king, was weakened through the jealousy and quarrelsomeness of his own servants. When we allow ourselves to become party to contention we greatly weaken the cause of the Lord.

Let us ask God to save us from being drawn into contention.

2 Sam. 3. 39; Prov. 6. 34; Col. 3. 13; Prov. 13. 10; Titus 3. 9

Spiritual Gifts

THE DISTRIBUTION OF SPIRITUAL GIFTS

October 8   Reading: Romans 12. 1-8

One of Paul's favourite ways of describing the church is as the Body of Christ. Each part of the human body has its own function and works in harmony with the rest. The health of the body is dependent upon the right functioning even of its lowliest members. So it is with the people of God. God has given some gift to each one of His children.

The word Paul uses for a 'gift' denotes something that a person could not acquire by himself. There are gifted speakers who can hold an audience spellbound. Other people may practise public speaking throughout their lives but never be able to grip the attention of others. The first have a gift of speaking, the others do not. Some people have a musical gift which others can never duplicate, however much they practise. A gift is more than an ability to do something. It is an ability plus an extra God-given capacity which makes it a gift.

Paul exhorts us to use the gifts God has given us (vs. 7-8). If we are going to use God's gifts we must first know what they are. Every believer is responsible to make an honest assessment of his capabilities, not in a spirit of pride claiming that he can do things of which he is not capable, or trying to excuse himself by saying that he has no gift at all.

We must also be ready to accept whatever gift God has given us, not to envy what God has given to others, but to be content to take our part whether it be prominent, lowly or unseen (v. 3). And whatever gift God has given must be used not for personal prestige, but as a duty to God in service for Him and for others.

Vs. 1-2 show the condition on which gifts can be used. The condition is that we give ourselves in all we do into the hands of the Lord. This is the opposite of the spirit of the world in which men live simply for their own ends. God-given gift is only of value when it is used in a spirit of submission to Christ.

Let us submit ourselves afresh to Him, spirit soul and body, that the gift He has given may be used to His glory.

Rom. 12. 1; Rom. 12. 2; Rom. 12.3; Rom. 12. 4-5; Rom. 12. 6

Spiritual Gifts

SPIRITUAL AND NATURAL GIFTS

October 9   Reading: Ephesians 4. 1-7

We have already seen that God's gifts to man are more than a man can acquire for himself. Yet we must not make such a distinction between natural and spiritual gifts that we despise anything that seems to us to be a natural talent. It is true as we have just said that God's gifts cannot be acquired by human means and practice, but that does not mean that they are of a completely different order from what we call natural gifts.

God is our Creator, and every faculty we possess has been given by Him, so it is wrong to relegate anything He has given us to some inferior level. Is there then any difference between natural and spiritual gift? The difference lies in the added factor of the grace of God. "Grace was given to each of us according to the measure of Christ's gift" (v. 7). A person may have a natural gift of oratory, a gift, remember, given by God as Creator, but grace transforms it into a spiritual gift so that it can be used, not as an entertainment or a means of furthering some worldly selfish cause; but as a means of bringing divine life to those who respond to the message proclaimed.

There are some believers who feel that any natural capability ought to be suspect, and who tend to look down upon the obvious gifts another believer may possess. If we understand what spiritual gift really is we will not do this. On the other hand we will not accept a gift of say oratory if there is obviously no flow of the grace of God. A further mistake some believers make is to decry the gifts they have, saying they have no spiritual gift and looking for something with a miraculous flavour. This too is wrong.

The initial verses of chapter four are a further emphasis of what Paul has said in Romans 12. He stresses the need of humility, patience and love (v. 2) in a concern to maintain the unity of the one body into which the Lord has brought us. All this is a manifestation of the grace through which God's gifts are effective. Let us pray for more grace.

Eph. 4. 3; Eph. 4. 4-5; Eph. 4. 7; 1 Cor. 8. 6; Rom. 11. 36

Spiritual Gifts

THE SPIRIT GIVES AS HE WILLS

October 10

Reading: 1 Corinthians 12. 4-11

Each of the three persons of the Godhead is mentioned in vs. 4-6. 'The same Spirit' (v. 4); 'the same Lord' (v. 5); 'the same God' (v. 6). This shows us that the triune God, in all His power, is vitally concerned with the care and growth of the assembly. He gives everything necessary for the church's well-being. If there is a lack within a local church, the lack is not in God's giving, but in man's receiving and using what has been given.

Paul shows that though there are varieties of service, gifts and their functioning, they all have a common origin in the 'same God' (v. 6), so should never lead to division or dissension. God gives them all and would control their functioning 'for the common good' (v. 7), not for the self gratification of any individual.

The distribution of the gifts is in the sovereign hand of God (v. 11). We cannot claim a gift to our own liking, nor have we any right to complain against what God has given us. On the other hand God, in giving gifts to His people, has not left out of account their natural abilities and temperaments. This is indicated by the use of the phrase 'to another' in v. 8 and in the middle of v. 10 where Paul says, "To another various kind of tongues." In Greek there are two words for 'another', both of which are used in vs. 8-11. One of these words signifies merely a numerical difference, another of the same sort. The second word is used in the two places already mentioned, and means another of a different sort. It expresses a qualitative difference. God gives gifts appropriate to the different types of people to whom He gives them.

Each gift is an equal manifestation of the Spirit (v. 7). While some gifts are more useful than others, no one gift is singled out as being a greater manifestation of the Spirit than any other. God does not give one particular gift to all His people, nor does He give all the gifts to any one of His people, but whatever He gives is an indication of His Spirit's working.

Let us thank the Lord for whatever gift He has been pleased to give us.

1 Cor. 12. 4; 1 Cor. 12. 5; 1 Cor. 12. 6; 1 Cor. 12. 7; 1 Cor. 12. 11

Spiritual Gifts

ALL GIFTS NOT FOR ALL TIME

October 11   Reading: 1 Corinthians 14. 20-25

Spiritual gifts are enumerated in three portions of the New Testament, 1 Cor. chs. 12-14, Rom. 12. 3-8, and Eph. 4. 11-16. The Corinthians in their enthusiasm over the miraculous and spectaular gifts had lost any sense of discernment as to God's real purpose in giving gifts to His people. Paul rebukes them with the words, "Brethren, do not be children in your thinking: be babes in evil, but in thinking be mature' (v. 20).

Only in Corinthians are the miraculous signs and gifts mentioned, healing, miracles, tongues, interpretation (12. 9-10). They appear neither in Romans nor in Ephesians. Paul, of the gifts mentioned in Ephesians, says that they are to function 'until we all attain to the untiy of the faith and of the knowledge of the Son of God, to mature manhood, to the measure of the stature of the fulness of Christ' (Eph. 4. 13). In the Corinthian and Roman accounts of the gifts there is no suggestion that the lists are either exhaustive or permanent.

In Corinthians Paul looks upon the gifts as given by the Spirit through whom God works out His purposes here upon the earth. The implication is that God gives gifts acording to the local contingencies. They are given for a specific purpose and cease to function when that purpose has been accomplished. The gifts mentioned in Ephesians as being given by the ascended Christ (Eph. 4. 8) are, on the other hand, of permanent importance for the life of the church.

Paul's mention of the gift of tongues in 14. 21-24 demonstrates the temporary value of some of the gifts. His Old Testament quotation in v. 21 is from Isa. 28. 11 and has reference to the Jewish people. Tongues were, therefore, principally a sign to the unbelieving Jews of the early church era (v. 22). In contrast, the gift of prophecy edifies the church and, rightly understood, is of more permanent value. Prophecy is ministry of the Word through which unbelievers also are convicted and brought to saving faith (vs. 24-25).

Let us thank the Lord for the way He gives gifts to meet our every need, temporary or permanent, and let us seek His help to understand them aright.

1 Cor. 14. 20; 1 Cor. 14. 21-22; 1 Cor. 14. 23; 1 Cor. 14. 24; 25

Spiritual Gifts

THE PURPOSE OF THE GIFTS

October 12   Reading: Ephesians 4. 8-14

In this list of gifts, or rather of gifted men, we have some of the Lord's permanent endowments to the church. They are imparted by the ascended Lord whose concern for the church is that it should attain 'the measure of the stature of the fulness of Christ' (v. 13). Until the church reaches that stage the gifts of the ascended Lord will be functioning within it.

Paul states the two related purposes of the gifts in v. 12 , "To equip the saints for the work of ministry, for building up the body of Christ." They are to bring the Lord's people and the church to a place of spiritual maturity, and to enable the Lord's people themselves to minister to others.

The first of these purposes is expanded in v. 13. The fulness of God's purpose will be finally attained only when we are with Christ. There is a state of maturity, however, which should be the present outcome of minstry to the Lord's people and the church. Maturity, in this sense, is not a final state of completeness, but an adult attitude which encourages a still greater growth in the things of God.

It is of great importance to realize that the purpose of God's gifts is not completed when individuals themselves are built up, or a church reaches a state of happy consolidated fellowship. The exercise of the gifts is 'to equip the saints for the work of ministry' (v. 12). A ministry which edifies someone else and stops there is incomplete. It has not fulfilled its purpose unless it has reproduced itself in others, so that those who are affected are not only edified themselves, but go out to edify others.

This is a great challenge to every child of God. It is a challenge not only to have a competent ministry, but to have a right attitude, an attitude which is ready to rejoice in seeing God use someone else, perhaps to a greater extent than He has used the minister Himself. It is a challenge to be rid of every vestige of jealousy, for jealousy is destructive to the gifts of God. Let us ask God to use us to encourage others to fulfil their ministry.

Eph. 4. 8; Eph. 4. 11; Eph. 4. 12; Eph. 4. 13; Eph. 4. 14

Spiritual Gifts

DESIRING THE BEST GIFTS

October 13   Reading: 1 Corinthians 14. 1-5

In 1 Cor. 12. 31 Paul writes, "But earnestly desire the higher gifts." Here in 14. 1 he gives a further exhortation to 'desire the spiritual gifts', and then goes on to explain why one gift, in this case the gift of prophecy, is more profitable than another, here the gift of tongues (vs. 2-5).

Paul's criterion of a 'higher' gift is quite plain. It is a gift which is intelligible to the mind and whose message, therefore, can be applied to every day living. He sees little point in the use, within the church, of a gift which cannot be understood (vs. 3-4). Always remember that right action is based on right understanding. We cannot live the truth if we do not understand the truth. In His Word God has set down truth in an intelligible fashion, and one of the chief purposes of the gifts is to communicate that truth intelligibly to others.

In contrast, Paul speaks of the gift of tongues which he relegates to an inferior place. Unless the message is made understandable through interpretation, it neither edifies the individual (v. 2) nor the church (v. 5). If such a gift is used privately as an expression of worship to God, it may be of value to the person who uses it, but its place is of doubtful value in any gathering of the Lord's people.

The believer is exhorted to desire the gifts of God, but his desire should be accompanied by a sense of responsibility to live as befits one who has been privileged to receive a gift from God, and the dispensing of the gifts is always in God's sovereign hands.

But beyond all there should be a pursuit of love. This is the point of ch. 13 set in the middle of Paul's discourse on gifts. Without love none of the gifts can function to the end for which God gave them. To be more concerned for gifts than for the love and unity of the Lord's people is to make the gifts themselves worthless. "Make love your aim" (14. 1).

Let us 'earnestly desire the higher gifts', but above all let us pray that love may be our aim.

1 Cor. 12. 31; 1 Cor. 14. 1; 1 Cor. 14. 2; 1 Cor. 14. 3; 1 Cor. 14. 4

287

Spiritual Gifts

ELDAD AND MEDAD

October 14

Reading: Numbers 11. 24-30

The children of Israel had complained about the manna which was God's provision for them in the wilderness. They wanted meat. Moses took their complaint to the Lord and God promised to give them their desire. In announcing God's word to the people Moses gathered seventy of the elders and 'placed them round about the tent' (v. 24). God's Spirit came upon the seventy and they prophesied (v. 25).

There were, however, two elders, Eldad and Medad who had not left the camp, but they prophesied where they were. In the camp there was consternation at this unorthodox behaviour. One young man ran and told Moses (v. 27), while Joshua asked Moses to forbid Eldad and Medad to prophesy further. Nobody suggested the prophesying was false, nor did they question the calling of Eldad and Medad as elders. What Joshua and others objected to was that their anointing was not manifested in the same way as that of the others.

Moses sweeps aside Joshua's complaint with the words "Would that all the Lord's people were prophets, that the Lord would put His Spirit upon them" (v. 29). Moses quite rightly silenced the critics. He was happy that the Lord should work any way He pleased without being restricted to a preconceived pattern.

Man is always apt to stereotype the working of God. Even those who boast of allowing 'freedom for God to work can make that free expression a limiting from beyond which they imagine God cannot work at all. Often when God has blessed His people in a particular way they think that if only they can hold on to the pattern they claim God has shown, they will be able to hold on to the blessing. But it is not so. We must be willing to allow God to use people and bless people in the way He chooses, and to realize that He is much greater than our limited concepts of His working. The gifts He gives cannot be reduced to a stereotyped form, or a stereotyped lack of form.

Let us pray for a heart always ready to accept God's working, even in ways that are new.

Num. 11. 29; 2 Cor. 3. 17; Rom. 11. 29; Jer. 7. 4; Job 9. 10

Cleanliness and Order

RESPECT FOR GOD'S CREATION

October 15   Reading: Psalms 95. 1-7

The Psalms form the greatest book of praise in the Bible, and it is significant that, in the midst of expressions of worship, the Psalmist has so much to say about God's creation. Some people, when they think of worship, think only of the realm of the spirit and the unseen, but the Bible does not do this. The Bible sees creation as part of the revelation of God's glory. We would know very little about the character of God apart from His working in nature and in people around us.

The Psalmist here calls upon us to worship God not only as the Creator of the world around us, but as the one who has made us ourselves (v. 6). It is true that everything has been distorted by the fall, but we must never, because of this make the mistake of despising the created world or looking upon man as no more than dirt. When God created the world He saw that everything was good, and the greatest of all His creations was man. Far from despising God's creation, we should sorrow at the way it has been misshapen through sin, and we should labour together with God to bring about the restoration that is going to be fully completed one day.

As God's children we must learn to respect all that He has made. In our homes we have little decorations made by the hands of man, and we value them, particularly if a piece has been made by someone we love and respect. God has given us a world that is far more beautiful than anything man could ever make, and to treat it with disdain is to insult God Himself.

Man in his sin goes on abusing and destroying the natural world in his own selfish interests. He has no respect for the creatures, the plants, the resources that God has made. When God's own people do this it is a great tragedy, for they thereby show that they do not recognize the greatness of the Lord they claim to worship.

Let us pray that God will give us a greater respect for the wonderful world He has made.

Ps. 95. 1; Ps. 95. 2-3; Ps. 95. 4; Ps. 95. 5; Ps. 95. 6-7

Cleanliness and Order

GLORIFYING GOD IN EVERYTHING

October 16   Reading: Ephesians 5. 15-20

The first three chapters of Ephesians are given over to doctrine, and in the final three chapters Paul goes on to apply to daily living what has already been taught. "Walk," he says, "not as unwise men but as wise" (v. 15). By 'wisdom' Paul does not here mean an intellectual accomplishment, but a way of life based on the knowledge of God and which seeks, therefore, to avoid all that would be displeasing to Him. This, of course, includes a mental understanding of God's will, as v. 17 makes clear.

This attitude of spiritual wisdom has a bearing on every aspect of living, on our use of time (v. 16), on our use of the world's material resources (v. 18), in fact on the way we view all our circumstances (v. 20). God has created the material world and the spiritual world. He has created time itself and all should be used to His glory.

In v. 15 Paul uses a word from the market place which means literally 'buying up' the time. God has given us time and opportunity in which to do so much for Him. Do we use our time aright, or do we fritter it away in useless pursuits, idle talk, or in doing nothing at all? How important it is to understand what God wants us to do with our time.

God has given us wonderful resources in the world He has made. These resources can be used wisely or abused. The worldly man uses things for his own personal pleasure. The child of God's concern should be that his life is so ordered that everything is used to God's glory (v. 18). A mark of spiritual wisdom is self-control, and self-control to the believer should mean the control of Christ.

Our circumstances too are in the hands of a sovereign God. In a fallen world men manipulate their circumstances to their own selfish ends, but God's people should see in their circumstances an opportunity of glorifying Him and should thank Him for it, whether circumstances be easy or difficult.

Let us pray for grace to glorify God more and more in all things.

Eph. 5. 15; Eph. 5. 16; Eph. 5. 17; Eph. 5. 18-19; Eph. 5. 20

Cleanliness and Order

THE SANCTITY OF THE MATERIAL ORDER

October 17   Reading: John 21.4-14

This was the third appearance of our Lord to His disciples after the resurrection (v. 14). At Peter's instigation six other disciples joined him and spent a fruitless night on the sea of Galilee (vs. 1-3).

As day was breaking, Jesus revealed Himself to them on the shore. he did not preach to His disciples a sermon on the unreality of the material order. His first question was whether they had caught anything (v. 5). When they told Him that they had caught nothing, He told them where to cast the net, and the result was a huge catch. Finally they drew near to the shore. The Lord was preparing a meal for them and they are together.

This is a particularly significant story because it shows how our Lord in His resurrection body related Himself to the material world. Our Lord's resurrection body was in some respects similar to our human bodies. In the present incident He was recognized by His disciples, conversed and acted as an ordinary person, and ate with them. At the same time, His. body was not subject to some of the limitations of mortality. He could, for example, suddenly appear to His disciples through closed doors (John 20. 19).

The main point is that He did not denigrate the body. In fact, in taking upon Himself a body after His death and identifying Himself with His disciples in the tasks of everyday living, He has shown the sanctity of the material order. Our Lord's resurrection was a physical resurrection, and one day we ourselves are going to have a new resurrection body as Paul clearly explains in 1 Cor. 15. The Bible never looks upon man as existing apart from a body, even in the life to come.

Our Lord's resurrection appearances demonstrate that the eternal state is not a disembodied existence. It is foreshadowed in the present material order, although it will be higher by far and free from present limitations which exist because of sin. To the extent that we know victory over sin now, the present material order of our lives can show forth the glory of God. Let us pray that it may be so more and more.

John 20. 19; John 20. 26; John 21. 1; John 21. 4-5; John 21. 12

Cleanliness and Order

ORDER IN THE CHURCH

October 18   Reading: 1 Timothy 3. 8-15

What we have been concerned to show over the past three days is that the material order does matter. Our Lord in His life before and after His resurrection demonstrated its importance, and we must realize its importance also. From the earliest days of the church there have been people who have said that the material world is unimportant or even sinful. Then they have gone on to say that conduct or the way we live is not all that important as long as we are in touch with God. This, of course, is wrong. The material order is important, and it is very very important indeed how we live.

The passage we have just read has to do with the way we live together in the fellowship of the church. In any community of people there has to be order, otherwise there will be confusion. In the church we have the opportunity, by the way we live together, of showing the respect all children of God should have towards one another and towards God's creation.

Some of the practical services of the chruch are in the hands of deacons and their women helpers (v. 11). Their duties are important ones. Deacons and deaconesses should be people of high spiritual calibre. In v. 8 Paul says they should not be 'double-tongued.' This is an interesting observation. It means that, in dealing with the members of the congregation, deacons and deaconesses should be able to resist the temptation to resort to insincerity and diplomacy in order to please everyone. They must be absolutely straightforward in their dealings.

This shows a real respect for fellow believers as part of God's purposeful creation. Deacons should be self-disciplined and selfless (v. 3), not using people and things for their own personal gain. In this way they should be an example to their own families (v. 12) and to others, leading the Lord's people on to a life where every relationship, every task is used for His glory as it ought to be.

Let us thank the Lord for the opportunity of being examples to others, through the church, of the way we should live. Let us pray that others may see in us a real respect for all of God's creation.

1 Tim. 3. 8-9; 1 Tim. 3. 11; 1 Tim. 3. 12; 1 Tim. 3. 13; 3. 14-15

Cleanliness and Order

CLEANLINESS

The children of Israel were given strict instructions regarding personal cleanliness, and they were told they should be clean 'because the Lord your God walks in the midst of your camp' (v. 14). Many people have the idea that personal cleanliness has nothing to do with spirituality, but this is obviously not true. Even a matter such as sanitation finds a mention here in the Bible, and we as believer should certainly be no less concerned about these things that God expected the people to be in Old Testament times.

The fact is that everything we do is a reflection of the kind of God we worship. If we really believe in a God of order, then we will have order in our own personal lives. On the other hand, if we are untidy and unclean in our personal habits, we are liable to be the same in our thinking and in our service for the Lord. If we do not observe a proper measure of cleanliness we will soon find that our health will suffer and, as a consequence, our witness for the Lord will suffer. If people in India observed the simple rules in our reading, India would be a much cleaner and healthier country. God's people ought to be an example in such things as part of their testimony to the purity and holiness of God.

If some highly respected person were to visit our home, we would be concerned that our home should be as clean and tidy as we could make it. It may be a very humble home, and we may have no money to spend on elaborate furnishings, but cleanliness, and order does not require a great deal of money. It requires a right attitude and a little personal effort.

Do we really believe that the sovereign, holy God dwells with us His people? If we really do believe it, would it not make a great difference to the cleanliness and order of our homes, as well as a difference in our conduct towards others? He is much greater than any earthly king.

Let us ask the Lord, that in our personal habits and in our homes we may establish order and cleanliness which will be an honour to the Lord who dwells with us.

Deut. 23. 14; 1 Cor. 14. 40; 2 Cor. 7. 1; Prov. 30. 12; Lev. 20. 7

Cleanliness and Order

ORDERED AND DISCIPLINED LIVING

October 20   Reading: Hebrews 12. 7-15

Cleanliness and order entail discipline, and conversely, if we are disciplined people, there will be cleanliness and order in our lives. Many people have the idea that discipline means correction or punishment. Basically, discipline means learning, and correction or punishment are but a part of dicipline which may sometimes be necessary in order that we might learn. The writer to the Hebrews tells us that the aim of God's discipline is 'that we may share his holiness' (v. 10), and that it might yield 'the peaceful fruit of righteousness' (v. 11).

So we see that God's discipline is purposeful. To attain any purpose in life, order is necessary, whether the purpose is lofty or something essentially simple. To write a letter, thoughts have to be ordered, and then the words put in order on paper. To cook a meal, various ingredients have to be ordered and combined in a specific way. To gain a degree, thoughts have to be ordered, facts marshalled, and conclusions reached in a disciplined fashion. Without order no aim can be attained.

God has the highest of all aims for His children, and He requires a very high degree of order and discipline. The sad fact is that so many believers resent God's discipline, or they use the plea of 'spiritual liberty' to refuse to order their lives aright. The result is that after many years of knowing the Lord they have advanced very little along the road to the purpose God has for them.

Let us always remember that spiritual liberty is not licence to do as we please under the pretext that 'the Spirit leads us'. Spiritual liberty is freedom from ourselves so that we can subject ourselves to the discipline and order of God as He sets it forth in His Word. God, as a good Father, recognizes our need of discipline (v. 7). How much, therefore, we ourselves should recognize our need of self-discipline.

Let us pray that the Lord may establish His order in our lives so that, through His discipline, His aim for us might be fulfilled.

Heb. 12. 7; Heb. 12. 8; Heb; 12. 9; Heb. 12. 10; Heb. 12. 11

Cleanliness and Order

LEVITES

When Aaron led the children of Israel into apostasy in the worship of the golden calf, the rest of the tribe of Levi remained faithful to the Lord. As a result, God gave them special responsibilities as ministers in the tabernacle. Only Aaron's sons were permitted to serve as priests, and the Levites, who were the remaining members of the tribe of Levi, took charge of the manual labour entailed in maintaining the tabernacle and transporting it from place to place. Each of the three families of Levi, the sons of Kohath, the sons of Gershon, and the sons of Merari were allotted specific duties in this connection. The Levites also had the very important ministry of acting as representatives of the first-born of all the tribes of Israel. They represented God's ideal of a people totally surrendered to Him.

Our reading today deals with the restoration of true worship under king Hezekiah. The ministrations of the temple had been discarded under the faithless king Ahaz (v. 19), and the temple itself was deserted and dirty. The Levites set about the task of bringing cleanliness and order into the temple, and preparing it again to be a place of worship to the glory of God.

The first thing the Levites did was to sanctify or cleanse themselves (v. 15). The job in which they were engaged was a humble one, but it was an important one, and they did the work as unto the Lord. It was inconceivable that the worship of God should be carried on in a careless and untidy manner. They were concerned that, in the smallest details, the dignity of the Lord should be upheld.

On the plea that the worship of God is 'spiritual' it is very easy for believers to neglect the material arrangements, the way they dress and deport themselves, saying that it is 'the heart that matters'. We need to remember that what we are outwardly is usually a reflection of what we are inwardly. This is one of the lessons we can learn from the Levites. Let us ask the Lord to help us to learn it well.

2 Chron. 29. 5; 2 Chron. 29. 15; 2 Chron. 29. 16; 2 Chron. 29. 17; 2 Chron. 29. 18

Wrong Doctrine

A PERVERSION OF TRUTH

October 22   Reading: Jeremiah 3. 19-25

Wrong doctrine has plagued the life of the church from the earliest years, and continues to do so. But what do we mean by wrong doctrine? It is very easy to accuse others of wrong doctrine in matters which are trivial and at the same time fail to understand what wrong doctrine really is.

In Old Testament times the children of Israel again and again went astray and God called them back through His prophets. At times they did openly worship pagan gods, but often they continued to offer lip service to Jehovah though their hearts were far from Him. The inroads of error was gradual.

Wrong doctrine does not usually take over all of a sudden. It makes its way slowly and unnoticed among the Lord's people in the guise of orthodox truth. Jeremiah uses a very interesting phrase when he says, "They have perverted their way" (v. 21). God's people had not been assailed by some new and heinous error. They had taken the truth of God as they understood it and perverted it to fit into their own low standards. The Lord says they were like a faithless wife who had left her husband (v. 20)..Their heart had grown cold towards the Lord, and wrong conduct and wrong belief had followed.

It is not difficult to understand how truth can be perverted. Many of the errors which exist today are the result of twisting the truth or drawing unwarrantable conclusions from it. The truth of the love of God can be perverted to mean that God will never punish sin, so people can live as they please. The truth of the judgement of God can be perverted to mean that God is lacking in grace and is just waiting to pounce upon the misdemeanours of His people. The truth of baptism can be perverted to mean that baptism of itself brings salvation. The truth of the Lord's table can be perverted to mean that it brings blessing however unworthy its reception may be.

Truth perverted by man's own self seeking can lead to wrong doctrine which can destroy the life and testimony of the church. Let us pray that the Lord will protect us from perverting the truth.

Jer. 3. 19; Jer. 3. 20; Jer. 3. 21; Jer. 3. 22; Jer. 3. 23

Wrong Doctrine

STARTS IN DISOBEDIENCE

October 23   Reading: Jude 1-8

Apparently Jude had been burdened to write a letter about 'our common salvation' (v. 3) when an urgent need presented itself 'to write appealing to you to contend for the faith which was once for all delivered to the saints' (v. 3). The word 'contend' is a strong one implying the need for mental effort to understand the faith, and moral effort to apply our understanding to every day living. The latter part of v. 3 shows that 'the faith' consists of a definite and final body of truth revealed by God which it is possible to understand and, therefore, to defend.

In opposition to this truth, as Jude warns the believers to whom he writes, certain 'ungodly persons' (v. 4) had infiltrated the fellowship of the church. They were perverting the truth, and the life of the assembly was being contaminated. Here is the same danger we saw yesterday, the danger of truth being perverted and becoming error.

Jude describes these intruders as 'ungodly'. The word indicates a basic lack of respect for God. Their lives were centred around themselves rather than on the will of God. They used the grace of God as an excuse for sin (v. 4). In doing so they were denying 'our only Master and Lord, Jesus Christ' (v. 4) though they continued to profess allegiance to Him.

Now Jude warns of their coming judgement, and in doing so warns the believers to whom he is writing of the peril of following them. He takes two examples, the children of Israel who came out of the land of Egypt (v. 5), and the angels (v. 6). Both had unique privileges, and the downfall of both was disobedience. They pleased themselves instead of pleasing God.

Very often wrong doctrine does not start with an intellectual difficulty. It starts with disobedience. It is initially a matter of the will, not of the mind. When disobedience is established, the mind is ready to accept anything that will justify it. We believe wrong because we start to do wrong.

Let us give ourselves afresh to the Lord and pray for grace to walk in obedience to His ways.

Jude 5; Jude 6; Jude 7; Jude 17-18; Jude 20-21

Wrong Doctrine

THAT WHICH DENIES BASIC TRUTH

October 24   Reading: 1 John 2. 18-25

In his first letter John explains three marks of the true child of God, right conduct, right fellowship and right belief. In vs. 18-19 he shows that there cannot be true fellowship between people who belong to the Lord and those who do not. Part of this lack of fellowship lies in a basic difference in belief. How do we distinguish right belief or doctrine from wrong?

John is quite definite in his contrast of truth with error (v. 21). All differences of opinion are not matters of different insights. They may be matters of right and wrong. There is certain basic truth which all true believers hold in common. To go beyond this basic truth is to move into heresy. There is no doubt in John's mind that it is possible to know this truth. Truth is not a matter of human speculation. It has been clearly and fully revealed by God.

The first facet of this basic truth is the truth concerning the person of our Lord Jesus Christ, His humanity and divinity. He was Jesus the man (v. 22) and also the Son, the second person of the divine trinity (v. 23). Anyone who denies this John calls a liar and the antichrist (v. 22).

A second factor of basic truth is the fact of revelation. "Let what you have heard from the beginning abide in you" (v. 24). God has given His revelation in an understandable way which is now embodied in the Bible. It is fundamental error to deny that such a revelation has been given.

The promise of eternal life (v. 25) is an indication of the work of redemption. Basic truth included an acceptance of the death and resurrection of our Lord, the work of the cross. Implicit in John's outline of doctrine is the truth about man. His concern with heresy is an admitting of man's fall, and the promise of eternal life would be meaningless if man had spiritual life already.

So fundamental truth can be summed up under four heads: the truth about man, the truth about Jesus Christ and God, the truth about redemption, and the truth about revelation. Let us ask the Lord to impress upon our hearts the importance of holding to the truth.

1 John 2. 20-21; 1 John 2. 22; 1 John 2. 23; 1 John 2. 24; 1 John 2. 25

Wrong Doctrine

OUR PARTIAL UNDERSTANDING

October 25   Reading: 1 Corinthians 13. 8-13

One of the problems with immature people is that they seldom recognize the extent of their limitations. Young people tend to see everything in terms of black and white. When they become a little older they begin to realize that problems are seldom so simple. The same is true in the spiritual realm, with one added difficulty, that the passage of years does not automatically mean a growth in spiritual maturity. Some people who have known the Lord a long time can be very spiritually immature. Yet spiritual immaturity and dogmatism often go together. People who are least competent to express an opinion are frequently the most self assured.

This was one of the problems which beleagured the Corinthian church. In relating their faith to practical daily living each one thought he knew best and criticized everyone else. All the time confusion reigned, but the Corinthians were unconcerned. Each one blamed someone else and absolved himself from responsibility.

Paul stresses the partial nature of our spiritual understanding. "Our knowledge is imperfect" (v. 9). "For now we see in a mirror dimly, but then face to face. Now I know in part, then I shall understand fully, even as I have been fully understood" (v. 12). As we saw yesterday, there is a body of basic truth of which we can be absolutely sure and on which all true believers should agree. But within this body of truth there is so much that we understand but partially. For example, we all understand broadly the functioning of the human body, the function of the brain, the heart and other organs, but in a particular sense we understand so little. There is so much that medical science has yet to learn. Amongst those who accept the basic truth we have been considering there are many differences of outlook and understanding, and as believers we should accept these differences with grace.

At the end of the chapter Paul tells us that greater than faith and hope is love. Our faith and hope will wither up unless we have the love which recognize our partial understanding of spiritual things and unites us together as God's people to learn more. Let us pray for a spirit of learning.

1 Cor. 13. 8; 1 Cor. 13. 9-10; 1 Cor. 13. 11; 1 Cor. 13. 12; 1 Cor. 13. 13

Wrong Doctrine

THE DEFENCE OF THE TRUTH

October 26   Reading: 1 Timomthy 4. 1-10

In His letters to Timothy and Titus Paul has much to say about the importance of sound doctrine in the life of the church. He is also concerned that sound doctrine should be properly defended. He had already seen the ravages wrong teaching can work amongst God's people, and he expressly warns Timothy here (vs. 1-3) that times will come when the churches will   be   assailed   by   people 'giving heed to deceitful spirits and doctrines of demons' (v. 1).

What is the answer to wrong doctrine in the church? The answer lies first in personal example. Timothy needs to be nourished in good doctrine (v. 6) if he is to withstand the dangers himself, and if he is to be able to help others withstand them. No man can be a true teacher unless he is constantly learning himself. An ignorant ministry is a dire threat to the spiritual life of the church. A sound understanding of Christian doctrine will help us to adopt a right attitude to those who are in danger of being led astray. It will also help us to avoid being taken up with side issues which detract from the cental facts of the faith (v. 7).

In v. 6 Paul says, "Put these instructions before the brethren." Paul uses an interesting word here. The surest method of driving people away is by an arrogant, dogmatic presentation of what we think is true. The word Paul uses is the very opposite of this. It is the suggestion of the teacher who knows his subject and is content to let the truth do its own work so that people are convinced of the truth for themselves.

We must be an example not only in our diligence to understand and teach, but also in our diligence to grow in godliness (vs. 7-8). The aim of spiritual fullness, or to use Paul's words, 'Our hope set on the living God' (v. 10), affects the whole man. The proof of any teaching is its effects. A godliness which compasses the whole person is the best advertisement for the Christian faith, and the surest antidote to error.

Let us pray that we may worthily defend the truth through what we teach and the way we live.

1 Tim. 4. 1; 1 Tim. 4. 4-5; 1 Tim. 4. 6; 1 Tim 4. 7; 1 Tim. 4. 8

Wrong Doctrine

JUDGEMENT OF WRONG DOCTRINE

October 27   Reading: Titus 3. 8-11

In this passage Paul stresses the need for action. There are people who are quick to condemn what they consider to be wrong doctrine in others, but they show very little of the impact of right doctrine in their own lives. Before we have a right to judge what is wrong in others we must exemplify what is right in our own living.

Greek philosophers and Jewish leaders spent endless time discussing religious problems, and some of them seemed to feel that there was merit simply in discussing these things. The same practice is fairly prevalent among some of the Lord's people today. People can become very heated in defending a pet doctrine or practice and yet can have little concern to work out what they so fervently claim to believe. All such is 'unprofitable and futile' (v. 9). We need to know what we believe, otherwise we will have no standards to guide us in our daily living, but the hall mark of the true believer is the way he lives, not what he professes to believe.

Having said this, we are responsible to exercise right judgement within the church. A certain body of truth is foundational to the life of any local church, and people who deny that truth have no place within the fellowship of God's people. The Authorised Version uses the word 'heretic' in v. 10, whereas the RSV uses 'factious'. The word Paul uses refers to a person who makes his own self-opinionated view the standard of all truth He has decided that what he says is right and everyone else wrong. He is closed to the fellowship of others, and is closed even to exhortation from the Word. "After admonishing him once or twice, have nothing to do with him," says Paul (v. 10).

It is a very serious thing for a man to hold to an idea which separates him from his fellow believers and closes his mind to what God wants to say through others. True faith always unites men. It makes a clear distinction between the believer and the unbeliever, but it does not separate believers from one another. Let us ask God to show us any ideas and attitudes in our own lives which require to be judged before we take upon ourselves the onerous responsibility of judging others.

Matt. 18. 15; Matt. 18. 16; Matt. 18. 17; Titus 3. 8; Titus 3. 10-11

Wrong Doctrine

JEHU

Reading: 2 Kings 10. 23-31

In these verses we see two sides of Jehu's character, his zeal for the Lord, and his pathetic weakness in ordering his own life aright.

Jehu was commander of Israel's army under king Jehoram, son of Ahab. While Jehoram was recovering from wounds received in battle, Elisha sent one of the sons of the prophets to anoint Jehu king, and he was given the task of exterminating the wicked house of Ahab. This Jehu did with all the vigour of his vigorous character, and perhaps went beyond the terms of the commission he was given.

Jehoram met his death at Jehu's hand, and Jezebel was thrown down into the courtyard of the palace to meet her end exactly as foretold by Elijah the prophet. Our reading tells of the destruction of the worshippers in the temple of Baal.

Jehu wiped out the worship of Baal from Israel (v. 28), and then his true character began to show itself in religious compromise. He tolerated the corrupt worship of God linked with 'the golden calves that were in Bethel, and in Dan' (v. 29). God commended him for ridding Israel of the evil of the house of Ahab (v. 30), but 'he did not turn from the sin of Jeroboam, which made Israel to sin' (v. 31). "Jehu was not careful to walk in the law of the Lord the God of Israel with all his heart (v. 31). It is not at all suprising that the nation did not prosper under his rule.

What was lacking in Jehu's zeal? It was purely negative. With great enthusiasm he tore down and destroyed what was evil, but when it came to positive obedience of the ways of the Lord he was woefully weak. We cannot build a life for the Lord on a foundation of evil. We must be ready to judge whatever is sinful within ourselves or within the church. But judgement of evil is not itself enough. True faith is always positive and must be directed to a life of obedience, establishing the standards of the Lord in our own lives and in the life of the church.

Let us pray that God will give us a heart not to stop at the judgement of sin, but to follow Him.

2 Kings 10. 16; 2 Kings 10. 31; Rom. 16. 17; Josh 22. 5; 2 Kings 19. 31

Church Elders

PLURALITY OF ELDERS

October 29   Reading: Acts 14. 19-23

The churches in New Testament times were governed by elders and in each local church there were always more than one. Two Greek words are used. The first, 'episkopos' is translated 'bishop' or 'overseer'. The second, 'presbuteros' is translated 'elder'. These two words indicate the same office and are used interchangeably. At Miletus, for example, Paul calls the 'elder's of the Ephesian church and exhorts them as those whom the Holy Spirit has made 'overseers' of the flock (Acts 20. 17, 28 NIV). In writing to Titus he asks him to appoint 'elders' in every city in Crete, explaining the qualities which should characterize those who are fit to occupy the position of an 'overseer' (Titus 1. 5-7 NIV).

The common practice today is for a local church or assembly to be governed by one man. Where elders exist they often have no real authority. They are there merely to carry out the wishes of the person who exercises the controlling power.

The significance of Paul and Barnabas' return visit to places in which they had previously ministered was that 'they appointed elders for them in every church' (v. 23). Notice the plural 'elders', and also the fact that there was no higher authority within the local church apart from the Lord Himself.

It is always easier for one person to exercise authority than for a number of people to exercise authority as a group, but we are not called always to take the easier way. To work harmoniously with others requires a great measure of humility and willingness to adjust.

One of the most important aspects of our life in Christ is fellowship. It removes the old spirit of self-centred living and gives us a new concern for the interests of the Lord and for others. The leaders of the church should, above all, be examples of this fellowship to other less mature believers. If more mature believers are not able to work in harmony and fellowship with one another, how can less mature believers be expected to do so? This is one of the challenges of eldership, and one of the reasons for plural eldership within the local church. Let us pray for a greater sense of the responsibilities and privileges of fellowship.

Acts 14. 22; Acts 14. 23; Phil. 1. 1; Acts 20. 17; 1 Pet. 5. 1

The Church Elders

THE APPOINTMENT OF ELDERS

October 30   Reading: Acts 20. 25-32

How are elders in a local church appointed? There is surprisingly little in the New Testament on this subject. In Acts 14. 23 there is one specific reference to elders being set apart by Paul and Barnabas in the cities of Lystra, Iconium and Pisidian Antioch. Writing years later to Titus, Paul charges him 'to appoint elders in every town' (Titus 1.5). No hint is given as to how the elders at Jerusalem, Ephesus and Philippi came to occupy their position, while it appears that, in other places, Corinth and Thessalonica for example, elders were recognized without any formal appointment.

The New Testament cites no instances of setting apart elders which could justifiably form a precedent for all time. Paul and Barnabas did set apart elders in certain places as we have already seen but this is not mentioned as a regular aspect of their ministry. There is no support in Scripture for the idea that appointment to the office of eldership was an apostolic prerogative.

Our reading recounts Paul's exhortaion to the elders of the church at Ephesus. Paul was passing through the port of Miletus and called the elders to meet him there. Whether they had originally been appointed by Paul we have no idea. No indication of how they were set apart is given. There is, however, an interesting and important pointer to the Scriptural emphasis in v. 28 where Paul says, "Take heed to yourselves and to all the flock, in which the Holy Spirit has made you guardians"

The emphasis of the Scriptures is that elders are the appointment of the Spirit. They were marked out as the divine choice by their life and conduct, a choice accepted by all who were spiritual in the assembly. Relegation of the choice directly to the Spirit according to the standard laid down in the Word effectively debars the self assertive from assuming a position of authority, and also protects the work of God from the fallibility of human judgement.

Let us thank God for His wisdom in ordering the life of the church, and let us pray that we may be protected from adopting human expedients.

Acts 20. 27; Acts 20. 28; Acts. 20. 29; Acts. 20. 31; Acts. 20. 32

Church Elders

QUALIFICATIONS FOR ELDERS (1)

October 31   Reading: 1 Timothy 3. 1-7

To desire the office of an overseer in New Testament days meant to be ready for sacrifice. Persecution was apt to break out at any time, and the elders would be the first to suffer. Ambition is not wrong provided it is ambition to serve, not ambition for the reputation of serving.

It is obvious from a reading of these qualifications that an elder should be a man of character and maturity. Yet the moral qualities which Paul enumerates are no more than should be found in any person who is settled in the faith and growing in the Lord. An elder in his character should be an example of what the grace of God can do in any believer. The qualities are such that none of them can afford to be waived. The word 'must' in v. 2 is a clear indication of a standard which cannot be relaxed. It is the minimum to be expected in a man whom aspires to eldership.

We have here an example of the relatedness of different aspects of Christian living. The sphere of Christian responsibility does not begin and end in the church. The believer has responsibilities in his own home and in the world. If he fails in these he will certainly fail in his responsibilities in the church. The elder should be a man respected by the church itself (vs. 2-3), a man 'above reproach' (v. 2). This sums up the qualities that follow.

Special mention should be made of the second condition, 'The husband of one wife.' It means that an elder should be faithful to his one and only marriage partner. He should not be divorced. Chastity was a distinctive Christian virture. On it depended, and still depends, the sanctity of the family and, therefore, to a large extent the stability of the church. The man who fails to see the standard of Christ exhibited in his own household is not in a fit position to share in the oversight of the church.

An elder should also have a good testimony in the world (v. 7). Few things are more damaging to the cause of Christ than men in the councils of the church whose business and social life is inconsistent with the faith they profess.

Let us ask God to give us the ambition to serve.

1 Tim. 3. 1; 1 Tim. 3. 2-3; 1 Tim. 3. 4-5; 1 Tim 3. 6; 1 Tim. 3. 7

Church Elders

QUALIFICATIONS FOR ELDERS (2)

November 1   Reading: Titus 1. 5-11

The testimony of a local church to a large extent depends on the quality of its eldership, so it is appropriate to note the emphasis which Paul makes again here in his letter to Titus.

An elder should be a man deservedly held in high esteem, and one whose family and household are a testimony to the faith he professes (v. 6). Spiritual confusion often enters the church through the disruption of family life. If the households of the elders are not a good testimony, there can be little encouragement for stable families among less mature believers. The obvious tenor of the present passage is that elders should rule by example rather than by decree.

Vs. 7-9 contain a list of negative and a list of positive characteristics for elders. In the latter (vs. 8-9) the emphasis is that both in deed and in teaching an elder should be a means of edification to others.

These characteristics form the basis for discipline within the church. Influences which would destroy the testimony of Christ are not to be looked upon lightly, but they are to be quenched not by argument alone, but by the indisputable evidence of Christian character. Paul says of those who are disturbing the church's life, "They must be silenced" (v. 11). The word he uses means to 'muzzle'. Where a profession of faith is demonstrated by living example, those who oppose it are left speechless. One Greek word is translated 'confute' in v. 9 and 'rebuke' in v. 13. It signifies an exhortation which carries conviction with it because it is backed by the transparent sincerity and godly character of the elder.

The spiritual life of the local church may be beset by constant problems, but the combination of faith, character and sound teaching demonstrated in a stable eldership forms a solid basis from which these difficulties can be dealt with.

Let us thank God for His order for the church, and pray that our lives may be a strength to the church's testimony and a rebuke to those who disobey the ways of the Lord.

Tit. 1. 5-6; Tit. 1. 7-8; Tit. 1. 9; Tit. 1. 10; Tit. 1. 11

Church Elders

THE AUTHORITY OF ELDERS

November 2   Reading: 1 Timothy 4. 11-16

Authority is an inevitable part of living, whether in the family, the church, or in society. Wherever people are called to relate to others there must be a recognition of authority. There are two types of authority, authority based on position, and authority based upon character. The authority of an elder is, or should be, based upon character. When purely positional authority is established within a church the result is tension, dissension and spiritual powerlessness.

In our reading Paul's emphasis is the importance of authority based upon character and the ministry which flows from it. From v. 11 he stresses the need of consistent spiritual living and of diligently teaching the Word. There can be no doubt that much failure in the life of a church can be attributed to a lack in these two respects. Where there is not a good example set in Christian character by a church's elders, the life of the church falls rapidly into decay. Where there is not a competent teaching ministry, and that is impossible apart from the character of the teacher, the door is wide open to all types of error.

What we teach must be backed up by our conduct (v. 12). Christian character should be marked by a concern for others, a loyalty to the Lord, and a respect for the high standards of the Word (v. 12). We must be diligent in using the gift God has given (v. 14). Living a consistent life and learning to present the Word of God adequately requires constant effort and concentration (v. 15). This self-discipline is the road to an effective and an authoritative ministry. The Christian leader cannot demand the respect of others. He must win it by his obvious spiritual calibre and growth in the things of the Lord.

The final exhortation of the chapter, "Take heed to yourself and to your teaching" (v. 16), is a warning to live consistently with what we profess to believe. Only when we grow in Christ ourselves will we be able to minister Christ to others. All spiritual authority is dependent upon spiritual character. An elder's position can never be a substitute for an elder's character.

Let us pray that, by our character, we may earn the right to minister to others.

1 Tim. 4. 11-12; 1 Tim. 4. 13; 1 Tim. 4. 14; 1 Tim. 4. 15; 1 Tim. 4. 16

Church Elders

THE DISCIPLINE OF ELDERS

November 3   Reading: 1 Timothy 5. 17-22

If the conditions laid down for eldership are not strictly observed, the church will sooner or later be the scene of confusion. Where they are observed and worthy elders are in office, the church should remember its responsibility to them. Particularly should the congregation honour an edifying ministry. To teach and to preach competently requires hard and consistent labour. The Christian minister is not a recipient of charity. He earns what he receives (v. 18).

It is inevitable that, at times, elders should be the targets of malicious talk. If they are men chosen because they obviously possess the qualities of elders, then a charge should never lightly be accepted against them. The question here is not of accepting a conviction against an elder, but even of admitting a charge against him. This should never be done unless there are at least two reliable witnesses (v. 19).

No elder, however, enjoys an immunity from reprimand. Where any Christian leader feels he should not be corrected, the church is in a very dangerous state. The duty of correcting belongs to those of spiritual status and must be exercised with great care.

Where an elder persists in sin, his public position demands that he should suffer public rebuke (v. 20) in order that he himself might be convicted, as a warning to others, and as a testimony to the church's stand for righteousness. The importance of this is emphasized by the serious way in which Paul makes his charge to Timothy (v. 21) and his warning against partiality. The sin of partiality is a particular temptation in dealing with those who have occupied places of spiritual prominence and authority. The health of any church depends to a large extent on the exercise of impartial discipline. Few things do more harm to a local testimony than the idea that some people can do no wrong, and others can do no right.

No position that we may occupy within the church frees us from subjection to godly discipline and correction. Let us always be open to correction, and pray that we may be kept from ever thinking that we are above the need for it.

1 Tim. 5. 17; 1. Tim. 5. 18; 1 Tim. 5. 19; 1 Tim. 5. 20; 1 Tim. 5. 21

Church Elders

DAVID

November 4   Reading: 1 Samuel 16. 6-13

God sent Samuel to anoint a king in the place of Saul God told him that the new king would be one of the sons of Jesse the Bethlehemite. When Samuel arrived at Bethlehem he prepared to offer a sacrifice to the Lord and invited Jesse with his sons.

Jesse had eight sons, and seven of them passed before Samuel (v. 10). His first impression was that Eliab, the first son to be brought before him, was God's choice, but the Lord warned him, "Do not look on his appearance or on the height of his stature, because I have rejected him; for the Lord sees not as man sees; man looks on the outward appearance, but the Lord looks on the heart" (v. 7).

Man always needs to beware of superficial judgements, and this is just as true of men of spiritual experience as it is of anyone else. Samuel, for all his experience and knowledge of God, was not infallible, and was in danger of being deceived by appearances. He was saved from a tragic error because he still had an open ear to God's voice.

It is very easy to be enamoured of a striking personality, or perhaps with a man of good organizational ability, and to think that he is the one to further the work of God. In doing so we may fail to see inner weaknesses that are serious disqualifications from God's point of view.

This does not mean that the outer man is unimportant, and that the man with no personality or initiative is the one God chooses, but it means that God wants something more than a man's natural, fallen abilities. Eliab had plenty of apparent potential, but he obviously did not possess the humble spirit which would have made his potential useful to the Lord.

It had never crossed Jesse's mind that his youngest son David might have any special place in God's purposes, but God thought otherwise. David had a pleasing character. "Now he was ruddy, and had beautiful eyes, and was handsome" (v. 12). But more than these things, he had a heart that was right with God and a will that was open to God's working. These were the qualities that were to make him a fit elder in Israel.

Let us ask God to make us truly usable in His hands.

1 Sam. 2. 3; 1 Sam. 16. 13; 1 Kings 8. 39; 1 Chron. 28. 9; Lk. 16. 15

Authority

AUTHORITY BASED ON POSITION

November 5   Reading: Luke 22. 24-27

Authority is one of the most crucial problems facing the individual believer and the church. Within every person are two paradoxical traits, the desire for an authority to which he can submit, and the desire to wield authority in however limited a sphere. It is very important, therefore, to understand what true spiritual authority is. An authority which is not based on the teaching of Scripture can be devastating in its consequences, both for those who wield it, and for those who are subject to it.

The disciples were very far from being impervious to the desire for authority. All of them would claim to bow before the authority of the Lord, but among themselves they were disputing about which one of them was the greatest (v. 24). It would seem that some of their claims were based on seniority, others on experience (v. 26). Their idea of authority was based on the superior position these things gave them.

Our Lord shows them that all authority is not equally valid in the sight of God. The basis of authority in the world is completely different from the basis of true spiritual authority. This is what Jesus points out so forcibly in the illustration of v. 25. "The kings of the Gentiles exercise Lordship over them." A king occupies a position from which he exercises authority quite independent of his character. In the realm of Christian work some people win a following and become leaders by virtue of their character. Often, however, this leads to their being given a position which may become the sole basis of their authority. Though they may lose out spiritually, their authority is retained because it is now basically dependent upon the position they occupy.

In the military world a man possessees authority because of his rank. He may or may not be a person of principle and moral integrity. In the political world people vie for position because position means authority. Even in the life of the church, authority may be in the hands of people who have assumed position or been voted into it without any spiritual qualifications. In this way a worldly concept of authority, based on position, invades the life of the church. Let us pray that we may be people of spiritual authority whom others follow because we are like Christ.

Luke 22. 25; Luke 22. 26; Luke 22. 27; Acts 5. 36. 1 Cor. 15. 24

Authority

THE AUTHORITY OF SPIRITUAL CHARACTER

November 6   Reading; 1 Thessalonians 1. 1-7

Yesterday we saw how our Lord explained to His disciples that their authority would be based not on any position they might occupy, but on their spirit of service to others. In other words, spiritual authority is based upon spiritual character. To a believing Christian, position should always be subservient to character.

The authority of spiritual character is seen supremely in the life of our Lord Himself. "He taught them as one who had authority, and not as the Scribes" (Mark 1. 22). Our Lord had no position here upon the earth. He was not a leader of the synagogue or the head of any religious order. Yet He had authority because of the quality of His character. In contrast, the Scribes were leaders in an authoritative position from which they could make demands upon others, but their teaching did not have that ring of divine authority which was so obvious in our Lord's words.

In Paul's relationship with the Thessalonians we again see the authority of spiritual character. It is true that he was an apostle, but he could make no legal claim on the obedience of others. Paul's stay in Thessalonica had been little more than three weeks (Acts 17.2) but his character had made a powerful impression upon the people. As he tells them, the gospel was not only preached before them, it was lived before them. "You know what kind of men we proved to be among you for your sake" (v. 5). The result was they accepted the word even 'in much affliction' (v. 6) and themselves became an example to all the believers in Macedonia and the adjoining province of Achaia (v. 7). Such was the spiritual authority of Paul. Its influence transformed the lives of others to the glory of God.

Elders held positions of authority within the churches, but the qualifications for elders clearly show that they had to be men of spiritual character first of all (1 Tim. 3. 1-8; Titus 1. 6-9). Their character was the source of their authority, and if they should lapse from the godly standard according to which they once lived, they were no longer entitled to hold the position.

God expects all His children to be people of spiritual authority who influence others because they themselves live for Christ.

Mark 1. 22; 1 Thess. 1. 5; 1 Thess. 1. 6; Luke 19. 17; Dan. 12. 3

Authority

THE AUTHORITY OF CHRIST

November 7   Reading: 1 Corinthians 2: 1-8

Paul was a man of spiritual authority. His message invoked a vital response from those who heard it. Yet it is equally clear that he never used his authority as a means of gathering people around himself. He even refused to administer baptism lest people should become his followers instead of followers of Christ (1 Cor. 1. 14-15). The great purpose of his ministry was to focus the attention of the believers upon Christ.

In our reading Paul emphasises the supremacy and authority of the Lord. Paul was learned in philosophy, but he had not come to propound a philosophic theory (v. 1). He was unconcerned to hide his own fears and weaknesses (v. 3). He had come to proclaim Jesus Christ and Him crucified (v. 2). He made no claim to any final authority for himself. He wanted the Corinthians to realize that all authority belonged to God, "That your faith might not rest in the wisdom of men but in the power of God" (v. 5).

"Yet among the mature we do impart wisdom... But we impart a secret and hidden wisdom of God" (vs. 6, 7). The depths of the gospel can only be understood by those who are 'mature', people who see beyond the authority of a man to the authority of God. Then and only then will they be able rightly to interpret the ministry God communicates through His servants. They will be able to discern between 'plausible words of wisdom' and the 'demonstration of the Spirit and of power' (v. 4), for in the ministry of any man these are liable to be mixed.

Authority belongs to our Lord Jesus Christ because He is God, and authority is given to His people to the extent in which they manifest His character. So the authority of a believer is derived from the authority of Christ. Respect is due first to the authority of Christ, but the person who recognizes authority in Christ Himself will recognize it also in the measure in which it exists in His servants. Submission to one another, to the church, to its eldership, is a duty for all believers, but it cannot be total, unquestioning submission, because none of these are God. All are fallible. Final authority belongs to the Lord alone. May the Lord help us to submit directly to Him and to His authority wherever it is truly manifested.

1 Cor. 2. 1; 1 Cor. 2. 2; 1 Cor. 2. 3; 1 Cor. 2. 4; 1 Cor. 2. 5

Authority

DELEGATED AUTHORITY

November 8   Reading: 1 Peter 5. 1-5

Peter speaks to elders to whom God has delegated authority within the local church. Then he counsels those who are younger to be subject to them (v. 5). Notice, however, that all authority ultimately goes back to God. the flock is God's flock (v. 2); It does not belong to any man. The elders are shepherds who tend the flock of God for Him, not for themselves. One day the chief Shephered will come and the under shepherds will have to give an account of their stewardship (v. 4).

It is a very serious thing to be answerable to God. This is what Peter here tries to emphasize. Human nature is such that there is an inborn tendency to domineer over others. Even the most timid person who seems to bend at the least sight of authority will try to show his superiority by venting his spite on some weaker creature.

This spirit of petty tyranny is frequently found within the church. Self-styled leaders domineer over those under them and look for an unquestioning obedience which they themselves will give to no one, not even to the Lord. This happens whenever believers fail to recognize the seriousness of their commission and their responsibility to God. As soon as a person takes seriously the fact that he is answerable to God, and begins to order his daily life accordingly, he will be an example to the flock (v. 3). His authority will be the authority of character which others will gladly follow, not the domineering authority which breeds resentment.

Spiritual authority is humble (v. 5) because the person who wields it knows that its source is nothing within himself. Its source is Christ, and it will remian only as long as he himself is under authority to Christ.

It is significant that alongside his exhortation to the younger to submit themselves to the elders (v. 5), Peter says, "Clothe yourselves, all of you, with humility toward one another." The elder is himself under authority to God, and God may speak through any one of His flock He chooses, even through the youngest. The elder must have his ear atune to the voice of God through whatever channel it may come. Let us pray for a more ready ear to hear God's voice and a more ready spirit to submit to Him.

1 Pet. 5. 4; Matt. 16. 19; Isa. 22. 22; 2 Cor. 5. 20; Prov. 13. 17

Authority

THE MISUSE OF AUTHORITY

November 9   Reading: Galatians 2. 11-16

Here we have the spectacle of an open confrontation between two great apostles, Paul and Peter (Cephas). Peter had been an apostle before Paul (1. 7). He had been entrusted with the gospel to the circumcised (2. 7). He was a pillar of the church (2. 9). A good case could have been put up for Peter's superior authority, but Paul was not to be intimidated. Peter had misused his authority and had, therefore, forefeited it. He had to be opposed.

No servant of God automatically maintains his spiritual authority, nor does any servant of God ever reach a position where it is impossible for him to mususe it. Unlike uninspired biography, Scripture is meticulously honest in portraying the lives of God's people. The failures as well as the strengths of men like Peter and Paul are faithfully recorded for our learning.

Here Paul recounts a twofold misuse of authority, first on the part of 'certain men' who came down from James (v. 12), and then on the part of Peter himself. Whether the pressure group that so intimidated Peter was actually backed by the authority of James and the Jerusalem church we do not know. It certainly claimed to be. When we consider the Judaizing tendencies within the church at Jerusalem, it is by no means impossible that they favoured the imposition of Jewish laws upon believers who had come from a Gentile background. If this was so, then they, as well as those who came to Antioch were guilty of the misuse of the authority God had given them to preach the gospel.

The influence of those men from Jerusalem so troubled Peter that he too lost his spiritual balance. His action was not of conviction but of fear (v. 12). Paul says he was 'not straightforward about the truth of the gospel' (v. 14). Peter used his apostolic position to spread teaching which in his own heart he did not believe, with the result that 'even Barnabas was carried away by their insincerity' (v. 13).

God had His hand upon the situation, and necessary rebuke and correction were administered, but the incident shows how easily spiritual authority can be misused, and the grave dangers that result.

Let us pray that God wil help us to use aright the authority He has given us to minister His Word.

Gal. 2. 11; Gal. 2. 12; Gal. 2. 13; Gal. 2. 14; Gal. 2. 15-16

314

Authority

THE MOTIVATION OF AUTHORITY

November 10   Reading: Hebrews 13. 17-21

What motivates people to seek authority? It has already been pointed out that true spiritual authority is based upon character. To a large extent, therefore, spiritual authority is wielded unconsciously. Yet our witness and service for the Lord are fruitless apart from spiritual authority, and there can be no such witness and service apart from a conscious motivation. So authority, witness and motivation are all closely linked together.

It is a sad fact that ulterior motives often characterize the scramble for authoritative positions in the church. The writer to the Hebrews asks for prayer on this very count, that he and others with responsibility among the people of God might be protected from wrong motivation and might 'have a clear conscience, desiring to act honourably in all things' (v. 18).

People of the world desire authority in order that they may gain by it. The purpose of spiritual authority, on the other hand, is to serve. Much of what we have already said over the past few days is summed up in the present passage. Leaders are those who watch over the souls of others as men who will have to give an account (v. 17). They look for the opportunity to serve and recognize that they have been entrusted by God with responsibilities for which they will one day have to answer to Him. THe prayer of v. 18 shows a concern that they should be an example to others by the character of their daily lives.

The great benediction of vs. 20-21 calls our Lord Jesus Christ the 'great Shepherd of the sheep'. Spiritual authority cannot exist apart from humility and submission to Him. The Great Shepherd's motive and purpose in caring for His sheep is wonderfully expressed in v. 21. It is to 'equip you with everything good that you may do his will, working in you that which is pleasing in his sight, through Jesus Christ; to whom be glory for ever and ever.' The purpose and motive of the under-shepherds can only be the same if they are true to their calling and accept the authority of the One who has commissioned them.

Let us ask God to keep us from wrong motives, and that we may have a clear conscience. desiring to act honourably in all things (v. 18).

Heb. 13. 17: Heb. 13. 18-19: Luke 16. 2; 2 Cor. 1. 12; 1 Thess. 2. 10

Authority

ZERUBBABEL

Reading: Zechariah 4. 1-11

Zerubbabel, son of Shealtiel, was governor of Judah. He had an unenviable task. The work of rebuilding the temple had been commenced, but was stopped shortly afterwards, and nothing was done for a period of about fifteen years. As the time went by, people became less and less concerned with the work of God and more immersed in their own interests. Zerubbabel's concern was to dispel the spiritual lethargy which had settled upon the nation and to rekindle the fire of enthusiasm to work for God.

Born in Babylon, Zerubbabel, along with Joshua the high priest, was active in the restoration of spiritual worship on the people's return from captivity (Ezra 3. 2), and under their leadership the foundation of the temple was restored (Ezra 3.8-10). Zerubbabel does not seem to have been an outstandingly gifted man. He was neither a statesman nor an orator, but he was faithful in his burden to further the Lord's cause. As governor of Judah (Hag. 1. 1) he apparently occupied a position of some authority, but this alone was not sufficient to restore to the cold hearts of the people a warmth of devotion to the Lord. Authority which stems only from a position can at best deal with things on a superficial level. It cannot deal with the things of the heart, emotions, attitudes, motives.

Zerubbabel needed all the encouragement God could give him. Zechariah's vision shows that human ability and position of themselves are quite insufficient to accomplish the purposes of God. The authority which will bring life and vitality must have its source in God Himself (v. 6).

The golden lampstand (v. 2) represents a testimony in righteousness for God here upon the earth. It cannot be sustained by human effort and ingenuity, but by the oil (v. 3) of the Holy Spirit of which there is a constant, free supply for those whose dependence is wholly upon the Lord.

Zerubbabel laboured with God (v. 8) and nothing could withstand him (v. 7), but the power and authority were the Lord's, and Zerubbabel, God's channel. Let us thank God for the privilege of being his channel, and let us pray that we may never usurp the power and authority that are His alone.

Zech. 4. 2-3; Zech. 4. 6; Zech; 4. 7; Zech. 4. 8; Zech. 4. 9-10

The Great Commission

THE COMMISSION TO THE DISCIPLES

November 12   Reading: Matthew 28. 16-20

The great commission which our Lord gave initially to the eleven disciples (v. 16) was the starting point of a witness to the gospel which has spanned the world. It began in Jerualem, and in the book of Acts, Luke traces the spread of the gospel into the Gentile world. It continued to spread down through the centuries, and today the church of Jesus Christ is established on every continent.

Yet our Lord's commission is as applicable to us today as it was in the time of the disciples. There are still multitudes who have never heard the name of Jesus Christ and have had no opportunity consciously to receive His saving grace.

The word 'disciple' means a pupil, one who learns. All who have received the saving grace of God are disciples, and all have some responsibility in fulfilling our Lord's commission. The disciples went forth realizing that they were backed not by the authority of man, but by the authority of God Himself (v. 18). The result was that, amidst all the opposition and persecution they endured, nothing could withstand the power of the gospel they preached. We today represent the same God and are backed by the same resources.

Jesus instructed His disciples to 'make disciples' (v. 19), to baptize (v. 19), and to teach those who believed to observe all that He had commanded (v. 20). These are three important aspects of our commission. Our witness for Christ does not end when a person has made a profession of faith in Him. We must encourage that person himself to become one who is constantly eager to learn from the Lord. And we will be able to do this only if we are learners ourselves.

The second responsibility of witness is demonstrated in baptism. Baptism is an open confession of faith and identification with Christ who was different from all the world around. A believer in Christ cannot hold on to past associations which would separate him from other believers. He must identify himself with Christ alone, where all who own Him are truly one and old distinctions of background are gone for ever. The third responsibility of witness is to teach the ways of the Lord that those who trust Him will grow in lives of true righteousness.

Let us ask God to make us faithful to the great commission He Has given us.

Mark 16. 15; Luke 24. 45-46; Luke 24. 47-48; Luke 24. 49; Luke 24. 50-51

317

The Great Commission

RESPONSIBILITY TO THE WORLD

November 13   Reading: Romans 4. 16-25

In spite of our Lord's clear teaching, there was an idea among some in the early church that the gospel was only for the Jews. The idea that the Jews had a place of special privilege before God simply because of the fact of their race was something Paul had to combat again and again in the course of his ministry. He himself, though a Jew and a Pharisee, had been particularly chosen of God as the apostle to the Gentiles. Paul knew that the gospel was for the world.

Here in Rom. 4 he shows that God's grace was not limited to the race bound by the Mosaic law, because God had given His promise of blessing to Abraham centuries before Moses was born. The promise was based not on law, but on faith which works righteousness (vs. 13, 16). Abraham was called to be father of a spiritual people composed of all those, of whatever race they might be, who had the same faith as he had himself (vs. 23-24). God made him the father of many nations (vs. 17, 18).

In this way Paul shows that the gospel is for all mankind, and our Lord's great commisson bids us reach out beyond our own community or race with the message of salvation. Jesus said, "God so loved the world" (John 3.16). He Himself came with the message for the world. Paul realized the tremendous implications of this. His vision reached out to Rome and to Spain, the great centres of influence in the world of his day. God would have us catch something of the same breadth of vision.

The Jews and the Gentiles harboured a traditional enmity against one another which went back for hundreds of years. Writing to the Ephesians, Paul shows that in Christ neither Jew nor Gentile exists any longer. Their place has been taken by 'one new man'. The wall of hostility has been broken down. The hostility has been brought to an end (Eph. 2. 14-16).

How important it is for us to see beyond the limitations of our background. There are some believers who would hardly dream of witnessing to anyone outside their own community. This is entirely wrong, for as believers in Christ we have a responsibility for the world. Let us ask God to enlarge our vision, and help us minister His truth irrespective of class or community.

Rom. 4. 16; Rom. 4. 17; Rom. 4. 18; Rom. 4. 19; Rom. 4. 21-22

The Great Commission

SUPPORTING THE WORK OF GOD

November 14   Reading: 1 Corinthians 9. 8-14

God calls some of His people to devote the whole of their time to the ministry of the Word. It is the privilege of the rest of God's people to support these by their prayers, effort and giving. Paul's life was given over to the preaching of the gospel, and he never made any claim for support upon the Corinthians or anyone else (v. 12). Nevertheless, he clearly sets out before them their responsibility. Giving for the furtherance of the great commission he sees as a clear spiritual principle and duty.

In v. 9 Paul quoted from the book of Deuteronomy. "You shall not muzzle an ox when it is treading out the grain" (Deut. 25. 4). Then in v. 13 he speaks of those who were employed in the service of the temple, and who were supported by the gifts of the people (Num. 5. 9-10). The conclusion he draws is plain. Those who serve in the things of the Spirit should not be denied needful material support (v. 11). "Those who proclaim the gospel should get their living by the gospel" (v. 14).

In Old Testament times a tithe or tenth was given for the support of the Levites and the tabernacle services (Num. 18. 21-24). There is no tabernacle or temple today, nor is the giving of a tenth any longer a legal requirement, but since our Lord more than fulfilled the law in all He did and taught, surely the giving of believing Christians today should be no less than the giving of Old Testament times. Rather should it be more.

The servant of God is obliged to do his work faithfully. The ox works hard (v. 9). So does the ploughman (v. 10). So do those who proclaim the gospel (v. 14). In the world everybody expects to pay for the services from which he benefits. We pay for the service of public transport. We pay for those who serve us in numerous ways. Likewise, if we accept the spiritual services of a minister of God's Word, we should feel a responsibility to give him necessary support. He too has to eat and live.

Paul, as do many servants of God, ministered to those beyond the circle of the church. It is the believer's privilege and responsibility not only to support the life of the local church, but to support the spread of the gospel as well. Let us ask God's direction in our giving, and let us be faithful in supporting His work.

Mal. 3. 10; 1 Cor. 9. 9; 1 Cor. 9. 11; 1 Cor. 9. 13; 1 Cor. 9. 14

The Great Commission

STUDYING TO FULFIL THE COMMISSION

November 15   Reading: Ezra 7. 1-10

Among those who returned to Jerusalem from captivity in Babylon was Ezra. He was 'a scribe skilled in the law of Moses' (v. 6). He was the man whom God used to bring His Word back into its place of rightful pre-eminence in the midst of His people. God had given Ezra a commission, and he had a great burden to fulfil it.

Ezra was a man well prepared for his task, and a man who was also aware of the need of continual preparation. When he returned from Babylon he was already learned in the law of Moses. He had a background of knowledge through which the Lord was able to impart increasing insights and build him up steadily in the understandiing of His ways.

It is evident from v. 10 that Ezra gave himself diligently to the study of God's Word. But he was much more than a scholar. What he learned was no mere abstract truth. It was applied practically to his own personal situation and worked out in his daily walk. From his knowledge of the truth and his practice of the truth Ezra was able 'to teach his (God's) statutes and ordinances in Israel' (v. 10).

The three factors mentioned in v. 10 go essentially together, the knowledge of the truth, the practice of the truth, and the teaching of the truth. In our Lord's great commission the Lord has called us to teach men to observe all that He has commanded (Matt. 28. 20). We can only do this adequately if we are constant students of the Word, and people who live according to the Word.

The Lord's commission is a challenge to us to be people of the Word. We cannot act aright unless we know the Word and what it means. Believers often get into grave difficulties simply because they do not know what God's Word says and, therefore, do not act according to it. Our witness to others will only be effective when people see that the Word of God provides us with a sure guide for our daily living. Let us make a greater effort to set time apart to study the Word, and let us pray for wisdom not to interpret it according to our own desires, but to understand it aright.

Ezra 7. 6; 2 Tim. 2. 15; Prov. 18. 2; Isa. 40. 8; Luke 11. 28

The Great Commission

A PERSONAL AND CORPORATE RESPONSIBILITY

November 16   Reading: Acts 8. 1-8

Following the death of Stephen a great persecution rose against the church in Jerusalem with the result that many of the believers were scattered throughout Judea and Samaria (v. 1). The church, however, was not thus destroyed. God, in His own sovereign way, used the scattering of His people to spread the good news.

The centre of the initial witness to the gospel was the church at Jerusalem. On the day of Pentecost when the church was founded, God had forged the disciple together in a wonderful love and unity. To this united company the Lord added such as should be saved (2. 47). The power of the early church lay in its unity and the concern of God's people one for another.

The New Testament has a great deal to say about the important place of the local church as a testimony to the reality of the gospel. In fact the witness of the church was an answer to the last great prayer of our Lord when He prayed 'that they may all be one, even as thou, Father, art in me, and I in thee, that they also may be in us, so that the world may believe that thou hast sent me' (John 17. 21) We do well to remember that our responsibility to one another in the church and our responsibility to fulfil the Lord's great commission go together. To the extent that our unity in the local church is marred, to that extent our witness is weakened.

But each believer also has an individual responsibility in fulfilling the great commission. Perhaps in the wisdom of God it was necessary that the church should be scattered in order that each believer should learn his own personal responsibility and not be content to hide within the anonymity of the group. Notice that the ordinary believers were scattered, not the apostles, but wherever they went they preached the Word (v. 4). Luke cites the example of Philip who proclaimed Christ in a city of Samaria (v. 5). Persecution had not silenced him. May the Lord give us a like sense of personal responsibility to live and speak His Word.

Acts. 8. 1; Acts 8. 4; Acts. 8. 5; Acts 8. 6; Acts 15. 35

The Great Commission

THE DIGNITY OF SERVING THE LORD

November 17   Reading: 2 Corinthians 5. 16-21

In 2 Corinthians Paul is writing not only to the church in Corinth but to the believers throughout the province of Achaia (1.1). His subject is the marks of the Christian ministry.

In some parts of the world little dignity is attached to the Christian ministry, but in the present passage Paul shows that the service of Christ is a calling of the highest honour and privilege. He likens it to an ambassadorship, but we are representatives not of some earthly nation, but of the King of kings (v. 20). With what seriousness then we should view this great responsibility.

A worthy ambassador is a man who has undergone an exacting training. He should be a man of insight, ability and self-discipline. As representatives of Jesus Christ we should be learning constantly in the school of the Holy Spirit, growing in spiritual capacity and understanding, ready to order our lives not according to our own pleasing, but in a manner which will commend Christ to others.

"God was in Christ reconciling the world to himself" (v. 19). We are serving one whose ministry was a ministry of reconciliation. He came to reconcile man to God and man to man. Reconciliation, therefore, is the principle aim of the Christian ministry. It is the end to which all our preaching and living should be directed. It is vitally important, therefore, that we as God's servants should be seen to be people who are at one with God and with one another.

There is a dignity in unity which vanishes immediately the unity is broken. It is not difficult to see how the dignity of the gospel and God's servants is lost when a church is riven by quarrelling and dissension. How important it is, therefore, to see every believer as the Lord sees him, as one who has been united to God and to us through the reconciling work of Christ. "If any one is in Christ, he is a new creation" (v. 17), and we regard him no longer from a human point of view (v. 16). Through faith in Christ we have been given a completely new standpoint, His standpoint, and when we view His people as He views them the dignity and worth of the proclamation of the gospel will be evident to all. Let us ask the Lord to give us a fresh sense of the dignity of serving Him.

2. Cor. 5. 16; 2 Cor. 5. 17; 2 Cor. 5. 18; 2 Cor. 5. 19; Eph. 6. 19-20

The Great Commission

PAUL

Paul's obedience to the great commission eventually took him to Rome. He had long desired to visit Rome, the centre of the Empire, but he hardly anticipated that he would finally reach the capital city as a prisoner. Yet throughout his imprisonment his sense of God's purpose for him never left him. He was, right to the end, an ambassador for Christ.

When he arrived in Rome Paul called for the local leaders of the Jews (28. 17) and 'they came to him at his lodging in great numbers' (v. 23). To them he proclaimed Jesus as the Messiah. Some were convinced while others disbelieved (v. 24). His witness went forth beyond the Jewish community (v. 28). Writing from prison to the Philippians he says that the gospel became known throughout the whole praetorian guard, the elite regiment of soldiers who had apparently been allotted the task of guarding him (Phil. 1. 13).

Vs. 30-31 tells us that Paul lived for two years in his own hired house. During that period he received many visitors both from the locality of Rome and from farther afield. To them he preached the kingdom of God and taught about the Lord Jesus Christ. He introduced some to the Lord. He built up others in their faith. Never did he feel that he had fulfilled all that the great commission required of him.

Along with his concern to witness in person to those who came to him, Paul carried a great spiritual burden for the assemblies he knew so well. At times he would receive a visitor from one of these churches as Epaphroditus came from Philippi. These visitors brought news which Paul must have eagerly devoured. To some of the assemblies he wrote letters, and the spiritual wealth of these letters written from his imprisonment is immediately obvious to any student of the Scriptures. In them he continues to advise and teach, to apply the gospel as it had been revealed to him to the diverse circumstances of the Lord's people. Never does he complain of his confinement. Instead, he sees the sovereign hand of God working in him and through him to the furtherance of the gospel.

Paul was a man constantly alive to the responisibilities of the great commission, and constantly pursuing them. Let us pray for a like spirit.

Acts 28. 23; Act 28. 30-31; 1 Tim. 1. 12; 1 Cor. 1. 8; Rev. 2. 10

The Second Coming

THE CERTAINTY OF HIS COMING

November 19   Reading: Acts 1. 1-11

Luke here recounts the last resurrection appearance of our Lord to the disciples. The minds of the disciples were filled with thoughts far different from our Lord's concerns. They ask Him if now He is going to restore the kingdom to Israel (v. 6). In spite of all that Jesus had taught them, they were obsessed with the idea of an earthly kingdom. Jesus does not try to explain to them their error. He had already given them positive instructions to remain in Jerusalem for the coming of the Holy Spirit (vs. 4-5), and He further stresses the Spirit's coming (v. 8). The power they are to recive is a spiritual power, not the power of an earthly, material kingdom. In this way our Lord prepares them for the founding of the church in which He as the Head is going to rule over His people, the body.

When He finished speaking to them 'He was lifted up, and a cloud took Him out of their sight' (v. 9). Then two men in white robes stood by the disciples (v. 10) and gave the glorious promise of our Lord's return. The two angels confirm words spoken earlier by the Lord (John 14. 3), and speak of the manner in which He will come back. "This Jesus who was taken up from you into heaven, will come in the same way as you saw him go into heaven" (v. 11).

There are many theories and mistaken ideas about our Lord's return. Some have claimed that He comes at death. It is true that at death the Lord come to take His own, but that is not the coming of which this passage speaks. The word spoken to the disciples was quite specific. The Lord is going to return 'in the same way' as He went. This has been the hope and expectation of the church for nearly two thousand years, the visible return of our Lord to the earth. Though the Lord in grace has tarried, yet His coming is sure.

It is a pity that the truth of the Lord's second coming has to a great extent been lost sight of amongst God's people. God is not heedless about the condition of the world and of the church. His coming is certain when each of us shall give account of himself to God. Let us pray that we may be found ready on that day.

Acts 1. 7; Acts 1. 9; Acts 1. 10; Acts 1. 11; Rom. 14. 12

The Second Coming

THE TIME OF HIS COMING

November 20   Reading: 1 Thessalonians 5. 1-11

The Thessalonian believers were very young in the faith, but Paul was greatly encouraged by their zeal for the Lord. In their enthusiasm, however, they tended to hold unbalanced views on some aspects of Christian truth, and in this letter of encouragement Paul also includes a word of correction.

It is not surprising that the Thessalonians should be filled with expectancy at the glorious truth of the second coming, but they were so convinced that that great event would take place at any moment, that some of them had even stopped working (4. 11-12). Paul seeks to restore their balance. There is no doubt whatsoever about the second coming of the Lord, but Jesus Himself stated that the time of His coming was known to the Father alone (Matt. 24. 36).

Many people down through the centuries have attempted to establish the date of the Lord's coming. Every one of them has been proved wrong. Yet there are still some who, through fanciful interpretations of the Scripture, make pronouncements about the signs of the times and claim that the Lord will appear on such and such a date. No believer should take any notice of such prophecies.

We know that the Lord's coming is nearer than it was when Paul wrote to the Thessalonians, and it may well be that the present day world confusion will head up in the great event, but it is not our business to speculate. Our job is to be ready. The Lord will come at a time when we least expect Him (v. 2), but His coming should hold no terrors for us. If we are sons of light He will not find us acting like thieves, doing things we ought not to be doing (vs. 4-5).

The believer looks to the second coming for the consummation of his salvation (v. 9), so here and now he should be concerned with growing in faith and expressing his love by witnessing to others (v. 8) This will mean that he continues to play his normal part diligently and honestly in the society in which he lives. We know the Lord is coming. Let us be ready when He appears.

Matt. 24. 36; 1 Thess. 5. 2; 1 Thess. 5. 4; 1 Thess. 5. 8; 1 Thess. 5. 9

The Second Coming

THE PURPOSE OF HIS COMING

November 21   Reading: 1 Corinthians 15. 51-55

The coming of the Lord will mean a radical overhauling of the whole system of life upon the earth. In some respects it will be like the owner of a business returning from a long absence to find his business in confusion. Some of his workers have been faithful. Many have not. Signs of ineptness and mismanagement are everywhere. The process of restoration will be a complicated one. Many tasks will have to be undertaken, some of them extremely unpleasant. There will be a calling to account of those who have been unfaithful as well as a rewarding of those who have sought to discharge their responsibilities honestly. Dismissals and promotions, destroying and conserving, all will be required in the work of restoration.

Paul is here concerned with the one ultimate purpose of the Lord's return. It is to make all things new, to work a final change in His people from that which is subject to corruption to that which is imperishable (v. 53). Imperfection is to give way to perfection. What was temporary is to give place to what is eternal (v. 54).

"We shall all be changed" (v. 51). What does this change entail? Those who have tasted of the grace of God have already been changed. At the very beginning of the letter Paul addresses the Corinthians as 'those sanctified in Christ Jesus, called to be saints' (1. 2). The Corinthian believers had known a radical change from their old lives, yet they still had problems, many of them because they were still limited in understanding, in growth, in spiritual capacity through the effects of the fall. Through the work of the Holy Spirit these limitations were gradually being overcome and their problems answered, but their limitations would never be fully overcome as long as they were bound to a fallen world.

The second coming is going to change all this. It will bring the change of final emancipation from the limitations of a fallen world. It will bring translation into a new eternal state of fullness and perfection. Truly death will be swallowed up in victory.

1 Cor. 15. 51; 1 Cor. 15. 52; 1. Cor. 15. 53; 1 Cor. 15. 57; 1 Cor. 15. 58

The Second Coming

RESPONSIBILITY IN VIEW OF HIS COMING

November 22   Reading: 2 Peter 3. 1-18

In the Bible 'the last days' (v. 3) generally refer to the final period of world history, that bounded by the first and second comings of our Lord. Scoffers existed in Peter's day, and will continue to exist right up to the end. They claimed that all things continued as they had done before and would do so for ever. The promises of God were unreliable (v. 4). In such a stable world events like the second coming just do not happen.

Peter in answer takes them back to the destruction by a flood of the world God had created (vs. 5-6). God is both Creator and Judge. He has made the world with a moral purpose and, as He intervened once before, will intervene again in His own good time (v. 7). God sees time from a different perspective than we do (v. 8). The delay of the Lord's coming is due to God's grace, not to any slackness concerning His promise (v. 9).

Having stressed the fact that the Lord is coming, Peter sets out to emphasise the responsibilities which now devolve upon the people of God (v. 11). The second coming show us that God is moving to a definite purpose. Believers are not, like the godless world, people who have nothing to live for. In the light of God's purpose, His people have definite responsibilities.

It is easy to imagine that the world is more permanent than the people who live in it. The world continues while people are born, live and die. This, however, is a mistaken idea. People are more important than things. The world as we know it will one day be dissolved (v. 11), but the people of God will continue in a new and glorified existence.

The hope of the Lord's coming should always inspire the Lord's people to live holy lives, for only righteousness will survive in the new heavens and the new earth (v. 13). If we have no concern for righteousness, we will be unfitted for the only life the Lord's return offers to His people.

How do we hasten 'the coming of the day of the Lord' (v. 12)? We prepare for it by godliness (v. 11), by witness (Mark 13. 10), by prayer (Matt. 6. 10), by repentance and obedience (Acts 3. 19-21). There lie our responsibilities. Let us heed Peter's warning in v. 17 and let us grow in the grace and knowledge of our Lord and Saviour Jesus Christ.

2 Pet. 3. 9; 2 Pet. 3. 10; 2. Pet. 3. 11; 2 Pet. 3. 13; 2. Pet. 3. 14

The Second Coming

JUDGEMENT AT HIS COMING

November 23   Reading: 2 Thessalonians 2. 7-16

Paul presents a picture of increasing lawlessness before the coming of the Lord. John's definition of sin is, "Sin is lawlessness" (1 John 3. 4). Sin is the assertion of man's will against the will of God. This is to be increasingly evident in the last times and will come to a head in 'the coming of the lawless one' (v. 9) who is the antichrist of John's first letter (1 John 2. 18).

Just who this 'lawless one' is, it is impossible to say. Since New Testament times there have been many evil men who have defied God and done Satan's work. There will no doubt be others before the antichrist himself appears. Paul makes no attempt to satisfy idle curiosity about this person. What he is concerned to emphasise is that this rebellion, and indeed every defiance of God, comes under His judgement. Immediately after mentioning the revelation of the lawless one Paul speaks of his destruction (v. 8).

Then Paul turns his attention to the followers of the antichrist (vs. 9-12). There is an evil power at work in the world and many follow it. Most people who take 'pleasure in unrighteousness' (v. 12) never see beyond the present enjoyment of their sin. But no sin is forgotten. It is either absolved through the atoning work of the Lord Jesus Christ, or it comes under God's personal judgement. When our Lord comes again, all evil is going to be finally dealt with.

In contrast to the judgement of those who defy the truth, Paul rejoices in the prospect before the Thessalonian believers. The redeemed life begins with God's call (vs. 13-14) but it continues as a person labours together with God (v. 15). God takes the initiative in salvation, but man has the responsibility of responding to Him in obedience, guided by the Word and the fellowship of other saints (v. 15). He is helped also by God himself (vs. 16-17). The purpose God has in view is that we 'may obtain the glory of our Lord Jesus Christ' (v. 14), a glory in which all sin is finally and completely dealt with. Our sin has been judged on the cross, but at the second coming we will have to give an account of our lives to God (Rom. 14. 10). The Lord grant that we will not be ashamed on that day.

2 Thess. 2. 8; 2. Thess. 2. 9-10; 2 Thess. 2. 11-12; 2. Thes. 2. 14; 2 Thes. 2. 16-17

The Second Coming

RESTORATION AND GOD'S RULE

November 24   Reading: Revelation 21. 1-8, 22-27

The book of Revelation deals with God's final triumph over all the forces of evil. This triumph will be consummated at the second coming of our Lord when the last judgement will come and His rule will be established over His people for ever.

John in his vision sees a new heaven and a new earth (v.1). He sees a new Jerusalem (v. 2). He hears a voice saying, "Behold I make all things new" (v. 5). Greek has two words for 'new'. One means new in point of time. The other means new in nature or quality. It is the second of these words that is used here. That which has been marred God is going to restore completely, and so institute a new order in which 'former things have passed away' (v. 4), a new order free from all sin and evil (v. 27).

In redemption God has already restored our relationship with Him, but the relationship is going to find a greater fulfilment when all His people are gathered around Him and He dwells in their midst (vs. 3, 22-23).

The earth is going to be restored (v. 1). One of the results of the fall was disharmony between man and the earth God made for him. Man has misused God's creation, but God is going to restore what has been so sadly despoiled, and a restored earth will have a place in God's eternal plan.

More than this, man and his relationships with others are going to be completely restored. God says He will wipe away every tear. There will be no more death, mourning, crying or pain (v. 4). Why do these things at present exist? Much sickness and pain is due to man's inner complexities. He is full of strains, tensions and fears, and these things affect his physical health. Another reason for distress, or 'mourning and crying' as v. 4 puts it, is the breakdown in relationships which exists often even among the people of God. When the Lord comes again man will be one with himself and with his brethren. The evil effects which disharmony produced will be gone for ever.

Yet God is working towards that full restoration now. Let us not wait till His coming again to allow Him to do His work in us.

Rev. 21. 3; Rev. 21. 4; Rev. 21. 5; Rev. 21. 6; Rev. 21. 7

The Second Coming

JOHN THE BAPTIST

November 25

Reading: Matthew 3. 1-6

John the Baptist was a strange man, yet he occupies a place of great importance in the story of the gospel. Luke records the events surrounding his birth as he does with the birth of our Lord, an importance accorded to the birth of no other person in Scripture. Our Lord commended John in the highest possible terms, "Among those born of women there has risen no one greater than John the Baptist" (Matt. 11. 11).

John was the forerunner of our Lord, preparing the way for the first coming of the Messiah (v. 3). We today are awaiting His second coming, and can learn much from John's life and character. As Luke tells us, he was born into a priestly family (Luke 1.5), but John cast aside all the privileges and prospects of his upbringing. He reacted violently against the luxury and hypocrisy of the religious world of his day (v. 4), and called people back to that which is most essential of all, a personal relationship with God.

"Repent, for the kingdom of heaven is at hand" (v. 2). This was John's message. He had a right sense of priorities. He did not live for worldly wealth and security, but to fulfil the commission God had given him in preparation for the coming of His Son. John the Baptist was single-eyed in vision, uncompromising in the message he preached. He was not like 'a reed shaken by the wind' (Matt. 11. 7), someone swayed easily by the popularity of the crowd. He was set on doing the will of God, and was heedless of the criticism of the world around.

John was a man with a message. There was an inner compulsion to preach and live for God; like Amos who said, "The lion has roared; who will not fear? The Lord God has spoken; who can but prophesy?" (Amos 3. 8); or like Paul who wrote, "Necessity is laid upon me. Woe is me if I do not preach the gospel!" (1 Cor 9. 16).

As we look forward to the second coming of the Lord, what is our attitude? Do we have right priorities? Are we more concerned about God's will than our own welfare? Do we put loyalty to the Lord before popularity? Have we a sense of divine urge to live for Christ?

Matt. 3. 1-2; Matt. 3. 3; Matt. 11. 7; Matt. 11. 11; John. 3. 30

The Use of Time

GOD'S USE OF TIME IN CREATION

November 26   Reading: Genesis 1. 14-19

In different parts of the world, or in varying circumstances, we find widely different attitudes to the use of time. The highly organized West is usually much more time conscious than the East. People who live in cities are normally more time conscious than those who live at the more leisurely pace of a country village. Those who work in industry are more time conscious than those who work in the fields.

Is there a specific spiritual attitude to time? Not uncommonly, believers in India tend to criticize those in the West for their attitude to time. Worship, prayer, everything is subject to the clock, and it is easy to develop an attitude of superiority where it is imagined that spirituality should take no thought of time whatsoever. Both attitudes, the one in which every act is inflexibly bound to a timetable, and the other which takes no account at all of time, are wrong.

In the Genesis account of creation we read that God made both sun and moon (v. 16), and so created time. The course of the sun determines the seasons, the course of the moon the months, and earth's revolving upon its axis determines day and night (v. 14). So time is an integral part of God's creation. His own creative programme was carried out according to a divine time-table. All was completed in six days, and the seventh was a day of rest.

God, of course, is sovereign over time as He is over all creation. He can stay the movement of the heavenly bodies according to His own pleasure. He did this in the notable incident recounted in the book of Joshua when He gave victory over the Amorites (Josh. 10. 12-14). Yet God does not often set aside the laws He has made. God is a God of order, and time is an essential feature in an ordered world. He respected it and expects us to do so also. The example He set in creation is an example applicable for all time of ordered working and living.

Time is for man's use. God did not give it to tyrannize us, but neither did He give it that we might neglect it at will. He gave it to help us fit in to the orderliness of His creation. Let us pray that we might use our time aright.

Gen. 1. 14; Gen. 1. 15; Gemn. 1. 16; Gen. 1. 17-18; Gen. 1. 19

The Use of Time

A MEANS OF SELF DISCIPLINE

November 27   Reading: Ecclesiastes 3. 1-11

Life brings many and varied experiences. Time brings constant change, youth and old age, discipline and reward, sowing and reaping, joy and sorrow. What does all this mean? To the person who does not know the Lord, all the experiences of life are little more than filling in time till the end comes. Which experience follows which is of no importance. Each experience of itself is impermanent and has, therefore, no ultimate meaning. To use time profitably is no better than to waste it, and to waste it no worse than to use it to advantage. Men without God can see time only as a tyranny, and the experiences it brings as of no lasting value.

So the preacher here shows two things. He shows the uselessness of time to the godless. "What gain has the worker from his toil?" (v. 9). The answer is that he has none, for time will give way to eternity, and all he has worked for will be gone for ever. But he also shows the importance of time to the believer. "He has made everything beautiful in its time; also he has put eternity into man's mind, yet so that he cannot find out what God has done from the beginning to the end" (v. 11). The believer may not be able to see clearly the end from the beginning, but he knows that God has an end, a purpose, and all that happens in between is meaningful and is a preparation for that purpose. Man vitalized by the Spirit of God has consciousness of a purposeful eternity. All that takes place till that age comes is 'beautiful in its time', for through it God is making us ready to enjoy eternity.

Time gives us the opportunity to savour the varied experiences God plans for our good. It gives us the opportunity to learn, and having learned, to moved on the next lesson God wishes to teach us. It gives us the opportunity to know the will of God and to do it, to rejoice with those who rejoice and weep with those who weep.

God has so much to show us, yet there can be no learning without discipline. We need to know how much time to allot to one subject and then be ready to pass on to the next. Time gives us the opportunity for self-discipline so that we may grow in the ways of the Lord. Let us pray for wisdom to use our time to His glory.

Eccl. 3. 1; Eccl. 3. 2; Eccl. 3. 4; Eccl. 3. 7; Eccl 3. 11

The Use of Time

A MEANS OF HELPING OTHERS

November 28   Reading: John 9. 1-7

The right use of time is a means of self-discipline. It is possible, however, to discipline our time for a variety of reasons, some of which may be entirely selfish. A person who lives a strictly ordered life can do so without any thought of others. This, of course, is very different from what the Bible teaches.

Jesus Himself lived a life of balanced order. He devoted time to personal prayer. He also took part in the corporate worship of the synagogue. He devoted much time to teaching the disciples. He also engaged in public preaching among the crowds who followed Him. At the same time He gave time to catering for individual needs, as in the incident we have just read where he healed the man who was born blind.

There was nothing haphazard about our Lord's living. He was guided in what He did by divine wisdom, but that did not lead to a disordered effect. He did not so exhaust Himself among the crowds that there was no time left for quiet meditation. He did not spend so much time in His personal devotional life that He had to neglect the teaching of the disciples. His ministry to the disciples did not crowd out His service for the needy people who surrounded Him. He saw each part of His ministry as contributing to the others, so each was apportioned its time. Without prayer there could have been no adequate ministry. Without His teaching there could have been no adequate motive for the service of others.

Our Lord said that He came 'not to be served but to serve' (Mark 10. 45), but true service can never be isolated from other aspects of living. If we are not right with God we cannot properly serve our fellow men. Nor can we serve them if we ourselves are not taught in the principles of the Word. If, like our Lord, we are going to live to serve, our time has to be disciplined to give room for these other important things without which our service cannot be directed aright.

We must work while it is day (v. 4), and so use our time that it will be a means of helping others. Let us pray for wisdom to order our lives that we may serve others to the opening of their spiritual eyes.

John 9. 1-2; John 9. 3; John 9. 4; John. 9. 5; John 9. 25

The Use of Time

STEWARDS OF TIME

November 29   Reading: Romans 13. 8-14

We all face eternity, and the time God has given us here upon the earth is a preparation for the time when we shall be with Him in heaven. We are stewards of time, obliged to use it to God's glory.

In the light of the consummation of our salvation, Paul urges us to take stock of the way we use our time (vs. 11-12). Are we using it as a means of witness for the Lord by our personal character (v. 13)? Are we concerned to grow in Him, casting aside our own selfish desires (v. 14)? We are called to use our time so that the order and purpose of our personal lives may speak to others of Christ.

There is, however, another very important side to the stewardship of time. We cannot use our time properly if we are concerned only about our own individual spiritual growth. The spiritual life can never be divorced from our relationship with others. As we saw yesterday, time should be used as a means of helping others. In vs. 8-10 Paul speaks of love as the fulfilling of the law. The law forbids a person to use his time commmitting certain wrong acts against his neighbour. Love goes far beyond what the law lays down. "Love does no wrong to a neighbour" (v. 10). Love does not stop at forbidding acts which may be considerd definitely sinful, acts such as adultery and theft. Love will not wrong a neighbour in much less conspicuous ways. It will not deprive him of any opportunity of spiritual progress. It will encourage him to be a good steward of time just as we should be good stwards of time ourselves.

There is a sense, therefore, in which we are stewards of others' time as well as of our own. There are people who seem never to waste a minute. They are desperately busy in the service of the Lord. All their time is taken up with prayer, ministry or service. But their well ordered lives show no respect for order in the lives of others. Others are expected to disrupt the order of their lives to fit into their wishes, while they themselves make no attempt to adjust to others. To be good stewards of time, we need to ask God to help us respect the responsibilities of our brethren to be good stewards also.

Rom. 13. 9-10; Rom. 13. 11; Rom. 13. 12; Rom. 13. 13; Rom. 13. 14

The Use of Time

THE LIFETIME PERSPECTIVE

November 30   Reading: 1 Peter 1. 18-25

God's perspective spans the whole of eternity. Christ 'was destined before the foundation of the world but was made manifest at the end of the times for your sake' (v. 20). In these words Peter tells us that at the beginning of eternity God planned the incarnation and the work of redemption for His glory and the welfare of His people in an eternity to come. In contrast to God's view, we who belong to a fallen, perishable past, tend to look upon everything in life as temporary. Millions of people never look beyond the present day. The most far sighted have a perspective which does not see beyond this earthly existence. Security and wealth become their main aims. Moral qualities such as truth and righteousness become secondary considerations. On these principles they live their own lives, educate and map out the future for their children.

Peter says that these are the futile ways from which we have been ransomed, not by some perishable offering (v. 18), but by an imperishable offering, the precious blood of Christ (v. 19). God has emancipated us from sin and self seeking. He has given us a new view of life which sees beyond our earthly existence to the glory which lies ahead (v. 21). Peter repeats this glorious fact. The flesh, self seeking, is no more permanent than the grass that withers away (v. 24) but life founded on the word of the gospel will abide for ever (v. 25).

The priorities of a life which is a preparation for the glory to come will be vastly different from the priorities of a life which ends with the grave. The believer who expends his time and energies seeking material security and prosperity to the neglect of truth and righteousness is denying the gospel he professes to accept. God has given us the abilities we possess. He expects us to develop and use them, but the time spent in doing so is mere waste if they contribute to no more than material comfort.

Let us face honestly the question of whether our ambitions, those things to which we give our time, are related to the glory of God. Are we concerned first for the glory of God in our ambition for our families? Do we encourage our children to seek first the kingdom?

1 Pet. 1. 20; Eccl. 12. 13; Eccl. 12. 14; Mark 10. 29-30; Rom. 14. 17

335

The Use of Time

TIME FOR LEISURE

December 1   Reading: Deuteronomy 5. 12-15

It is true that, as believers, we are no longer under the Mosaic law as a system, but that does not mean that the ten commandments have no relevance for us today. The Jewish Sabbath has been replaced for us by the first day of the week, the day of resurrection on which it is our privilege, in a special way, to give ourselves to worship and witness as did the early believers.

The fourth commandment, however, expresses a very important principle, the principle that man needs both work and relaxation. God's creation was completed in six days, and on the seventh day He rested, thus hallowing for every believer the need of leisure. In these days of strikes for shorter working hours and more pay for less work, it is necessary to remember that the Bible hallows work as well as rest. God worked, and so should we. Only as we are faithful in our work do we have the need of leisure and earn the right to it. There is a time to work and a time to play.

Some believers are quick to condemn any form of physical or mental relaxation. But this is wrong. Our bodies and minds require exercise and rest if they are to function as God intends they should. There is a time to sleep and a time to pray. It may be of great benefit on occasion to devote a night to prayer, but habitually to deny ourselves the sleep we need is no sign of spirituality, for it weakens both the physical and mental reserves God wants to be used to His glory. On the other hand, we should restrict sleep to what is necessary.

Many people find physical refreshment in walking or taking part in some vigorous game. In this way bodies are kept healthy, to be used for the Lord. Mental relaxation can be found in reading good books, in such things as painting and music. Minds are thus refreshed to be applied efficiently to the more important duties of life. Leisure, however, should not occupy the chief place in our living. It should fit us to work for the glory of God.

Let us thank God for the privilege of working for Him, and also for times of leisure. Let us pray that these too may be used to His honour.

Deut. 5. 13; 1 Cor. 6. 13; 1 Cor. 6. 19; 1 Cor. 6. 20; 1 Thess. 5. 23

The Use of Time

NEHEMIAH

December 2   Reading: Nehemiah 2. 11-16

Nehemiah had travelled a long distance from Susa, Artaxerxes' capital
(1. 1; 2. 1) to Jerusalem. He was a man with a purpose, determined to
restore the city of God which lay in ruins, and to bring life again to a
testimony which, at best, was weak and faltering. King Artaxerxes gave
him permission to return, and Nehemiah set a time for carrying out his
investigations (2. 6).

All we read of Nehemiah indicates that he was a methodical man,
and no less spiritual for it. On the other hand, he was not inflexible. He
was not a captive to his own sense of order. Had he been so it would have
been well nigh impossible for him to accomplish his task, considering the
opposition and unforseen circumstances with which he had to contend.

Arriving in Jerusalem, he remained for three days before commencing
his work (vs. 11-12). Exactly what he did during these three days we are
not told. He no doubt needed some rest after a journey which had taken
him about three months, and it was necessary that he should be fresh in
mind and body for the task that lay ahead of him. Considering the great
burden with which he had returned to Jerusalem he certainly spent time
thinking and praying. Already he knew that the work was not going to
go forward unopposed (2. 10) and that he needed the wisdom and strength the Lord alone could give. Nehemiah's time was well and wisely used.
His three days preparation for the survey he was going to make had
strengthened him in body, mind and spirit, as subsequent events abundantly
show.

The initial reconnaissance took place at night. Nehemiah allotted the
night for his purpose in order to avoid idle curiosity and to allow him to
view the situation in the light of the burden which God had placed on his
own heart (v. 12). Having methodically completed his task, he returns
(v. 15) and starts on the job of organizing the reconstruction.

Nehemiah was a man of devotion to God and resolute purpose. He
was a good steward of time. He had time to seek God's face, time to do
the work God had given him, time to rest that he might be fit to fulfil the
task. Let us pray that God will make us good stewards of our time like
Nehemiah.

Neh. 1. 4; Neh. 1. 11; Neh. 2. 3; Neh. 2. 5; Neh. 2. 17

Faith and Righteousness

THE MEANING OF FAITH

Reading: Matthew 18. 1-6

'Faith' is one of the most familiar words in our Christian vocabulary. Yet do we know what faith really means?

The disciples had been discussing among themselves who would be greatest in the kingdom of heaven. Not being able to reach any conclusion, they bring their question to the Lord. Jesus does not answer them immediately, but calling a little child to Him, he sets him down in the midst of them, and then says to His disciples, "Truly, I say to you, unless you turn and become like children, you will never enter the kingdom of heaven" (v. 3).

The word Matthew uses for a child means a small child, yet he was old enough to respond to the call of Jesus and to come to Him. Obviously he was not a babe in arms, but a child with a developed will who could walk, communicate to some extent with others, and was able to respond intelligently to what others said. At the same time, he was a small child not yet able to live an independent life. He was perhaps three or four years of age.

A child of this age may have a strong will and boundless self-confidence, although he is totally unable to cope with life alone. In a spiritual sense unregenerate man is the same. He thinks he is quite self-sufficient, having no need of other people or even of God, but in reality he is as powerless to face the real issues of life alone as a three year old child.

"Unless you turn and become like children, you will never enter the kingdom of heaven," said Jesus. He was calling His disciples to turn from their own sense of self-sufficiency and to cleave to Him in the dependence of a child upon its parents. This is an illustration of faith.

Faith is more than a mental assent to the facts of the gospel, that Jesus lived, died, rose again, and did so to save us from our sins. These are great and glorious truths but faith is more than an acceptance of these facts. Faith is an act of the will whereby we cast ourselves in absolute and constant dependence upon Christ. It is more than a momentary experience. It is an experience of continual submission to the Lord.

Matt. 18. 1-2; Matt. 18. 3; Matt. 18. 4; Matt. 18. 5; Matt. 18. 6

Faith and Righteousness

FAITH INSEPARABLE FROM RIGHTEOUSNESS

December 4   Reading: James 2. 18-26

James wrote this letter because of a tendency, which began to appear very early in the history of the church, to separate faith from practical living. In our own experience we know how easily this can be done. We can maintain all the language of faith and yet have no concern to relate what we say we believe to practical every day living. Such a faith, James tells us, is like 'the body apart from the spirit' (v. 26). It is dead.

The Bible often places together truths which our finite minds find it impossible to reconcile. The classical example is, of course, the sovereignty of God and the free will of man. To our limited understanding these are two irreconcilable facts, but both are nevertheless true. Some people have thought that James' emphasis on works is inconsistent with a belief in salvation through faith alone, but the fact that inspired Scripture places faith and righteous works side by side should prevent us from trying to separate them. When God puts two truths together, they should always be held together.

In this passage James shows that righteousness is the inevitable outcome of a true faith. He quotes the instance of Abraham who, he says, was justified when he offered his son Issac upon the altar (v. 21). It is quite clear, however, that Abraham's obedience was due to his deep faith, a faith first shown in his obedience to the call of God to leave his father's house and go out he knew not whither (Gen. 12. 1, 4).

Our Lord Himself showed that true faith will result in a concern for righteousness when He said, "You will know them by their fruits" (Matt. 7. 20). Paul emphasises the same truth in writing to the Ephesians. He quite clearly states that we are saved by faith, not by good works (Eph. 2. 8), but in salvation we are 'created in Christ Jesus for good works, which God prepared beforehand, that we should walk in them' (Eph. 2. 10). John bears his testimony to the same truth by saying that one of the marks of a child of God is his obedience to God's ways (1 John 2. 3-6).

We have no Scriptural right to accept a profession of faith in Christ as genuine if the person does not show evidence of righteousness and a concern for righteousness in his daily living. May God help us to show our faith through the righteousness of our lives.

James 2. 20; James 2. 21; James 2. 22; James 2. 23; James 2. 26

Faith and Righteousness

FAITH IN PRAYER

Reading: Mark 11. 20-25

Peter was startled at the rapidity with which our Lord's cursing the fig tree had taken effect. The Lord uses the incident as an opportunity to teach His disciples the principles of prevailing prayer. He tells them that prevailing prayer is dependent upon two conditions, one a person's relationship with God (v. 22), the other his relationship with his brethren, a relationship of forgiveness (v. 25).

Faith and forgiveness go together, and a lack of either is a fatal hindrance to our prayers. God has forgiven us all through Christ and is deeply concerned for His people. If our relationship with Him is right, we will have something of the same concern for our brethren that He has, and the same spirit of forgiveness. If we cannot forgive, it means we really do not believe the Lord can do the same in our brother as we claim He has done in us through His forgiveness. John too shows how our relationship with our brother is essentially linked with our relationship with the Lord. He says, "He who does not love his brother whom he has seen, cannot love God whom he has not seen" (1 John 4. 20).

If I believe that God, having forgiven my brother, can fully accomplish His purpose in him, then I can forgive my brother also, however hard or even impossible it may have seemed to be from a human standpoint. Similarly, if I believe that God wills to accomplish a certain purpose, however difficult it may humanly appear to be, then I can believe that He will do it. A faith for God to do the seemingly impossible is dependent upon a confidence that it is His will, but nothing is impossible with a God who can implant a spirit of forgiveness in a hard, human heart. If I myself have experienced this, there is every reason to trust God to do all He wants. Jesus says that the potentials of faith according to the will of God are limitless (v. 23).

With ourselves, within the family, within the church, within the wider sphere of our Christian witness, we all have our problems. Every one of them can be touched and solved by faith. The reason we remain defeated is that our faith is small. Lord, increase our faith.

Mark 11. 23; Mark 11. 24; Mark 11. 25; 1 John 4. 20; 1 John 4. 21

Faith and Righteousness

FAITH IN ALL CIRCUMSTANCES

December 6   Reading: Habakkuk 2. 1-4

Habakkuk lived at a tumultuous time in the history of Israel. He had seen good king Josiah defeated and killed in battle against the Egyptian Pharaoh, his son Jehoahaz deposed after a reign of only three months, and another son Jehoiakim ascend the throne. Jehoiakim was a godless man, a cruel tyrant who, with the rich and powerful of the land, oppressed the people and plunged the nation into a state of disorder.

The book of Habakkuk is a record of Habakkuk's problems and God's answer. Why should a good king like Josiah be prematurely taken away and God's people have to suffer the oppression of a man like Jehoiakim? Why should their cries for deliverance go apparently unheeded, and the wicked prosper at the expense of the righteous? In answer to Habakkuk's complaint God says He is going to do an astounding thing (1. 5). He is going to use the Chaldeans to judge the wickedness of the wicked Judeans (1. 6).

This answer only compounds Habakkuk's problems. Why should God use as an instrument of judgement a people more wicked than those He is going to judge? (1. 13). Unable to understand, Habakkuk retires to his 'tower' (v. 1), his place of quietness and meditation from which he is able to view his problems in a wider perspective, as one can view a landscape from a high point. Faith is not the isolated trust or experience of a moment. It must learn to see the whole of life from God's perspective, and trust Him in the inscrutability of His ways.

The gist of God's answer is in v. 4. "The righteous shall live by his faith," or 'faithfulness' as the word really means. True faith results in faithfulness to God, whatever the circumstances. God told Habakkuk to wait (v. 3). Impatient man looks for immediate answers, but it may be a long time before we know the true meaning of events even in our own lives. Faith understands this. Ultimately 'he whose soul is not upright in him will fail' (v. 4). Pride and tyranny are self-destructive. This principle is true of believer and unbeliever alike. God is faithful. The one who through faith remains faithful to Him whatever happens will find his faith abundantly justified. Let us pray for a faith which trusts the Lord in every situation.

Hab. 1. 5; Hab. 2. 1; Hab. 2. 2; Hab. 2. 2; Hab. 2. 3; Hab. 2. 4

Faith and Righteousness

FAITH AND UNBELIEF

December 7   Reading: Mark 9. 17-27

Who was the man who brought his son to Jesus? We do not know. Mark does not even mention his name. Yet surely he is one of the most honest men in the Bible. There is no great faith obvious in his request, "If you can do anything, have pity on us and help us" (v. 22). Jesus replied that all things are possible to one who believes (v. 23). Immediately the father cried out, "I believe; help my unbelief!"(v. 24).

If we are honest with ourselves, do we not have to admit that this man's experience is our own? Not one of us can boast of a faith that is free from any shadow of doubt or is never at any time mixed with self-seeking. Whether this father was educated or uneducated, rich or poor, we do not know, but instinctively he mistrusted himself. We have no reason to doubt the sincerity of his profession when he said to the Lord, "I belive." Yet in the midst of his faith he knew there was a lingering doubt. He did not try to excuse his unbelief. He asked for help to overcome it. Jesus did not condemn him. He answered his faith by healing his son, and in doing so answered his doubt also.

There are some believers who would never dare to admit that they doubt. They are usually believers who have more doubts than others. It may be humbling to realize that our faith has not reached perfection point, but we are never likely to overcome our failures if we refuse to admit that they exist. Habakkuk's faith was sorely tried as he viewed the situation around him. Like the father in our reading, he was a man of faith and unbelief, but as he continued to watch God's ways from his tower, God answered his doubts and strengthened his faith.

Peter likens our faith to gold tried in the fire (1 Peter 1.7), and through being tested emerging purified, free from the doubts and mixed motives which so often characterize it. Let us thank God for having delivered us from the rank ubelief of those who deny Him. Let us pray for humility to recognize how far we yet have to go before our faith is as pure gold, and let us not be content till every shadow of unbelief is banished.

Mark 9. 23; Job 23. 10; Ps. 66. 10; Prov. 17. 3; 1 Cor. 3. 12-13

Faith and Righteousness

THE DISCIPLINE OF FAITH

December 8   Reading: Hebrews 12. 1-6

The writer to the Hebrews urges us forward to 'run with perseverance the race that is set before us' (v. 1). Jesus is the pioneer and perfecter of our faith (v. 2). As we move to ward the goal, He who has initiated our faith is going to perfect it. The goal before our Lord was to fulfil the work of redemption. In pursuing it He endured the hostility of men (v. 3) and the shame of the cross (v. 2). We have not yet been called to suffer as He suffered (v. 4), but our Lord has, by His example, shown us that any purpose which God has for His people is abundantly worth the trial which may precede it.

God has called His people unto glory (1 Thess. 2. 12). Glory is final perfection, and an important part of glory is a perfect faith. In His perfecting process God now disciplines His children. All His discipline is purposeful and in love (vs. 5-6). It is no sign of love if a father refuses to correct and discipline his children. Similarly God's dealings, though they may at times be unpleasant, are for our good.

There is a great similarity between the subject of this passage and the experience of Habakkuk as he viewed the working of God from his tower (Hab. 2.1). The difference is that, whereas Habakkuk had a perspective of God's working in the history of the nation, the writer to the Hebrews is emphasising the importance of God's working in us as individuals. Only in retrospect can we fully understand God's working in history, and only in retrospect will we be able fully to understand the way He has led us as individuals. But we do know that all His dealings are purposeful, and the discipline of our faith is always meant to strengthen it, not to destroy it.

The writer tells us to run the race 'with perseverance'. This is a very significant phrase which is almost impossible to translate accurately. 'Perseverance' is the spirit which recognizes the sovereignty and purposefulness of God in every experience. It may not understand God's ways, but it accepts them all as expressions of His grace and, therefore, learns through them. As God disciplines our faith, let us realize the love of His dealings. Let us pray that we may learn from them and that our faith may be strengthened.

Heb. 12. 2; Heb. 12. 4; Heb. 12. 5; Heb. 12. 6; 1 Cor. 11. 32

Faith and Righteousness

ELIEZER

December 9   Reading: Genesis 24. 34-48

Eliezer had been given a very responsible task, to find a wife for Isaac the son of Abraham, and it is not surprising that he should have voiced his doubts. "Perhaps the woman will not follow me," he said (v. 39). What was he to do then? Abraham assures him that the Lord will go before him, and in faith Eliezer set out on his long journey.

As he approached the city in which Nahor, Abraham's brother, lived, Eliezer prayed to God for guidance. We are given no details of the long journey which led him to this spot, but from what we know of Eliezer's character he must have committed his mission many times unto God during the course of his travel, and if he still harboured his fears, he had a faith greater than his fears, a faith which urged him steadily forward.

Eliezer believed that God was guiding him in every step he took. The hand of God was upon him working out the purpose on which he had been sent. He does ask for an indication of God's favour, that the woman chosen to be Isaac's bride should respond in a pariticular way to his request for a drink (vs. 43-44). Yet he believes also that his circumstances are ordered by God's sovereignty, and through them God will show His will. Eliezer did not look for an outstanding miracle. He had a solid faith in God's constant presence and grace. God can break into a situation in a miraculous way when He pleases, but what carries us through life in victory is a constant confidence in Him and our submission of faith in matters of everyday living, big or small.

When God answered, Eliezer did not forget to give thanks (v. 48). Faith does not take the blessings of God for granted. It does not treat our confidence in God's goodness as an act of merit which compels God to respond. It recognizes that all God's responses flow from His grace, and the only response we can make is one of worship.

It is easy to imagine that God blesses us because of the strength of our faith, and to pride ourselves in it. God blesses us because of His grace, and true faith is always humble. Let us ask God to give us Eliezer's humble faith.

Ps. 118. 6; Prov. 14. 26; Isa. 30. 15; 1 Kings 18. 37; Isa. 25. 1

Relationships

RESPECTING ONE ANOTHER

December 10   Reading: 1 Peter 2. 11-17

Life is made up of relationships on many levels, from the relationships within a family to relationships within a nation or within the international community of men. We live in a world beset with problems, big problems. Day after day we read news of international jealousies, tensions and strife. Yet all of these problems which affect the stability of the world in which we live have their origin in the relationships of individuals one with another. The first personal relationships of which we are conscious are those within our own family circle, and what we learn there may have an effect upon the whole of our own future lives and the lives of others as well. It also makes its contribution to the stability or the instability of the world around us.

"Maintain good conduct among the Gentiles," says Peter (v. 12). Good conduct and good relationships are inseparable, and they are the basis of our testimony in the world. It is not difficult to see how the testimony for God is ruined when relationships are not right, whether it be within the family, in the church, or on a wider level.

We are called to 'be subject for the Lord's sake to every human institution' (v. 13). Peter then goes on to talk of our relationship with the State (vs. 13-14), but his words have a much wider application as subsequent verses show (vs. 17-18). Everyone, from youngest to eldest, occupies a position in the family or in society which should be respected. No one has any right to think that the whole of life should revolve around him. In a family the needs of all have to be taken into consideration. The needs and wishes of children cannot and should not be fulfilled in total disregard of the needs and wishes of the parents. Nor, on the other hand, can parents live their lives in total disregard of their children. Each has to learn to respect the other.

One of the results of the fall is a spirit of self-centredness and, therefore, a lack of respect for the experience and responsibilities of others. This problem is solved only in Christ who gives us a spirit of concern for others, and brings harmony into our relationships.

1 Pet. 2. 11; 1 Pet. 2. 12; 1 Pet. 2. 15; 1 Pet. 2. 16; 1 Pet. 2. 3

Relationships

HONOURING GOD IN EARLY YEARS

December 11   Reading: Ecclesiastes 12. 1-7

"Remember also your creator in the day of your youth" (v. 1). The Preacher enforces the thought of these words by embarking on a highly symbolic but pointed explanation of mortality. Vs. 2-6 are a picture of declining faculties until the body returns to the dust from which it was made, and life is taken back by God who gave it (v. 7).

This is a picture which in youthful years seems very remote, but draws nearer and nearer with an alarming swiftness. The point of this description is not to draw us down into despair, but to rouse us to action. Death has not yet laid hold of us, and until it does let us be working for God who, if we will let Him, is preparing us for something much greater beyond the grave. The time to begin the preparation is as soon as at all possible, in the days of youth.

It is a subtle lie of the devil that God wants to take everything from us, all joy, all meaning, all life. The Preacher's title for God in v. 1 'Creator' is significant in this respect. We are called to remember the One who has made us, the One who alone sees the end from the beginning, the One to whom all resources belong. We were His workmanship, but have destroyed it by our own self-sufficiency. However, He still has the power to create us anew if we will allow Him to do so.

To 'remember' our Creator is more than a mere mental act. It means to commit ourselves to Him, recognizing how puny and foolish we have been, and how helpless we are on our own to make anything really worth while out of our lives. This short lifetime is not too much to give over to God who wants to do so much in us. The book of Ecclesiastes shows the tragic possibility of spending years in self-indulgence and self-seeking only to find that it has all been a waste, and most of life has gone. This is the cry of the Preacher, "Vanity of vanities, says the Preacher; all is vanity" (v. 8).

When, in our early years, we give heed to the Preacher's advice, we find that all else begins to take its proper place. Relationships may pose their problems, but when God and His will are central, relationships begin to fall into harmonious order. Let us remember now our Creator.

Eccl. 12. 1; Eccl. 12. 11; Deut. 8. 18; Eccl. 11. 1; Eccl. 11.5

Relationships

GROWING TO MATURITY

December 12   Reading: Ephesians 4. 15-24

Life means growth. Growth in spiritual things requires a readiness to be honest with others and to learn from others. V. 15 obviously implies the need to accept the truth in love as well as to speak it, for there is no point in speaking to a person who is unwilling to listen.

Paul outlines the way of the godless world (vs. 17-19) and says that one of the marks of the godless world is 'futility' (v. 17). They do not know where they are going, and the reason is that they are 'darkened in their understanding, alienated from the life of God because of ignorance' (v. 18). It may seem rather startling to use terms such as 'darkened in understanding' and 'ignorance' of our modern world. Science has made such tremendous strides. Knowledge has increased to a phenomenal extent. But has there been any real growth?

Today we hear much talk of 'development', but what is development? What is the advantage of growth in scientific knowledge if man does not know how to use it, or uses it only to his own destruction? 'Futility' (v. 17) is an apt description of the feeling of many of the most knowledgeable people in our world today. The truth is that there is no real growth.

In contrast to this Paul says, "You did not so learn Christ!" (v. 20), and he speaks of the believer as having put off the way of the old godless world, and put on the new life given us in Christ (vs. 22-24). This alone is the basis of true growth.

Growth means a willingness to learn, and a willingness to learn means that we have not yet learned everything. Growing means having a mind open to new things. All of us can stop growing spiritually by thinking that we have learned everything of importance already. How many older believers have closed minds to any further truth. But the idea of 'knowing it all' is also a mark of youth. It sweeps aside impatiently the experience of older people and listens to their opinions only to refute them. It speaks what it considers the truth, not in love, but in self-assurance. Growth is both painful and painfully slow. Let us ask the Lord for grace to listen, grace to learn, and grace to grow.

Eph. 4. 16; Eph. 4. 17; Eph. 4. 18; Eph. 4. 20-22; Eph. 4. 23-24

Relationships

THE DANGER OF PRIDE

December 13   Reading: Proverbs 13. 1-10

"A scoffer does not listen to rebuke" (v. 1). "He who opens wide his lips comes to ruin" (v. 3). "One pretends to be rich, yet has nothing" (v. 7). "By insolence the heedless make strife" (v. 10). All these sayings suggest pride, the subtle, besetting temptation which assails us all in one form or another.

Pride, beyond everything else, ruins relationships and hinders spiritual growth. If the troubles of local churches were carefully examined, it would be found that the great majority of them are caused by pride.

The relationship between youth and age is an extremely delicate one, but it is one of great importance to the life and health of the church. Ideally the church should be governed by men of mature spiritual experience which implies, among other things, a certain experience which comes only with year. But the youth of today are the leaders of tomorrow, and their fitness for future leadership is to a great extent dependent upon their relationship now with those who are older and more mature in the faith.

A scoffer (v. 1) is fit neither to lead nor to be prepared for leadership. The young man who, filled with pride in his own superior understanding, scorns the insights of his elderly brother, has a mind closed to correction and cannot, therefore, learn anything beyond the little he knows as long as his attitude persists. The elder who scorns the opinion of his younger brother will most likely be the last of his line. He will never succeed in encouraging others to assume efficiently responsibility within the church.

The person who 'opens wide his lips' (v. 7), who with a pitying smile dismisses the work of others as so much rubbish, should take warning from this verse. Similarly, the person who professes to have the answer to every problem should ask first whether he has found the answers to his own problems. It is easy to make professions of great wisdom when, in reality, we have nothing (v. 7). All of these manifestaiions of pride lead to strife (v. 10). They do not build up relationships. They break them down.

The young pride themselves in their fresh approach to life, the old in their experience. Both freshness and experience and, above all, humility, are needed if we are to learn. Let us ask God for a humble spirit.

Prov. 13. 1; Prov. 13. 3; Prov. 13. 4; Prov. 13. 7; Prov. 13. 9

Relationships

CARING FOR ONE ANOTHER

December 14   Reading: Ephesians 4. 25-32

Healthy relationships depend upon the genuine care we have for one another. It is the lack of this spirit of care that so often causes the lamentable breakdown of relationships within the family or the local church a spirit of care is part of our inheritance in Christ. It has to be developed, and in the process of growth it is not surprising that, in our limitations and ignorance, we should at times display the opposite, a spirit of harshness and carelessness. When we are at the receiving end of this attitude of lovelessness, the temptation is to react in the same manner with the result that all grace is gone and the family or church becomes embroiled in a problem very difficult to solve.

In these verses Paul urges us to grow in a spirit of mutual concern, and warns us against being contaminated by a spirit of bitterness which has taken hold of another brother.

If we are truly concerned for one another, we have to learn to speak the truth (v. 25). When we try to hide things from one another, are evasive in what we say, or indulge in flattery, disharmony is sure to result, be it within the family or within the church. A child of God cannot remain unmoved in the presence of sin, and there is a legitimate anger against sin, but it seeks the deliverance of the sinner, as God's wrath led to the judgement of sin and salvation through faith. Anger which results in resentment is, however, itself sin (v. 27). To harbour resentment is to give place to the devil.

What is our reaction when we are badly treated by a brother in the Lord? Do we lose the care we previously had for him? Does evil talk begin to take the place of what used to be a desire to edify him? (v. 29). Do we react in bitterness, a bitterness which gives way to slander and a desire to hurt? (v. 31) God in Christ forgave us (v. 32). Caring for one another will always be accompanied by a spirit of forgiveness.

"Be kind to one another" (v. 32) is a simple word of advice, but how often simple kindness is forgotten, and how often it would restore a relationship that is in danger of breaking. Let us ask the Lord to strengthen our relationships with Him and His people, to keep us from giving place to the devil, and to make us responsive constantly to the Spirit.

Eph. 4. 26; Eph. 4. 28; Eph. 4. 29; Eph. 4. 31; Eph. 4. 32

Relationships

RESPONSIBILITY OF A CONSISTENT EXAMPLE

December 15   Reading: 2 Timothy 1. 1-7

The way we live affects other people for good or evil. None of us live unto ourselves. As children of God we have a constant responsibility to set a godly example before those with whom we live and work. The importance of this within the family, within the church, or in the broader sphere of society can hardly be overestimated.

Paul here refers to his own background, and to Timothy's as well. We know very little about Paul's early life, but it is apparent that he came from a very religious family. He speaks here of serving God with a clear conscience 'as did my fathers' (v. 3). No doubt his parents passed on to him something of their own religious zeal and devotion to God. It is clear, however, that there had also been another type of religious influence in Paul's life, and that from the example of others he had imbibed the bigotry which led to his vigorous persecution of Jesus and His followers. By God's grace Paul was delivered from the baneful influence of his co-religionists, but it remains as a warning to us how our attiudes and actions can affect others for worse.

Of Timothy's father we know nothing apart from the fact that he was a Greek (Acts 16. 3). The formative influence in Timothy's early life came through his mother Eunice and his grandmother Lois (v. 5). His father may have been a 'God-fearer' or a proselyte. He certainly posed no threat to the religious influence upon his son, so the likelihood is that he himself had been enlightened by the knowledge of the true God whom his wife worshipped.

Paul speaks of Timothy's 'sincere faith' (v. 5) as an inheritance from his mother and grandmother. The word translated 'sincere' means lacking in all guile or pretence. No doubt Eunice and Lois spoke to Timothy about their faith, but their lives demonstrated the faith they professed. They were the type of people who impressed others at once as being folks of sincere faith and godly character. Their influence was obvious first of all in their own household, and from there it no doubt spread much farther afield.

How many people are stumbled, some for life, through the inconsistent living of those who profess to know the Lord. May the Lord give us a sense of our responsibility to live lives which are a godly example to others.

2 Tim. 1. 3; 2 Tim. 1. 4; 2 Tim. 1. 5; 2. Tim. 1. 6; 2 Tim. 1. 7

Relationships

SAMUEL

December 16   Reading: 1 Samuel 3. 1-12

Elkanah and Hannah dedicated their son Samuel to the service of the Lord, and Samuel was ministering to the Lord under Eli (v. 1). The sons of Eli, Hophni and Phinehas, who were acting as priests, had brought disgrace to the priesthood by their evil behaviour. They would listen to no one, least of all to their father who was very old and had lost all semblance of authority over his family.

Samuel was but a boy, but even so he could hardly have been totally ignorant of the evil of Eli's house, and he was well acquainted with Eli's own wavering character which was unable to deal with his sons whose sins were such a terrible stain on their sacred office. Nevertheless Samuel did not rebel against his situation as youthful impulse might have tempted him to do. He gave to Eli the respect due to him, and in doing so learned a very basic and valuable lesson.

Samuel had not previously received any divine revelation, so when he first heard the voice of God he thought that Eli was calling him (vs. 4-5). It would have been quite easy for him to ignore the call and more so the second time as it must have seemed to him that Eli was calling but was unaware of what he was doing. Nevertheless, three times Samuel rose from his bed and ran to Eli ready to do his bidding. Eli at last realized that the Lord was calling the boy, and told Samuel what he should do if the call should come again (vs. 7-8). The call did come again, and God told young Samuel of the judgement that was about to befall Eli's house. God had already warned Eli through one of His prophets (2. 27), but the warning had fallen on deaf ears. In Samuel God found someone who was ready to listen to Him.

In the service of Eli, Samuel had learned to listen, and he was ready to respond to a call when it came. God speaks through His people, and if we cannot listen to man it is unlikely that we will hear the voice of God. Eli, though old and experienced, had lost his ability to listen. Let us pray that God will give us Samuel's listening ear.

1 Sam. 2. 25; 1 Sam. 2. 26; 1 Sam. 3. 9; 1 Sam. 3. 10; 1 Sam. 3. 19

Miracles

THE NATURE OF MIRACLES

December 17   Reading: Psalm 135. 5-12

The Old and New Testaments use a number of different words to refer to God's activity in nature and history. They are translated by such words and phrases as 'signs' (John 20. 30), 'miracles' (Acts 8. 13), 'mighty acts' (Ps. 150. 2), 'wonders' (Exod. 3. 20). They signify acts which are the result of the power of God, are distinctive and wonderful, and have a particular significance. These may be said to be the marks of a miracle.

Scripture does not make any hard and fast distinction between God's sovereign power through which He orders and sustains His creation, and particular acts of His power. So in our reading the Psalmist passes easily from the work of creation and nature (v. 7) to the signs and wonders God wrought in Egypt (v. 10). All are works of his power, wonderful and significant. As believers we should learn to see the whole of creation as a miracle of God's sustaining grace (Col. 1.16-17).

In a narrower sense, a miracle is an event which cannot be explained in terms of ordinary natural forces as we understand them. A further important factor in Biblical miracles wrought by the power of God is that they are part of God's revelation of Himself, and teach a lesson which calls for a personal response to the Lord. They are never performed merely to incite wonder. God is a God who is doing wonders all the time, and not least when they are familiar things to us, as maintaining the order of the world in which we live.

The majority of the miracles in the Bible occur during three periods. First are the miracles which surrounded the exodus and the entry into the Promised Land. Then comes a long period of spiritual decline under the Judges followed by the establishment of the kingdom. During this period miracles were very few, but they again appear during the ministry of Elijah and Elisha (1-2 Kings). Following this period there are again but few miracles till the time of Christ and the apostles.

At certain important times in history God has been pleased to grant these special signs. Always, however, there are the signs of His sovereign power in nature and in His regenerating work. These are the greatest miracles of all.

Ps. 135. 6; Ps. 135. 7; John 20. 30; Ps. 150. 2; Rom. 1. 20

Miracles

THE MIRACLES OF OUR LORD

December 18   Reading: Mark 2. 1-12

Our Lord's earthly life began in the miracle of the virgin birth, and ended in the miracles of the resurrection and ascension. In fact these miracles are absolutely basic to our faith. If Jesus Christ is not God manifested in the flesh, then our faith is no more than a myth. If Jesus did not rise from the dead, then we are still in our sins and of all men most to be pitied (1 Cor. 15. 17, 19). These miralces are the great signs of who He is and of His saving work.

The gospels record only a selection of our Lord's miracles (John 20.30). All who knew Him best, even His enemies (Mark 3. 22), believed that He worked miracles, yet He never performed a miracle to dazzle people. He refused to give in to the temptation to cast Himself down from the pinnacle of the temple (Matt. 4. 5-7). To the Pharisees who sought a sign He said, "No sign shall be given to this generation" (Mk. 8. 12). He never sought the reputation of a worker of wonders. Again and again, after performing a miracle, He asked those who had seen it to tell no one (Matt. 8. 4; Mk. 8. 30; 9.9).

The miracles of Jesus were the works of the Messiah, and they were performed as an integral part of His mission of proclaiming the kingdom of God. When John the Baptist questioned whether He was in fact the Messiah, He replied, "The blind receive their sight and the lame walk, lepers are cleansed and the deaf hear, and the dead are raised up, and the poor have good news preached to them" (Matt. 11.5). These words are a reflection of Isa. 35. 5-6. Our Lord's miracles were a fulfilment of Old Testament predictions, and a sign to those who had eyes to see that He was the Saviour He claimed to be.

Jesus' power over demons was a sign that the kingdom of Satan had been overcome (Luke 11. 20-22). His power over the elements was a sign that He was one with the God of the Old Testament (Mark 4.41; Psa. 107. 29). His power over disease, as in our reading of the healing of the paralytic, was, to a people who believed that sickness was a punishment for sin, a sign of His authority to forgive sin.

Our Lord did not criticize those who beheld his miracles for not wondering, but for not repenting (Matt. 11.21). His miracles were all directed to the end that people might find in Him a personal Saviour. He wanted them, and He wants us, to look not for wondrous acts, but for forgiveness and grace.

Mark 2. 10-11; Mark 8. 12; Matt. 11. 5; Mark. 4, 41; Matt. 11. 21

Miracles

MIRACLES IN THE EARLY CHURCH

December 19   Reading: Acts 3. 1-10

Here we have a record of one of the earliest miracles of the apostolic age. It is the healing of a man lame from birth, and is a miracle very similar to many that the Lord Himself performed. During His earthly ministry Jesus had delegated His power to His disciples (Luke 9. 1-2), and He affirmed that this power would remain with them after His resurrection (John 14. 12; Acts 1. 8).

It was necessary that the church should begin its life with a demonstration of the power of the Lord in the midst of His people similar to the demonstration He gave in His own public ministry. The miracles of the apostles sprang from their union with Christ, and they were performed in his name (v. 6). They were not an end in themselves, but were a continuation of our Lord's proclamation of the kingdom.

As the story of the early church progresses, miracles become less and less common. In the latter part of the book of Acts they are rare. The final miracle recorded in Acts is the healing by Paul of Publius' father on the island of Malta (Acts 28.8). What is the significance of this apparent lessening of miraculous power? It would appear that miracles continued till the church was well established, and possibly till the New Testament Scriptures were being freely circulated. Then they ceased to be an important factor in the church's life.

God is the same yesterday, today and for ever. He is always able to break into the experience of an individual or of the church in a miraculous way, but we should not assume that it is always His will to do so, or to refrain permanently from doing so. He is always the sovereign Lord.

The miracles of the early church were certainly different from all subsequent miracles as they were immediately connected with the revelation of the incarnate Son of God. They were part of the original revelation and were not, therefore, sufficient ground for holding that miracles must always accompany the proclamation of the gospel. We have already seen that there have been long periods in Biblical history when God did not use miracles in dealing with His people. We would be wise not to insist that God should work in a specific way. There is always the miracle of grace, conclusive proof that God still works today as He wills. Let us thank Him for it.

Acts 3. 6; Luke 9:1; Luke 9. 2; Heb. 2. 2-3; Heb. 2. 4

Miracles

THE MIRACLE OF REGENERATION

December 20   Reading: Ephesians 2. 1-10

The greatest of all miracles is the miracle of grace (v. 8). Paul pictures it as life from the dead (vs. 1, 5). In doing so he is using no mere metaphor. The fall brought spiritual death (v. 1), and through grace God has made us 'alive together with Christ' (v. 5). We easily agree that the raising of Lazarus from the dead was one of God's mighty acts, but the work of regeneration is no less so, and this is a miracle which is constantly being repeated.

Paul contrasts what we once were, following our own self-centred ways (vs. 2-3), with what we may become through the saving work of Christ (vs. 8-10). God changes people. How exactly He does it we will never fully understand, but that He does do it is a fact substantiated by the lives and testimonies of countless thousands down through the years. Speaking to Nicodemus the ruler of the Jews, Jesus likens the regenerating work of the Holy Spirit to the wind. "The wind blows where it wills, and you hear the sound of it, but you do not know whence it comes or whither it goes; so it is with every one who is born of the Spirit" (John 3. 8). We may not understand the origin or the destination of the wind, but we see its effects. There is a divine and obvious effect upon every one who is born of the Spirit.

In any discussion on miracles it is all too easy to get our perspective wrong. When a spectacular event takes place which is not in line with ordinary natural forces as we understand them, we wonder and applaud. People will congregate in thousands, in the hope of physical healing or in the hope of observing a healing miracle. The spectacular is always impressive to man. It may be much less impressive to God.

Jesus paid a higher compliment to John the Baptist than he paid to any other man when He said, "I say to you, among those born of women there has risen no one greater than John the Baptist" (Matt. 11. 11). Yet it is recorded of John, "John did no sign" (John 10. 41). He worked no miracle. God was interested in something greater, the quality of John's character.

There are Christians who profess miraculous powers, but they are unable to make bad men good. This is the miracle God wants to perform. There is no greater miracle than the miracle of regeneration.

Eph. 2. 1-2; Eph. 2. 3; Eph. 2. 4-5; Eph. 2. 6-7; Eph. 2. 8-9

Miracles

MIRACLES IN THE OLD TESTAMENT

December 21   Reading: 1 Kings 19. 1-8

This may seem to be the least outstanding miracle of Elijah's life, but it is an outstanding example of the grace of God. God not only sustained Elijah physically, He also lifted him up from the very depths of despair.

It should be remembered that there are no long, unbroken periods of Biblical history characterized by a continuous performance of miracles. In the Old Testament there are two main periods during which outstanding miracles occurred, the first is the period of the exodus from Egypt, and the second is the period of the ministry of Elijah and Elisha. Apart from these two periods spectacular miracles were of infrequent occurrence.

Miracles have characterized the crises of sacred history. This is obviously so in the New Testament where they accompany the redemptive work of Christ and the founding and establishing of the church. The greatest miracle of all history, the resurrection of our Lord, was also the greatest crisis of all history. In the Old Testament the greatest of God's mighty acts was the deliverance at the Red Sea (Exod. 14. 21-28). This was an obvious crisis at the beginning of the life of a new nation. Without the miracle at the Red Sea there would have been no Israel, no Old Testament, no Jewish faith. The Old Testament Jewish faith was not developed from some human theory about the power of God. It was based on an actual manifestation of God's power. To the Jews, the deliverance at the Red Sea became a type of all God's deliverances throughout their subsequent history. God is still the God of deliverance.

The ministry of Elijah and Elisha took place during another crisis period in the history of the nation. The spiritual life of the people had degenerated. Compromise with Baal worship was rampant, and it seemed likely that the country would sink into complete apostasy. During this time God worked a series of remarkable miracles as a demonstration of His continuing power, and a reminder to the people that they were to have no other gods besides Him.

In our reading God intervenes miraculously in Elijah's personal crisis to bring new life and to maintain him in time of trial. God can do the same today. He is still God, and calls upon all men to worship Him. This is what the Old Testament miracles teach us.

1 Kings 19. 4; 1 King 19. 5; 1 Kings 19. 8; Ex. 14. 13; Ex. 14. 14

Miracles

SPURIOUS MIRACLES

December 22   Reading: Deuteronomy 13. 1-8

Many people are easily carried away by anything spectacular. Anything in the nature of the miraculous they at once assume to be the work of God. The Bible warns us strongly against such an attitude. Jesus spoke out clearly about the possibility of being deceived by spurious miracles (Matt. 7. 22-23). Paul did the same (2 Thess. 2. 9). In our reading there is a similar strict warning.

In a previous study we remarked how Jesus refused to perform a miracle simply for its own sake. The mere ability to work a miracle is no guarantee that a person receives his power from God. When Aaron performed a miracle before Pharaoh (Exod. 7. 10), Pharaoh called his sorcerers, and they duplicated the miracle 'by their secret arts' (Exod. 7. 11-12). The sequel proves the authenticity of the sign Moses and Aaron gave (Exod. 7. 12). Nevertheless the fact remains that Pharaoh's sorcerers did perform a miracle.

The present passage in Deuteronomy highlights an important factor about the working of miracles. It is that the spiritual authenticity of a miracle is proved by whether or not it draws people into a close relationship with the Lord (vs. 1-3). What we generally call a miracle should contribute to the miracle of grace, God's regenerating and transforming work. If it does not, it is worthless or positively dangerous. The words used to describe miracles in both the Old and New Testament clearly show that only miracles which are significant are valid. They must result in glory to God, not only in the excitement of the moment, but by the greater devotion and obedience they produce in the lives of those who experience them.

In these days many claims to miracle working powers are made in the name of the Lord. They attract large crowds, but seldom do they result in deeper spiritual living, godliness of character and a more effective witness. They should, therefore, be rejected. Miracles in the Bible were never offered as a mere spectacle. The greatest miracles are those performed in the hearts of men. Let us ask the Lord to keep transforming us by the miracle of His grace.

Deut. 13. 3; Deut. 13. 4; Matt. 7. 22-23; Matt. 24. 24; Ex. 7. 12.

Miracles

AHASUERUS

December 23   Reading: Esther 6. 1-11

'Ahasuerus' was a royal title, like 'Pharaoh' the title of the Egyptian rulers in the early period of Old Testament history. The name of the Ahasuerus mentioned in the book of Esther was Xerxes. He was like many other rulers of his time, despotic and violent, but God rules in the affairs of men, and He uses even the tyrants of this world to work out His purposes.

Looking superficially at the incident we have just read, it may not appear that any great miracle is involved. Most of us pass a sleepless night now and again, and so did Ahasuerus. Like the capricious man he was, he roused his servants from their sleep and ordered them to read to him an account of some of the memorable events of his own reign. One of these told how Ahasuerus had been saved from an assassination attempt through Mordecai the Jew (v. 2), yet Mordecai had gone unrewarded (v. 3).

At the precise moment the king was discussing the service Mordecai had rendered him, Haman, Ahasuerus' prime minister had entered the outer court of the palace. He was coming to request the king for Mordecai's execution (4.4). So sure was he that the king would accede to the request that he had already erected a gallows on which to hang his victim. But the king had other thoughts in mind. "What shall be done to the man whom the king delights to honour?" he asked Haman. Haman, thinking the king was referring to him (v. 6), outlined an extravagant programme of adulation which, to his dismay, he was ordered to perform for Mordecai his enemy.

Some people long and pray for dramatic miracles, but very often the greatest miracles are contained in the most ordinary events. Ahasuerus had a sleepless night, not an astounding event, but it had outstanding consequences. What would have happened had his insomnia overtaken him one night earlier or one night later? What would have happened had Haman entered the court of the king's palace but one hour later than he did? God's timing was the miracle, and God's timing was perfect. God performs miracles for us countless times, and we are not even aware of them. Let us thank Him for them.

Ps. 31. 15; Dan. 2. 20; Dan. 2. 21; Ps. 66. 7; Col. 1. 29

The Life of Our Lord

HIS BIRTH

December 24   Reading: Luke 2. 1-7

Caesar Augustus issued a decree that a census should be taken (v. 1), and in compliance with the order Joseph and Mary set out from Nazareth for the town of Bethlehem (v. 4). Bethlehem had been the home of Joseph's forefathers. There in that little Palestinian town, took place the most significant event in the history of the world. Jesus was born.

The incarnation will always remain a mystery to us, how God became man. Wisely, the writers of the New Testament do not treat it as a philosophic problem, but as the coming of a divine Saviour, and that is the way we should view this most wonderful of all events.

The teaching of the New Testament is that the eternal Son of God became human, and doing so did not in any way diminish His divine nature. The story of the babe of Bethlehem, born of a virgin, emphasises our Lord's humanness. "She gave birth to her first born son and wrapped him in swaddling clothes, and laid him in a manger" (v. 7). Jesus came into the world as a helpless infant requiring the same attention as any other new born child. It was not that God came to dwell in a human being as the Holy Spirit comes to dwell in us at regeneration. It was that God the Son began to live a life which was fully human. This meant that He was subject first to His human parents, and also to His heavenly Father. He grew as we grow. Luke tells us that 'Jesus increased in wisdom and in stature, and in favour with God and man' (v. 52).

Because Jesus was a man, He passed through every human experience just as we do. He passed through experience of temptation and moral conflict which are common to all men, and because He did, He is able to help us in our times of trial (Heb. 2. 18). Yet because He was God there was nothing in Him which responded or could respond to temptation. He was without sin (2 Cor. 5. 21). Being without sin, He had no need to die for sins of His own, but He died for the sins of others.

Let us thank God for the wonder of the incarnation, and for His grace which made Him come to the earth in the person of His Son to live and die for us. Let us pray for grace to allow Him to do all He came to do in us.

Luke 2. 4-5; Luke 2. 6-7; 1 Tim. 3. 16; Matt. 1. 23; Matt. 1. 21

The Life of Our Lord

ADORATION OF SHEPHERDS AND WISE MEN

December 25   Reading: Matthew 2. 7-12; Luke 2. 15-20

Christmas day. Today thousands of people in many parts of the world are remembering in a particular way the birth of our Lord Jesus Christ. The birth of our Lord was revealed in a special way to two different sets of people, to the wise men as we have read in Matthew's gospel and to the shepherds as we have read in Luke.

Who these wise men were, or where exactly they came from we do not know. Tradition says there were three of them and that they were kings, but the Bible does not tell us this. We do know, however, that they were rich, learned, and had hearts open to God's revelation. The word Matthew uses to describe them (Matt. 2. 7) indicates that they were astrologers. Now we know that astrology is a heathen superstition, and although astrology is very widely practised today, no believer should have any part in it whatsoever. The wise men of course, were heathen people, and Jesus came not only for the Jews but for them as well. It is not surprising that God should have heralded the birth of the Saviour of the world by some extraordinary astronomical sign, and He used this to bring the wise men to worship the new born king.

The wise men brought gifts to Jesus, gold and frankincense and myrrh; gold signifying holiness; frankincense worship; and myrrh suffering. In this way, though they could not have understood the significance of what they were doing, the wise men paid tribute to Jesus' perfect manhood, His divinity which calls for worship, and His redeeming work on the cross.

The shepherds watching their flocks on the hills of Judea were humble Jewish people. In many ways they were totally different from the wise men, but they too had a heart for God's revelation, and God privileged them with an angelic visitation to announce Jesus' birth. The shepherds were also among the first to worship the new born king (Lk. 2. 20).

These two incidents teach us that the Lord Jesus came for the rich and the poor, the educated and the uneducated, for people of every class and race and tongue. He came for them all, that anyone who trusts Him might find eternal life. Let us make this day a day of joy in the birth of the Saviour of the world, and a day of worship.

Luke 2. 8; Luke 2. 11; Luke. 2. 15; Luke 2. 16; Luke 2. 20

The Life of Our Lord

HIS BAPTISM

December 26   Reading: Matthew 3. 13-17

Apart from one incident recorded by Luke (Luke 2. 41-52), the gospels are silent about the life of our Lord from the time of His birth till He took up His public ministry when He was about thirty years of age (Luke 3. 23). Then He came from Galilee to John the Baptist at the river Jordan and asked him for baptism (v. 13). John at first demurred. Here was Jesus putting Himself in a position of inferiority to John who well knew that he himself was the inferior one. "I need to be baptized by you, and do you come to me?" he said.

John's baptism was a baptism of repentance (v. 6). Why, therefore, should the One who did no sin wish to be baptized? We can understand this when we realize why our Lord came. He came to bring redemption to the world, and in doing so He first identified Himself completely with those He came to save. He was no sinner in need of repentance, but He accepted the baptism of repentance for us just as later He died for us, though, as the sinless One, He had no need to die.

As Jesus came up from the water the heavens were opened, the Spirit of God revealed Himself like a dove, and a voice from heaven said, "This is my beloved Son with whom I am well pleased" (vs. 16-17). In this way God testified to the sinlessness of His Son. Our Lord, of course, was at the very beginning of His public ministry, but during the previous thirty years, growing up and labouring in a humble home, surrounded by all the sins and problems of a sinful world, He lived a life of perfect righteousness. Thus the Father could say He was well pleased with Him.

The Holy Spirit's descending on Jesus was the sign of His commissioning. He was ready to take up the task for which He had come into the world, the task of bringing peace and redemption. The dove is a symbol of peace, so in our Lord's commission at His baptism there is a reflection of the words spoken at His birth, "Glory to God in the highest, and on earth peace among men with whom he is pleased" (Luke 2. 14).

So three factors emerge at our Lord's baptism, His commissioning, His holiness, His identification with sinners. God has commissioned us also to take forth the gospel, and our commission can only be fulfilled as we live holy lives and are ready to identify ourselves with those to whom He has sent us.

Matt. 3. 13; Matt. 3. 14; Matt. 3. 15; Matt. 3. 16; Matt. 3. 17

The Life of Our Lord

THE TEMPTATION

Immediately following His baptism, our Lord was subjected to Satan's temptation. His ability to fulfil His commission had to be put to the test. God does this with all of us. Luke tells us He was lead by the Spirit for forty days IN the wilderness (vs. 1-2). Matthew says He was led by the Spirit INTO the wilderness (Matt. 4.1). Both are true. Jesus was led by the Spirit to the place of temptation, but throughout the period of temptation the Spirit was bearing Him up.

In this first great temptation our Lord won the crucial victory over Satan, but it was not the last temptation. The devil 'departed from him until an opportune time' (v. 13). He was always looking for an opportunity to return. Temptation is a constant factor in our spiritual lives, but victory in the first temptaion, which is always the hardest, strengthens us to combat the temptation which follow.

Jesus was tempted along three specific line, and all temptation falls into one of these three categories. He was first tempted to make material things His priority. "If you are the Son of God, command this stone to become bread" (v. 3). Satan did not tempt Him to do something wrong of itself. It is perfectly all right to take legitimate steps to supply our material needs. It is not wrong to eat. But if we put material things first in our lives, before the will of God, then it is sin.

The second temptation was for Jesus to compromise with Satan to obtain what He had come to receive, all power and dominion (vs. 5-7). Satan, of course, lied to our Lord in saying that this was his to give (v. 6). Often we are tempted to think that compromise with evil or the world will help us the quicker to do something for God, but this is always a lie.

Finally, Satan tried to lure our Lord to do something spectacular, to throw Himself down from the pinnacle of the temple (vs. 9-10). How often we are tempted to show off our own abilities, or to engage in a little showmanship, but none of these accomplish the will of God. Jesus withstood all these temptations by quoting the Scripture (vs. 4, 8, 12). If we remain true to God's Word, Satan's temptations can never defeat us.

Luke 4. 1-2; Luke 4. 4; Luke 4. 8; Luke 4. 12; Luke 4. 13

The Life of Our Lord

JESUS AND THE KINGDOM

December 28   Reading: Luke 17. 20-21

The kingdom of God or the kingdom of heaven is mentioned more than a hundred times in the gospels. The Kingdom forms the essence of our Lord's ministry. It figures at the very beginning of His ministry (Mark 1. 15), and it does so also at the end. After the resurrection, during the forty days in which He appeared to His disciples, Jesus spoke of the kingdom of God (Acts 1.3).

In the time of our Lord the kingdom was the subject of great misunderstanding as it is today. The Jews looked for the coming of an earthly Messiah who would reign over them as a king, and this false idea persisted in the minds of the disciples even though Jesus had specifically told them that His kingdom was something much different (cf. Acts 1. 6). Speaking to the Pharisees, Jesus tells them, "The kingdom of God is not coming with signs to be observed" (v. 20). That is, it is not an outward, earthly kingdom, but, "The kingdom of God is in the midst of you," or 'in you' (v. 21). The words Jesus used can mean both 'in you' and 'in the midst of you', and both are true.

The kingdom of God is first of all God's rule in the hearts of His people. In the sermon on the Mount where Jesus says much about the kingdom, He emphasises the importace of the inner man, his attitudes and motives from which all his actions flow. The kingdom of God is His rule in these innermost recesses of our beings which no one sees or knows but God and ourselves.

God's kingdom is also His rule in the midst of His people. This is often where we experience the greatest difficulty, in allowing God to have His place in relationship with our fellow believers in the church. Yet the greatest testimony to the world of the reality of the gospel is the peace and unity which flow from God's dwelling in the midst of His people and having His place of rightful supremacy among them.

In a wider sense, the kingdom of God is His rule in the affairs of men. God rules this world in the interest of His glory and His people. This is true in history. It is also true in the events of our personal lives. God rules. A time is coming when every knee will bow to Him and His kingdom will be established for all eternity. Let us thank the Lord for bringing us into His kingdom, and let us afresh give to Him the full control of our lives, our relationships, our all.

Luke 17. 20; Luke 17. 21; Dan. 4. 25; John 18. 36; Rev. 11. 15.

363

The Life of Our Lord

JESUS AND HIS DISCIPLES

December 29   Reading: Mark 3. 3-19

One of the most important parts of our Lord's short ministry was His training of the twelve. He ministered to many others in many different ways,
but His main energies were poured into teaching the disciples. Mark tells
us that the twelve were chosen to be with the Lord (v. 14), to be sent out
to preach (v. 14), and to have authority to cast out demons (v. 15). The
apostles, as our Lord called the twelve, occupied a special place at the beginning of the church age, but the three guiding principles Jesus gave them
are applicable to us all. The Lord call us to spend time with Him, to witness
to others of His saving power, and to have authority over everything that
is of the evil one first of all in ourselves, and through obedience to the
Word in others also.

Mark here gives us a list of the twelve disciples' names. Those of whom
we have some information were all about as different from one another
as could be. They were not easily moulded together into a fellowship, but
their ultimate unity seen so clearly at the foundation of the church shows
how the Lord can unite in love the most diverse characters. When we think
we cannot get along with another believer, let us remember that the power
of the gospel can make us one if we are but willing to allow the Lord to
do His work within us.

Of some of the disciples we know no more than their names, James
son of Alphaeus for example, and Thaddaeus. About others such as Peter
and John we know a good deal. The opposite characteristics of some of
the twelve are not difficult to see. Simon the zealot, the patriotic Jew, and
Matthew the tax collector for the Roman government; impulsive Peter, and
John the apostle of love (though there was also another side to his
character); Andrew the man of faith and Thomas the doubter.

Jesus did not choose twelve people who were alike, yet with all the
possibilities of difficulties in their relationship, He sent them out two by two
(Mark 6. 7). He knew the problems they would face, but they could find
victory in Him.

The twelve disciples are a miniature of the church. They show us the
need of fellowship and the Lord's power to maintain His people together
in love. Let us pray for a deeper fellowship in our own lives with all who
are the Lord's children.

Mark 3. 13; Mark. 6. 7; Lk. 22. 28-29; John 20. 27-28; Matt. 16. 15-16

The Life of Our Lord

JESUS AND PRAYER

December 30   Reading: Mark 1. 29-39

"And in the morning a great while before day, he rose and went out to a lonely place, and there he prayed" (v. 35). Jesus was divine, yet He was also fully man, and prayer played a very important part in His life. He was dependent always upon the Father (John 5. 30), and through prayer found strength to do the Father's will (Mark 14. 36).

Jesus was teaching in the synagogue at Capernaum (1. 21) when a man with an unclean spirit entered. Jesus healed him (v. 25). Leaving the synagogue He went to the house of Simon and Andrew. There He healed Simon's mother-in-law (vs. 29-30). News spread rapidly, and by evening people with their ailments had gathered at the home from throughout the city. Jesus healed many (v. 34).

Morning, however, found Jesus alone in a deserted place praying (v. 35). Exhausted both physically and spiritually from the ministry of the previous day, He was in need of renewed spiritual refreshing and strength. We are not told what He prayed for, but almost certainly He prayed for strength to fulfil the purpose for which He had been sent.

Simon and those who were with him pursued our Lord to His place of prayer (v. 36). "Everyone is searching or you," they said (v. 37). No doubt many more had arrived with their ailments in the hope of being healed. Probably others were looking for the Lord merely out of curiosity. But our Lord did not go back to them. He said, "Let us go to the next town, that we may preach there also" (v. 38).

Our Lord's great concern was the preaching of the good news. He preached from a heart of compassion, and the healings and deliverances He wrought were all an outflow of His love. Yet they were secondary to the purpose for which He had come, which was to proclaim the kingdom. Through prayer He kept this purpose ever before Him, and found strength to minister the gospel when all around were people clamouring for physical healing. Physical need there certainly was on every hand, but Jesus resisted the temptation, to be so completely occupied with doing good that what was most necessary would be left undone. We too need to maintian a close communion with the Lord, in the midst of all the calls which come to us, that we may know His will and be strengthened to do it.

Mark 1. 21; Mark 1. 27; Mark 1. 35; Mark 1. 38; John 5. 30

The Life of Our Lord

THE TRANSFIGURATION

December 31   Reading: Mark 9. 1-8

The transfiguration took place six days after Jesus' great self-disclosure at Caesarea Philippi (8. 27). It was there that Peter made his confession, "You are the Christ" (8. 29), and Jesus told the disciples that He had to suffer, be rejected, die, and after three days rise again (8. 31). This was too much for Peter who rebuked the Lord (8. 32), only to be rebuked himself in turn with the words, "Get thee behind me, Satan! For you are not on the side of God, but of men" (8. 33). The thought of a suffering Messiah was incredible to the disciples. What Jesus had just told them was a severe blow to their faith.

Peter, James and John were with Jesus when He was transfigured before them. Then Moses and Elijah appeared, talking to Jesus. A cloud overshadowed them, and from the cloud a voice proclaimed, "This is my beloved Son; listen to him" (v.7). Whatever the disciples felt in their fear (v. 6), it was clear that God had set His seal of approval upon His Son and the choice He had made, the choice of the cross. What Jesus had told the disciples at Caesarea Philippi was not to mean the end of everything. In the suffering, rejection and death that lay ahead, the power and love of God were at work to bring triumph out of apparent defeat, a triumph gloriously revealed in the resurrection.

Moses and Elijah represented the law and the prophets. Jesus had come to be the fulfilment of what they proclaimed. The tradition of the law and the prophets had fashioned the mental attitude of the disciples, but Jesus brought something more. He brought not merely a law, but a life which touched the very foundations of man's being, and to make that life available to others He now had to tread a lonely road beyond anything the prophets of old had ever done.

Up to the transfiguration Jesus had stood in the long tradition of the Old Testament prophets, but now He leaves them to pursue His own unique path, consecrating Himself afresh to the will of the Father which meant the sacrifice of the cross.

As we come to the end of one year and look ahead to the beginning of another, God calls us to step out on untrodden paths as Jesus Himself did. God goes before, and whatever the future may hold, the end is victory. Let us thank Him for it.

Mark 8. 31; Mark 8. 32-33; Mark 9. 2; Mark 9. 3-4; Mark 9. 7

Index of Scripture Portions

11.	19-26	Apr.	29
12.	1-11	June	8
14.	19-23	Oct.	29
15.	6-21	Mar.	22
16.	6.12	Mar.	21
16.	25-33	June	1
17.	10-15	Mar.	18
19.	21-28	Feb.	23
20.	4-7	Sept.	4
20.	25-32	Oct.	30
21.	7-9	Aug.	25
28.	21-30	Nov.	18

Romans

1.	1-16	Apr.	23
1.	18-21	Feb.	14
2.	12-16	July	19
3.	9-18	Feb.	15
3.	21-26	Apr.	25
4.	1-16	Apr.	26
4.	16-25	Nov.	13
5.	1-5	Apr.	27
5.	12-21	Feb.	16
6.	1-11	Sept.	5
6.	12-16	Feb.	29
6.	17-23	May	7
7.	1-6	May	10
7.	7-12	Feb.	28
7.	13-25	May	8
8.	1-8	Mar.	1
8.	9-17	May	9
8.	18-27	Apr.	28
8.	28-39	Feb.	17
9.	14-21	July	2
12.	1-8	Oct.	8
12.	9-21	Jan.	24
13.	1-7	Apr.	16
13.	8-14	Nov.	29
14.	1-13	June	29
15.	1-6	Sept.	18

1 Corinthians

1.	18-25	Oct.	5
1.	26-31	Oct.	2
2.	1-8	Nov.	7

3.	1-15	Oct.	1
5.	1-8	July	12
6.	1-11	Oct.	3
7.	1-9	July	10
7.	10-16	May	4
8.	1-13	Feb.	20
9.	8-14	Nov.	14
9.	15-18	July	28
9.	19-27	May	23
10.	1-13	May	19
10.	16-24	Sept.	8
11.	17-22	Feb.	24
11.	23-32	Sept.	7
12.	4-11	Oct.	10
12.	12-26	Aug.	3
13.	1-7	Feb.	6
13.	8-13	Oct.	25
14.	1-5	Oct.	13
14.	20-25	Oct.	11
15.	1-14	Jan.	18
15.	17-26	Apr.	13
15.	51-55	Nov.	21

2 Corinthians

3.	1-6	Sept.	19
5.	16-21	Nov.	17
6.	1-13	May	17
6.	14-18	May	5
8.	1-7	Aug.	11
9.	1-15	Aug.	9
10.	1-6	Feb.	10
10.	7-12	Aug.	15
12.	1-10	May	31

Galatians

1.	1-9	Mar.	3
1.	10-17	June	19
2.	11-16	Nov.	9
3.	19-29	Feb.	27
4.	1-7	May	12
5.	13-26	Feb.	5
6.	1-10	Aug.	22
6.	11-18	June	30

Ephesians

1.	1-10	Jan.	1

1.	11-23	July	30
2.	1-10	Dec.	20
2.	11-22	Aug.	2
3.	1-13	June	20
3.	14-21	June	13
4.	1-7	Oct.	9
4.	8-14	Oct.	12
4.	15-24	Dec.	12
4.	25-32	Dec.	14
5.	15-20	Oct.	16
5.	21-33	May	2
6.	1-4	Aug.	24
6.	10-13	May	21
6.	14-20	May	22

Philippians
1.	1-11	Jan.	22
1.	12-21	Mar.	24
2.	1-13	Apr.	9
2.	14-29	Jan.	26
3.	1-11	Apr.	14
3.	12-21	July	6
4.	1-7	Jan.	28
4.	8. 13	July	13
4.	14-20	Aug.	8

Colossians
1.	1-14	July	22
1.	15-29	July	26
3.	5-17	Feb.	8
3.	18-4.6	July	25

1 Thessalonians
1.	1-7	Nov.	6
2.	1-12	June	28
5.	1-11	Nov.	20
5.	12-23	Jan.	8

2 Thessalonians
1.	3-12	Feb.	9
2.	7-16	Nov.	23
3.	6-13	Apr.	19

1 Timothy
3.	1-7	Oct.	31
3.	8-15	Oct.	18
4.	1-10	Oct.	26

4.	11-16	Nov.	2
5.	1-2	July	9
5.	3-8	Apr.	20
5.	17-22	Nov.	3
6.	3-10	Aug.	6

2 Timothy
1.	1-7	Dec.	15
1.	8-14	June	2
2.	1-10	Sept.	20
2.	14-22	Jan.	23
3.	10-17	Mar.	16
4.	1-8	Aug.	18

Titus
1.	5-11	Nov.	1
2.	1-15	Aug.	21
3.	1-7	Feb.	3
3.	8-11	Oct.	27

Philemon
1.	1-25	May	13

Hebrews
1.	1-9	Jan.	17
2.	1-9	June	7
3.	1-15	Sept.	2
4.	14-5.10	Jan.	16
8.	1-7	Aug.	31
9.	23-28	July	21
10.	1-10	Apr.	10
10.	11-18	Aug.	14
10.	19-25	Jan.	11
12.	1-6	Dec.	8
12.	7-15	Oct.	20
13.	10-16	Apr.	11
13.	17-21	Nov.	10

James
1.	1-11	May.	14
1.	12-18	May	15
1.	19-25	Sept.	17
2.	8-17	Apr.	18
2.	18-26	Dec.	4
3.	1-12	July	24
3.	13-18	Oct.	4
4.	1-10	June	5

372

Index of Bible Characters

A name printed in capitals indicates that the character is the subject of the reading on the date immediately following his name.

Aaron, Mar 4, Aug 27, Sept 15, Oct 21, Dec 22.
ABNER, Oct 7.
ABRAHAM, Jan 7, Feb 4, Apr 26, June 23, Nov 12, Dec 4, 9.
ABSALOM, May 6, Jan 4, Aug 12, Oct 7.
Adam and Eve, Feb 14, Apr 13, 30.
Agabus, Aug 16.
Ahab, June 10, Oct 28.
AHASUERUS, Dec 23.
Ahaz, Sept 30.
Ahaziah, June 10.
Ahimelech, Mar 11.
Amaziah, July 29.
Amon, Sept 23.
AMOS, July 29, Nov 25.
ANDREW, June 24, Dec 29, 30.
ANNANIAS, Aug 5.
Artaxerxes, Dec 2.
ATHALIAH, June 10.
Augustus, Dec 24.

BALAAM, Mar 25.
Balak, Mar 25.
BARNABAS, Apr 29, Mar 22, May 23, Oct 29, Nov 9.
BARZILLAI, Aug 12.
Bathsheba, Mar 7, July 11.
Belshazzar, Apr 1.
BEREANS, Mar 18.
Bilhah, July 22.

CENTURION, Jan 21.
Chimham, Aug 12.

DAN, July 22.
DANIEL, Apr 1, June 7.

Darius, Apr 1.

DAVID, Nov 4, Jan 4, Feb 4, Mar 11, May 6, 25, June 7,
July 11, 29, Aug 12, Sept 26, Oct 7.

Demetrius, Jan 25.

Demetrius the silversmith, Feb 23.

Diotrophes, Jan 25.

DOEG, Mar 11.

EBED MELECH, Feb 11.

ELDAD, Oct 14.

ELI, Aug 26, Jan 14, Dec 16.

Eliab, Nov 4.

ELIEZER, Dec 9.

Elihu, May 28.

ELIJAH,July 8, June 7, 14, Aug 19, Oct 28, Dec 21, 31.

Eliphaz, May 28.

ELISHA, Aug 19, Oct 28, Dec 21.

Elkanah, Jan 14, Dec 16.

Epaphroditus, Jan 22, 26, Nov 18.

Esau, July 1, Sept 13.

Esther, Sept 12.

Eunice, Dec 15.

EUODIA, Jan 28.

Ezra, May 26, Sept 27, Nov 15.

Gaius, Jan 25, Aug 10.

Gamaliel, Apr 21.

Gershon, Oct 21.

Goliath, May 6.

Habakkuk, Dec. 6.

Haggai, Mar 26.

Haman, Sept 12, Dec 23.

HANNAH, Jan 14, Dec 16.

Herod the Great, June 6.

HEZEKIAH, Sept 30, Sept. 14, Oct 21

Hilkiah, Sept 23.

374

Hophni, Aug 26, Dec 16.
Hosea, Sept 10.

Isaac, June 23, Dec 9.
Ishbosheth, Oct 7.
Ishmael, June 23.

JACOB, Feb 25, June 8, July 1, 22.
Jahaziel, May 27.
James, brother of John, Feb 19, Mar 13, Apr 15, June 8, Dec 31.
James, elder of Jerusalem Church, Mar 22, Nov 9.
James, son of Alphaeus, Dec 29.
Jehoahad, Dec 6.
Jehoiada, June 10.
Jehoiakim, Dec 6.
Jehoram, Oct 28.
JEHOSHAPHAT, May 27.
Jehosheba, June 10.
JEHU, Oct 28.
JEREMIAH, June 3, Feb 11, Sept 13.
Jeroboam, Oct 28.
Jeroboam II, July 29.
Jesse, Nov 4.
Jezebel, June 10, July 8, Oct 28.
JOAB, Oct 7, May 25.
Joash, June 10, Aug 19.
Job, May 28, July 7.
Joel, Sept 16, 24.
JOHN, Apr 15, Jan 25, Feb 19, Mar 13, Apr 21, June 15, Dec 29, 31.
John Mark, Apr 29, May 23.
JOHN THE BAPTIST, Nov 25, June 21, July 3, Sept 24, Dec 18, 20, 26.
Jonah, Mar 28.
Joram, June 10.
Joseph, husband of Mary Aug 20, Dec 24.
JOSEPH, July 15, Mar 3, May 19, June 8.
JOSEPH OF ARIMATHEA, Jan 21.
Joshua, Mar 6, Sept 21, Oct 14.

375

Joshua the High Priest, Mar 26, June 4, Nov 11.
JOSIAH, Sept 23, Sept 14, Dec 6.
Judas Iscariot, Apr 6, June 5. 6.

Kohath, Oct 21.

LABAN, July 1, Feb 25.
LEVITES, Oct 21.
Lois, Dec 15.
Lot, Jan 7, June 16.

Maachah, May 6.
Manasseh, King of Judah, Sept 23.
MANOAH, Apr 22, July 22.
Mary Magdalene, Apr 5.
Mary, mother of our Lord, Apr 15, Aug 20, Dec 24.
Matthew, Dec 29.
MEDAD, Oct 14.
Merari, Oct 21.
Mordecai, Sept 12, Dec 23.
MOSES, Mar 4, June 7, July 2, 8, 22, Sept 1, 15, 21, Oct 14, Dec 22, 31.

Nahor, Dec 9.
Naomi, Mar 30.
Nathan, Mar 7.
Nebuchadnezzar, Apr 1.
NEHEMIAH, Dec 2.
Nicodemus, Apr 24, Dec 20.

Obadiah, Sept 13.
Onesimus, May 13.
Orpah, Mar 30.

PAUL, Nov 18, Jan 22, 26, Mar 16, 18, 21, 22, 24, Apr 14, 19, 27, 29,
    May 13, 17, 23, 30, 31, June 19, 28, July 28, Oct 29,
    Nov 6, 9, 25, Dec 15
PETER, Feb 18, Mar 3, 13, 22, Apr 7, 15, 21, June 4, 8, 15, 24,
    Sept 4, Nov 9, Dec 29, 30, 31.

General Index

A

ADOPTION: under the control of Christ, May 12.

ANGELS: who they are, June 7; guardians of God's people, June 8, July 8; and the Lord Jesus Christ, June 9.

APOSTLES: Christ the great, Aug 13, Sept 2; ministry of, Aug 15, Dec 29; authority of, Nov 6.

ASSURANCE: through the Holy Spirit, Mar 22.

ATONEMENT: meaning of, Apr 4, through the cross, Apr 9, Nov 23; day of, Apr 4, Aug 28, 29, Sept 2.

ATTITUDES: need to foster right, June 24; effects of, Mar 1, Dec 15; sin exists in, Feb 15; law cannot deal with, Feb 27; changed through justification, Apr 27; sanctification of, May 10, Christ reigning over, Dec 28; right doctrine fosters right, Dec 26; fellowship hindered by wrong, Jan 24, Feb 5, 24, Sept 30; danger of unsurrendered, Oct 4; victory over wrong, Mar 2; worldly, Feb 23; of worship, Jan 13, June 16; of learning, Sept 17, 19; of truth, Mar 7; of service, Aug 23; of covetousness, Feb 26.

AUTHORITY: of Christ, Nov 7, Dec 18; of the Word, Mar 18; of apostles, Aug 15, Nov 7; of church elders, Oct 29, Nov 2; of God above that of man, Apr 21, July 20; of apostles subject to the Word, Mar 18; delegated, July 27, Nov 7, 8, 12; within the family, Aug 23; principle of human, Apr 16, Aug 13; limit of human, Apr 21; positional, Nov 5; spiritual, Nov 5, 6, 10; misuse of, Nov 9.

B

BAPTISM: instituted by Christ, Sept 3, Nov 12; meaning of, Sept 5, 6; Paul's refusal to administer, Nov 7; of the Holy Spirit, Jan 31; meaning of John's, Dec 26; of our Lord, Dec 26.

BEAUTY: God created, Nov 27; God's love of, Feb 22; God's people should love, June 26, 27.

BLOOD: meaning of, Aug 30; offering of Christ's, Nov 30; of Passover sacrifice, Sept 1, 30.

BODY: importance and sanctity of, Apr 8, 13; of resurrection, July 16, Oct 17; fitness of, Dec 1, 2.

BODY OF CHRIST: the church, July 26, Aug 3; Christ the Head, July 26, Aug 3, 15.

BUSINESS: our Lord and the world of, Feb 19; right attitude to, Feb 22; obsession with, Feb 23, July 1; witness in, June 22.

C

CHILDREN: parents' responsibilities for, Apr 20, Aug 20, Dec 10; parents' influence on, Feb 25; guidance of, Mar 21, May 1; discipline of, Dec 8; weakness in dealing with, Aug 26; attitude of world towards, Nov 30; their duties to parents, July 25, Aug 24; to be like, Dec 3; of God, Apr 12.

CHOOSING: God's sovereign, June 21; to accept truth, Mar 29; the way of the Spirit, May 9; suffering and the cross, Dec 31; responsibility in, July 3; factors which influence, July 3.

CHRIST, THE LORD JESUS

THE PERSON AND THE WORK OF: deity, Jan 15, Dec 25; humanity, Jan 16, Dec 25; authority, Jan 15, Nov 7; Mediator, Jan 17; Prophet, Priest and King, Jan 17, Aug 16, 28; Servant, Sept 11; Head of the Church, Aug 3, 15; incarnation, Jan 20; virgin birth, Dec 18, 24; ministry of, Aug 13; His redemptive work, Jan 20, July 20, Dec 26; perfect sacrifice of, July 21, Aug 14, 28, 29.

THE LIFE OF: His birth, Dec 24, 25; temptation, June 6; distinctiveness and sinless character, Jan 19, Dec 26; consistency, Jan 19; prayerfulness, June 11, Dec 30; joy in facing the cross, Feb 7; crucifixion, Jan 18, 26, Apr 3, 4, 11, May 30, Sept 9; resurrection, Jan 18, Sept 9; coming again, Apr 19, July 16.

CHURCH: universal, July 30; local, Jan 27, July 31; God's purpose for, Feb 17, July 30; Christ's pre-eminence in, July 30, Nov 19, Dec 28; foundation of, Aug 4, 5; under care of the triune God, Oct 10; body of Christ, Aug 3, Oct 8, Nov 19; house of God, Aug 4; one new man, Aug 2, Nov 13; marks of local, Sept 6; unity of, Jan 31, Nov 16; its holiness, Jan 10, July 30, Aug 5; importance of sound ministry in, Nov 2; gifts of the ascended Lord to, Oct 12; ministry of, Aug 21; a testimony to the reality of the gospel, Nov 16; witness of, July 26; authority in, Nov 4; order in, Oct 18, 29, Dec 13; judgment and discipline in, Oct 27, 28, Nov 1; answer to problems in, Nov 1; twelve disciples a miniature of, Dec 29; the family a miniature of, Aug 21, tabernacle a symbol of, Aug 31; responsibility of giving within, Aug 9; spirit of caring within, Dec 14; supporting the work of, Nov 14; miracles in, Dec 19.

CIRCUMCISION: spurious claims for, Mar 22, Apr 26, June 30.

COMMANDMENTS, TEN: importance of, Feb 26; breaking of, Mar 4; first, Sept 27; fourth, Dec 1; seventh, July 11; eighth, Feb 28; tenth, Feb 28.

COMPROMISE: sin of, Feb 20, Sept 8, 27, Oct 28; temptation to, Dec 27; may be based on fear, Nov 9; in marriage relationships, May 5.

CONSCIENCE: meaning of, July 19.

CONTENTION: Oct 1-7; a mark of carnality, Oct 1; causes of, Oct 4, 6; encouraged by truth without love, Mar 8; answer to, Oct 2.

CORRUPTION: Christian attitude in midst of, Feb 21; background of the Corinthian church, Oct 1.

CREATION: by the hand of God, July 2; of a moral world, Sept 10, 16; a revelation of God's power and greatness, July 19, Dec 17; of time, Nov 26; God's purpose in, June 18, Oct 18, Nov 22; respect for God's, Oct 15, 17; of the Church, Aug 2; new, Nov 24, Dec 11.

CRITICISM: often a mark of immaturity, Oct 25; which is wrong, Mar 9, Oct 14, Nov 26; reaction to, Mar 9, Nov 25; rejoicing in Mar 24.

CROSS: meaning of, Apr 11, 12, Oct 15; principle of contrary to natural thinking, Oct 5; scope of work of, July 26, Aug 2, Nov 23; forgiveness through, Sept 28; glorying in, June 30; satan defeated at, June 6.

D

DEACONS: qualifications of, Oct 18.

DEATH: meaning of, July 16; negation of everything qualitative, May 7; spiritual, Dec 20; powerless over Christ, Apr 5; of cross gateway of life, Apr 12; identification with our Lord's, Sept 5; no more, Nov 24.

DELIVERANCE: from evil, Sept 12; from legalism, Mar 3; type of God's, Dec 21.

DISCERNMENT: importance of, Jan 23, Mar 6, July 13, Nov 4; basis of true, Oct 2, Nov 7, 15; of God's people together, Mar 22; examples of, May 25, Sept. 15, 16.

DISCIPLE, DISCIPLESHIP: meaning of, Aug 24, Nov 12; basis of true, Mar 5; Jesus' concern for His, June 11; twelve a miniature of the church, Dec 29.

DISCIPLINE: of God is purposeful, Feb 2, 7, Oct 20, Dec 8; within the church, July 12, Aug 31, Oct 18; within the family, Aug 24; in ordinary living, Oct 20; by right use of time, Nov 27; of speech, Oct 4; of elders, Nov 3, 9; of children, Dec 8; must be impartial, Nov 3.

380

DIVISION IN THE CHURCH: sources of, Feb 24, Mar 8, Sept 7, Oct 2; concern for, Aug 3; destroys testimony, Nov 17; prayer heals, June 13.

DIVORCE: Apr 30-May 6; and the law of Moses, May 3; hated by God, May 4, July 14.

DOCTRINE: measured by Scriptures, Mar 16; of apostles, Apr 13; related to practical living, Sept 21; gradual inroads of wrong, Oct 22; importance of right, Oct 23, 26; distinguishing between right and wrong, Oct 24; answer to wrong, Oct 26.

E

ELDERS: plurality of, Oct 29; appointment of, Oct 30; qualifications of, Oct 31, Nov 1; authority of, Nov 2, 8: discipline of, Nov 3, 9; encouragement of younger men by, Dec 13.

EQUALITY: of man and woman, Aug 23; in marriage relationship, May 2.

ETERNAL LIFE: a term of quality, May 7, 16; the consummation of sanctification, May 7.

EVANGELIST: ministry of, Aug 17; responsibility to do the work of, Sept 20.

F

FAITH: Dec 3-9; meaning of, Dec 3; a continual experience, Dec 3, 6; results of, May 13, 14, July 21, Dec .15; inseperable from righteousness, Dec 4; inseperable from faithfulness, Feb 9, Dec 6; is humble Dec 9; produces obedience, July 18; practical implications of, Feb 23; shown by our words, July 24; unites God's people, Oct 27; walk of, Sept 1, 9; in God alone, Mar 4, 18, Aug 1; justification by, Apr 26, June 20, July 19; examples of, Apr 29; corruption of, May 8, 18; mixed with unbelief, Dec. 7; purifying of, Dec. 7.

FAITHFULNESS: fruit of the Spirit, Feb 5, 9; inseparable from faith, Feb 9; in proclaiming the Word, July 30, Nov 14; produces spiritual strength, July 9; prayer for, June 15; of God mirrored in marriage relationship, Apr 30; reward for, July 20.

FALL: of man, Feb 13, 16; its meaning, Apr 7; results of, Apr 28, July 3, 13, 31, Sept 16, Oct 15, Dec 20.

FAMILY: sanctity of, Apr 20, July 11, Aug 20, Oct 31; importance of stable, Apr 22, July 11, 14, Nov 1; God's purpose for, July 23; should live together, July 10; harmony within, May 1; influence of relationships within, Aug 22; discipline within, Aug 24; planning, Apr 20; providing for, Aug 6; ambitions for, Nov 30; the church in miniature, June 23, Aug 21; of God, July 26; debased in modern world, July 13; tragedy of David's, May 5.

FEAR: a natural emotion, May 27; can lead to sin, Nov 9; faith overcomes, Dec 9; Paul's human, Nov 7; of disciples, Dec. 31.

FELLOWSHIP: Jan 22-28; importance of, Jan 22, Sept 8; basis of, Jan 23; a test of true faith, July 18, Oct 24; of the church, Aug 1, Sept 6, 9; responsibilities of, Jan 23, Sept 8; its extent, Jan 27; self giving of, Jan 26; church elders an example of, Oct 29; with God, Feb 8; problems of, Jan 25; hindrances to, Mar 29, Sept 29; grounds of removal from, July 12.

FLESH: meaning of, May 10; impermanence of, Nov 30; works of, Feb 5; failure of acting in spirit of, May 26, Oct 6; a source of temptation, May 27; hinders sanctification, May 8; denial of, May 9.

FOREKNOWELDGE: of God, Feb 7.

FORGIVENESS: a part of the gospel, Apr 25; need of, Feb 16, June 12, Dec 14, 18; assurance of, Sept 26; of others, Sept 28; effective prayer dependent upon, Dec 5.

FORMALISM: danger of, Jan 13.

FREEDOM: result of salvation, Apr 28; from sin, Feb 29; from self-seeking, Nov 30; dependent on truth, Mar 5; not absolute, Feb 29, Mar 17, May 7; limits to personal, June 29, Oct 20; from limitations at second coming, Nov 21.

FRUIT OF THE SPIRIT: Feb 5-11; vine an illustration of, Feb 2.

G

GENTLENESS: fruit of the Spirit, Feb 5, 10.

GIFTS, SPIRITUAL: Oct 8-14; nature of, Oct 9; distribution of, Oct 8, 10; to the church, Oct 12; dangers to, Oct 12.

GIVING: Aug 6-12; spirit of, Aug 8; principles of, Aug 9; self-giving of our Lord, Aug 8; to the work of God, Aug 10, Nov 14; of ourselves, Aug 11, 12.

GLORY: meaning of, Apr 28, Nov 23, Dec 8; God's purpose for man, Feb 17, Apr 24, June 18; hope of God's people, Apr 27; of Christ, Apr 9; cross the gateway to, Apr 12.

GOD: Jan 1-7; one God, Jan 2; Creator, Jan 2, 6, Nov 22; personalness,

Jan 1, 7; trinity, Jan 2; omnipotence, Jan 7; omniscience, Jan 5; omnipresence, Jan 5, Oct 19; transcendance, Jan 5; providence, Jan 6, 7, Feb 10, Dec 17; sovereignty, Feb 17; supremacy, Jan 9; self-revealing, Jan 3, Mar 12; holiness, Jan 4; love, July 2.

THE FATHER: Jan 15; sovereignty of, Apr 3; relationship to the Son, May 2; caring for His people, July 14.

THE SON: Jan 15-21; relationship to the Father, May 2; the living Word, Jan 3; Messiah, Apr 2, Sept 10, Nov 18, Dec 18.

THE HOLY SPIRIT: Jan 29-Feb 4; personality and deity of, Jan 29; scope of His work, Jan 30, Feb 2; baptism of, Jan 31.

GOODNESS: fruit of the spirit, Feb 5, 9.

GOSPEL: the transforming power of, Feb 3, 15, 16, Apr 23, July 23, Aug 15, Oct 3, Nov 12, Dec 20, 29; greatness of, June 2; historical foundation of, Aug 15; ministry of, Apr 19, June 19, July 17; spread of, Mar 21, 24, Apr 17, May 22, July 5, Aug 10, Nov 12, Dec 30; meets the basic needs of man, Apr 18, July 27; victory over legalism through, Mar 3; manifested in lives of God's people, Sept 19, Nov 6; statements of, July 23, Aug 21, Sept 20; in Isaiah, July 5; for all mankind, Nov 13; hindrances to, Aug 23, Oct 31; denying the, Nov 30.

GOVERNMENT, HUMAN; relationships with, Jan 10, Dec 10.

GRACE: of God, Mar 28, May 15, Sept 7, 14, Dec 8; basis of relationship with God, Feb 29; power of, Feb 29, Aug 9; wrong conception of, May 24; emphasised by the prophets, Aug 16; justification through, Apr 26; salvation through, Feb 27; deliverance from evil through, Mar 2; life in Christ imparted through, Dec 20.

GROWTH, SPIRITUAL: through the Scriptures, Mar 16, July 23; through gift of teaching, Aug 18; to maturity, Dec 12; essential to effective witness, Aug 4, Nov 17; concern for, Nov 29; hindrances to, Mar 9, Oct 20, Dec 13; examples of, June 19, Nov 15.

GUIDANCE: Mar 19-25; basis of, Mar 19; through the Word, Mar 19, May 11, Sept 22, Nov 23; through the Spirit, Mar 20; through fellowship, Mar 21, Nov 23; through prayer, June 11, 12, 16, Dec 9; need of commitment in, Mar 23; need of constant, June 22; in ordering time aright, Nov 28.

GUILT: man's complex of, Apr 24; spiritual, Sept 7.

June 27; entrance into, Apr 24, Dec 3; need of repentance to enter, Sept 24; prayer for, June 12, 15.

385

Dec 11; temptation of, Dec 27; freedom from bondage to, June 28; preaching the gospel for, June 28.

MINISTRY: Aug 13-19; marks of, Nov 17; respect of, Nov 3, 14; purpose of, Nov 7; a balanced, Nov 28; gifts for the work of, Oct 12; reproductive, Aug 18; of the gospel, June 19, Aug 10; of reconciliation, Aug 17; calling to the, June 22; of Christ, Aug 13; of John the Baptist, June 21; of prophets, Mar 28; mixture of human and divine in, Nov 7; dangers of an ignorant, Oct 26.

MIRACLES: Dec 17-23; nature of, Dec 17; purpose of, Dec 22; faith not dependent on, Dec 8; gifts of, Oct 11; in O.T., Dec 21; of our Lord, Dec 18; in the early church, Dec 19; spurious Dec 22.

MONEY: Aug 6-12; the use of, Feb 22, Mar 26; love of, Aug 6, 7.

MOTIVES: right are part of right action, Mar 2; need of pure, Feb 28, Aug 6, Nov 10; incentives to right, July 4; of believers misunderstood, May 17; Christ reigning over our, Dec 28; temptation aimed at distorting, June 6.

MUSIC: a gift from God, July 13; used in worship, Jan 12.

MYSTERY: meaning of, June 20.

N

NEW BIRTH: the need of, Apr 24, Dec 20; a decisive experience, May 18.

O

OBEDIENCE: Mar 16-Apr 1; to God's Word, Sept 2, 17; faith produces, Dec 4, 16; proof of love, Feb 1; gives joy, Feb 7; produces thanksgiving, Jan 8; sacrifice of, Apr 10; affects a person's destiny, July 18; shallow, Mar 28; excuses for lack of, Mar 26; prayer not a substitute for, June 16; judgment according to, July 19, negative attitude a hindrance to, Oct 28.

P

PARENTS: responsibilities for their children, Apr 20, July 25, Aug 20, 24; Dec 10; influence upon their children, Feb 25; Jesus subject to, Dec 24.

PASTORS: their ministry, Aug 18; fatherly concern of, Aug 19.

PATIENCE: fruit of the Spirit, Feb 5, 8; under injustice, Feb 21; of God, Feb 18.

PEACE: fruit of the Spirit, Feb 5, 7; result of justification, Apr 27; in the church, Aug 2.

PENTECOST: meaning of day of, Jan 31, Apr 12, Nov 16; uniqueness of, Sept 6.

PRAYER: June 11-17; its nature June 12; giving time for, Nov 28; corporate, June 15, Aug 25; intercessory, Jan 8, June 13, 14, 15, July 25, Nov 11; within the family circle, Aug 23; faith in, Dec 5; faithfulness in, Apr 1; forgiveness in, Dec 5; in trials, June 1; of Jesus, Apr 7, 10, June 11, Dec 30; of Paul, Feb 9, June 13, July 23; of Hezekiah, Sept 30; selfish, May 18.

PREDESTINATION: by God, Feb 17, June 20, 21, July 6.

PRIDE: sin of, Mar 28, Apr 6, May 23, Sept 12, 13, Dec 13; basis of all sin, June 5; is satanic, June 4; in our accomplishments, May 25; mark of the world, June 25, 30; encouraged by sense of free will, July 3; is self-destructive, Dec 6; ruins relationships, Dec 13; destroyed through the work of the cross, July 31.

PRIESTHOOD: Christ's, Jan 16, 17, Aug 14, 28, Sept 2; work of, Jan 16; of O.T. Aug 27; Jewish high, Apr 4, July 21; corruption within, June 21; of believers, Aug 14.

PRIORITIES: basis of right, Mar 1, Nov 30; temptation to wrong, May 18, Dec 30.

PROMISE: sacredness of, Mar 6.

PURPOSE: of God, Feb 17, 18, May 17, June 12, 18, July 2, 26, Aug 1, Sept 10, 19, Nov 23, 27; of God cannot be thwarted, July 8; sense of, May 17, July 15, 23; discipline necessary to attaining, Oct 20, Dec 8; of ministry, Nov 7.

R

RECONCILIATION: the Gospel of, Apr 23, July 26, Aug 17, Nov 17; of the saints, June 13; need of concern for, Aug 3; through the cross, Aug 30, Oct 5; forgiveness brings, Sept 26.

REDEMPTION: planned by God, Nov 30; God's initiative in, Nov 23; through death of Christ, Jan 20, Apr 4; scope of, July 26, Nov 24, Dec 25; sealed for the day of, Dec 14; fulfilment of, Apr 28, June 18, 20; disunity a denial of work of, Aug 2; symbolized in tabernacle, Sept 1.

REGENERATION: work of the Holy Spirit, Feb 3, Sept 4; God's greatest miracle, Dec 17, 19, 20.

RELATIONSHIPS: with God, Feb 5, 26, Mar 4, Apr 25, 27, July 7, 15, 21, Aug 1, 29, Sept 3, 7, 14, Dec 5, 11; with one another, Feb 8, 10,

26, July 18, Aug 1, Sept 3, 9, 28, Nov 24, 29, Dec 5; powerfulness of relationship with God, Feb 29, Mar 1, June 11, Aug 6; the gospel of a new, Apr 23; between husband and wife, May 2, witness of right, July 25; with God broken through sin, Feb 15, Mar 4; with Adam, Mar 9, May 10; sins of, Feb 5; problems of, Aug 21; distorted by sense of guilt, Apr 27; restoration of, Apr 28.

REPENTANCE: Sept 24-30; need of, May 24, June 12, 17, Sept 10, 23; a continuing experience, Sept 25; is submission to the will of God, Sept 25; result of true, Mar 31; is aim of discipline, July 12.

RESPONSIBILITY: human, Feb 17, Apr 19, July 5, Sept 12; to live according to the faith we profess, June 14, Oct 13, Dec 15; to use aright what God has given, July 20, Sept 20, Oct 8, 16, Nov 2, 8, 18, 29, 30, Dec 2; extent of spiritual, Oct 31; of being ready for His coming again, Nov 20, 23; to our brethren, June 29; to respect the responsibilities of others, Nov 29; of intercession, June 14, Aug 14; to spread the gospel, July 17, 27, Aug 17, Nov 12, 13, 16; to judge righteously, Oct 27; in making right choices, July 3; of giving, Aug 10, Nov 14; to earthly government, Apr 16; within the family, Aug 22.

RESURRECTION: Apr 9-15; meaning of, Sept 5; of Christ, Jan 18, Apr 5, 13, Dec 18, 31; witness of, Aug 15; appearances, Sept 3, Oct 17, Nov 19, Dec 28, of saints, Apr 13.

REVELATION: of God in creation, Oct 15; of God in the Scriptures, Mar 12, June 19, Sept 10, 15, 24, Oct 24; of the Lord Jesus Christ, Apr 2, 5, July 26, Dec 25; through the church, Aug 5; of O.T., Mar 14, Sept 6; of N.T., Mar 15; partial, June 30.

RIGHTEOUSNESS: Dec 3-9; seek first, Feb 22; more than good actions, Mar 2; a matter of the heart, Feb 26; revealed in God's children, Apr 25, May 17, Sept 14; is bondage to Christ, May 7; faith inseparable from, Dec 4; through the Scriptures, Mar 16; world reacts against, May 30; incentive to, July 31.

S

SACRIFICE: Christ's perfect, July 22, Aug 14; of ourselves, Aug 11, 14; of obedient will, Apr 10; of Manoah, Apr 22; of O.T., July 22, Aug 27, 28, Sept 8; imperfection of O.T., Apr 10.

SALVATION : Apr 23-29; a sovereign act of God, Feb 17; God's initiative in, Nov 23; affects the entire person, Feb 3; repentance fundamental

388

to, Sept 24; not through the law, Feb 27; by faith, May 18, July 19, Dec 4; through grace alone, Feb 27, July 19; through the Scriptures, Mar 16; through the resurrection, Apr 5; a past, present and future experience, May 18; working out, July 6; consummation of, Nov 20.

SANCTIFICATION: May 7-13; meaning of, Feb 17, Apr 11, 25, May 7; process of, May 11, Dec 8; through the Holy Spirit, Apr 27; through trials, May 14; problems of, May 8.

SATAN: existence of, May 21; who he is, Feb 13, May 15, June 4; influence of Apr 6; victory over, June 6, Dec 18; giving opportunity to, Dec 14, 21.

SCRIPTURE (See also 'WORD OF GOD'): Mar 12-18; revealed to man, July 19; acceptance of, Sept 27; basis of right standards, Oct 27; respect for, Aug 5, Nov 2; rejected by the world, Aug 4.

SECOND COMING: Nov 19-25; certainty of, Nov 19; expectation of, Apr 19; time of, Nov 20; purpose of, Nov 21; delay of, Nov 22; judgement at, Nov 23.

SELF CONTROL: fruit of the Spirit, Feb 5, 10.

SELF DECEPTION: of Jacob, Feb 25.

SELFISHNESS: in business, Jan 8, Feb 23, 24, 25; a cause of wrong doctrine, Oct 23.

SERVICE: of God, Jan 24, July 5, 15, Sept 20, Nov 14; of others, Jan 24; a basic Christian attitude, Aug 23; ambition for, Oct 31, Nov 10; motives of, Mar 27, Dec 11; call to, June 21; dignity of, Nov 17; discipline of, Nov 28; basis of spiritual authority, Nov 5, 10; hindrances to, Apr 3; influence of personal cleanliness on, Oct 19.

SIN: Feb 12-18; sin and sins, Feb 16; meaning of, Feb 13, 16, 28, 29, Oct 17, Nov 23; its complexity, Feb 29; its effects, Feb 14; is against God, July 15; God's attitude to, Jan 18; Christ's death for, Apr 3, July 21; recognizing personal, June 14, in the 'inward parts', Mar 7, Aug 29, Sept 2; unconscious, Mar 27; of Adam, Apr 13; of the flesh, Feb 5; of adultery, July 11; of resentment, Mar 28; of silence, Feb 20; of litigation, Oct 3; conviction of, Sept 23, Nov 3; confession of, Sept 29; truth frees from, Mar 5; leaven a symbol of, July 12.

SON (See 'GOD' and 'CHRIST—THE PERSON AND WORK OF').

SOVEREIGNTY OF GOD: July 2-8; over all creation, Nov 26; in guidance, Mar 23; in circumstances, Mar 24, 30, July 7, Sept 12, Oct 16, Dec 8,

9, 19, 23, 28; in trials, May 14, 17, 31, Nov 16, 18; and free-will of man, Dec 4.

STANDARD, MORAL: need of Scriptural, Mar 16, July 15; and the law, May 8; permanency of God's, June 25, Nov 22; within the family, May 5; with opposite sex, July 9; instability of those without, Mar 17; rejected by the world, Aug 4; result of abandoning, July 14, Sept 10.

SUFFERING: a part of Christian living, May 14, June 22; reason for, Jan 10, May 16, 28, July 7, Dec 6; cause of, May 28; for Christian standards, Feb 21; discipline of, Mar 29; for the gospel, June 2; identification with the world's, May 30, June 3; of Christ, Jan 16, Mar 29, Apr 7, May 29, Aug 16, Sept 5; Christ our example in, May 16, Dec 7.

T

TABERNACLE: preceded by the tent of. meeting, Mar 4; worship in, Apr 4; ritual of, July 21; furniture of, Aug 27; symbolism of, Aug 31; Levites ministers of, Oct 21, Nov 14.

TEACHERS: our Lord the greatest of, Dec 29; the ministry of, Aug 18, Sept 11; elders should be, Nov 1; of the gospel, Nov 12.

TEMPLE: dedication of, June 17, restoration of, Nov 11; worship in, Apr 4; service of, Nov 14; ritual of, July 21, Sept 16; treasure of, May 26.

TEMPTATION: May 14-20; nature of, Mar 31, 15, 23, June 21, Nov 3; source of, Mar 27; our Lord's sympathy in, Jan 16; limited by God, May 19; resisting, May 19, July 10, 15; prayer in face of, Apr 7, June 12; personal responsibility for, May 15; recurring nature of, June 6, Sept 8; wrong attitude to, May 20; of Jesus, June 6, 9, Dec 18, 24, 27, 30; of Adam, Feb 13; in business life, Feb 20; of fashion, June 26.

TESTIMONY (See 'WITNESS').

TIME: Nov 26- Dec 2; created by God, Dec 23; God's use of, Dec 23; wise use of, Dec 2; priorities in using, Mar 26, Oct 16; stewards of, Nov 29; a means of helping others, Nov 28; for leisure, Dec 1; of second coming, Nov 20.

TRANSFIGURATION: meaning of, Mar 13, June 11, Dec 31; witness of, Apr 15.

TRANSFORMATION: miracle of, Dec 22; process of, Apr 25, May 10; through the gospel, Aug 21, Nov 21, Dec 20; through the Scriptures,

391

live for God, May 9, Nov 4; repudiating one's own, July 4; repentance an act of, Sept 24, 27; personal problems based on unsurrendered, Oct 5; wrong doctrine a matter of, Oct 23.

WILL OF GOD: Jesus' concern for, Apr 10; confidence in, Dec 5; fulfilling the, Sept 7, Nov 25; joy in, Feb 7; selfish desires hinder, May 18.

WITNESS: July 23-29; of personal life, July 23, Oct 31, Dec 15; of good personal relationships, Dec 10; of disciplined words, July 24; in secular life, June 22; in suffering, June 1; of prayer, Apr 1; of good citizenship, Apr 16, 17; of the family May 1, June 23; corporate, July 26; of church, Jan 31, June 20; of corporate worship, Jan 11; in an unjust world, Feb 21; prayer for boldness in, June 15; hindrances to, Oct. 3.

WORD OF GOD: the eternal, Jan 3; a revelation of God's character, Mar 12, Sept 19; inspiration of, Mar 13, 14, 15; given through the apostles, Aug 15; accepting the standard of, Sept 27; reliability of, Mar 16; sufficiency of, Mar 16, Sept 21; profitable for correction, Mar 16; importance of knowing, Mar 17; 21; Sept 17; sheds light into our lives, Mar 9, Sept 17; cleansing power of, Jan 11, May 11, Aug 29; guidance through, Mar 19, 20; its place in the church, July 30, Nov 15; its relationship to the Holy Spirit, Feb 1, 2; ministry of, Jan 23, 28, Aug 19, Oct 11, Nov 2; continuing in Jan 8; discipleship and, Mar 5; symbols of, Apr 24; distorting the, Mar 10.

WORK: need of, Dec 1; duty to, Apr 19; priorities in, Mar 26; witness in daily, June 22, July 25; the sin of avoiding, Feb 21.

WORLD: June 25 - July 1; meaning of, June 25, 29, Aug 8; its ruler, June 4, 5; our Lord distinct from, Apr 11; its injustice, Feb 21; deliverance from the power of, Mar 3, Dec 12.

WORSHIP AND THANKSGIVING: Jan 8-14; an attitude of heart, Jan 13; in all things, Jan 8; June 1 Dec 9; based on humility, Jan 9; corporate worship, Jan 11, Sept 16, Dec 1; order in, Oct 21; within the family, Aug 25; spurious, Apr 10; symbol of, Aug 27.